The Archie Wedding

Archie ®

in *WILL YOU MARRY ME?*

Cover Art:
Stan Goldberg & Bob Smith

Cover Colorist:
Tito Peña

Writer: **Michael Uslan**

Penciller: **Stan Goldberg**

Inker: **Bob Smith**

Letterer: **Jack Morelli**

Colorist: **Glenn Whitmore**

Co-CEO:
Jonathan Goldwater

Co-CEO:
Nancy Silberkleit

Co-President/Editor-In-Chief:
Victor Gorelick

Co-President/Director of Circulation:
Fred Mausser

Vice President/Managing Editor:
Mike Pellerito

Designer: Joe Morciglio

Production Manager: Stephen Oswald

Production: Ellen Leonforte,
Carlos Antunes, Paul Kaminski,
Suzannah Rowntree,
Duncan McLachlan

Table of Contents:

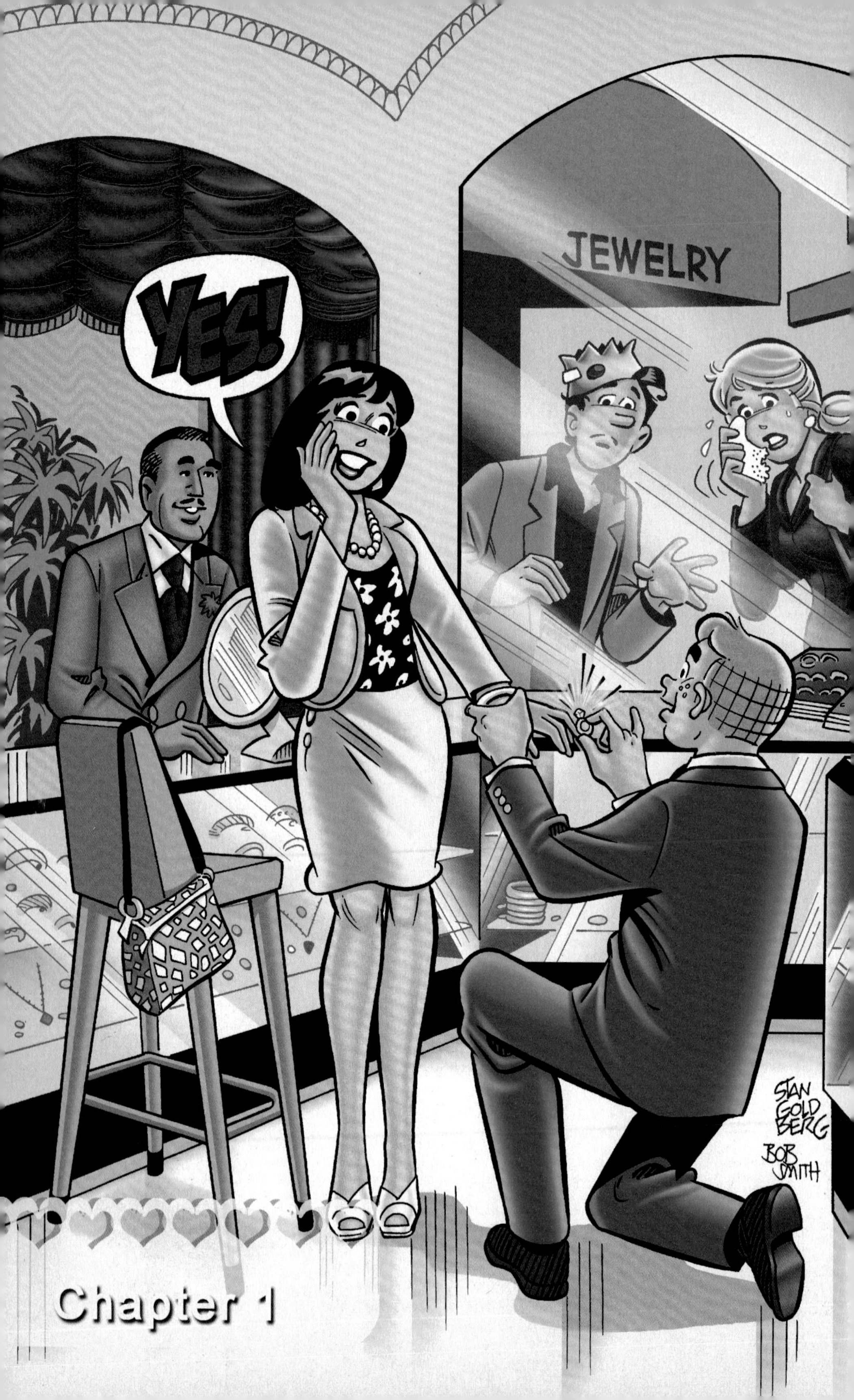
YES!
JEWELRY
STAN GOLDBERG
BOB SMITH

Chapter 1

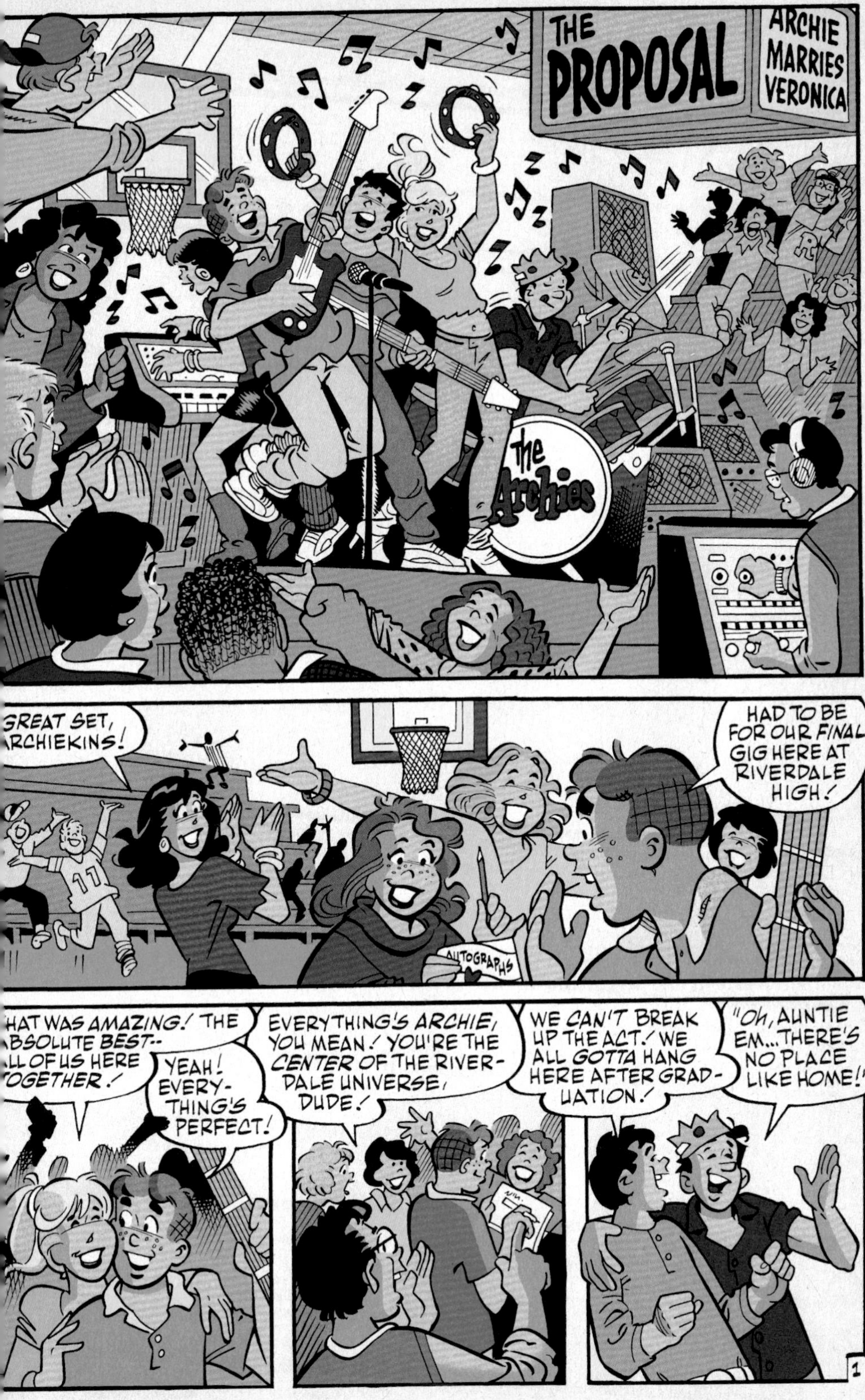
THE PROPOSAL
ARCHIE MARRIES VERONICA
the Archies
GREAT SET, RCHIEKINS!
HAD TO BE FOR OUR FINAL GIG HERE AT RIVERDALE HIGH!
11
AUTOGRAPHS
HAT WAS AMAZING! THE BSOLUTE BEST-- LL OF US HERE OGETHER!
YEAH! EVERY-THING'S PERFECT!
EVERYTHING'S ARCHIE, YOU MEAN! YOU'RE THE CENTER OF THE RIVER-DALE UNIVERSE, DUDE!
WE CAN'T BREAK UP THE ACT! WE ALL GOTTA HANG HERE AFTER GRAD-UATION!
"Oh, AUNTIE EM...THERE'S NO PLACE LIKE HOME!"
1

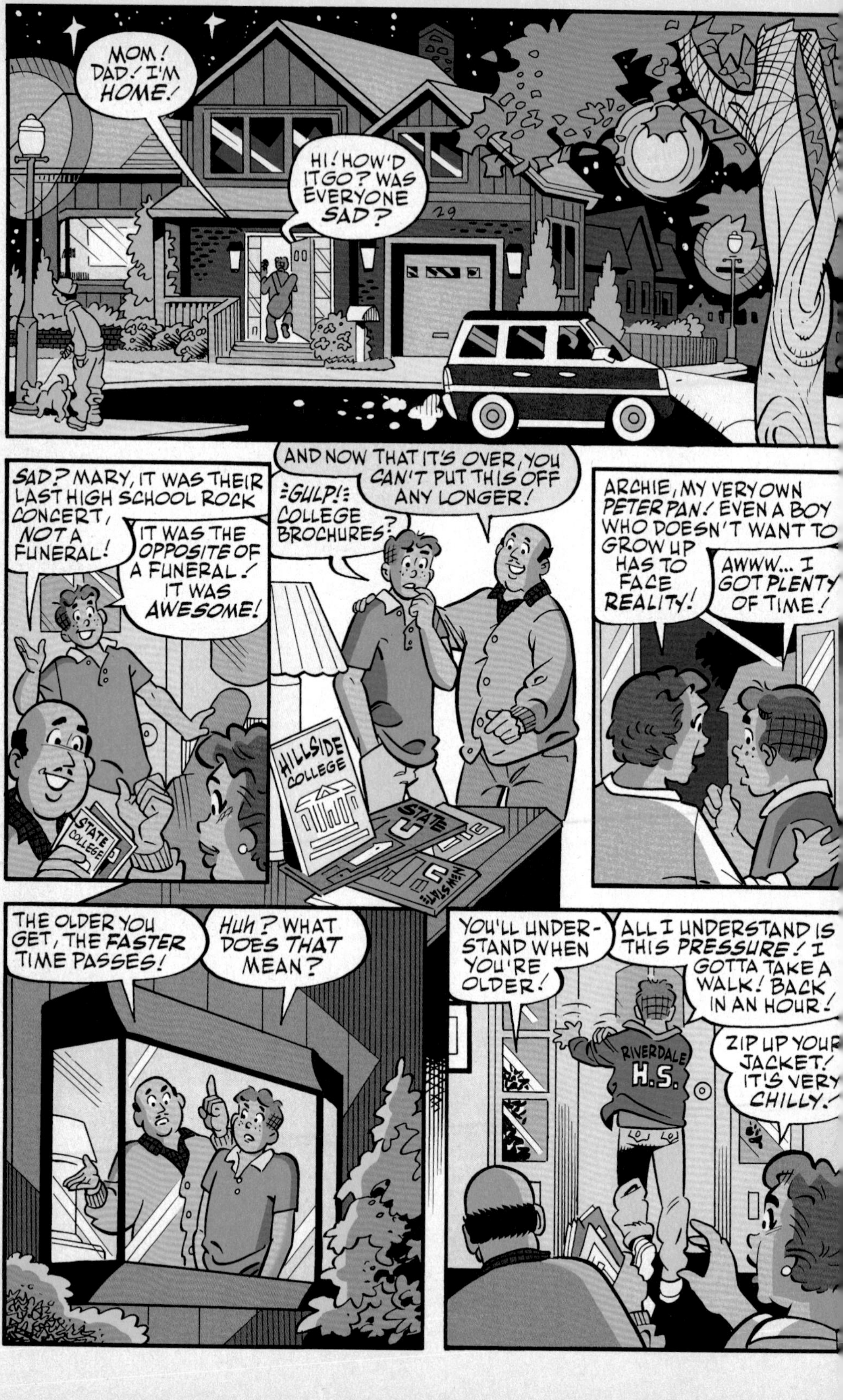
MOM! DAD! I'M HOME!
HI! HOW'D IT GO? WAS EVERYONE SAD?
29
SAD? MARY, IT WAS THEIR LAST HIGH SCHOOL ROCK CONCERT, NOT A FUNERAL!
IT WAS THE OPPOSITE OF A FUNERAL! IT WAS AWESOME!
STATE COLLEGE
AND NOW THAT IT'S OVER, YOU CAN'T PUT THIS OFF ANY LONGER!
GULP! COLLEGE BROCHURES?
HILLSIDE COLLEGE
STATE U
ARCHIE, MY VERY OWN PETER PAN! EVEN A BOY WHO DOESN'T WANT TO GROW UP HAS TO FACE REALITY!
AWWW... I GOT PLENTY OF TIME!
THE OLDER YOU GET, THE FASTER TIME PASSES!
HUH? WHAT DOES THAT MEAN?
YOU'LL UNDERSTAND WHEN YOU'RE OLDER!
ALL I UNDERSTAND IS THIS PRESSURE! I GOTTA TAKE A WALK! BACK IN AN HOUR!
RIVERDALE H.S.
ZIP UP YOUR JACKET! IT'S VERY CHILLY!

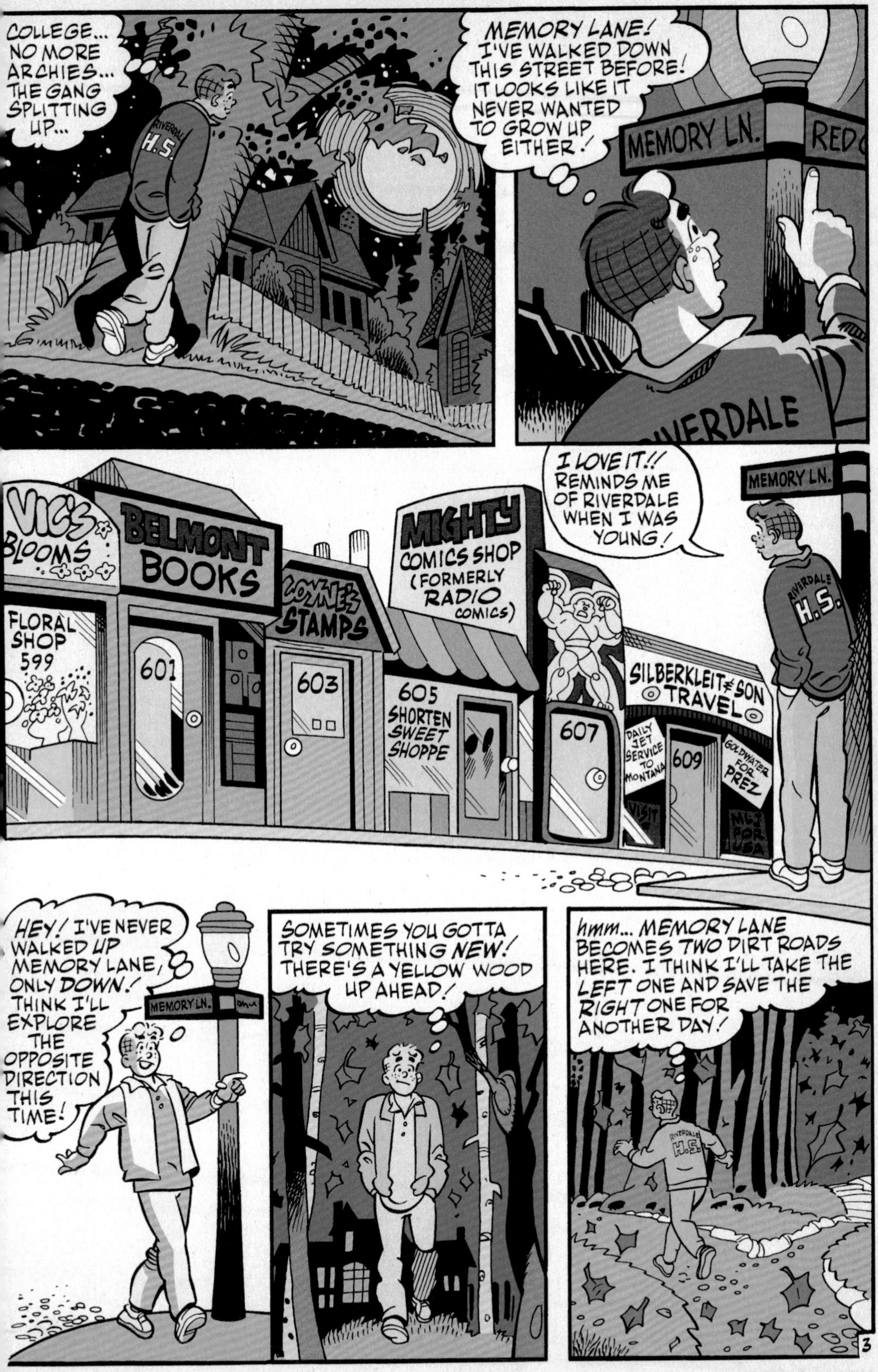
COLLEGE... NO MORE ARCHIES... THE GANG SPLITTING UP...
RIVERDALE H.S.
MEMORY LANE! I'VE WALKED DOWN THIS STREET BEFORE! IT LOOKS LIKE IT NEVER WANTED TO GROW UP EITHER!
MEMORY LN.
RED
RIVERDALE
I LOVE IT!! REMINDS ME OF RIVERDALE WHEN I WAS YOUNG!
MEMORY LN.
VIC'S BLOOMS
BELMONT BOOKS
COYNE'S STAMPS
MIGHTY COMICS SHOP (FORMERLY RADIO COMICS)
FLORAL SHOP 599
601
603
605 SHORTEN SWEET SHOPPE
607
SILBERKLEIT & SON TRAVEL
DAILY JET SERVICE TO MONTANA
609
GOLDWATER FOR PREZ
MLJ FOR USA
RIVERDALE H.S.
HEY! I'VE NEVER WALKED UP MEMORY LANE, ONLY DOWN! THINK I'LL EXPLORE THE OPPOSITE DIRECTION THIS TIME!
MEMORY LN.
SOMETIMES YOU GOTTA TRY SOMETHING NEW! THERE'S A YELLOW WOOD UP AHEAD!
hmm... MEMORY LANE BECOMES TWO DIRT ROADS HERE. I THINK I'LL TAKE THE LEFT ONE AND SAVE THE RIGHT ONE FOR ANOTHER DAY!
RIVERDALE H.S.
3

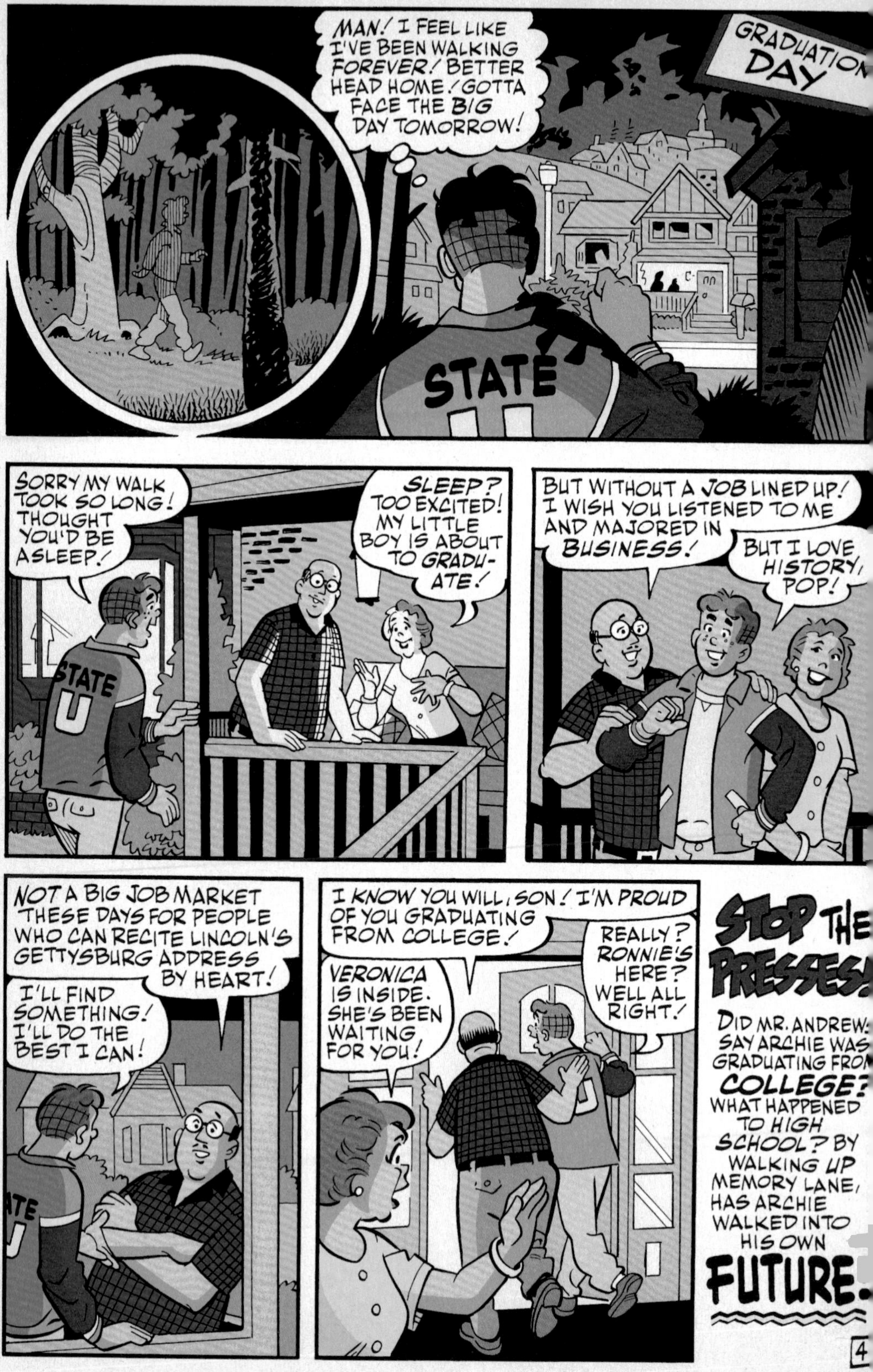
MAN! I FEEL LIKE I'VE BEEN WALKING FOREVER! BETTER HEAD HOME! GOTTA FACE THE BIG DAY TOMORROW!
GRADUATION DAY
STATE U
SORRY MY WALK TOOK SO LONG! THOUGHT YOU'D BE ASLEEP!
SLEEP? TOO EXCITED! MY LITTLE BOY IS ABOUT TO GRADUATE!
BUT WITHOUT A JOB LINED UP! I WISH YOU LISTENED TO ME AND MAJORED IN BUSINESS!
BUT I LOVE HISTORY, POP!
NOT A BIG JOB MARKET THESE DAYS FOR PEOPLE WHO CAN RECITE LINCOLN'S GETTYSBURG ADDRESS BY HEART!
I'LL FIND SOMETHING! I'LL DO THE BEST I CAN!
I KNOW YOU WILL, SON! I'M PROUD OF YOU GRADUATING FROM COLLEGE!
VERONICA IS INSIDE. SHE'S BEEN WAITING FOR YOU!
REALLY? RONNIE'S HERE? WELL ALL RIGHT!
STOP THE PRESSES!
DID MR. ANDREWS SAY ARCHIE WAS GRADUATING FROM COLLEGE? WHAT HAPPENED TO HIGH SCHOOL? BY WALKING UP MEMORY LANE, HAS ARCHIE WALKED INTO HIS OWN FUTURE?
4

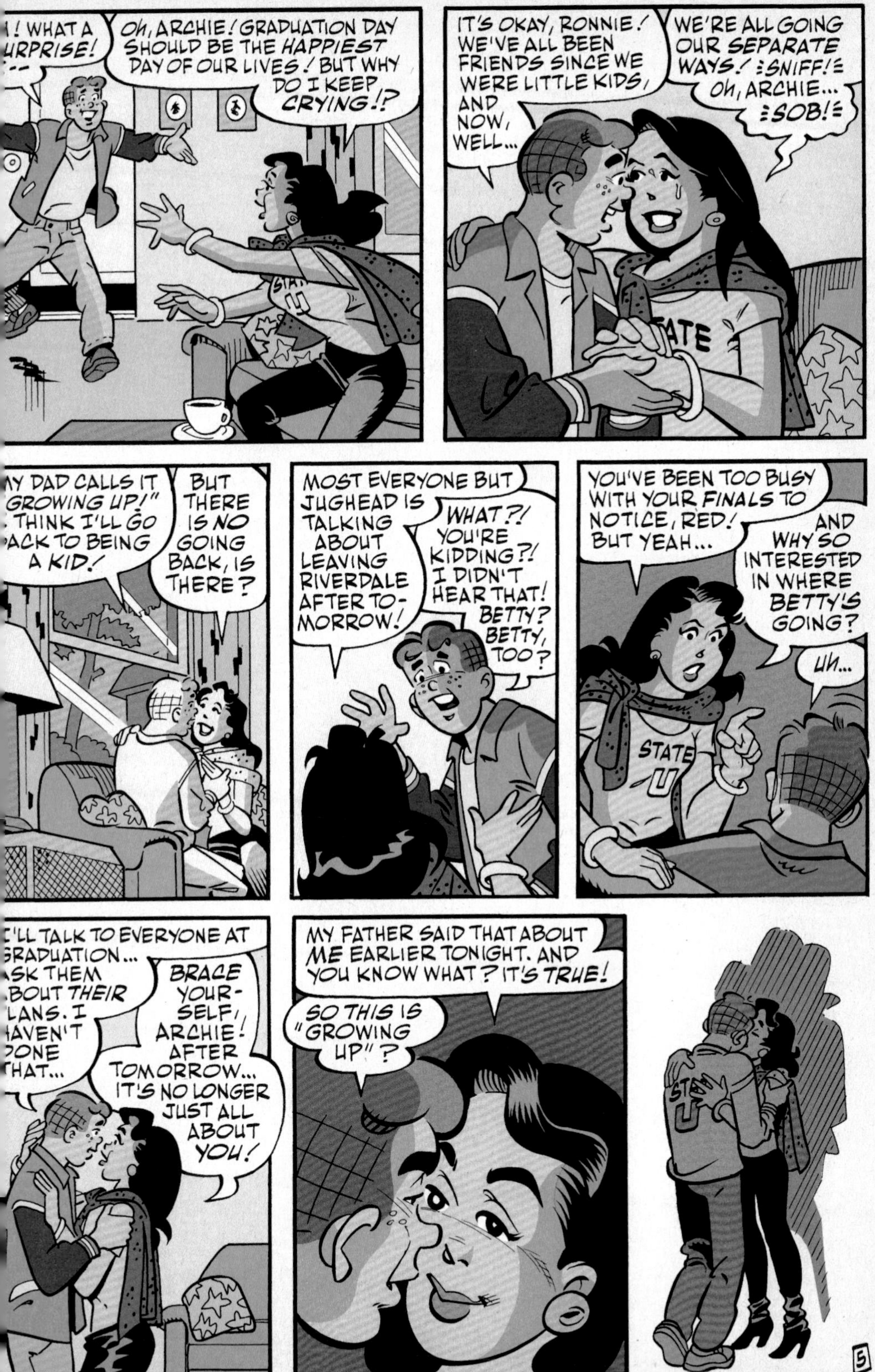
! WHAT A URPRISE!
OH, ARCHIE! GRADUATION DAY SHOULD BE THE HAPPIEST DAY OF OUR LIVES! BUT WHY DO I KEEP CRYING!?
IT'S OKAY, RONNIE! WE'VE ALL BEEN FRIENDS SINCE WE WERE LITTLE KIDS, AND NOW, WELL...
WE'RE ALL GOING OUR SEPARATE WAYS! SNIFF! OH, ARCHIE... SOB!
MY DAD CALLS IT "GROWING UP!" THINK I'LL GO BACK TO BEING A KID!
BUT THERE IS NO GOING BACK, IS THERE?
MOST EVERYONE BUT JUGHEAD IS TALKING ABOUT LEAVING RIVERDALE AFTER TO-MORROW!
WHAT?! YOU'RE KIDDING?! I DIDN'T HEAR THAT! BETTY? BETTY, TOO?
YOU'VE BEEN TOO BUSY WITH YOUR FINALS TO NOTICE, RED! BUT YEAH...
AND WHY SO INTERESTED IN WHERE BETTY'S GOING?
UH...
I'LL TALK TO EVERYONE AT GRADUATION... ASK THEM ABOUT THEIR PLANS. I HAVEN'T DONE THAT...
BRACE YOURSELF, ARCHIE! AFTER TOMORROW... IT'S NO LONGER JUST ALL ABOUT YOU!
MY FATHER SAID THAT ABOUT ME EARLIER TONIGHT. AND YOU KNOW WHAT? IT'S TRUE!
SO THIS IS "GROWING UP"?
5

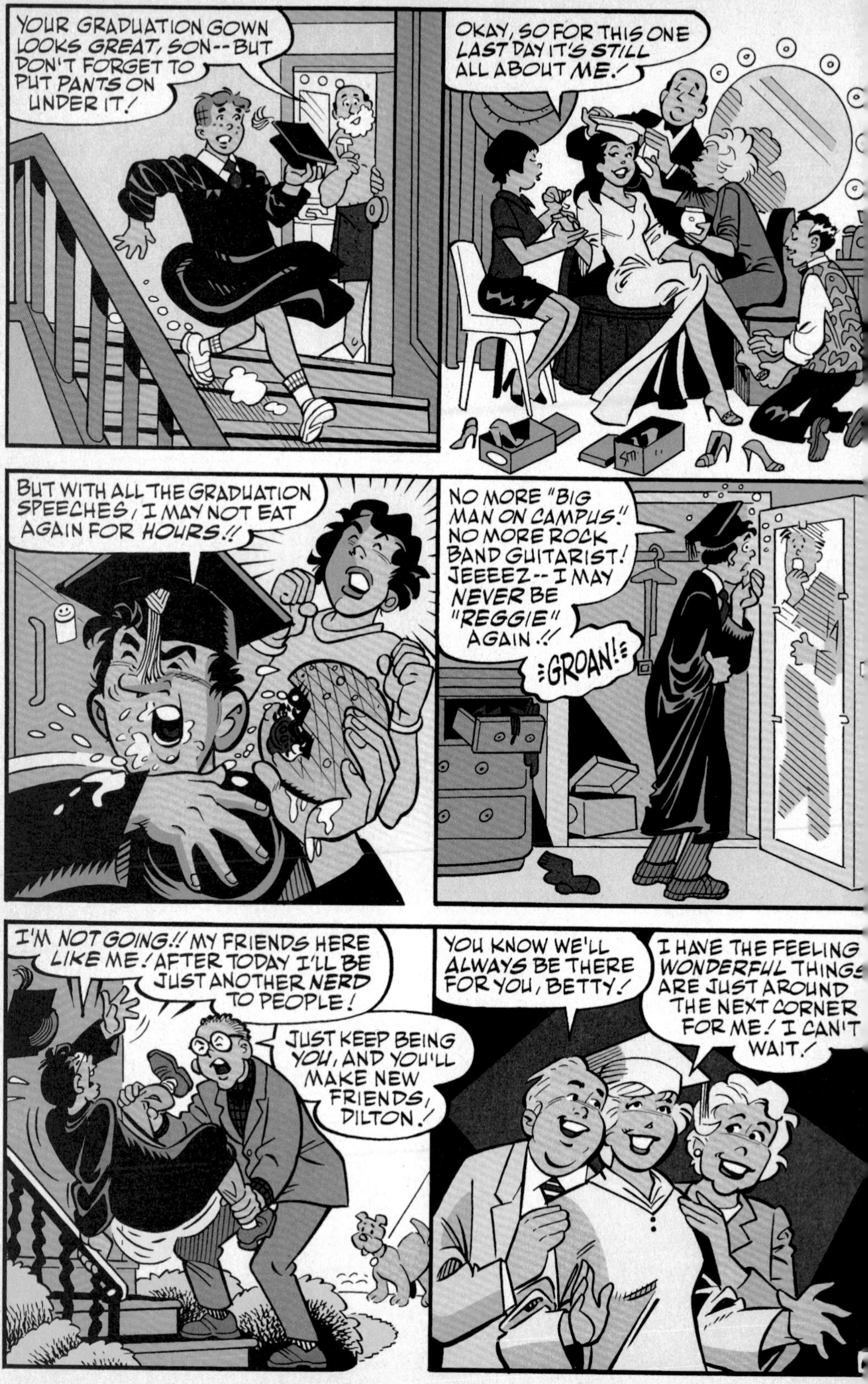
YOUR GRADUATION GOWN LOOKS GREAT, SON-- BUT DON'T FORGET TO PUT PANTS ON UNDER IT!
OKAY, SO FOR THIS ONE LAST DAY IT'S STILL ALL ABOUT ME!
BUT WITH ALL THE GRADUATION SPEECHES, I MAY NOT EAT AGAIN FOR HOURS!!
NO MORE "BIG MAN ON CAMPUS!" NO MORE ROCK BAND GUITARIST! JEEEEZ-- I MAY NEVER BE "REGGIE" AGAIN!!
GROAN!
I'M NOT GOING!! MY FRIENDS HERE LIKE ME! AFTER TODAY I'LL BE JUST ANOTHER NERD TO PEOPLE!
JUST KEEP BEING YOU, AND YOU'LL MAKE NEW FRIENDS, DILTON!
YOU KNOW WE'LL ALWAYS BE THERE FOR YOU, BETTY!
I HAVE THE FEELING WONDERFUL THINGS ARE JUST AROUND THE NEXT CORNER FOR ME! I CAN'T WAIT!

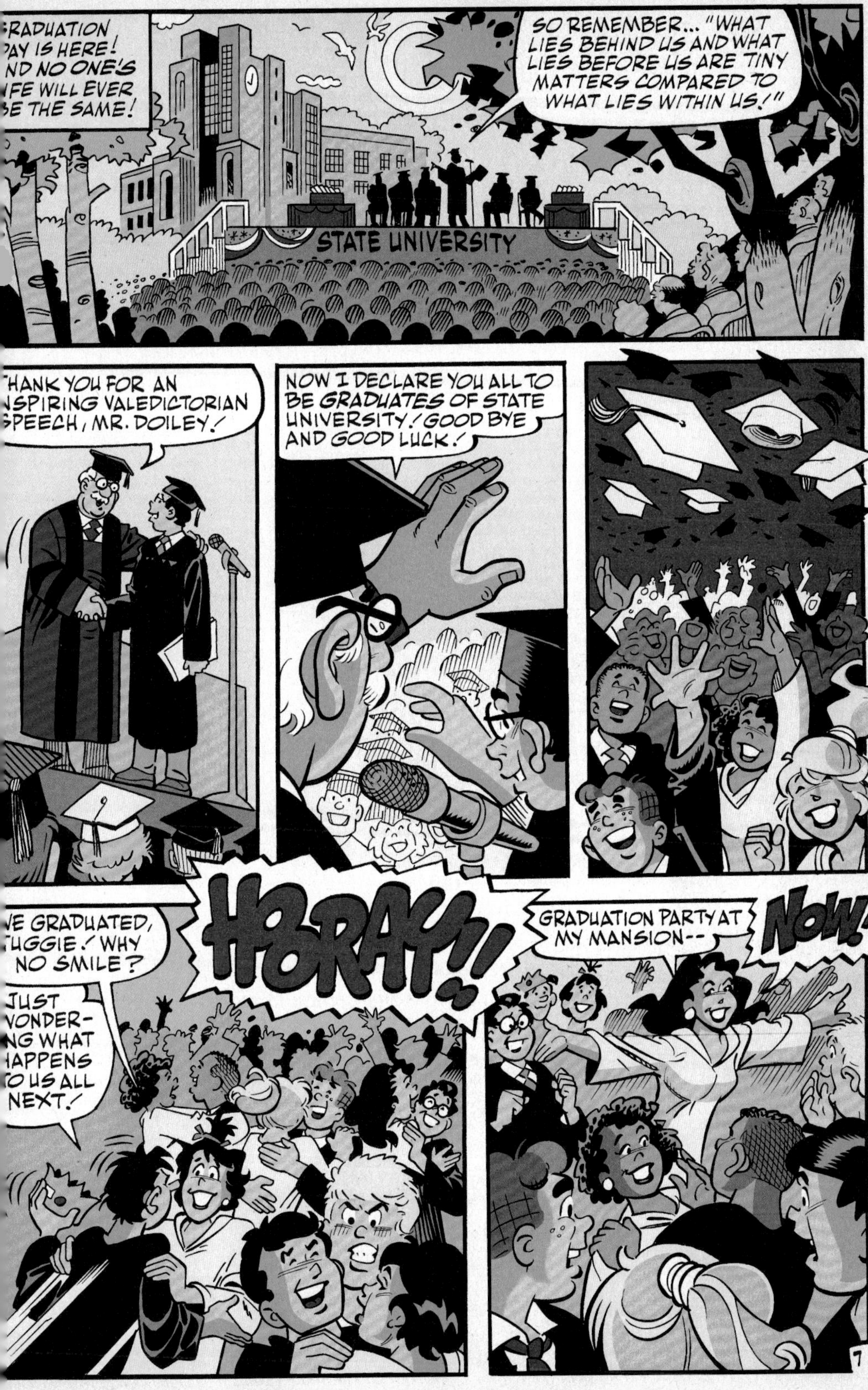
RADUATION
PAY IS HERE!
ND NO ONE'S
IFE WILL EVER
E THE SAME!
SO REMEMBER... "WHAT LIES BEHIND US AND WHAT LIES BEFORE US ARE TINY MATTERS COMPARED TO WHAT LIES WITHIN US!"
STATE UNIVERSITY
HANK YOU FOR AN NSPIRING VALEDICTORIAN PEECH, MR. DOILEY!
NOW I DECLARE YOU ALL TO BE GRADUATES OF STATE UNIVERSITY! GOOD BYE AND GOOD LUCK!
E GRADUATED, UGGIE! WHY NO SMILE?
HOORAY!!
JUST ONDER- NG WHAT APPENS O US ALL NEXT!
GRADUATION PARTY AT MY MANSION--
NOW!

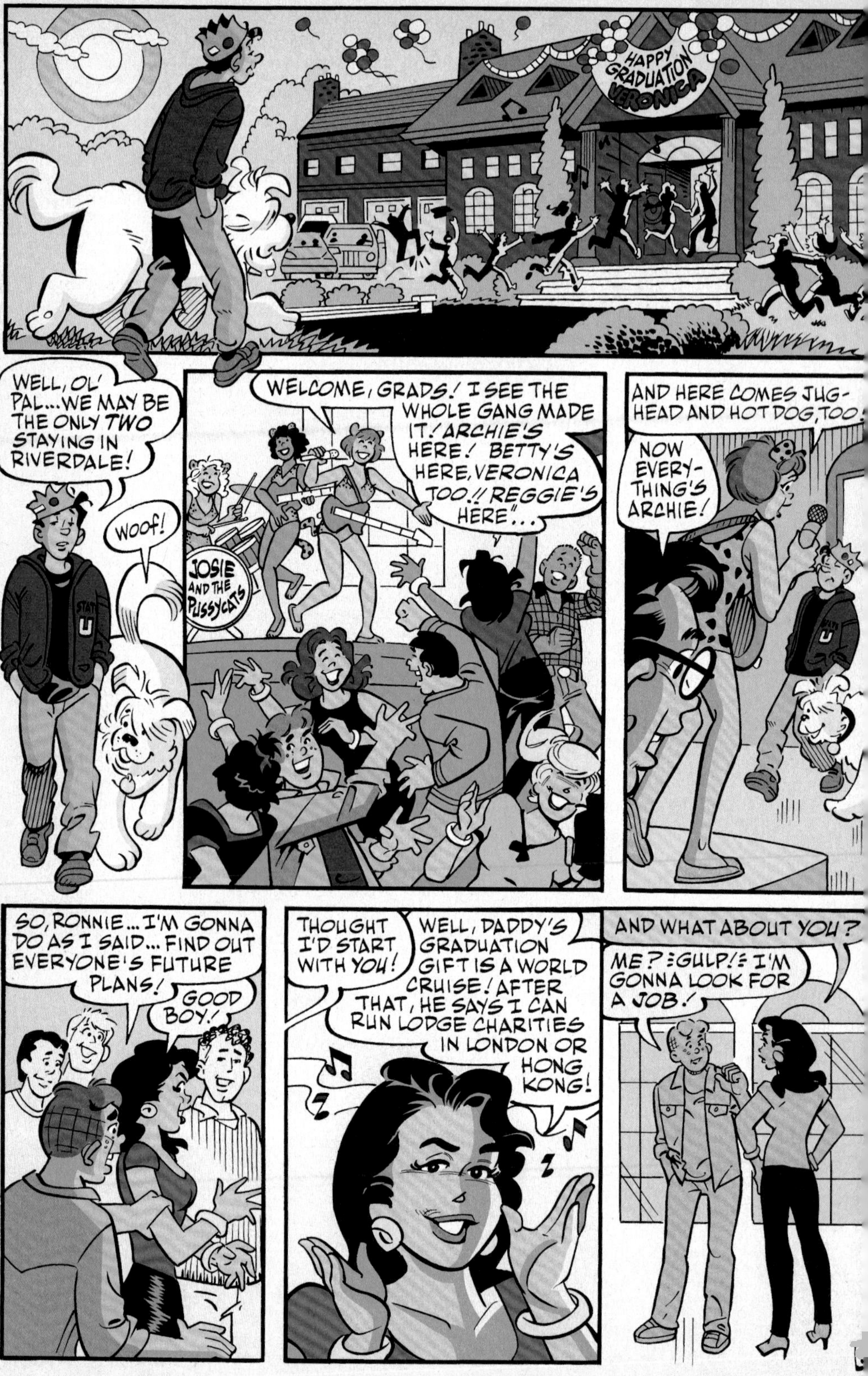
HAPPY GRADUATION VERONICA
WELL, OL' PAL...WE MAY BE THE ONLY TWO STAYING IN RIVERDALE!
WOOF!
WELCOME, GRADS! I SEE THE WHOLE GANG MADE IT! ARCHIE'S HERE! BETTY'S HERE, VERONICA TOO!! REGGIE'S HERE!...
JOSIE AND THE PUSSYCATS
AND HERE COMES JUGHEAD AND HOT DOG, TOO!
NOW EVERYTHING'S ARCHIE!
SO, RONNIE... I'M GONNA DO AS I SAID... FIND OUT EVERYONE'S FUTURE PLANS!
GOOD BOY!
THOUGHT I'D START WITH YOU!
WELL, DADDY'S GRADUATION GIFT IS A WORLD CRUISE! AFTER THAT, HE SAYS I CAN RUN LODGE CHARITIES IN LONDON OR HONG KONG!
AND WHAT ABOUT YOU?
ME? GULP! I'M GONNA LOOK FOR A JOB!

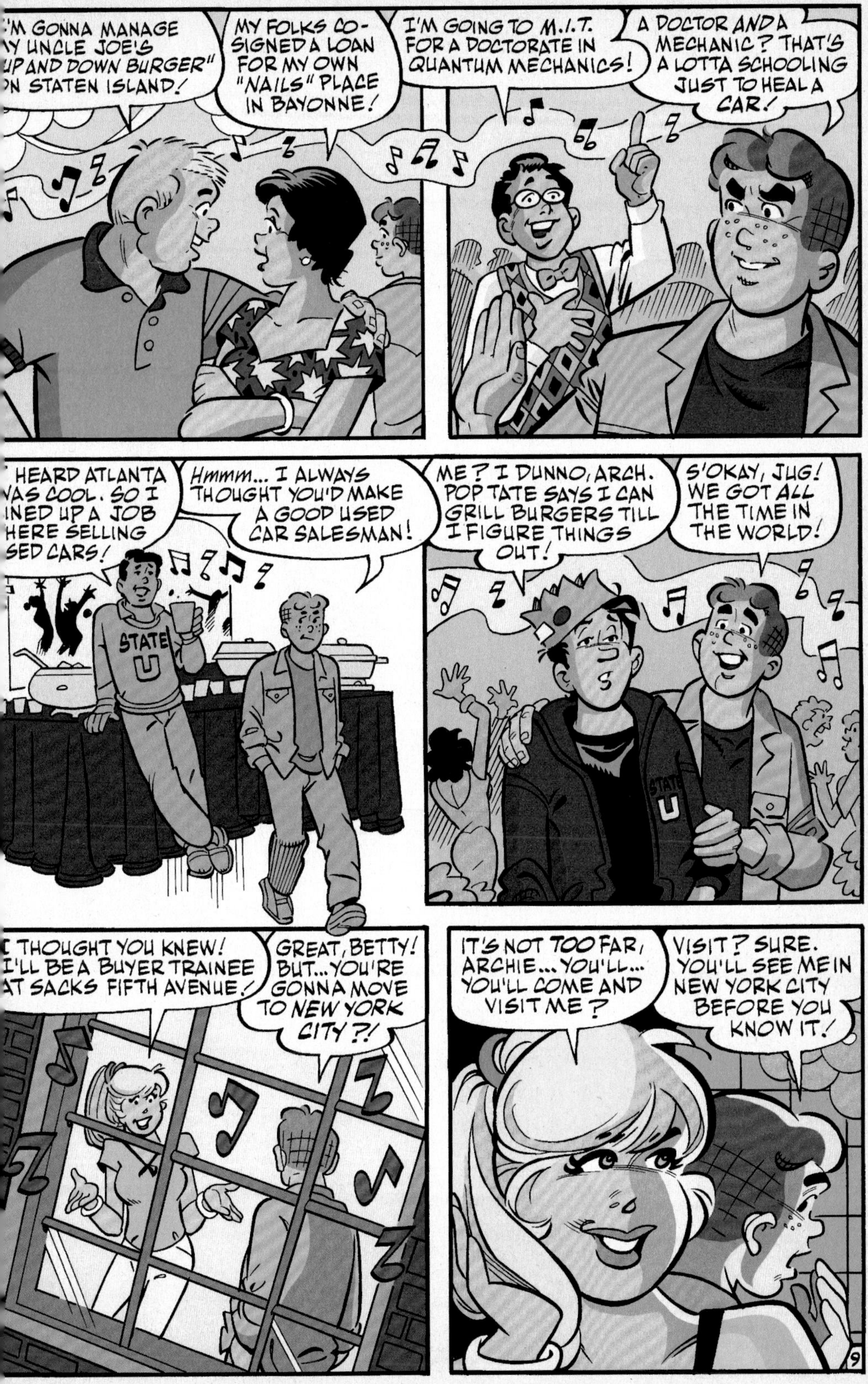
'M GONNA MANAGE
Y UNCLE JOE'S
UP AND DOWN BURGER"
N STATEN ISLAND!
MY FOLKS CO-SIGNED A LOAN FOR MY OWN "NAILS" PLACE IN BAYONNE!
I'M GOING TO M.I.T. FOR A DOCTORATE IN QUANTUM MECHANICS!
A DOCTOR AND A MECHANIC? THAT'S A LOTTA SCHOOLING JUST TO HEAL A CAR!
HEARD ATLANTA
VAS COOL. SO I
INED UP A JOB
HERE SELLING
SED CARS!
Hmmm... I ALWAYS THOUGHT YOU'D MAKE A GOOD USED CAR SALESMAN!
STATE U
ME? I DUNNO, ARCH. POP TATE SAYS I CAN GRILL BURGERS TILL I FIGURE THINGS OUT!
S'OKAY, JUG! WE GOT ALL THE TIME IN THE WORLD!
STATE U
I THOUGHT YOU KNEW!
'LL BE A BUYER TRAINEE
AT SACKS FIFTH AVENUE!
GREAT, BETTY! BUT... YOU'RE GONNA MOVE TO NEW YORK CITY?!
IT'S NOT TOO FAR, ARCHIE... YOU'LL... YOU'LL COME AND VISIT ME?
VISIT? SURE. YOU'LL SEE ME IN NEW YORK CITY BEFORE YOU KNOW IT!
9

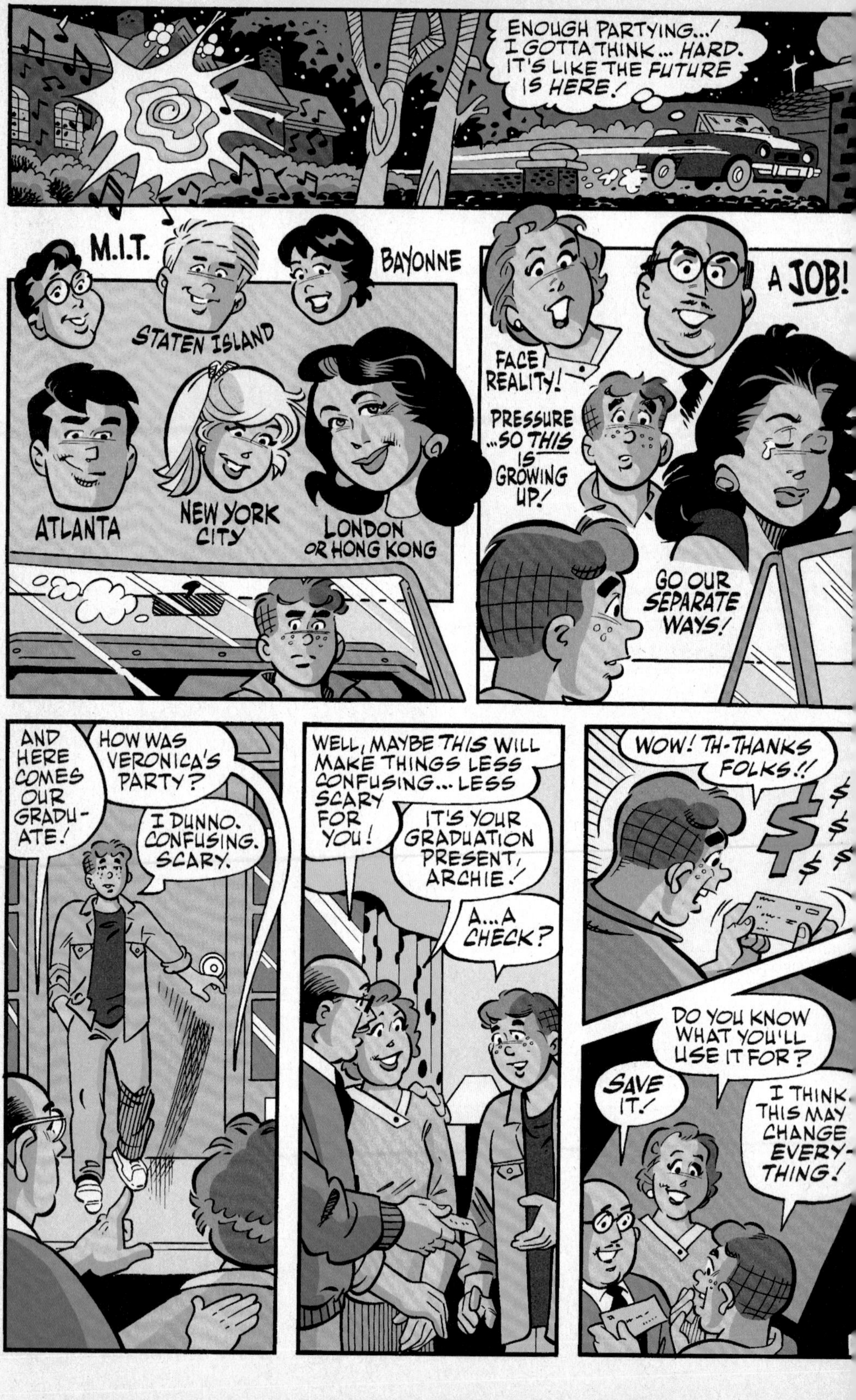
ENOUGH PARTYING...! I GOTTA THINK... HARD. IT'S LIKE THE FUTURE IS HERE!
M.I.T.
STATEN ISLAND
BAYONNE
ATLANTA
NEW YORK CITY
LONDON OR HONG KONG
FACE REALITY!
A JOB!
PRESSURE ...SO THIS IS GROWING UP!
GO OUR SEPARATE WAYS!
AND HERE COMES OUR GRADUATE!
HOW WAS VERONICA'S PARTY?
I DUNNO. CONFUSING. SCARY.
WELL, MAYBE THIS WILL MAKE THINGS LESS CONFUSING... LESS SCARY FOR YOU!
IT'S YOUR GRADUATION PRESENT, ARCHIE!
A...A CHECK?
WOW! TH-THANKS FOLKS!!
DO YOU KNOW WHAT YOU'LL USE IT FOR?
SAVE IT!
I THINK THIS MAY CHANGE EVERYTHING!

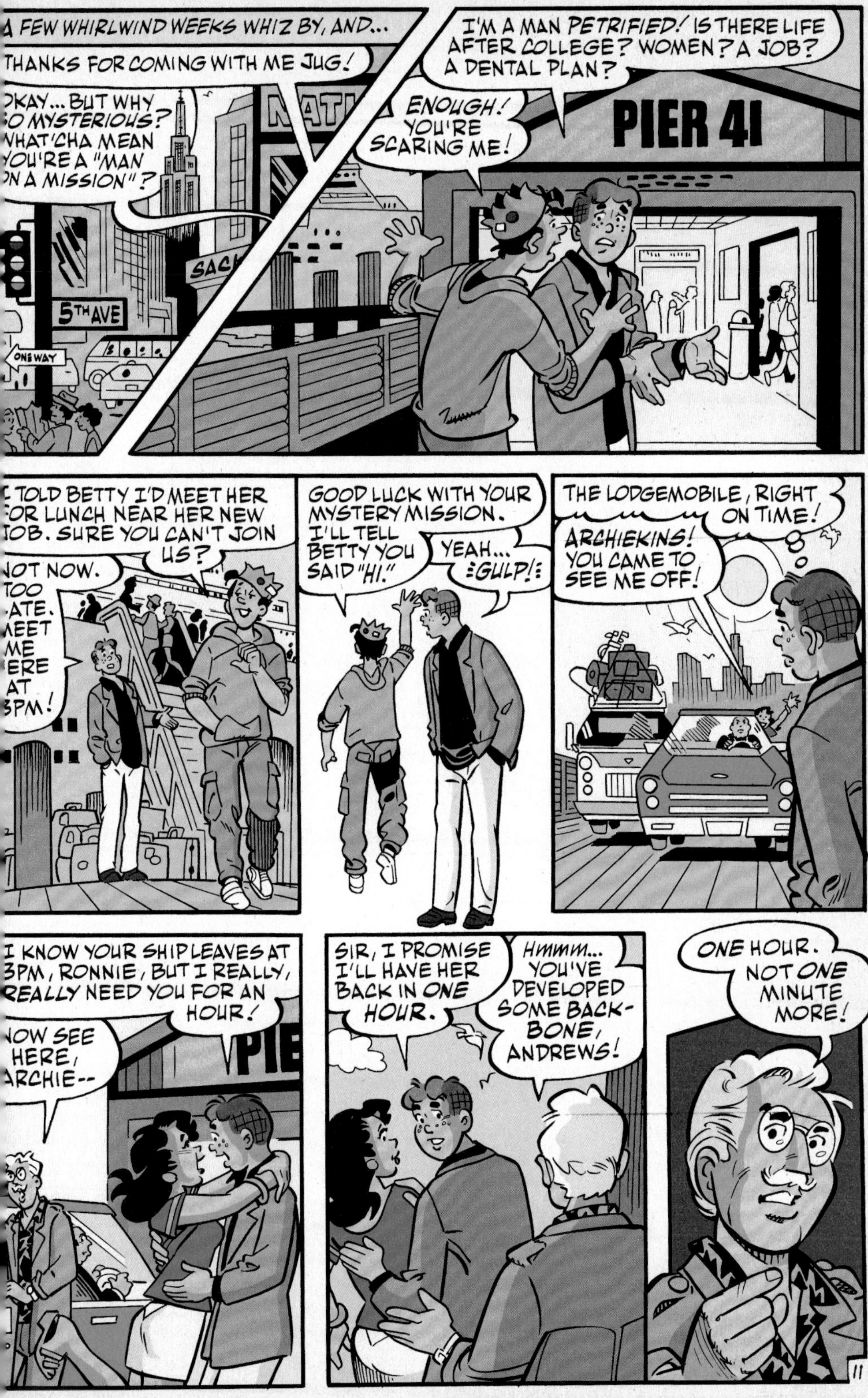
A FEW WHIRLWIND WEEKS WHIZ BY, AND...
THANKS FOR COMING WITH ME JUG!
OKAY... BUT WHY SO MYSTERIOUS? WHAT'CHA MEAN YOU'RE A "MAN ON A MISSION"?
5TH AVE
ONE WAY
I'M A MAN PETRIFIED! IS THERE LIFE AFTER COLLEGE? WOMEN? A JOB? A DENTAL PLAN?
ENOUGH! YOU'RE SCARING ME!
PIER 41
I TOLD BETTY I'D MEET HER FOR LUNCH NEAR HER NEW JOB. SURE YOU CAN'T JOIN US?
NOT NOW. TOO LATE. MEET ME HERE AT 3PM!
GOOD LUCK WITH YOUR MYSTERY MISSION. I'LL TELL BETTY YOU SAID "HI."
YEAH... GULP!
THE LODGEMOBILE, RIGHT ON TIME!
ARCHIEKINS! YOU CAME TO SEE ME OFF!
I KNOW YOUR SHIP LEAVES AT 3PM, RONNIE, BUT I REALLY, REALLY NEED YOU FOR AN HOUR!
NOW SEE HERE, ARCHIE--
SIR, I PROMISE I'LL HAVE HER BACK IN ONE HOUR.
HMMM... YOU'VE DEVELOPED SOME BACK-BONE, ANDREWS!
ONE HOUR. NOT ONE MINUTE MORE!
11

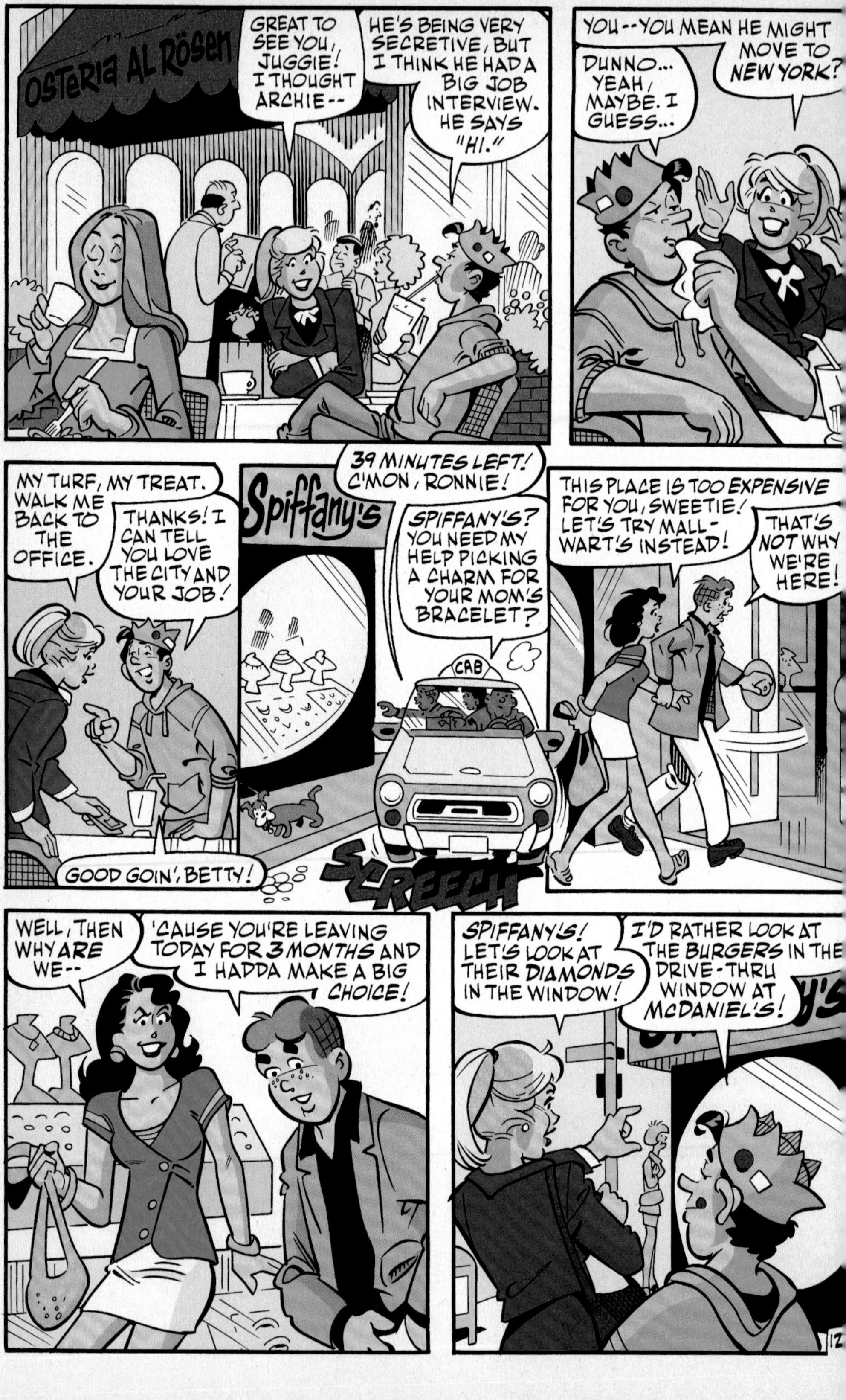
OSTERIA AL RÖSEN
GREAT TO SEE YOU, JUGGIE! I THOUGHT ARCHIE--
HE'S BEING VERY SECRETIVE, BUT I THINK HE HAD A BIG JOB INTERVIEW. HE SAYS "HI."
YOU--YOU MEAN HE MIGHT MOVE TO NEW YORK?
DUNNO... YEAH, MAYBE. I GUESS...
MY TURF, MY TREAT. WALK ME BACK TO THE OFFICE.
THANKS! I CAN TELL YOU LOVE THE CITY AND YOUR JOB!
GOOD GOIN', BETTY!
Spiffany's
39 MINUTES LEFT! C'MON, RONNIE!
SPIFFANY'S? YOU NEED MY HELP PICKING A CHARM FOR YOUR MOM'S BRACELET?
CAB
SCREECH
THIS PLACE IS TOO EXPENSIVE FOR YOU, SWEETIE! LET'S TRY MALL-WART'S INSTEAD!
THAT'S NOT WHY WE'RE HERE!
WELL, THEN WHY ARE WE--
'CAUSE YOU'RE LEAVING TODAY FOR 3 MONTHS AND I HADDA MAKE A BIG CHOICE!
SPIFFANY'S! LET'S LOOK AT THEIR DIAMONDS IN THE WINDOW!
I'D RATHER LOOK AT THE BURGERS IN THE DRIVE-THRU WINDOW AT MCDANIEL'S!
12

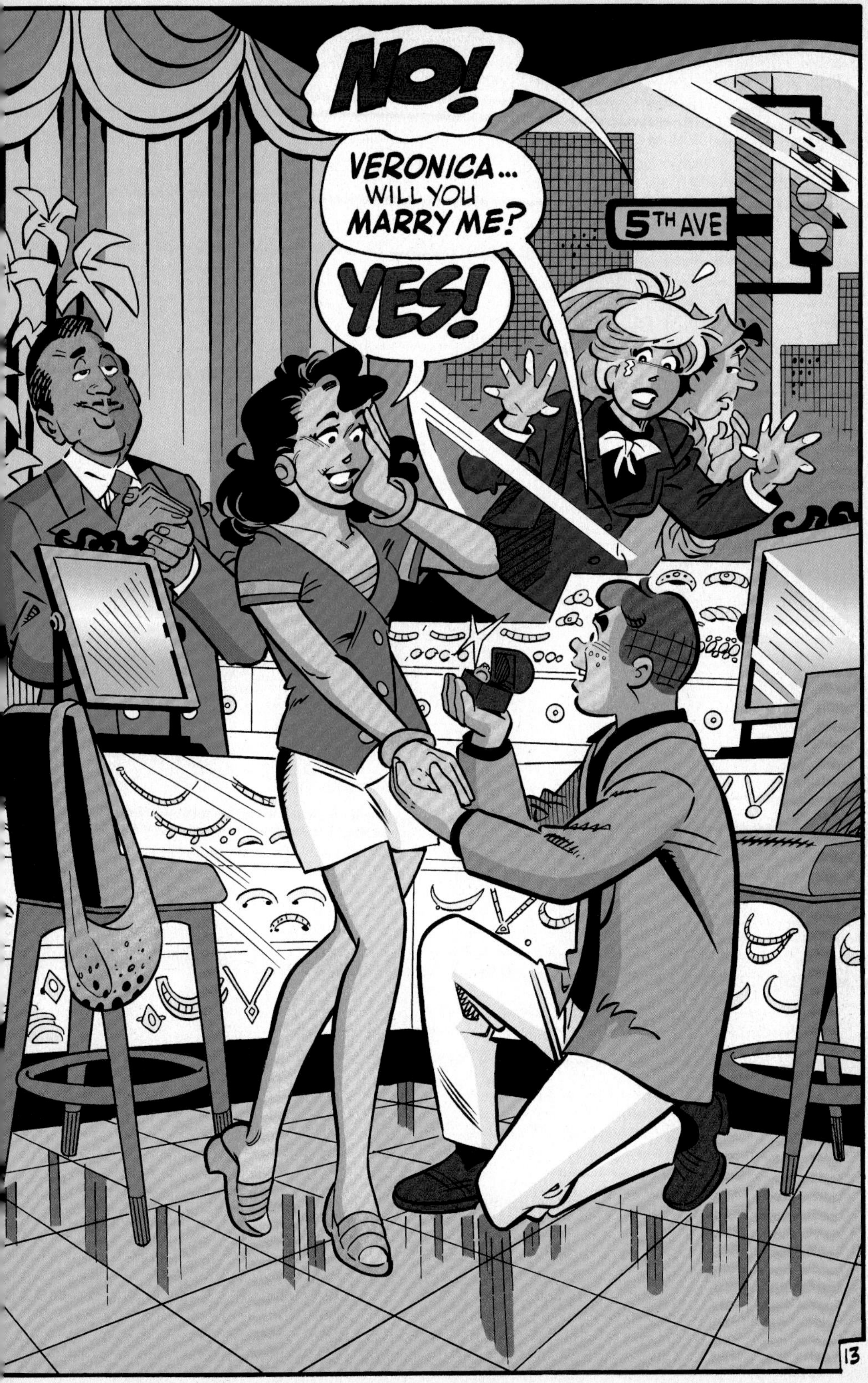
VERONICA... WILL YOU MARRY ME?
YES!
NO!
5TH AVE
13

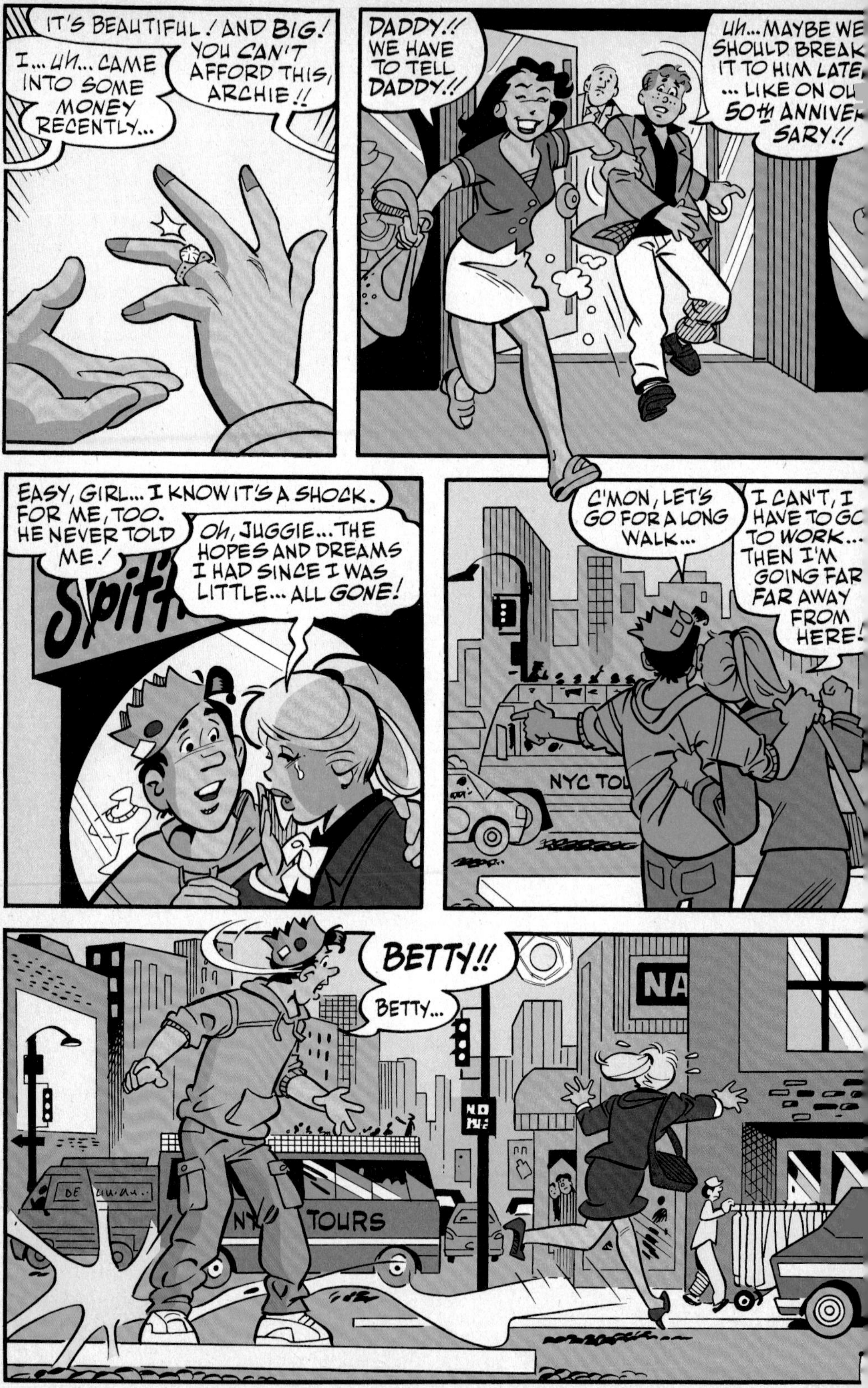
IT'S BEAUTIFUL! AND BIG! YOU CAN'T AFFORD THIS, ARCHIE!!
I... UH... CAME INTO SOME MONEY RECENTLY...
DADDY!! WE HAVE TO TELL DADDY!!
UH... MAYBE WE SHOULD BREAK IT TO HIM LATE... LIKE ON OU 50th ANNIVER SARY!!
EASY, GIRL... I KNOW IT'S A SHOCK. FOR ME, TOO. HE NEVER TOLD ME!
OH, JUGGIE... THE HOPES AND DREAMS I HAD SINCE I WAS LITTLE... ALL GONE!
C'MON, LET'S GO FOR A LONG WALK...
I CAN'T, I HAVE TO GO TO WORK... THEN I'M GOING FAR FAR AWAY FROM HERE!
NYC TOU
BETTY!!
BETTY...
NA
NO
NY TOURS

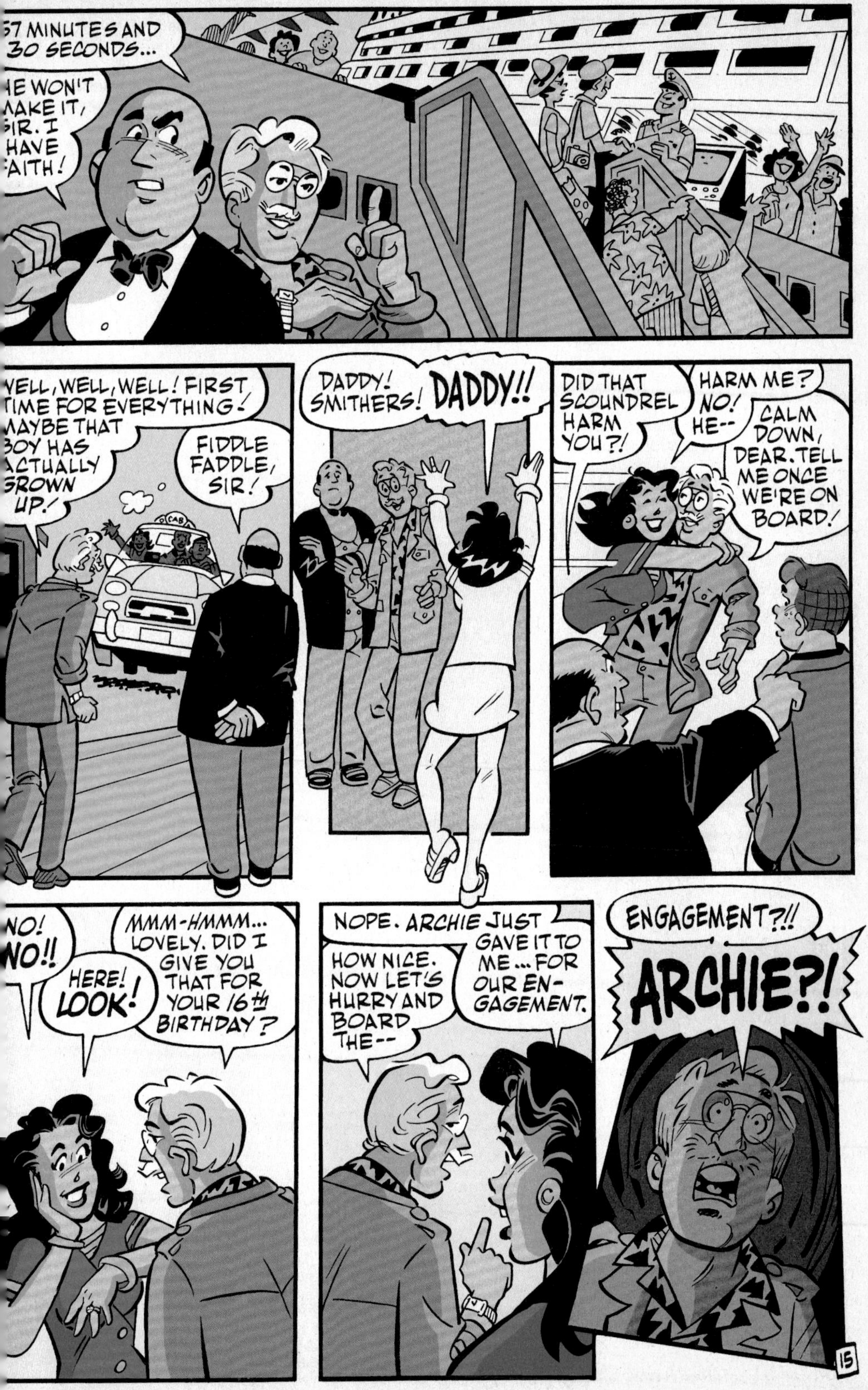
57 MINUTES AND 30 SECONDS...
HE WON'T MAKE IT, SIR. I HAVE FAITH!
WELL, WELL, WELL! FIRST TIME FOR EVERYTHING! MAYBE THAT BOY HAS ACTUALLY GROWN UP!
FIDDLE FADDLE, SIR!
CAB
DADDY! SMITHERS! DADDY!!
DID THAT SCOUNDREL HARM YOU?!
HARM ME? NO! HE--
CALM DOWN, DEAR. TELL ME ONCE WE'RE ON BOARD!
NO! NO!!
MMM-HMMM... LOVELY. DID I GIVE YOU THAT FOR YOUR 16th BIRTHDAY?
HERE! LOOK!
NOPE. ARCHIE JUST GAVE IT TO ME... FOR OUR ENGAGEMENT.
HOW NICE. NOW LET'S HURRY AND BOARD THE--
ENGAGEMENT?!!
ARCHIE?!
15

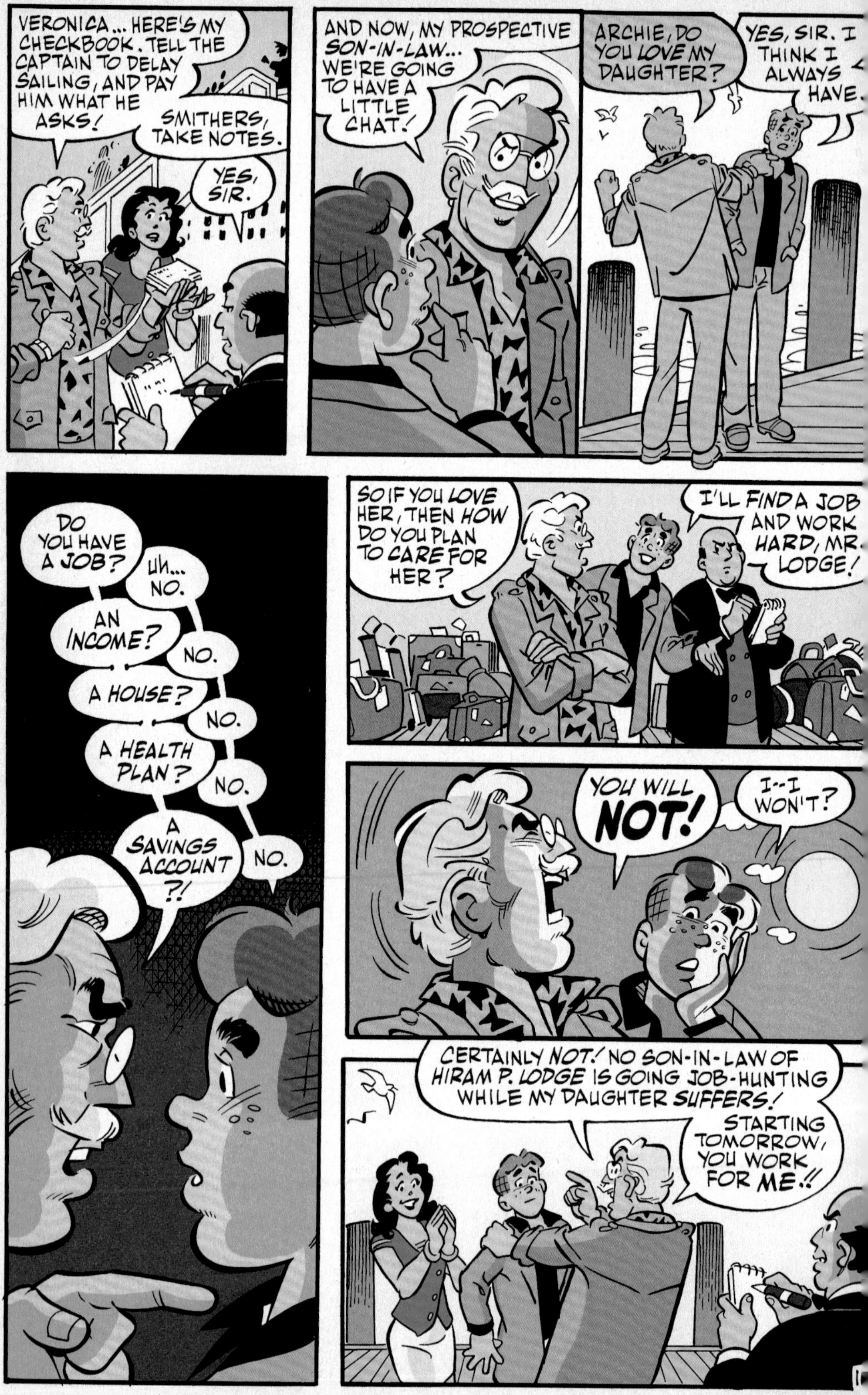
VERONICA... HERE'S MY CHECKBOOK. TELL THE CAPTAIN TO DELAY SAILING, AND PAY HIM WHAT HE ASKS!
SMITHERS, TAKE NOTES.
YES, SIR.
AND NOW, MY PROSPECTIVE SON-IN-LAW... WE'RE GOING TO HAVE A LITTLE CHAT!
ARCHIE, DO YOU LOVE MY DAUGHTER?
YES, SIR. I THINK I ALWAYS HAVE.
DO YOU HAVE A JOB?
UH... NO.
AN INCOME?
NO.
A HOUSE?
NO.
A HEALTH PLAN?
NO.
A SAVINGS ACCOUNT ?!
NO.
SO IF YOU LOVE HER, THEN HOW DO YOU PLAN TO CARE FOR HER?
I'LL FIND A JOB AND WORK HARD, MR. LODGE!
YOU WILL NOT!
I--I WON'T?
CERTAINLY NOT! NO SON-IN-LAW OF HIRAM P. LODGE IS GOING JOB-HUNTING WHILE MY DAUGHTER SUFFERS!
STARTING TOMORROW, YOU WORK FOR ME!!

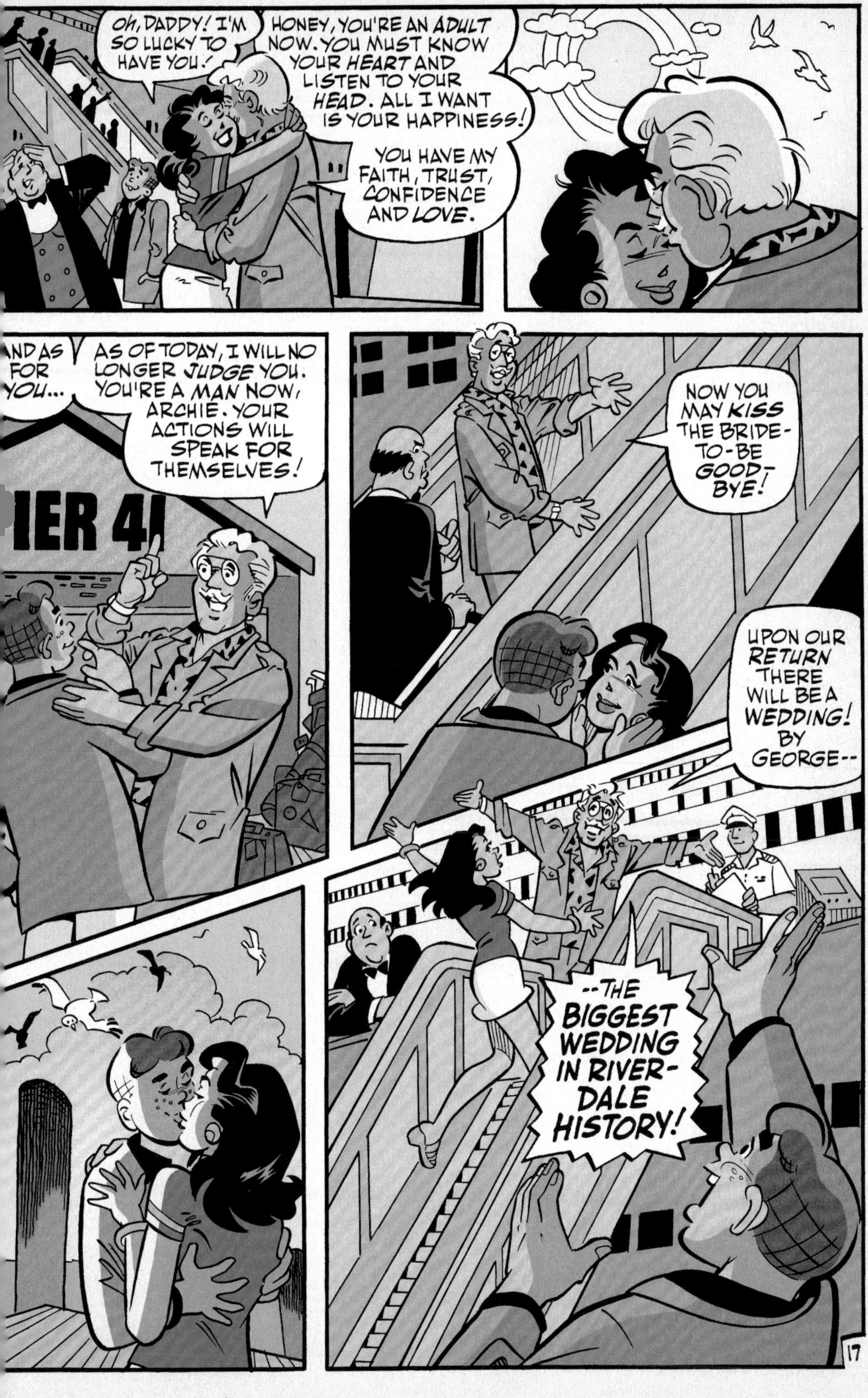
OH, DADDY! I'M SO LUCKY TO HAVE YOU!
HONEY, YOU'RE AN ADULT NOW. YOU MUST KNOW YOUR HEART AND LISTEN TO YOUR HEAD. ALL I WANT IS YOUR HAPPINESS!
YOU HAVE MY FAITH, TRUST, CONFIDENCE AND LOVE.
AND AS FOR YOU...
AS OF TODAY, I WILL NO LONGER JUDGE YOU. YOU'RE A MAN NOW, ARCHIE. YOUR ACTIONS WILL SPEAK FOR THEMSELVES!
IER 41
NOW YOU MAY KISS THE BRIDE-TO-BE GOOD-BYE!
UPON OUR RETURN THERE WILL BE A WEDDING! BY GEORGE--
--THE BIGGEST WEDDING IN RIVER-DALE HISTORY!
17

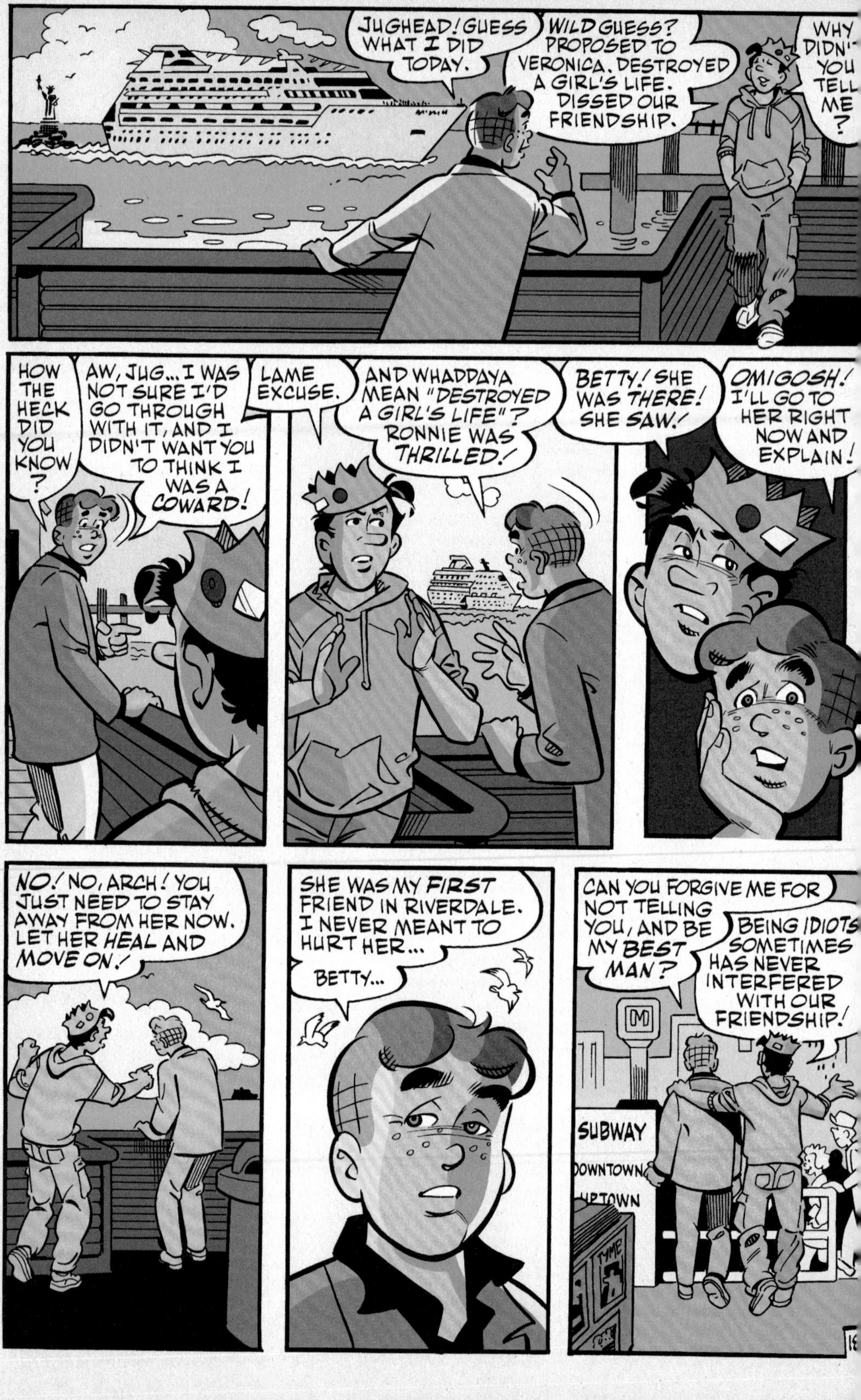
JUGHEAD! GUESS WHAT I DID TODAY.
WILD GUESS? PROPOSED TO VERONICA. DESTROYED A GIRL'S LIFE. DISSED OUR FRIENDSHIP.
WHY DIDN' YOU TELL ME?
HOW THE HECK DID YOU KNOW?
AW, JUG... I WAS NOT SURE I'D GO THROUGH WITH IT, AND I DIDN'T WANT YOU TO THINK I WAS A COWARD!
LAME EXCUSE.
AND WHADDAYA MEAN "DESTROYED A GIRL'S LIFE"? RONNIE WAS THRILLED!
BETTY! SHE WAS THERE! SHE SAW!
OMIGOSH! I'LL GO TO HER RIGHT NOW AND EXPLAIN!
NO! NO, ARCH! YOU JUST NEED TO STAY AWAY FROM HER NOW. LET HER HEAL AND MOVE ON!
SHE WAS MY FIRST FRIEND IN RIVERDALE. I NEVER MEANT TO HURT HER...
BETTY...
CAN YOU FORGIVE ME FOR NOT TELLING YOU, AND BE MY BEST MAN?
BEING IDIOTS SOMETIMES HAS NEVER INTERFERED WITH OUR FRIENDSHIP!
SUBWAY
DOWNTOWN
UPTOWN

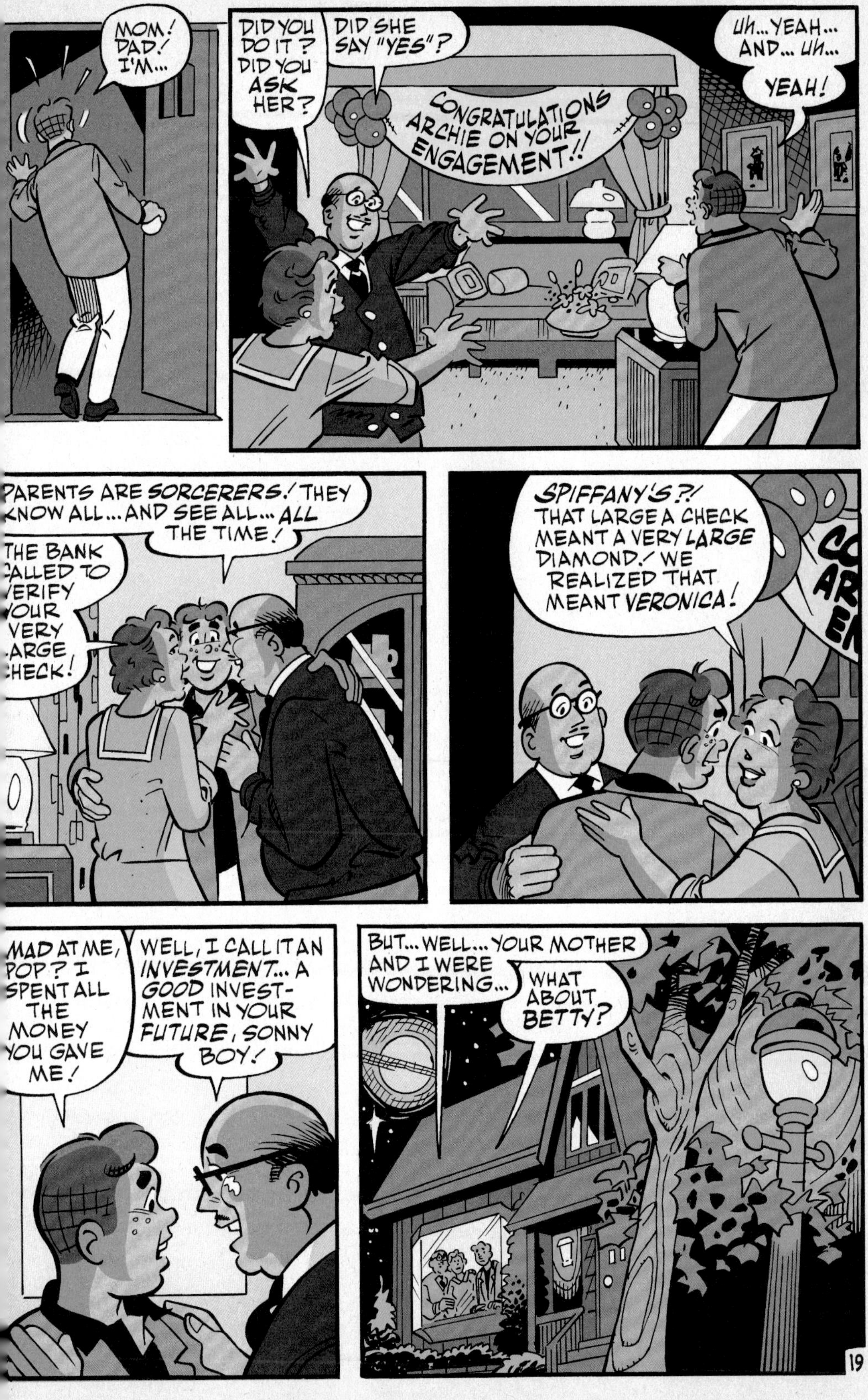
MOM! DAD! I'M...
DID YOU DO IT? DID YOU ASK HER?
DID SHE SAY "YES"?
CONGRATULATIONS ARCHIE ON YOUR ENGAGEMENT!!
UH... YEAH... AND... UH...
YEAH!
PARENTS ARE SORCERERS! THEY KNOW ALL... AND SEE ALL... ALL THE TIME!
THE BANK CALLED TO VERIFY YOUR VERY LARGE CHECK!
SPIFFANY'S?! THAT LARGE A CHECK MEANT A VERY LARGE DIAMOND! WE REALIZED THAT MEANT VERONICA!
MAD AT ME, POP? I SPENT ALL THE MONEY YOU GAVE ME!
WELL, I CALL IT AN INVESTMENT... A GOOD INVESTMENT IN YOUR FUTURE, SONNY BOY!
BUT... WELL... YOUR MOTHER AND I WERE WONDERING...
WHAT ABOUT BETTY?
19

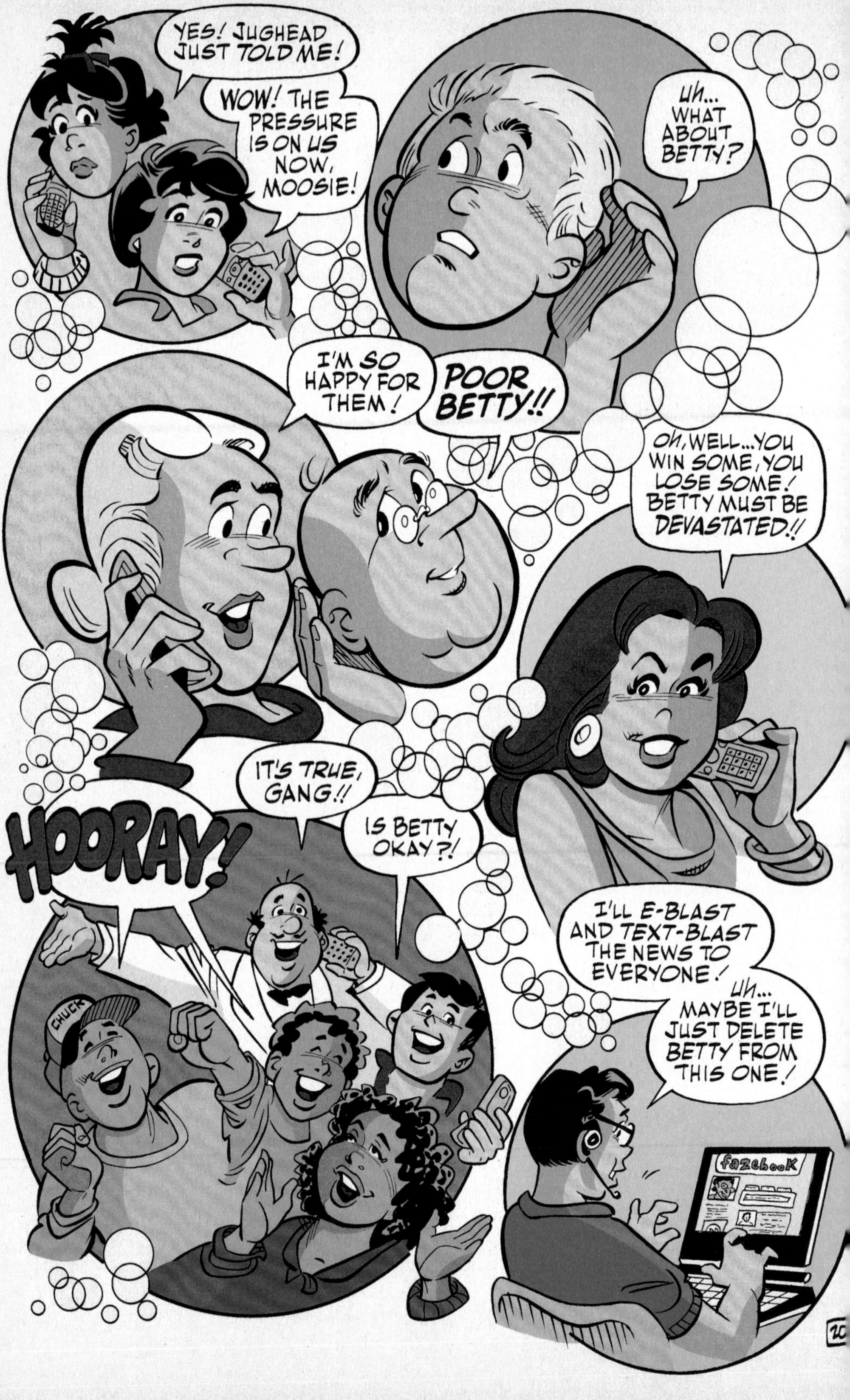
YES! JUGHEAD JUST TOLD ME!
WOW! THE PRESSURE IS ON US NOW, MOOSIE!
UH... WHAT ABOUT BETTY?
I'M SO HAPPY FOR THEM!
POOR BETTY!!
OH, WELL...YOU WIN SOME, YOU LOSE SOME! BETTY MUST BE DEVASTATED!!
IT'S TRUE, GANG!!
HOORAY!
IS BETTY OKAY?!
CHUCK
I'LL E-BLAST AND TEXT-BLAST THE NEWS TO EVERYONE!
UH... MAYBE I'LL JUST DELETE BETTY FROM THIS ONE!
fazebook
20

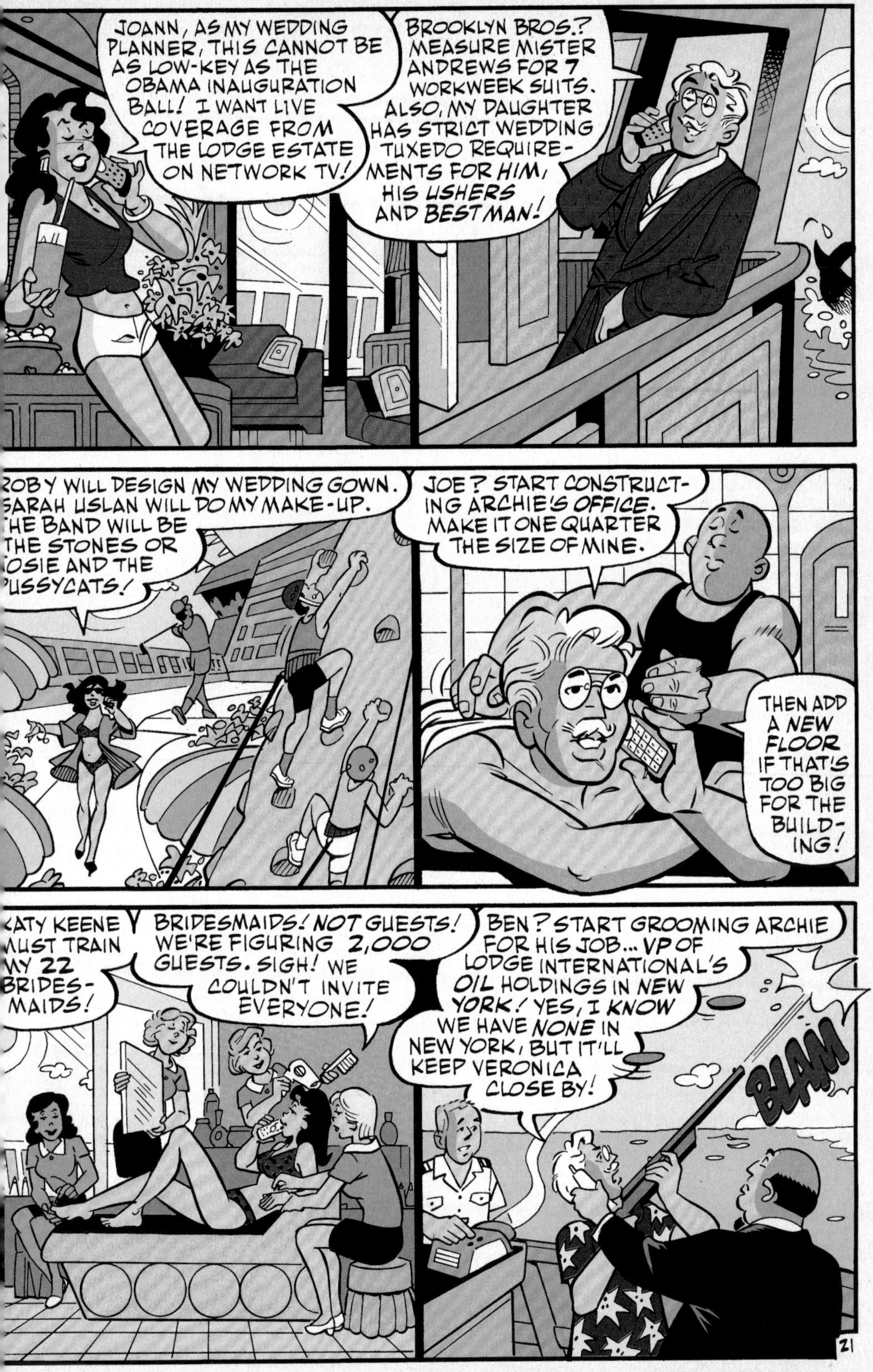
JOANN, AS MY WEDDING PLANNER, THIS CANNOT BE AS LOW-KEY AS THE OBAMA INAUGURATION BALL! I WANT LIVE COVERAGE FROM THE LODGE ESTATE ON NETWORK TV!
BROOKLYN BROS.? MEASURE MISTER ANDREWS FOR 7 WORKWEEK SUITS. ALSO, MY DAUGHTER HAS STRICT WEDDING TUXEDO REQUIREMENTS FOR HIM, HIS USHERS AND BEST MAN!
ROBY WILL DESIGN MY WEDDING GOWN. SARAH USLAN WILL DO MY MAKE-UP. THE BAND WILL BE THE STONES OR JOSIE AND THE PUSSYCATS!
JOE? START CONSTRUCTING ARCHIE'S OFFICE. MAKE IT ONE QUARTER THE SIZE OF MINE.
THEN ADD A NEW FLOOR IF THAT'S TOO BIG FOR THE BUILDING!
KATY KEENE MUST TRAIN MY 22 BRIDESMAIDS!
BRIDESMAIDS! NOT GUESTS! WE'RE FIGURING 2,000 GUESTS. SIGH! WE COULDN'T INVITE EVERYONE!
BEN? START GROOMING ARCHIE FOR HIS JOB... VP OF LODGE INTERNATIONAL'S OIL HOLDINGS IN NEW YORK! YES, I KNOW WE HAVE NONE IN NEW YORK, BUT IT'LL KEEP VERONICA CLOSE BY!
BLAM
21

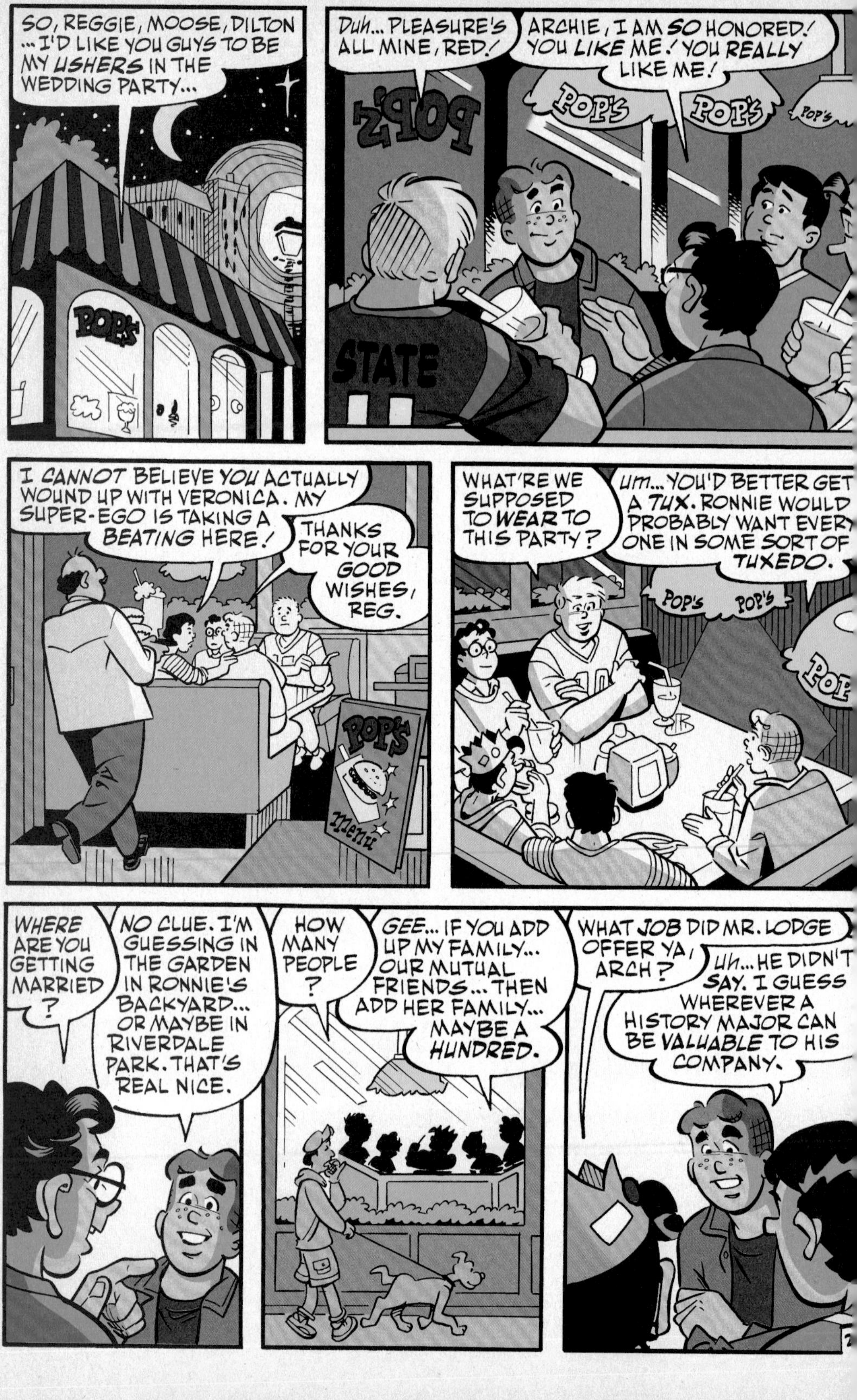
SO, REGGIE, MOOSE, DILTON ... I'D LIKE YOU GUYS TO BE MY USHERS IN THE WEDDING PARTY...
POP'S
DUH... PLEASURE'S ALL MINE, RED!
ARCHIE, I AM SO HONORED! YOU LIKE ME! YOU REALLY LIKE ME!
POP'S
STATE
I CANNOT BELIEVE YOU ACTUALLY WOUND UP WITH VERONICA. MY SUPER-EGO IS TAKING A BEATING HERE!
THANKS FOR YOUR GOOD WISHES, REG.
POP'S
MENU
WHAT'RE WE SUPPOSED TO WEAR TO THIS PARTY?
UM... YOU'D BETTER GET A TUX. RONNIE WOULD PROBABLY WANT EVERY ONE IN SOME SORT OF TUXEDO.
WHERE ARE YOU GETTING MARRIED?
NO CLUE. I'M GUESSING IN THE GARDEN IN RONNIE'S BACKYARD... OR MAYBE IN RIVERDALE PARK. THAT'S REAL NICE.
HOW MANY PEOPLE?
GEE... IF YOU ADD UP MY FAMILY... OUR MUTUAL FRIENDS... THEN ADD HER FAMILY... MAYBE A HUNDRED.
WHAT JOB DID MR. LODGE OFFER YA, ARCH?
UH... HE DIDN'T SAY. I GUESS WHEREVER A HISTORY MAJOR CAN BE VALUABLE TO HIS COMPANY.

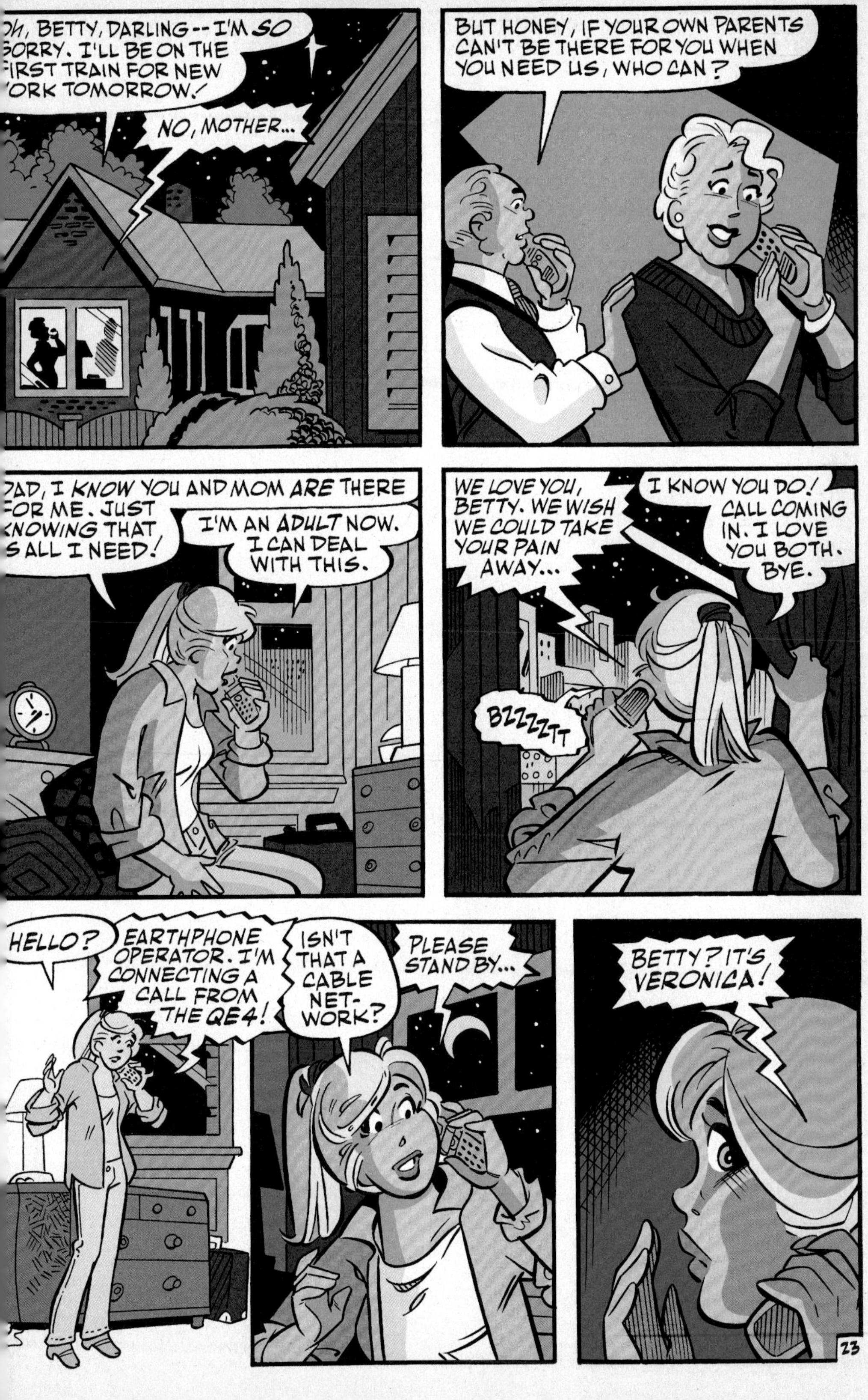
OH, BETTY, DARLING -- I'M SO SORRY. I'LL BE ON THE FIRST TRAIN FOR NEW YORK TOMORROW!
NO, MOTHER...
BUT HONEY, IF YOUR OWN PARENTS CAN'T BE THERE FOR YOU WHEN YOU NEED US, WHO CAN?
DAD, I KNOW YOU AND MOM ARE THERE FOR ME. JUST KNOWING THAT IS ALL I NEED!
I'M AN ADULT NOW. I CAN DEAL WITH THIS.
WE LOVE YOU, BETTY. WE WISH WE COULD TAKE YOUR PAIN AWAY...
I KNOW YOU DO! CALL COMING IN. I LOVE YOU BOTH. BYE.
BZZZZZTT
HELLO?
EARTHPHONE OPERATOR. I'M CONNECTING A CALL FROM THE QE4!
ISN'T THAT A CABLE NET-WORK?
PLEASE STAND BY...
BETTY? IT'S VERONICA!
23

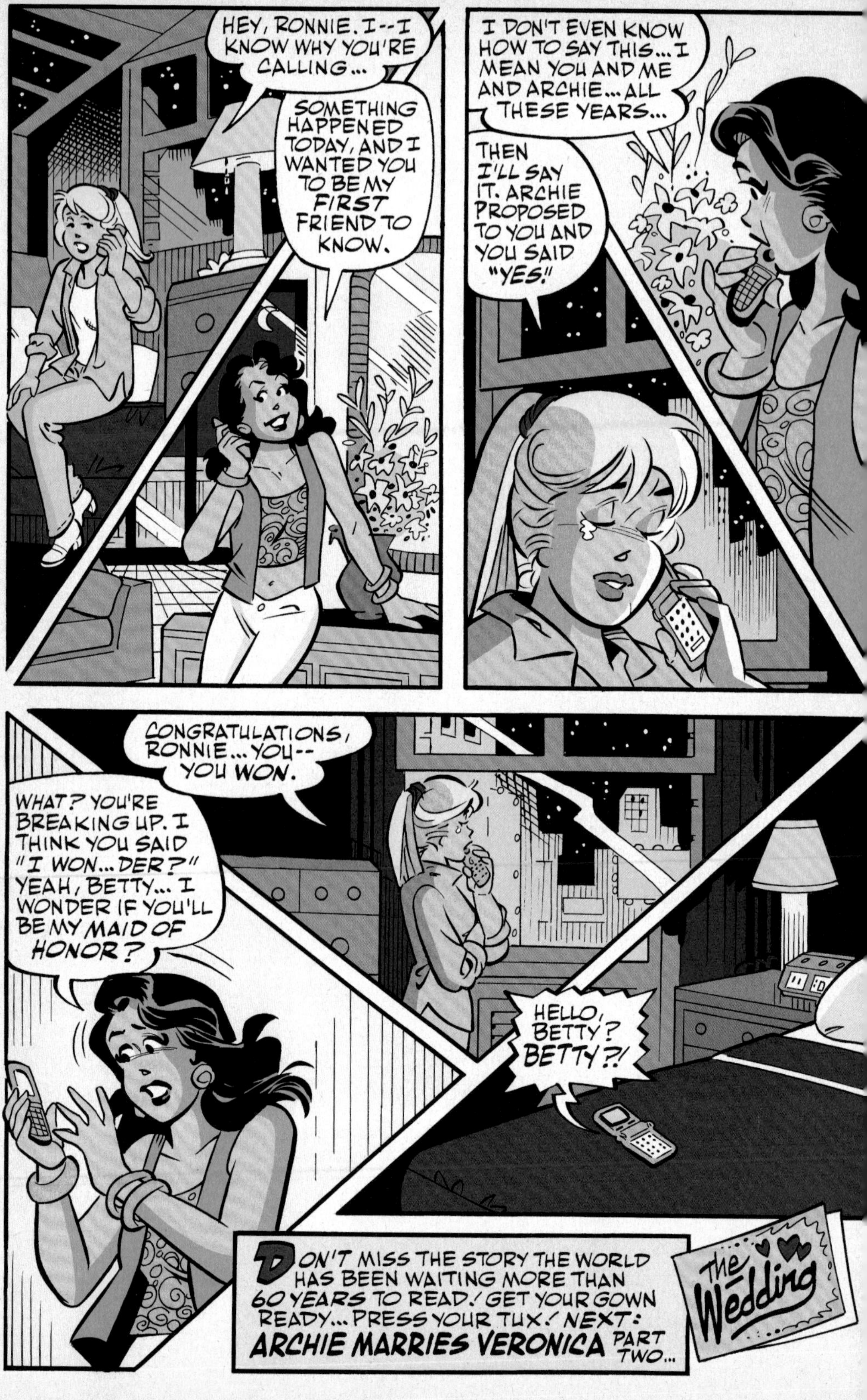
HEY, RONNIE. I--I KNOW WHY YOU'RE CALLING...
SOMETHING HAPPENED TODAY, AND I WANTED YOU TO BE MY FIRST FRIEND TO KNOW.
I DON'T EVEN KNOW HOW TO SAY THIS... I MEAN YOU AND ME AND ARCHIE... ALL THESE YEARS...
THEN I'LL SAY IT. ARCHIE PROPOSED TO YOU AND YOU SAID "YES!"
CONGRATULATIONS, RONNIE... YOU-- YOU WON.
WHAT? YOU'RE BREAKING UP. I THINK YOU SAID "I WON...DER?" YEAH, BETTY... I WONDER IF YOU'LL BE MY MAID OF HONOR?
HELLO, BETTY? BETTY?!
DON'T MISS THE STORY THE WORLD HAS BEEN WAITING MORE THAN 60 YEARS TO READ! GET YOUR GOWN READY... PRESS YOUR TUX! NEXT: ARCHIE MARRIES VERONICA PART TWO...
The Wedding

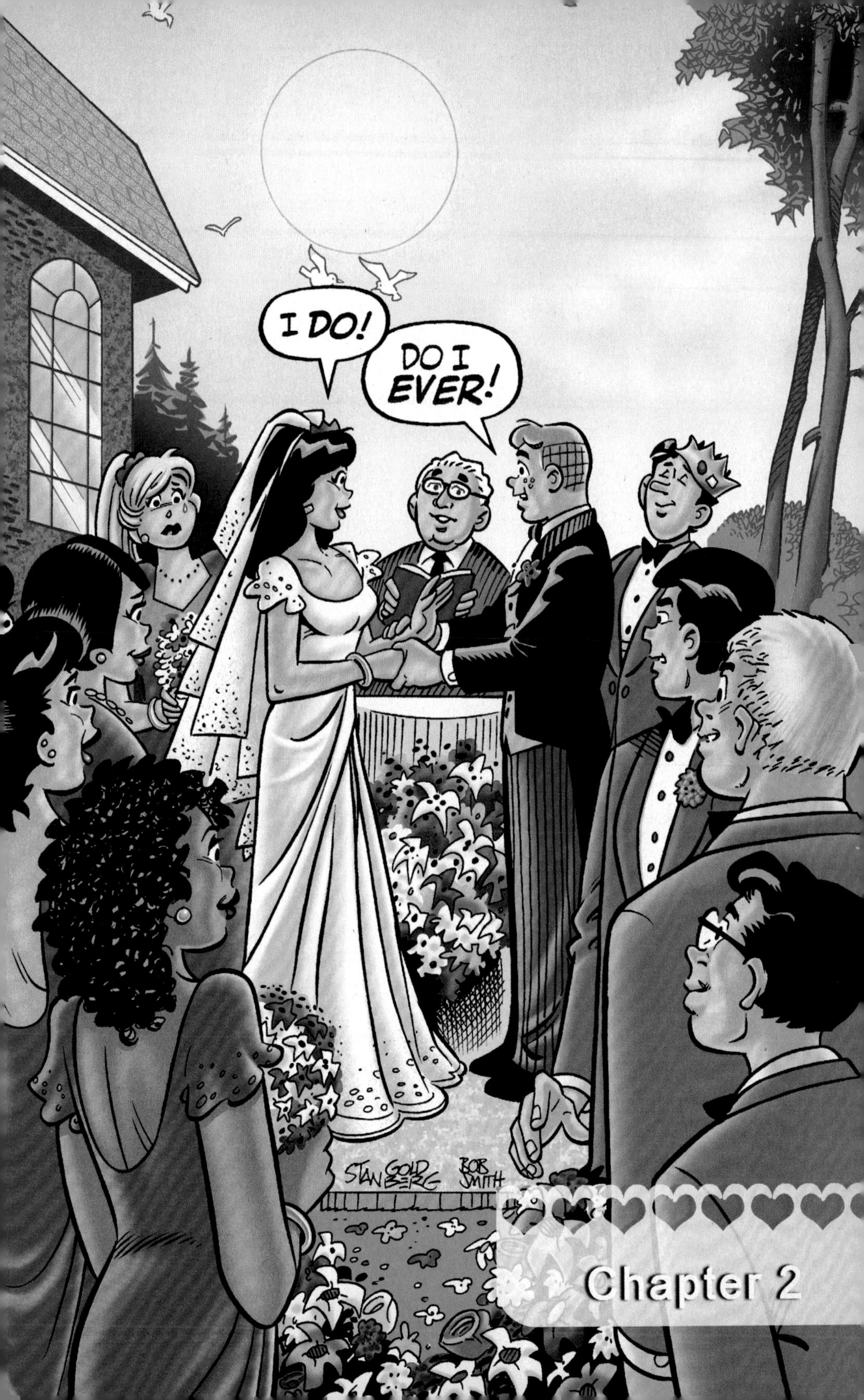
I DO!
DO I EVER!
STAN GOLDBERG
BOB SMITH

Chapter 2

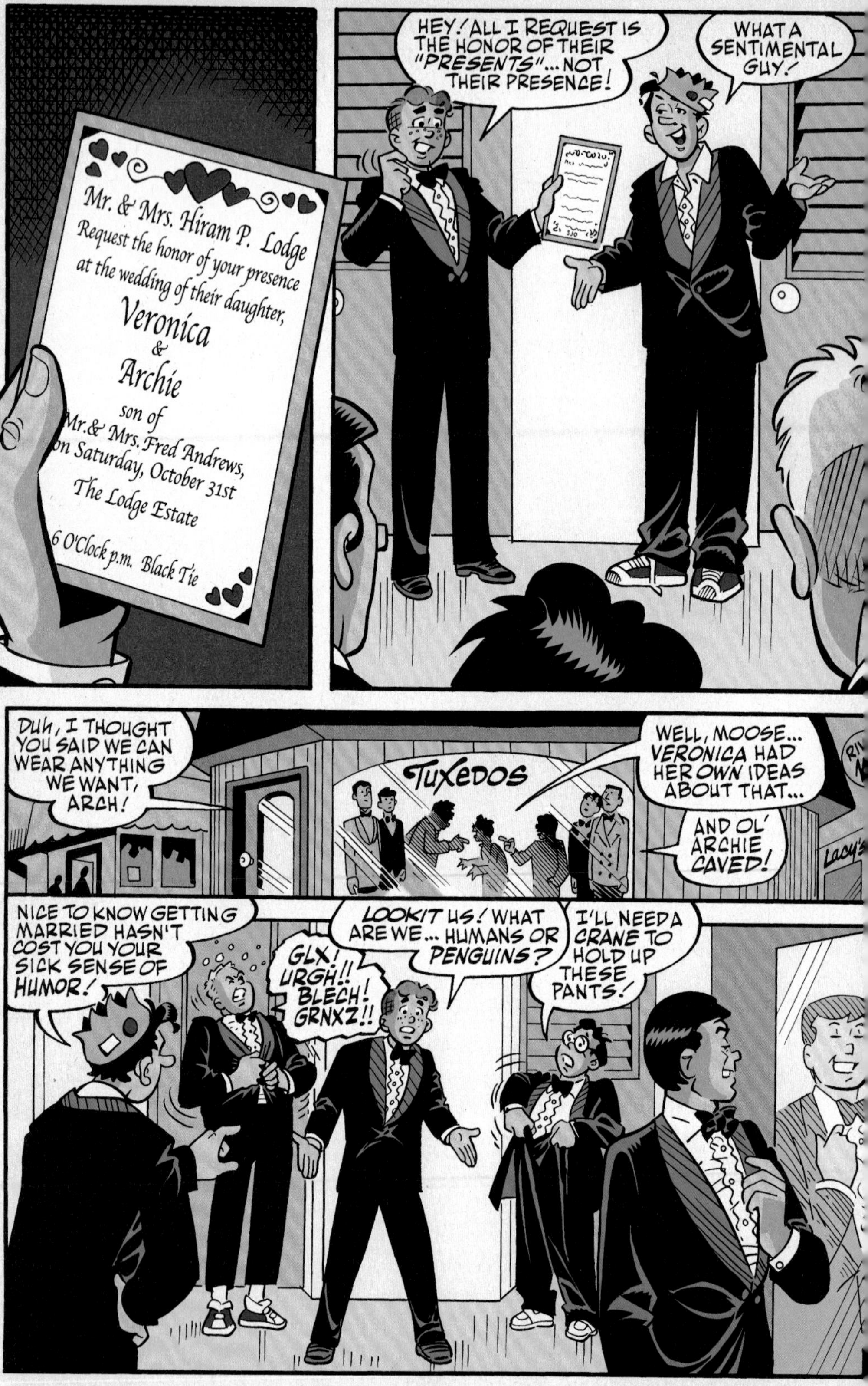

Mr. & Mrs. Hiram P. Lodge
Request the honor of your presence
at the wedding of their daughter,
Veronica
&
Archie
son of
Mr.& Mrs. Fred Andrews,
on Saturday, October 31st
The Lodge Estate
6 O'Clock p.m. Black Tie
HEY! ALL I REQUEST IS THE HONOR OF THEIR "PRESENTS"... NOT THEIR PRESENCE!
WHAT A SENTIMENTAL GUY!
DUH, I THOUGHT YOU SAID WE CAN WEAR ANYTHING WE WANT, ARCH!
TUXEDOS
WELL, MOOSE... VERONICA HAD HER OWN IDEAS ABOUT THAT...
AND OL' ARCHIE CAVED!
NICE TO KNOW GETTING MARRIED HASN'T COST YOU YOUR SICK SENSE OF HUMOR!
GLX! URGH!! BLECH! GRNXZ!!
LOOKIT US! WHAT ARE WE... HUMANS OR PENGUINS?
I'LL NEED A CRANE TO HOLD UP THESE PANTS!

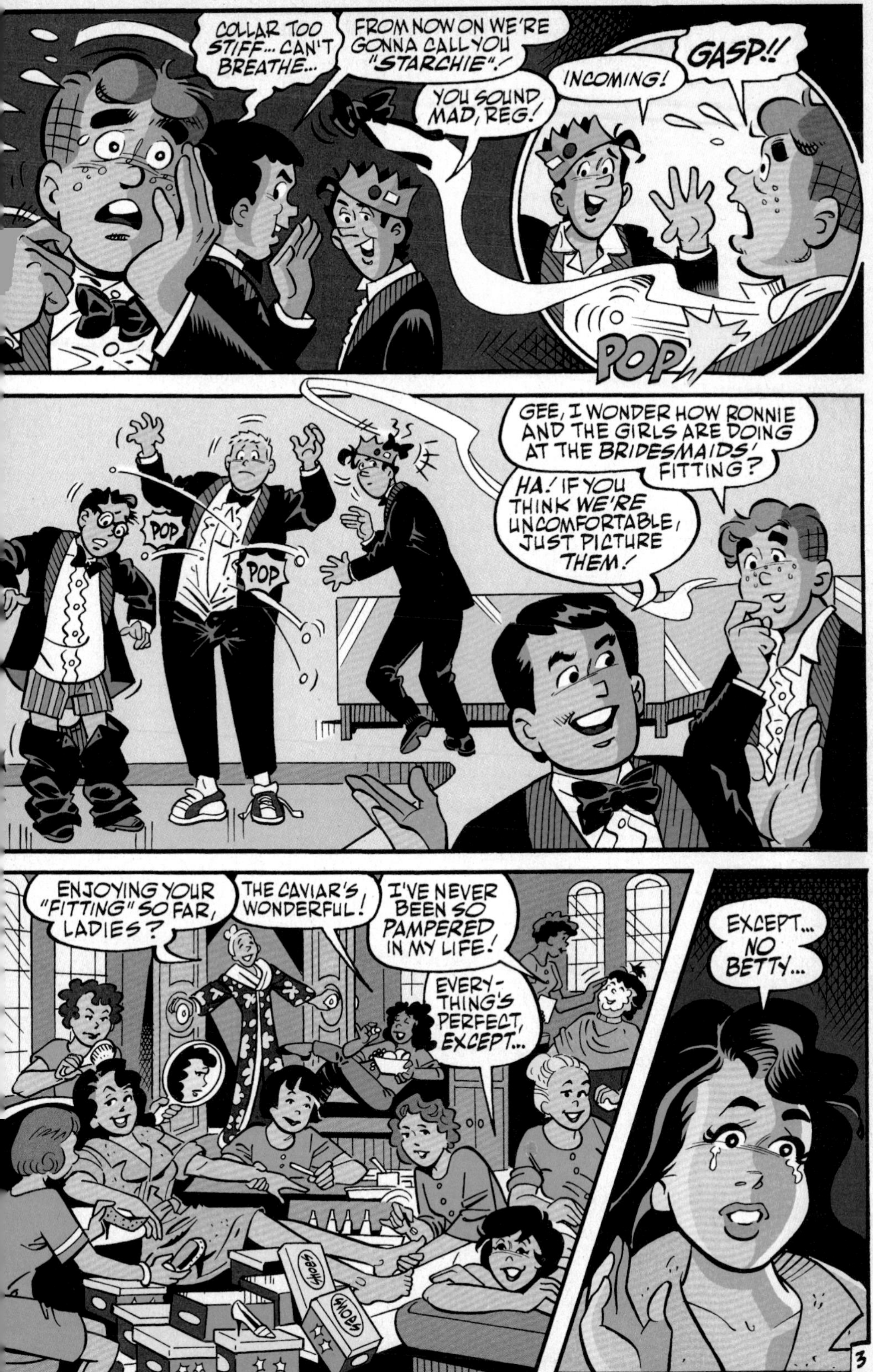
COLLAR TOO STIFF... CAN'T BREATHE...
FROM NOW ON WE'RE GONNA CALL YOU "STARCHIE"!
YOU SOUND MAD, REG!
INCOMING!
GASP!!
POP
GEE, I WONDER HOW RONNIE AND THE GIRLS ARE DOING AT THE BRIDESMAIDS' FITTING?
HA! IF YOU THINK WE'RE UNCOMFORTABLE, JUST PICTURE THEM!
POP
POP
ENJOYING YOUR "FITTING" SO FAR, LADIES?
THE CAVIAR'S WONDERFUL!
I'VE NEVER BEEN SO PAMPERED IN MY LIFE!
EVERY-THING'S PERFECT, EXCEPT...
SHOES
SHOES
EXCEPT... NO BETTY...
3

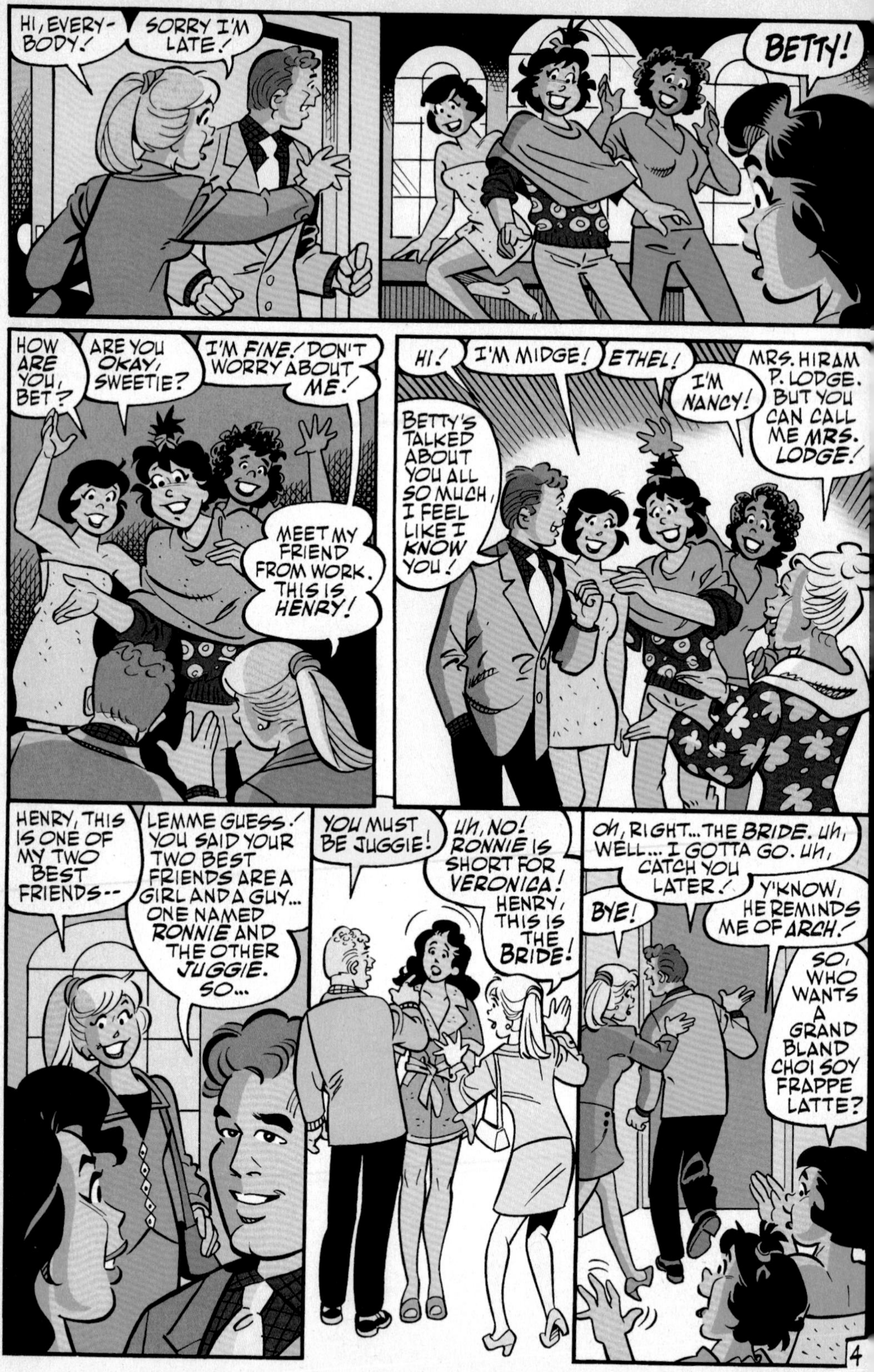

HI, EVERY-BODY!
SORRY I'M LATE!
BETTY!
HOW ARE YOU, BET?
ARE YOU OKAY, SWEETIE?
I'M FINE! DON'T WORRY ABOUT ME!
MEET MY FRIEND FROM WORK. THIS IS HENRY!
HI!
I'M MIDGE!
ETHEL!
I'M NANCY!
MRS. HIRAM P. LODGE. BUT YOU CAN CALL ME MRS. LODGE!
BETTY'S TALKED ABOUT YOU ALL SO MUCH, I FEEL LIKE I KNOW YOU!
HENRY, THIS IS ONE OF MY TWO BEST FRIENDS--
LEMME GUESS! YOU SAID YOUR TWO BEST FRIENDS ARE A GIRL AND A GUY... ONE NAMED RONNIE AND THE OTHER JUGGIE. SO...
YOU MUST BE JUGGIE!
UH, NO! RONNIE IS SHORT FOR VERONICA! HENRY, THIS IS THE BRIDE!
OH, RIGHT... THE BRIDE. UH, WELL... I GOTTA GO. UH, CATCH YOU LATER!
BYE!
Y'KNOW, HE REMINDS ME OF ARCH!
SO, WHO WANTS A GRAND BLAND CHOI SOY FRAPPE LATTE?
4

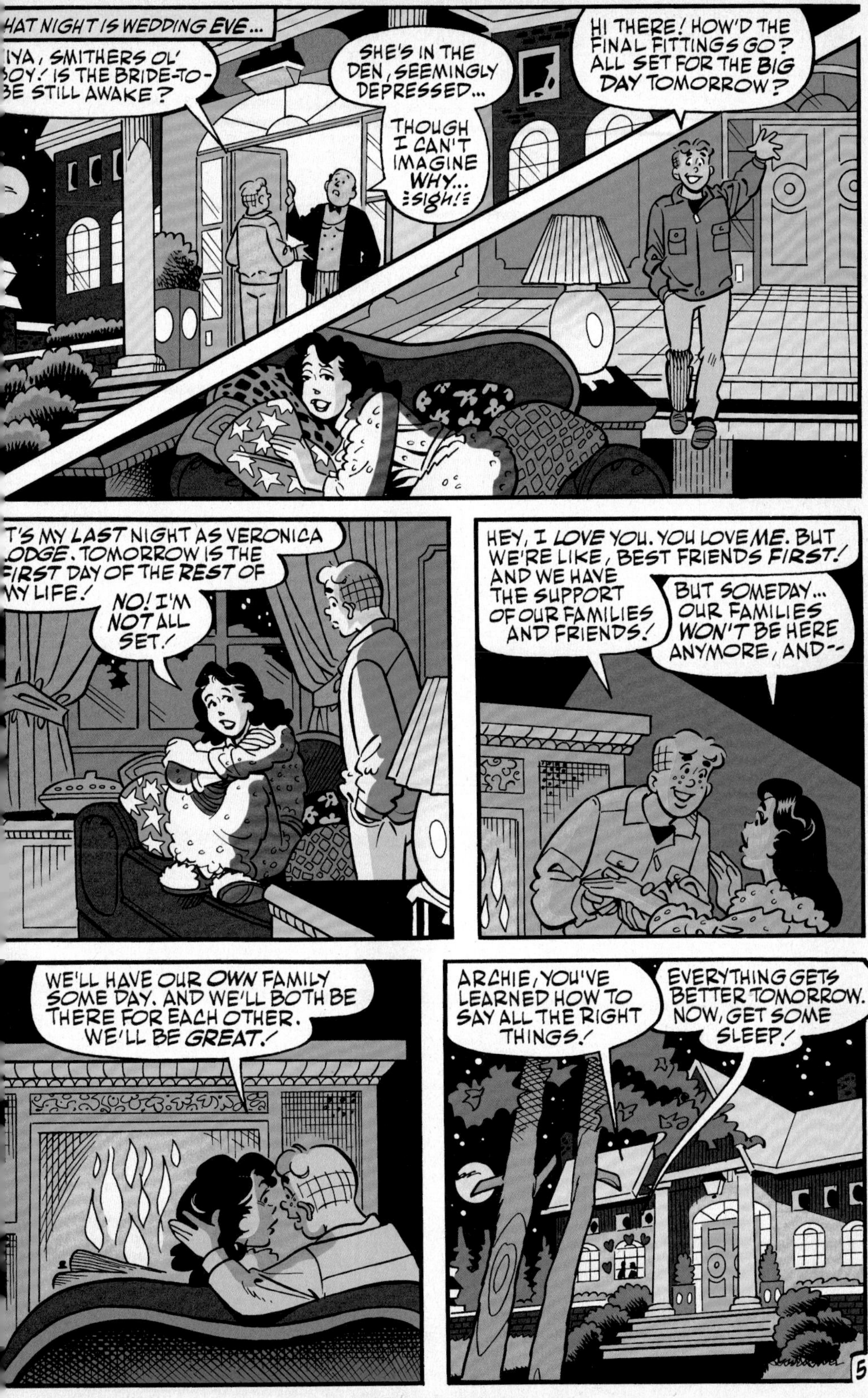
HAT NIGHT IS WEDDING EVE...
IYA, SMITHERS OL' BOY! IS THE BRIDE-TO-BE STILL AWAKE?
SHE'S IN THE DEN, SEEMINGLY DEPRESSED...
THOUGH I CAN'T IMAGINE WHY... sigh!
HI THERE! HOW'D THE FINAL FITTINGS GO? ALL SET FOR THE BIG DAY TOMORROW?
T'S MY LAST NIGHT AS VERONICA LODGE. TOMORROW IS THE FIRST DAY OF THE REST OF MY LIFE!
NO! I'M NOT ALL SET!
HEY, I LOVE YOU. YOU LOVE ME. BUT WE'RE LIKE, BEST FRIENDS FIRST! AND WE HAVE THE SUPPORT OF OUR FAMILIES AND FRIENDS!
BUT SOMEDAY... OUR FAMILIES WON'T BE HERE ANYMORE, AND--
WE'LL HAVE OUR OWN FAMILY SOME DAY. AND WE'LL BOTH BE THERE FOR EACH OTHER. WE'LL BE GREAT!
ARCHIE, YOU'VE LEARNED HOW TO SAY ALL THE RIGHT THINGS!
EVERYTHING GETS BETTER TOMORROW. NOW, GET SOME SLEEP!
5

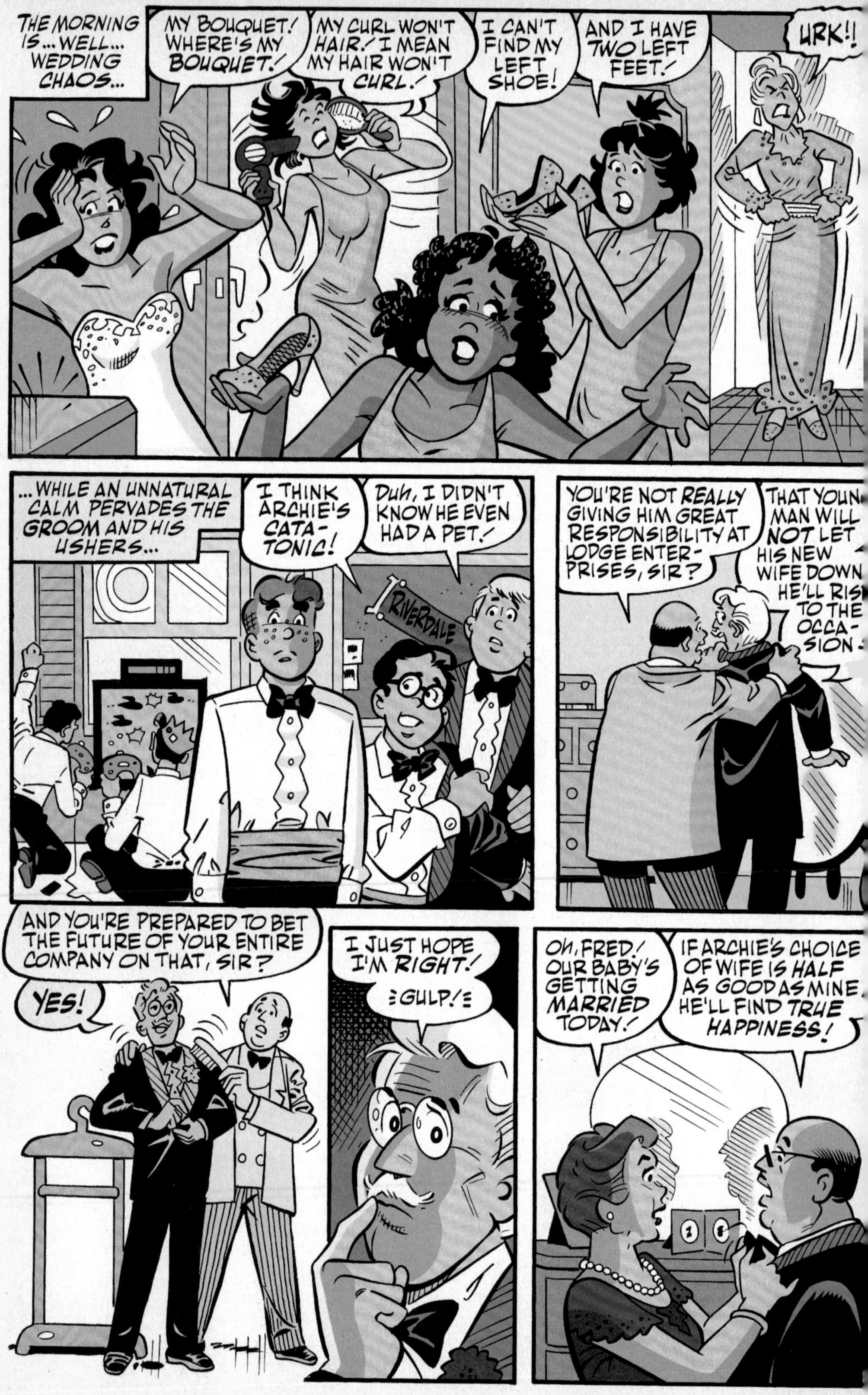
THE MORNING IS... WELL... WEDDING CHAOS...
MY BOUQUET! WHERE'S MY BOUQUET!
MY CURL WON'T HAIR! I MEAN MY HAIR WON'T CURL!
I CAN'T FIND MY LEFT SHOE!
AND I HAVE TWO LEFT FEET!
URK!!
...WHILE AN UNNATURAL CALM PERVADES THE GROOM AND HIS USHERS...
I THINK ARCHIE'S CATATONIC!
Duh, I DIDN'T KNOW HE EVEN HAD A PET!
RIVERDALE
YOU'RE NOT REALLY GIVING HIM GREAT RESPONSIBILITY AT LODGE ENTERPRISES, SIR?
THAT YOUN MAN WILL NOT LET HIS NEW WIFE DOWN HE'LL RIS TO THE OCCASION
AND YOU'RE PREPARED TO BET THE FUTURE OF YOUR ENTIRE COMPANY ON THAT, SIR?
YES!
I JUST HOPE I'M RIGHT!
GULP!
Oh, FRED! OUR BABY'S GETTING MARRIED TODAY!
IF ARCHIE'S CHOICE OF WIFE IS HALF AS GOOD AS MINE, HE'LL FIND TRUE HAPPINESS!

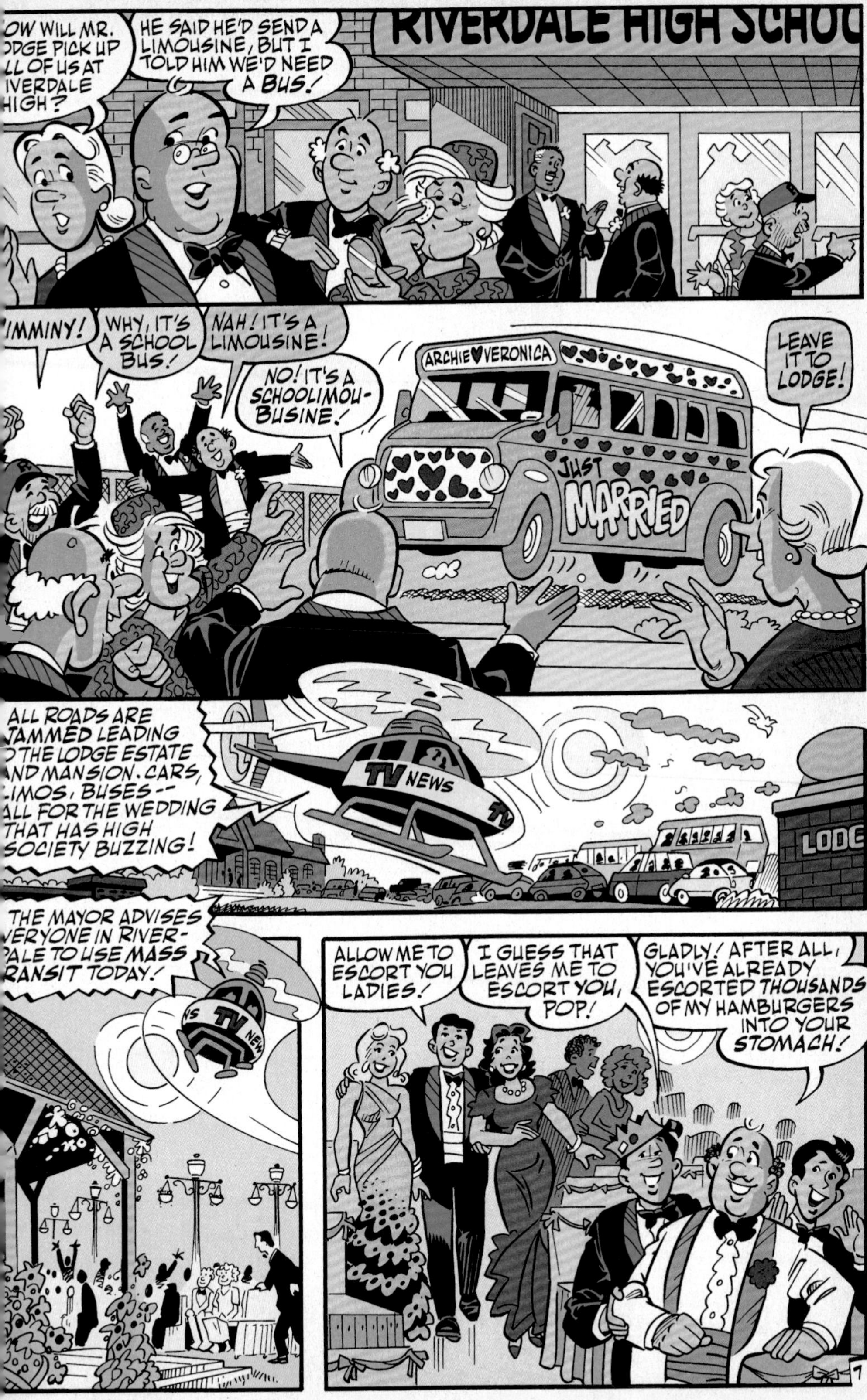
RIVERDALE HIGH SCHOO
OW WILL MR. ODGE PICK UP LL OF US AT IVERDALE HIGH?
HE SAID HE'D SEND A LIMOUSINE, BUT I TOLD HIM WE'D NEED A BUS!
IMMINY!
WHY, IT'S A SCHOOL BUS!
NAH! IT'S A LIMOUSINE!
NO! IT'S A SCHOOLIMOU-BUSINE!
ARCHIE♥VERONICA
JUST MARRIED
LEAVE IT TO LODGE!
ALL ROADS ARE JAMMED LEADING O THE LODGE ESTATE AND MANSION. CARS, LIMOS, BUSES -- ALL FOR THE WEDDING THAT HAS HIGH SOCIETY BUZZING!
TV NEWS
LODG
THE MAYOR ADVISES VERYONE IN RIVER-DALE TO USE MASS RANSIT TODAY!
ALLOW ME TO ESCORT YOU LADIES!
I GUESS THAT LEAVES ME TO ESCORT YOU, POP!
GLADLY! AFTER ALL, YOU'VE ALREADY ESCORTED THOUSANDS OF MY HAMBURGERS INTO YOUR STOMACH!
7

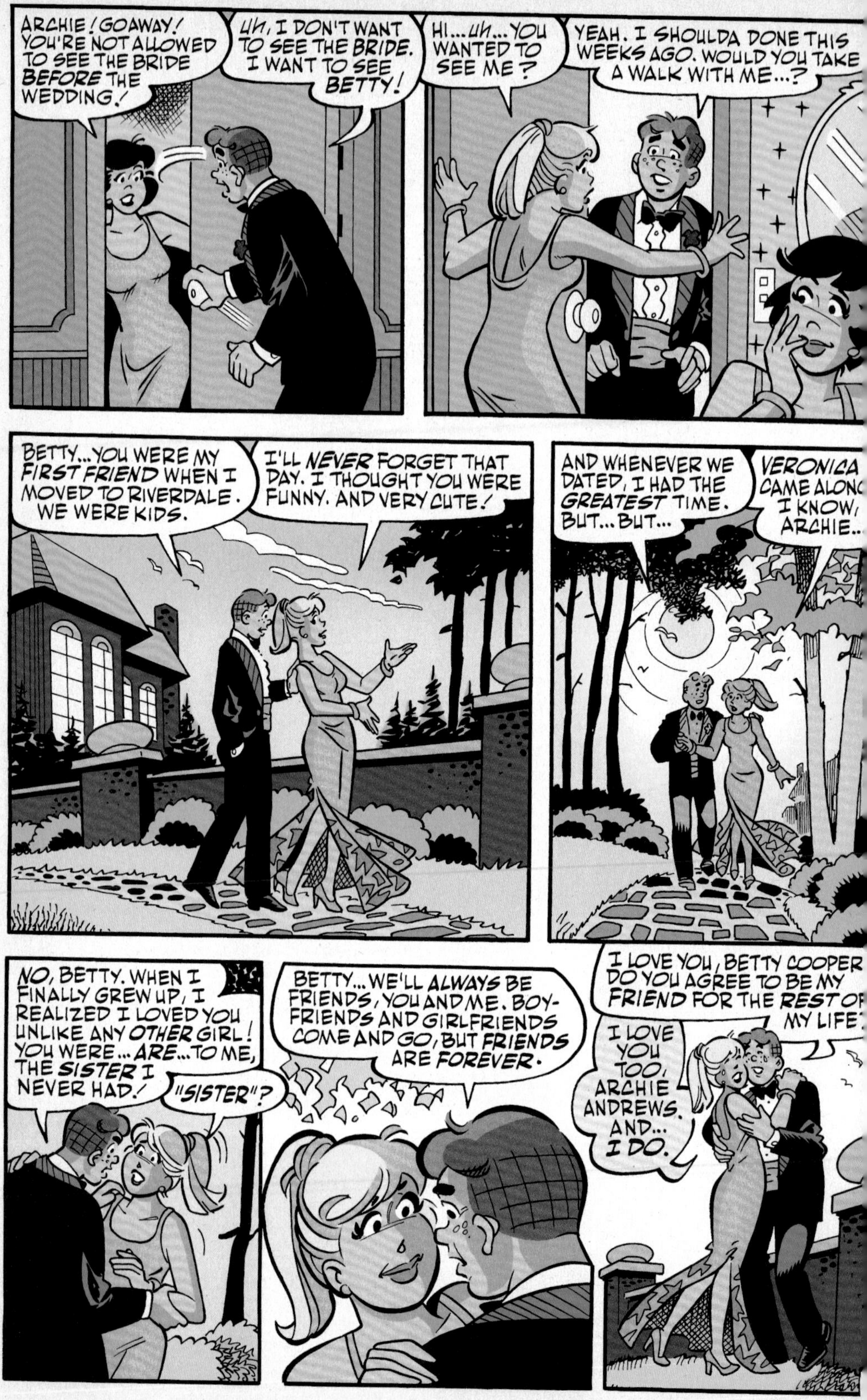
ARCHIE! GO AWAY! YOU'RE NOT ALLOWED TO SEE THE BRIDE BEFORE THE WEDDING!
UH, I DON'T WANT TO SEE THE BRIDE. I WANT TO SEE BETTY!
HI... UH... YOU WANTED TO SEE ME?
YEAH. I SHOULDA DONE THIS WEEKS AGO. WOULD YOU TAKE A WALK WITH ME...?
BETTY... YOU WERE MY FIRST FRIEND WHEN I MOVED TO RIVERDALE. WE WERE KIDS.
I'LL NEVER FORGET THAT DAY. I THOUGHT YOU WERE FUNNY. AND VERY CUTE!
AND WHENEVER WE DATED, I HAD THE GREATEST TIME. BUT... BUT...
VERONICA CAME ALON I KNOW, ARCHIE...
NO, BETTY. WHEN I FINALLY GREW UP, I REALIZED I LOVED YOU UNLIKE ANY OTHER GIRL! YOU WERE... ARE... TO ME, THE SISTER I NEVER HAD!
"SISTER"?
BETTY... WE'LL ALWAYS BE FRIENDS, YOU AND ME. BOY-FRIENDS AND GIRLFRIENDS COME AND GO, BUT FRIENDS ARE FOREVER.
I LOVE YOU, BETTY COOPER DO YOU AGREE TO BE MY FRIEND FOR THE REST O MY LIFE
I LOVE YOU TOO, ARCHIE ANDREWS. AND... I DO.

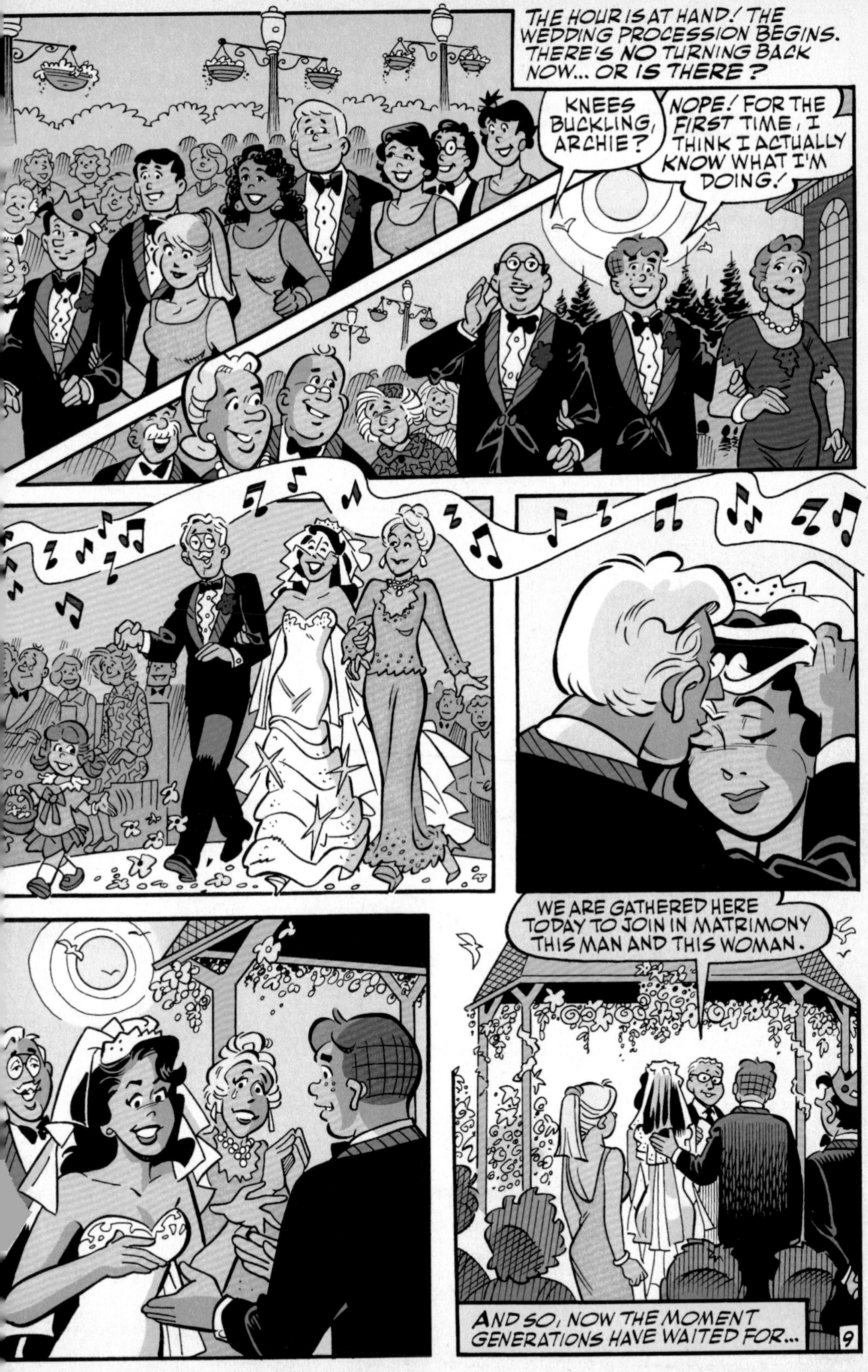
THE HOUR IS AT HAND! THE WEDDING PROCESSION BEGINS. THERE'S NO TURNING BACK NOW... OR IS THERE?
KNEES BUCKLING, ARCHIE?
NOPE! FOR THE FIRST TIME, I THINK I ACTUALLY KNOW WHAT I'M DOING!
WE ARE GATHERED HERE TODAY TO JOIN IN MATRIMONY THIS MAN AND THIS WOMAN.
AND SO, NOW THE MOMENT GENERATIONS HAVE WAITED FOR...
9

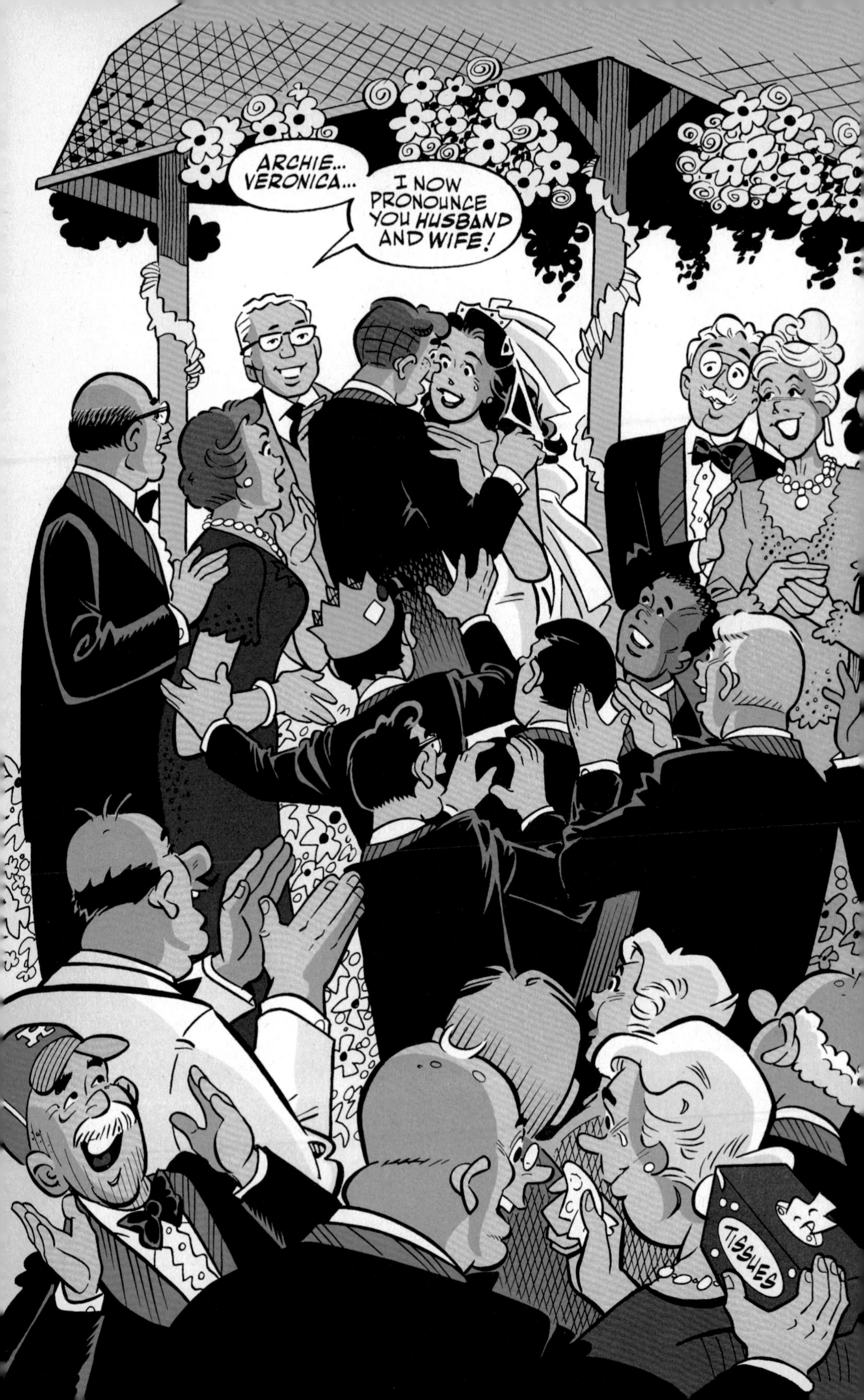
ARCHIE... VERONICA...
I NOW PRONOUNCE YOU HUSBAND AND WIFE!
TISSUES

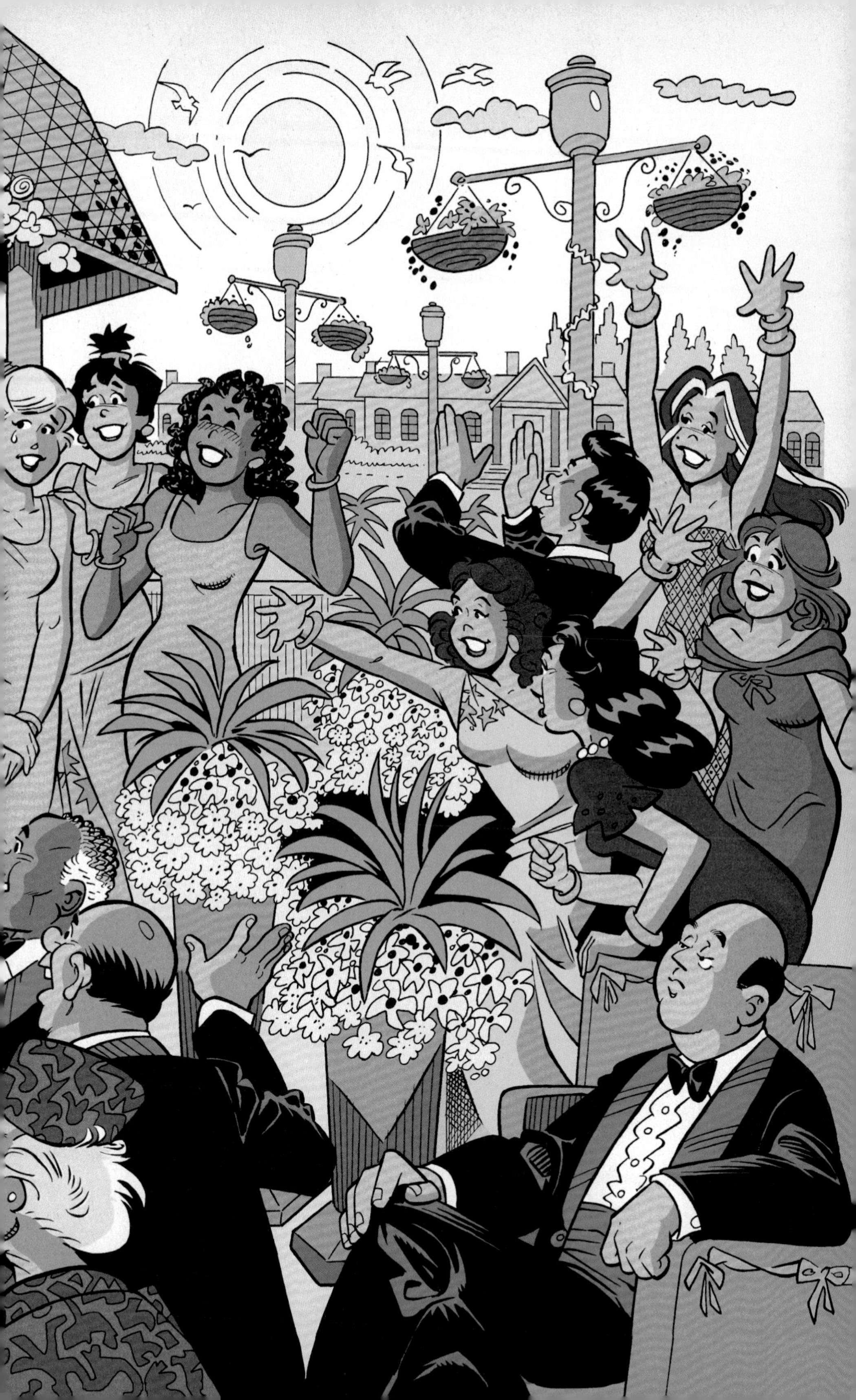

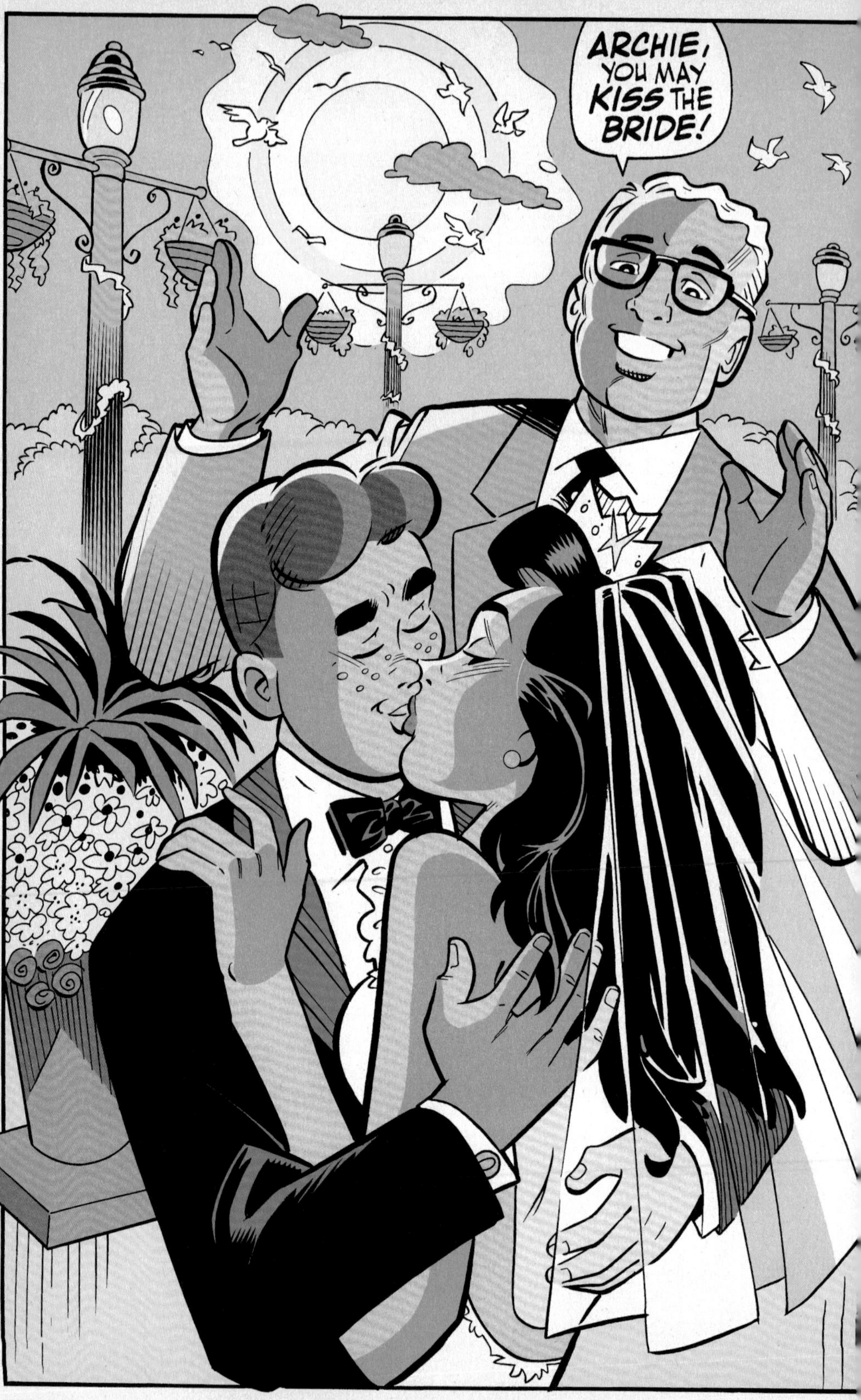
ARCHIE, YOU MAY KISS THE BRIDE!

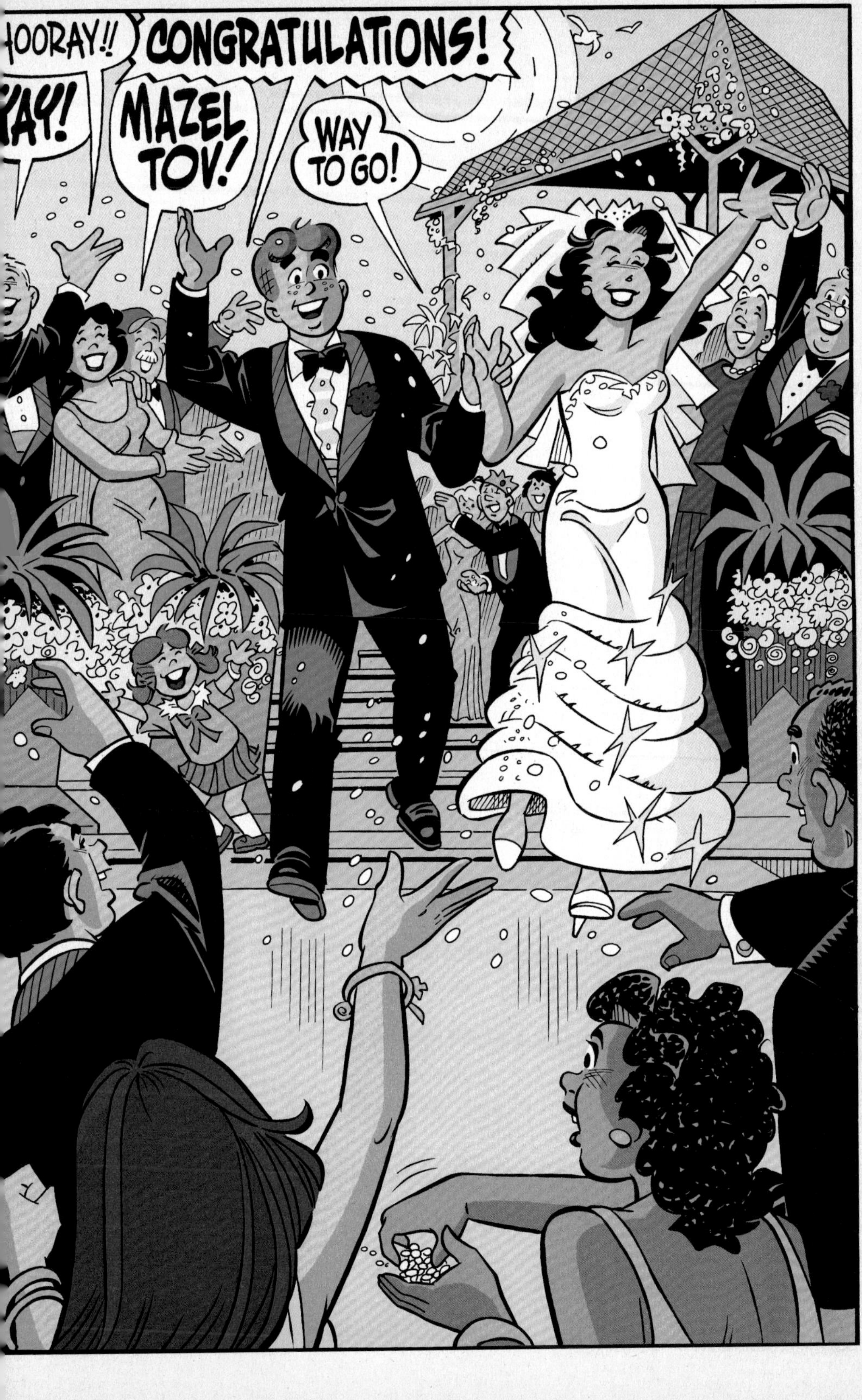
HOORAY!!
CONGRATULATIONS!
YAY!
MAZEL TOV!
WAY TO GO!

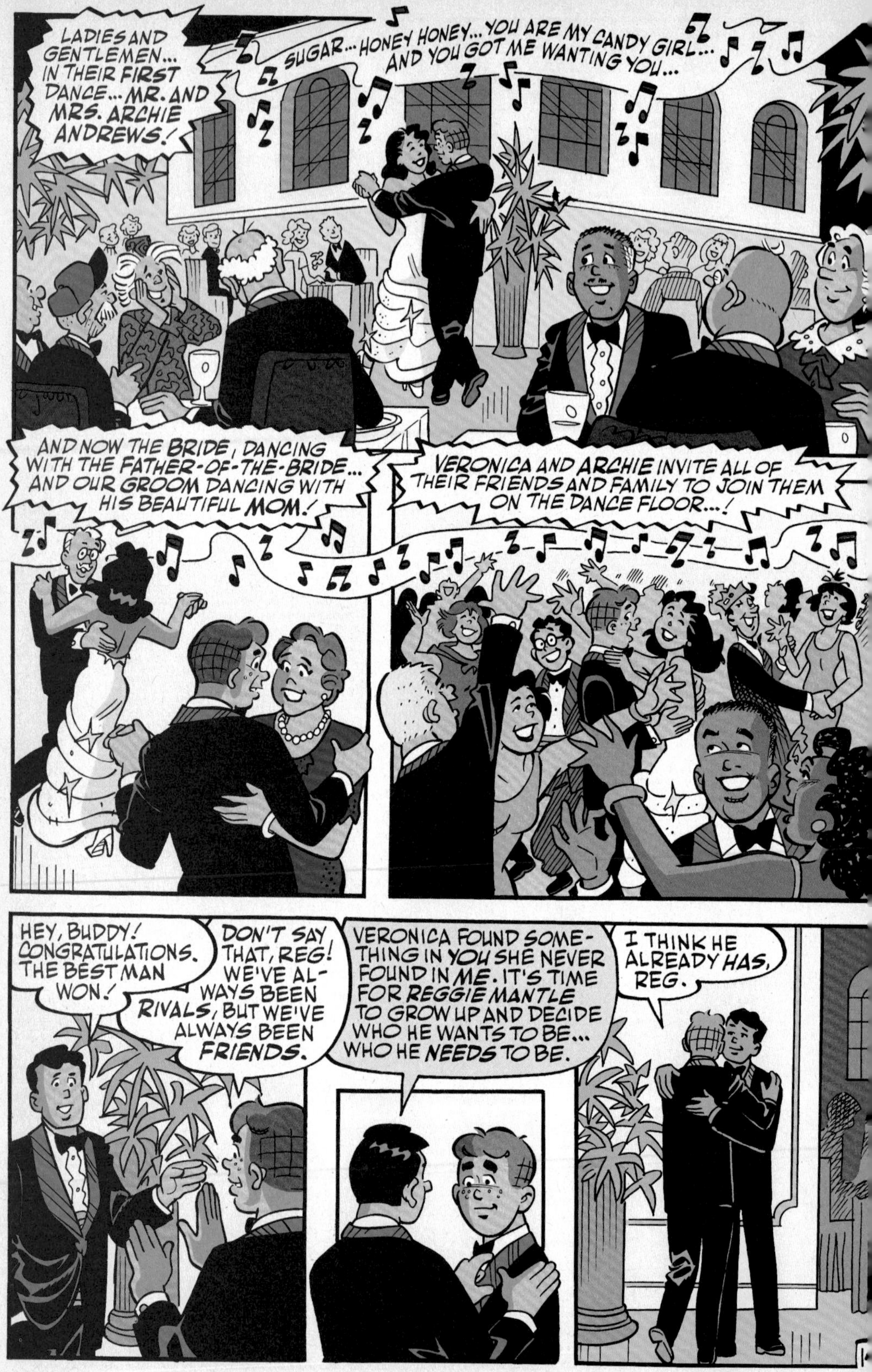
LADIES AND GENTLEMEN... IN THEIR FIRST DANCE... MR. AND MRS. ARCHIE ANDREWS!
SUGAR... HONEY HONEY... YOU ARE MY CANDY GIRL... AND YOU GOT ME WANTING YOU...
AND NOW THE BRIDE, DANCING WITH THE FATHER-OF-THE-BRIDE... AND OUR GROOM DANCING WITH HIS BEAUTIFUL MOM!
VERONICA AND ARCHIE INVITE ALL OF THEIR FRIENDS AND FAMILY TO JOIN THEM ON THE DANCE FLOOR...!
HEY, BUDDY! CONGRATULATIONS. THE BEST MAN WON!
DON'T SAY THAT, REG! WE'VE ALWAYS BEEN RIVALS, BUT WE'VE ALWAYS BEEN FRIENDS.
VERONICA FOUND SOMETHING IN YOU SHE NEVER FOUND IN ME. IT'S TIME FOR REGGIE MANTLE TO GROW UP AND DECIDE WHO HE WANTS TO BE... WHO HE NEEDS TO BE.
I THINK HE ALREADY HAS, REG.

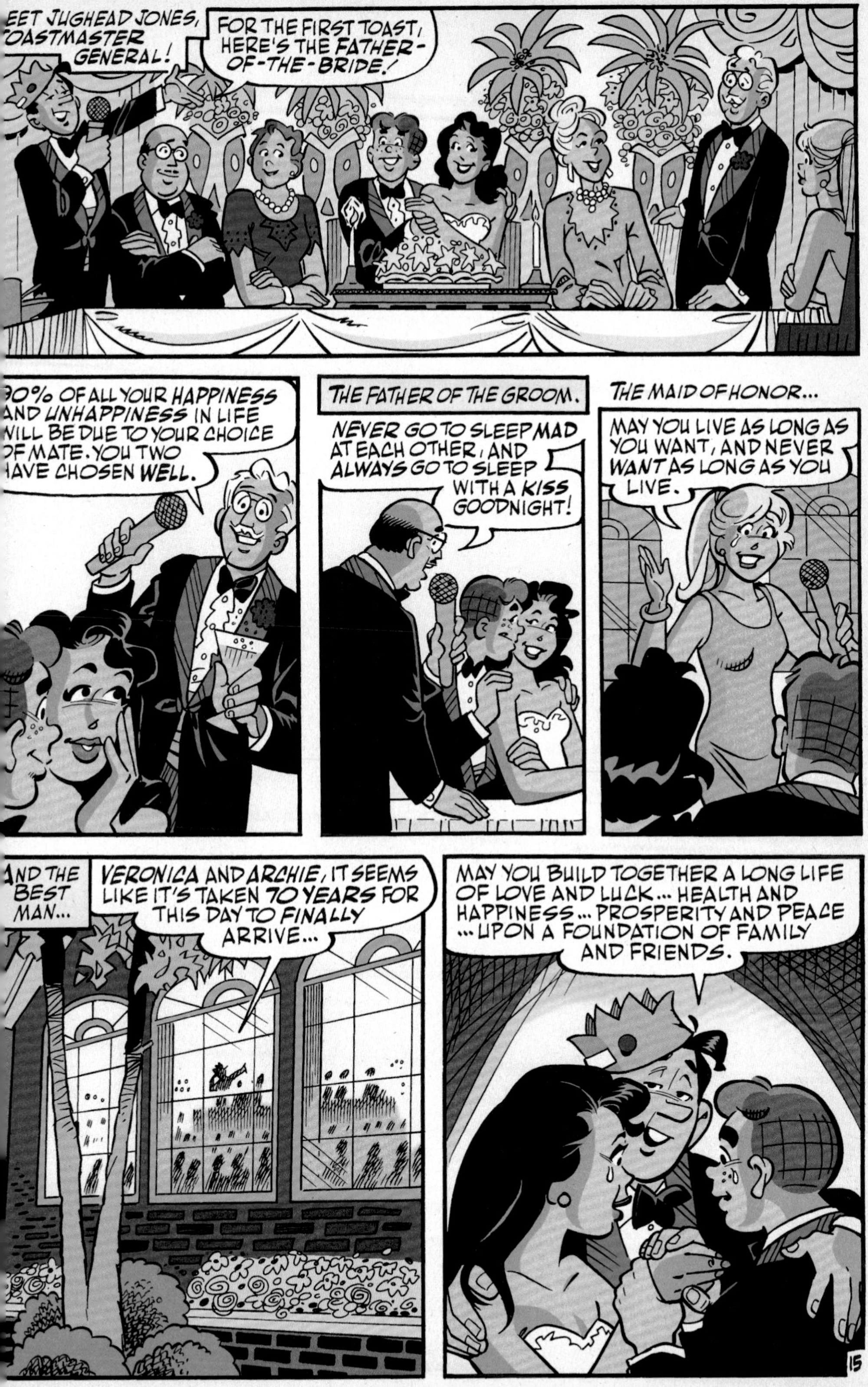

EET JUGHEAD JONES, TOASTMASTER GENERAL!
FOR THE FIRST TOAST, HERE'S THE FATHER-OF-THE-BRIDE!
90% OF ALL YOUR HAPPINESS AND UNHAPPINESS IN LIFE WILL BE DUE TO YOUR CHOICE OF MATE. YOU TWO HAVE CHOSEN WELL.
THE FATHER OF THE GROOM.
NEVER GO TO SLEEP MAD AT EACH OTHER, AND ALWAYS GO TO SLEEP WITH A KISS GOODNIGHT!
THE MAID OF HONOR...
MAY YOU LIVE AS LONG AS YOU WANT, AND NEVER WANT AS LONG AS YOU LIVE.
AND THE BEST MAN...
VERONICA AND ARCHIE, IT SEEMS LIKE IT'S TAKEN 70 YEARS FOR THIS DAY TO FINALLY ARRIVE...
MAY YOU BUILD TOGETHER A LONG LIFE OF LOVE AND LUCK... HEALTH AND HAPPINESS... PROSPERITY AND PEACE ...UPON A FOUNDATION OF FAMILY AND FRIENDS.
15

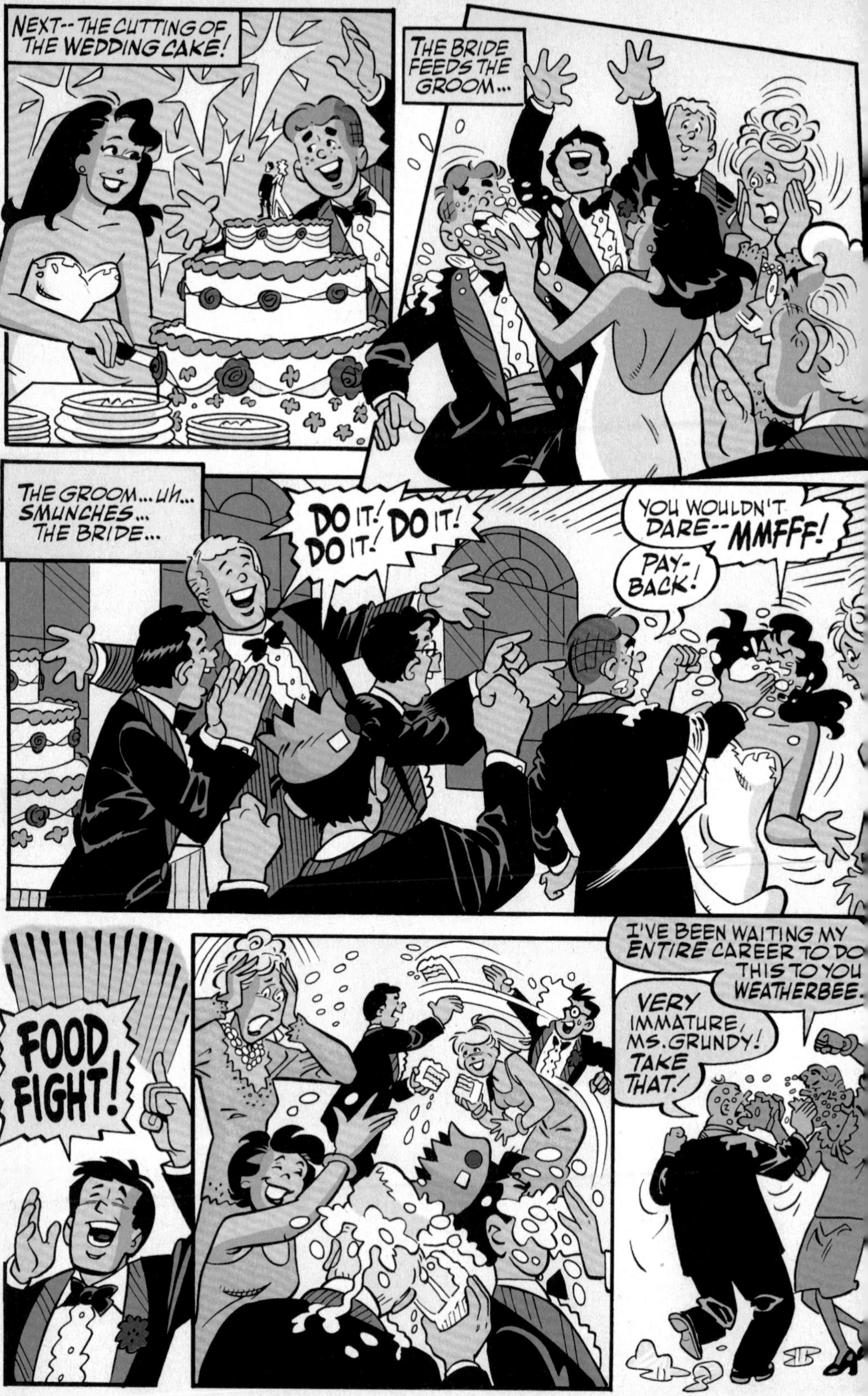
NEXT-- THE CUTTING OF THE WEDDING CAKE!
THE BRIDE FEEDS THE GROOM...
THE GROOM... uh... SMUNCHES... THE BRIDE...
DO IT! DO IT! DO IT!
YOU WOULDN'T DARE-- MMFFF!
PAY-BACK!
FOOD FIGHT!
I'VE BEEN WAITING MY ENTIRE CAREER TO DO THIS TO YOU WEATHERBEE.
VERY IMMATURE, MS. GRUNDY! TAKE THAT!

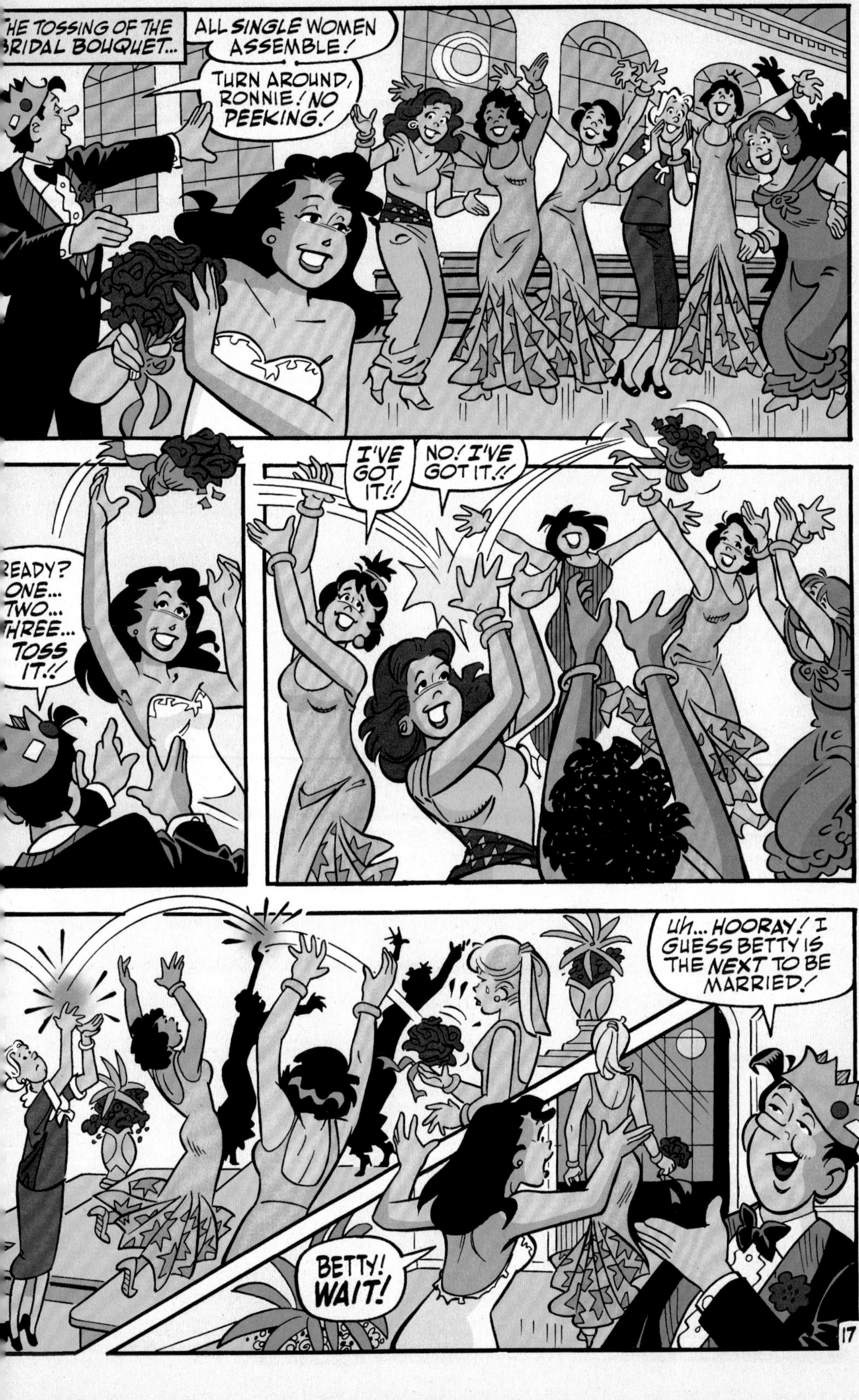
THE TOSSING OF THE BRIDAL BOUQUET...
ALL SINGLE WOMEN ASSEMBLE!
TURN AROUND, RONNIE! NO PEEKING!
READY? ONE... TWO... THREE... TOSS IT!!
I'VE GOT IT!!
NO! I'VE GOT IT!!
UH... HOORAY! I GUESS BETTY IS THE NEXT TO BE MARRIED!
BETTY! WAIT!

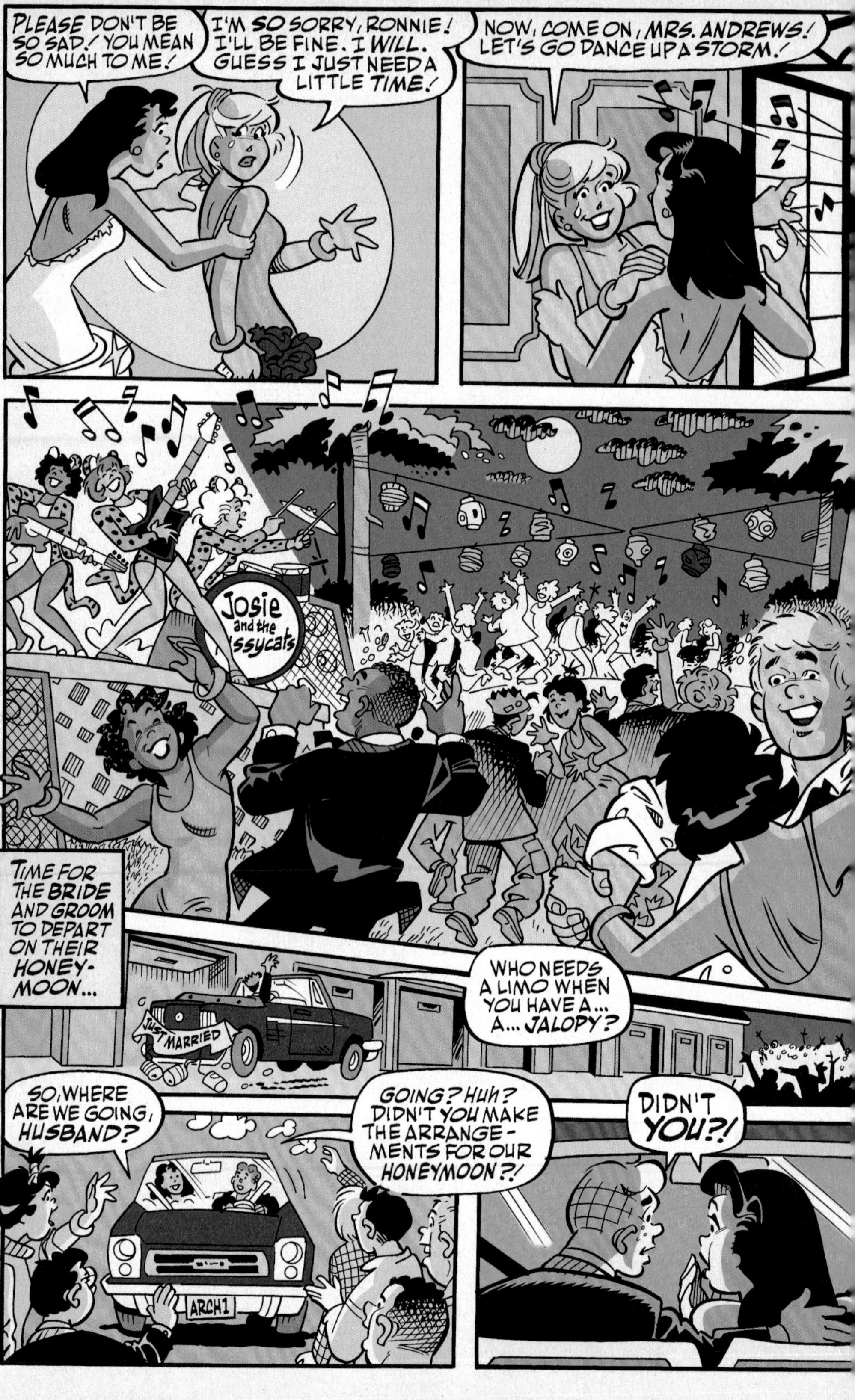
PLEASE DON'T BE SO SAD! YOU MEAN SO MUCH TO ME!
I'M SO SORRY, RONNIE! I'LL BE FINE. I WILL. GUESS I JUST NEED A LITTLE TIME!
NOW, COME ON, MRS. ANDREWS! LET'S GO DANCE UP A STORM!
Josie and the Pussycats
TIME FOR THE BRIDE AND GROOM TO DEPART ON THEIR HONEY-MOON...
JUST MARRIED
WHO NEEDS A LIMO WHEN YOU HAVE A... A... JALOPY?
SO, WHERE ARE WE GOING, HUSBAND?
GOING? Huh? DIDN'T YOU MAKE THE ARRANGE-MENTS FOR OUR HONEYMOON?!
DIDN'T YOU?!
ARCH1

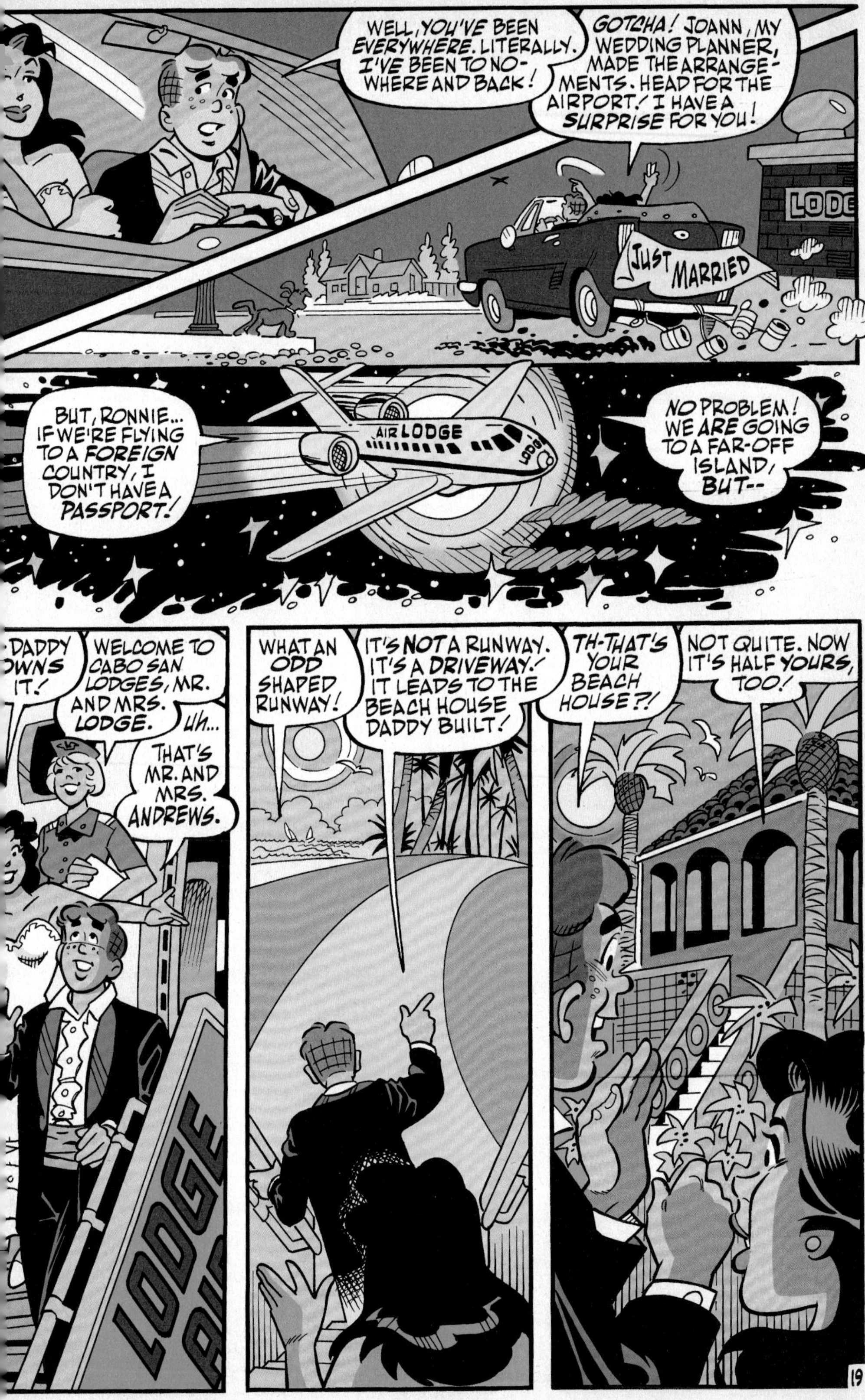
WELL, YOU'VE BEEN EVERYWHERE. LITERALLY. I'VE BEEN TO NO-WHERE AND BACK!
GOTCHA! JOANN, MY WEDDING PLANNER, MADE THE ARRANGE-MENTS. HEAD FOR THE AIRPORT! I HAVE A SURPRISE FOR YOU!
LODGE
JUST MARRIED
BUT, RONNIE... IF WE'RE FLYING TO A FOREIGN COUNTRY, I DON'T HAVE A PASSPORT!
AIR LODGE
LODGE
NO PROBLEM! WE ARE GOING TO A FAR-OFF ISLAND, BUT--
DADDY OWNS IT!
WELCOME TO CABO SAN LODGES, MR. AND MRS. LODGE.
uh... THAT'S MR. AND MRS. ANDREWS.
LODGE
WHAT AN ODD SHAPED RUNWAY!
IT'S NOT A RUNWAY. IT'S A DRIVEWAY! IT LEADS TO THE BEACH HOUSE DADDY BUILT!
TH-THAT'S YOUR BEACH HOUSE?!
NOT QUITE. NOW IT'S HALF YOURS, TOO!
19

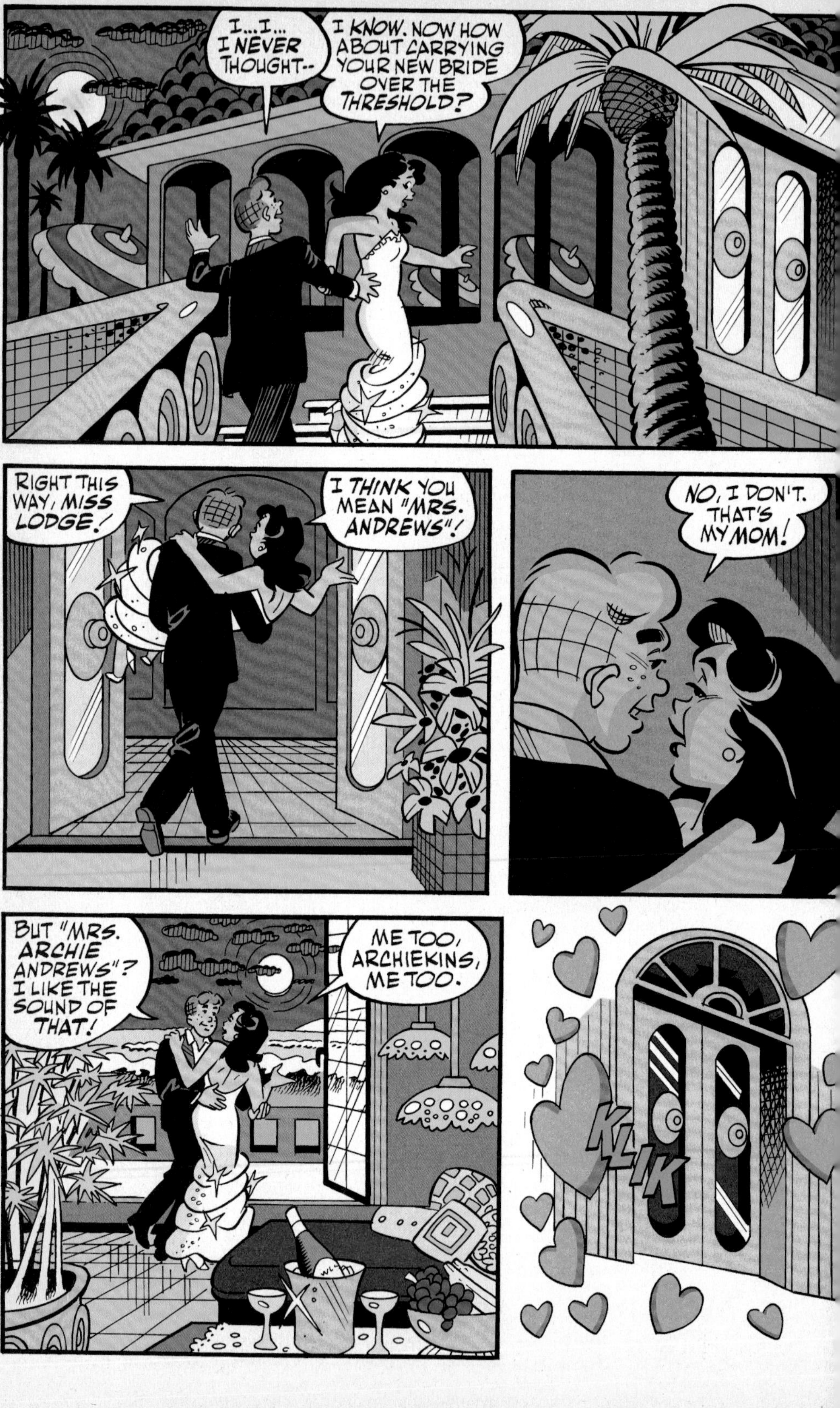
I... I... I NEVER THOUGHT--
I KNOW. NOW HOW ABOUT CARRYING YOUR NEW BRIDE OVER THE THRESHOLD?
RIGHT THIS WAY, MISS LODGE!
I THINK YOU MEAN "MRS. ANDREWS"!
NO, I DON'T. THAT'S MY MOM!
BUT "MRS. ARCHIE ANDREWS"? I LIKE THE SOUND OF THAT!
ME TOO, ARCHIEKINS, ME TOO.
KLIK

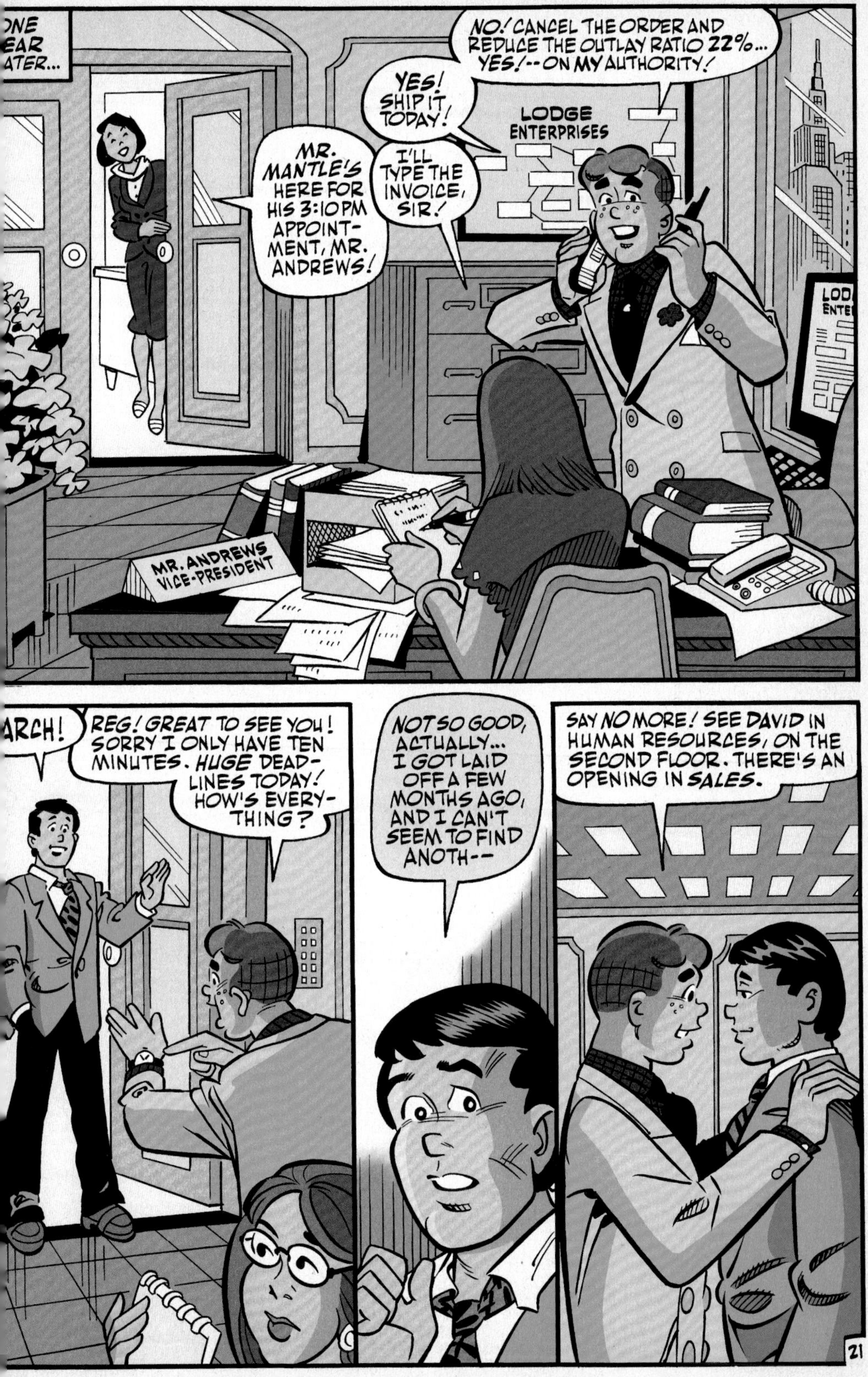

ONE
EAR
ATER...
MR. MANTLE'S HERE FOR HIS 3:10PM APPOINT-MENT, MR. ANDREWS!
YES! SHIP IT TODAY!
I'LL TYPE THE INVOICE, SIR!
NO! CANCEL THE ORDER AND REDUCE THE OUTLAY RATIO 22%... YES!--ON MY AUTHORITY!
LODGE ENTERPRISES
MR. ANDREWS VICE-PRESIDENT
ARCH!
REG! GREAT TO SEE YOU! SORRY I ONLY HAVE TEN MINUTES. HUGE DEAD-LINES TODAY! HOW'S EVERY-THING?
NOT SO GOOD, ACTUALLY... I GOT LAID OFF A FEW MONTHS AGO, AND I CAN'T SEEM TO FIND ANOTH--
SAY NO MORE! SEE DAVID IN HUMAN RESOURCES, ON THE SECOND FLOOR. THERE'S AN OPENING IN SALES.
21

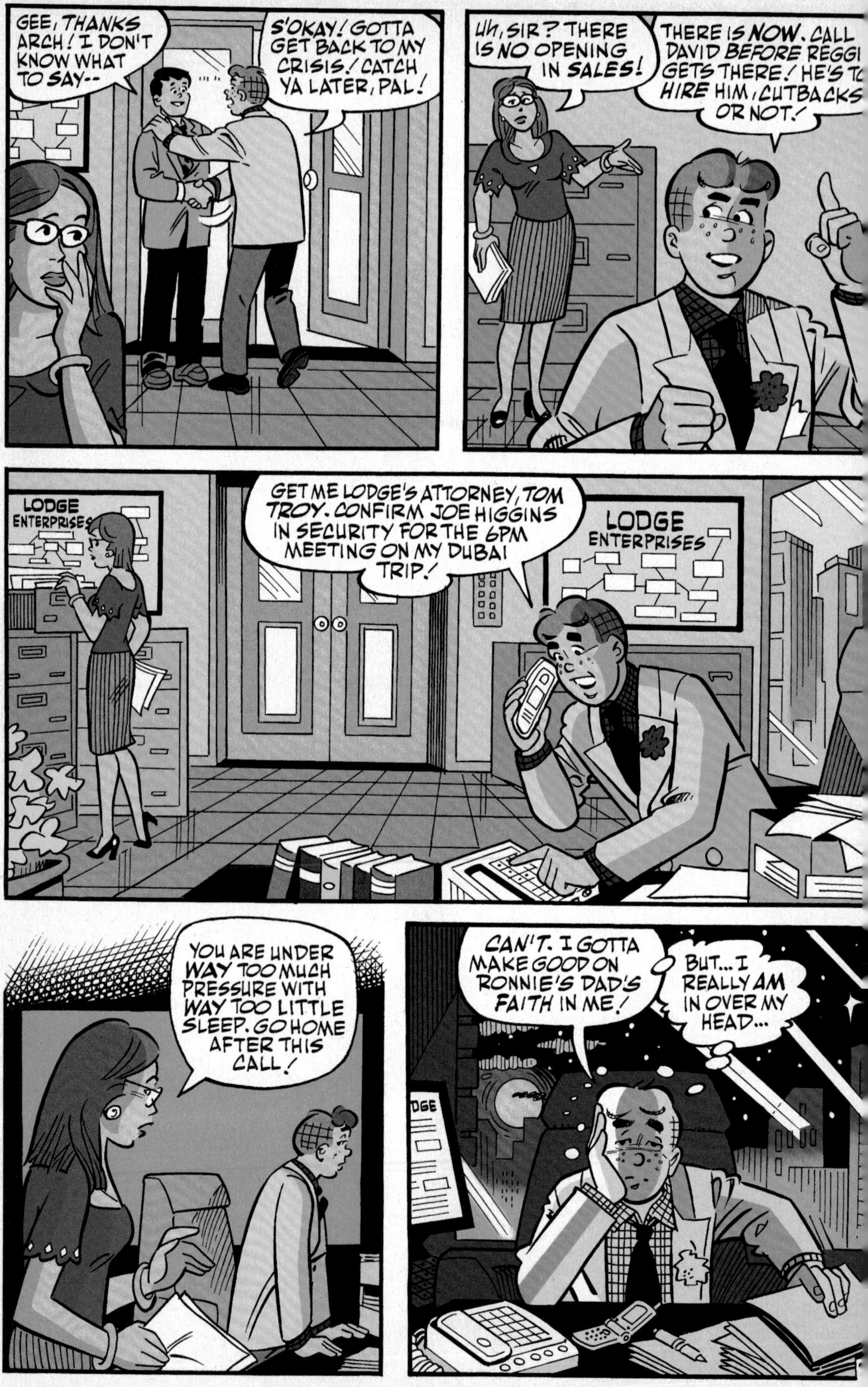
GEE, THANKS ARCH! I DON'T KNOW WHAT TO SAY--
S'OKAY! GOTTA GET BACK TO MY CRISIS! CATCH YA LATER, PAL!
UH, SIR? THERE IS NO OPENING IN SALES!
THERE IS NOW. CALL DAVID BEFORE REGGI GETS THERE! HE'S T HIRE HIM, CUTBACKS OR NOT!
LODGE ENTERPRISES
GET ME LODGE'S ATTORNEY, TOM TROY. CONFIRM JOE HIGGINS IN SECURITY FOR THE 6PM MEETING ON MY DUBAI TRIP!
LODGE ENTERPRISES
YOU ARE UNDER WAY TOO MUCH PRESSURE WITH WAY TOO LITTLE SLEEP. GO HOME AFTER THIS CALL!
CAN'T. I GOTTA MAKE GOOD ON RONNIE'S DAD'S FAITH IN ME!
BUT... I REALLY AM IN OVER MY HEAD...

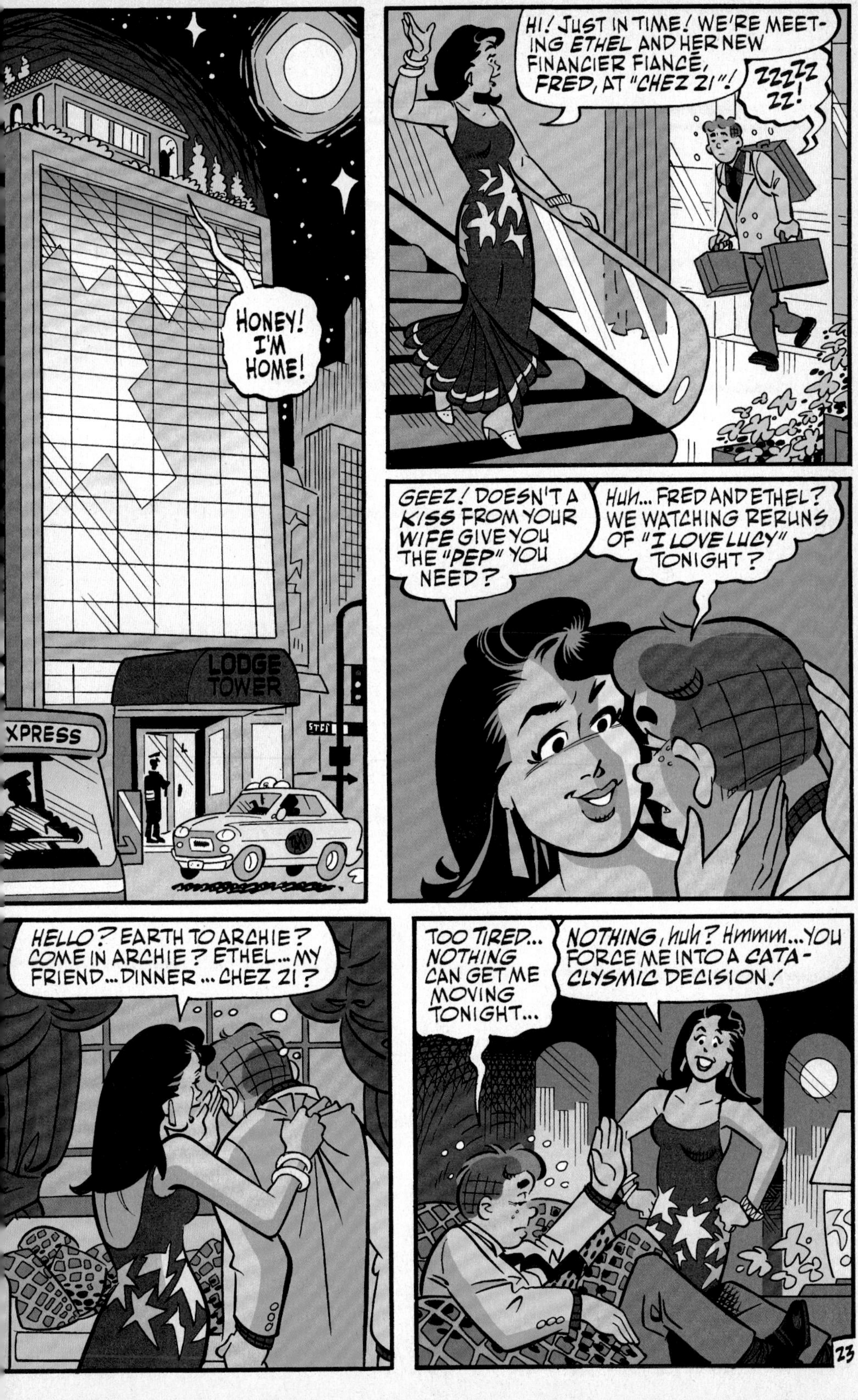
HONEY! I'M HOME!
LODGE TOWER
XPRESS
HI! JUST IN TIME! WE'RE MEETING ETHEL AND HER NEW FINANCIER FIANCÉ, FRED, AT "CHEZ ZI"!
ZZZZZ ZZ!
GEEZ! DOESN'T A KISS FROM YOUR WIFE GIVE YOU THE "PEP" YOU NEED?
HUH... FRED AND ETHEL? WE WATCHING RERUNS OF "I LOVE LUCY" TONIGHT?
HELLO? EARTH TO ARCHIE? COME IN ARCHIE? ETHEL... MY FRIEND... DINNER... CHEZ ZI?
TOO TIRED... NOTHING CAN GET ME MOVING TONIGHT...
NOTHING, HUH? HMMM... YOU FORCE ME INTO A CATACLYSMIC DECISION!
23

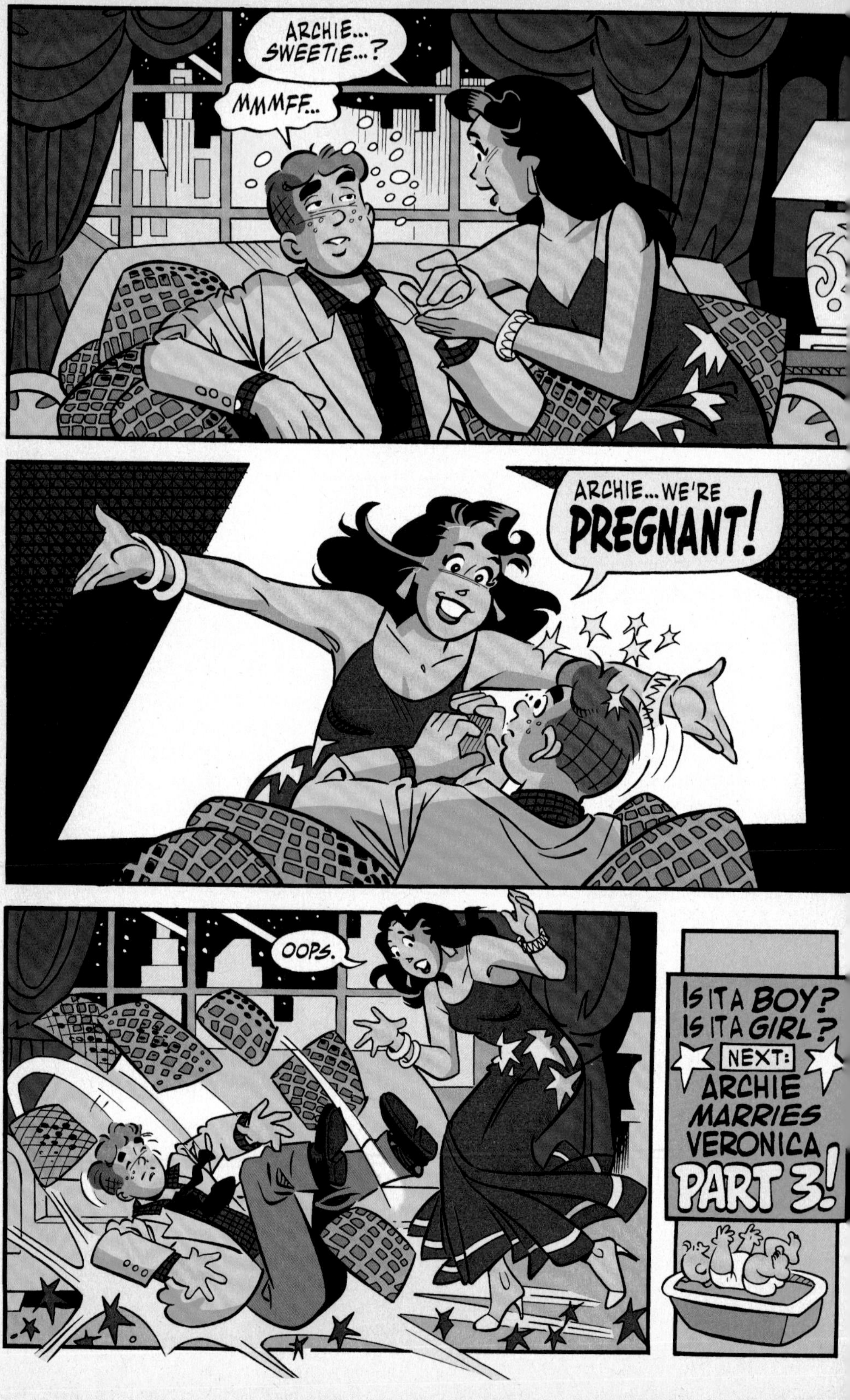
ARCHIE... SWEETIE...?
MMMFF...
ARCHIE... WE'RE PREGNANT!
OOPS.
IS IT A BOY? IS IT A GIRL?
NEXT:
ARCHIE MARRIES VERONICA PART 3!

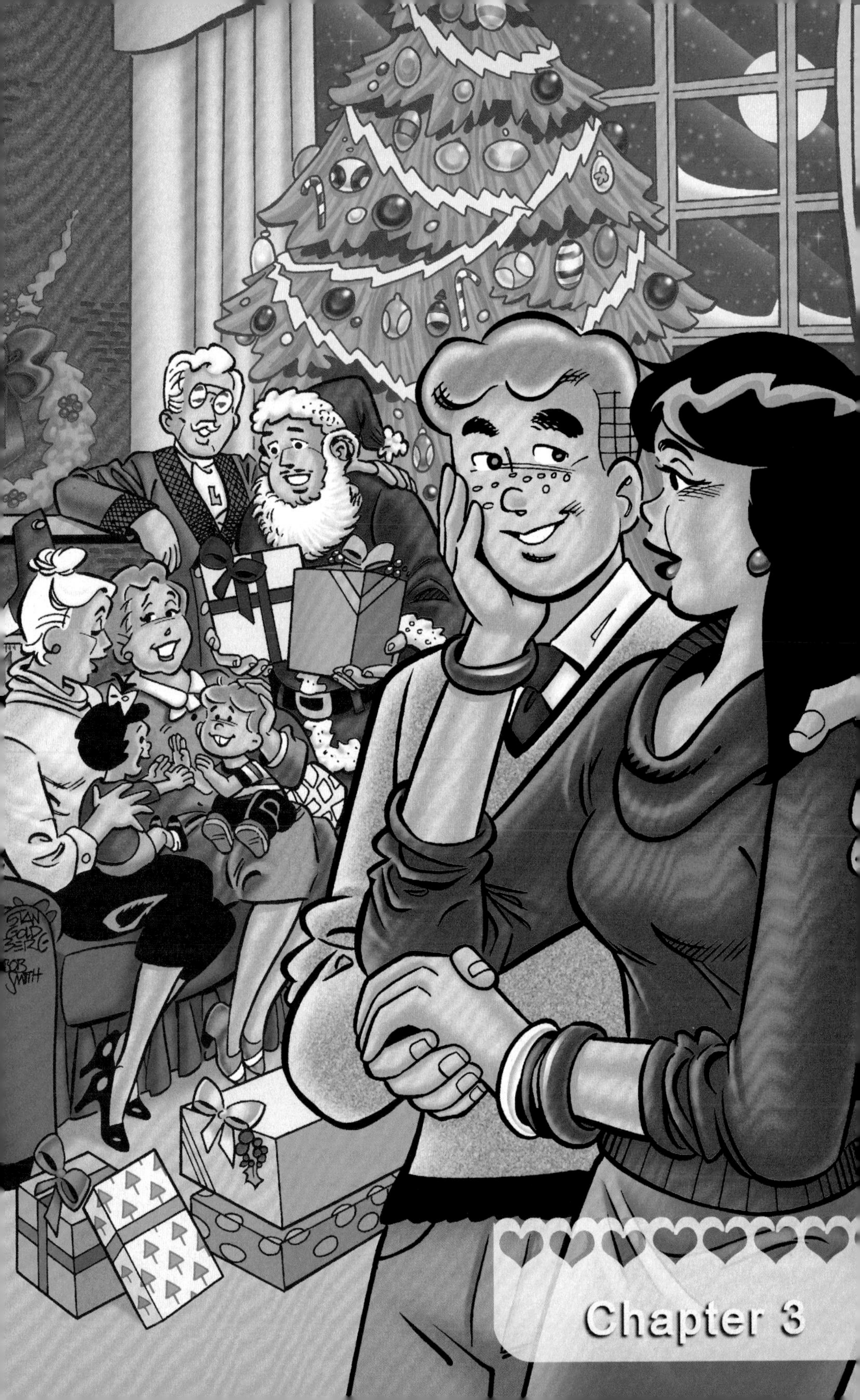
STAN GOLDBERG
BOB SMITH

Chapter 3

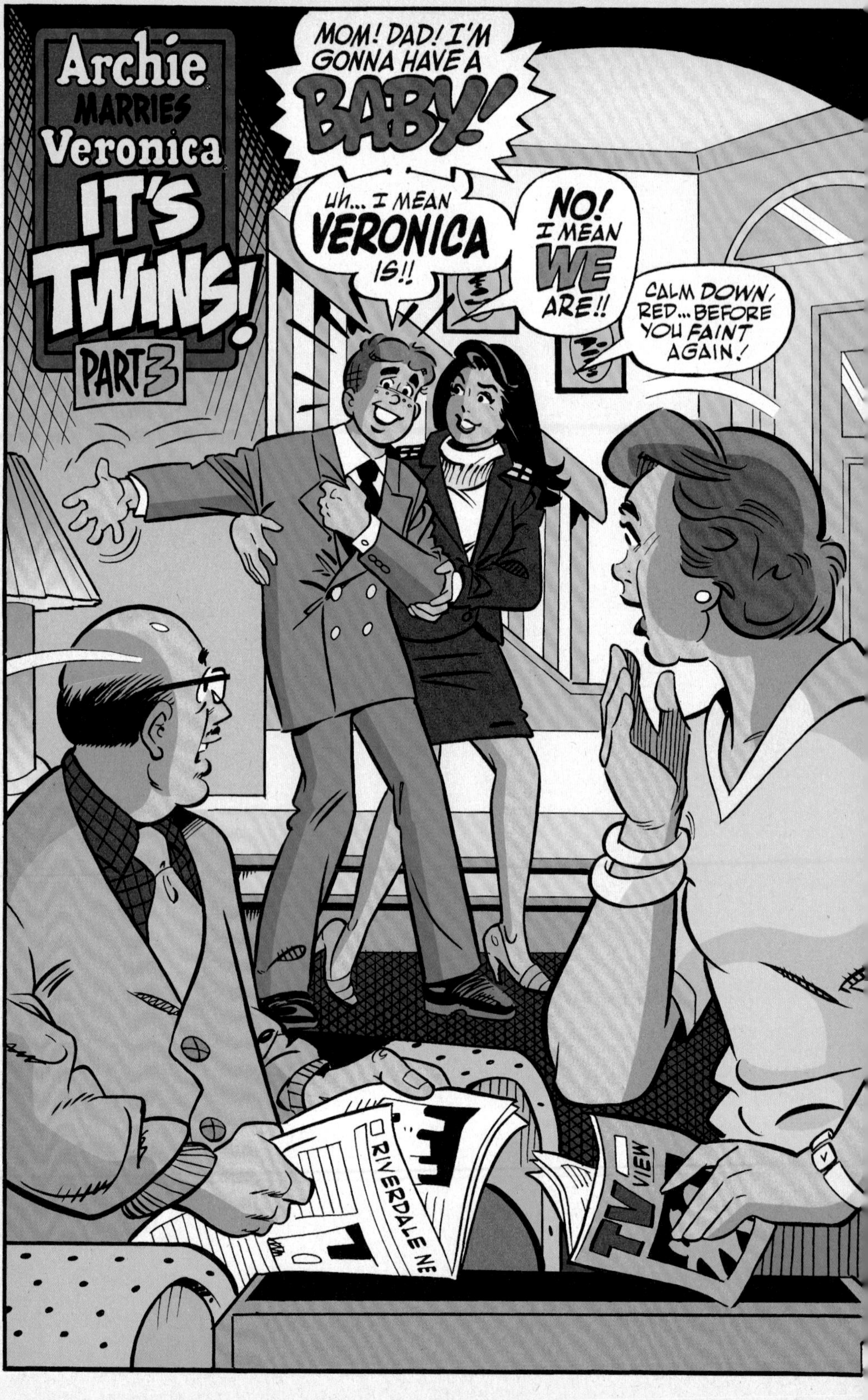
Archie MARRIES Veronica
IT'S TWINS!
PART 3
MOM! DAD! I'M GONNA HAVE A BABY!
UH... I MEAN VERONICA IS!!
NO! I MEAN WE ARE!!
CALM DOWN, RED... BEFORE YOU FAINT AGAIN!
RIVERDALE NE
TV VIEW

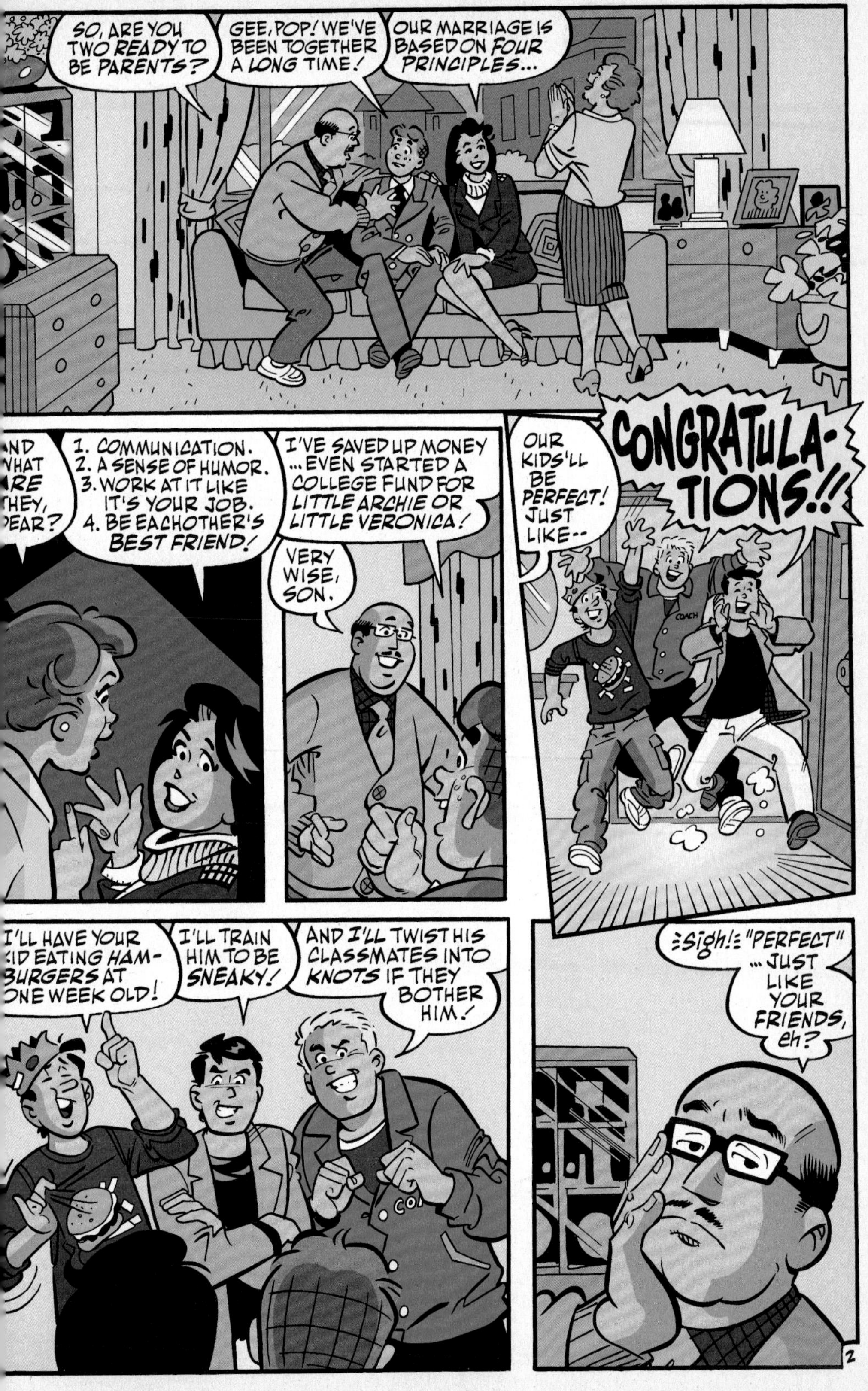
SO, ARE YOU TWO READY TO BE PARENTS?
GEE, POP! WE'VE BEEN TOGETHER A LONG TIME!
OUR MARRIAGE IS BASED ON FOUR PRINCIPLES...
1. COMMUNICATION. 2. A SENSE OF HUMOR. 3. WORK AT IT LIKE IT'S YOUR JOB. 4. BE EACHOTHER'S BEST FRIEND!
I'VE SAVED UP MONEY ...EVEN STARTED A COLLEGE FUND FOR LITTLE ARCHIE OR LITTLE VERONICA!
VERY WISE, SON.
OUR KIDS'LL BE PERFECT! JUST LIKE--
CONGRATULA-TIONS!!
COACH
I'LL HAVE YOUR KID EATING HAM-BURGERS AT ONE WEEK OLD!
I'LL TRAIN HIM TO BE SNEAKY!
AND I'LL TWIST HIS CLASSMATES INTO KNOTS IF THEY BOTHER HIM!
:Sigh!: "PERFECT" ...JUST LIKE YOUR FRIENDS, eh?
2

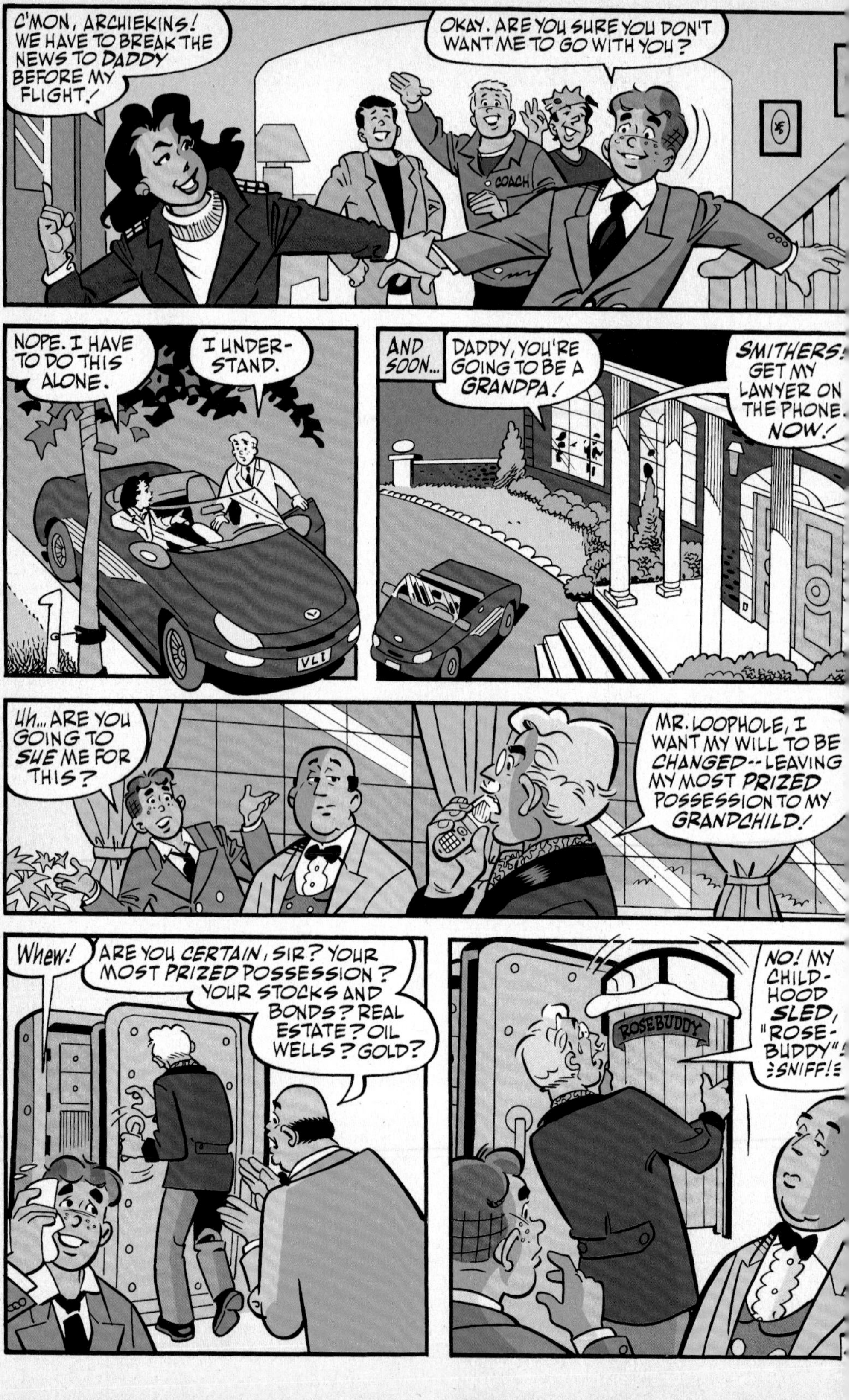
C'MON, ARCHIEKINS! WE HAVE TO BREAK THE NEWS TO DADDY BEFORE MY FLIGHT!
OKAY. ARE YOU SURE YOU DON'T WANT ME TO GO WITH YOU?
COACH
NOPE. I HAVE TO DO THIS ALONE.
I UNDERSTAND.
VLI
AND SOON...
DADDY, YOU'RE GOING TO BE A GRANDPA!
SMITHERS! GET MY LAWYER ON THE PHONE. NOW!
UH... ARE YOU GOING TO SUE ME FOR THIS?
MR. LOOPHOLE, I WANT MY WILL TO BE CHANGED-- LEAVING MY MOST PRIZED POSSESSION TO MY GRANDCHILD!
Whew!
ARE YOU CERTAIN, SIR? YOUR MOST PRIZED POSSESSION? YOUR STOCKS AND BONDS? REAL ESTATE? OIL WELLS? GOLD?
NO! MY CHILDHOOD SLED, "ROSEBUDDY"! SNIFF!
ROSEBUDDY

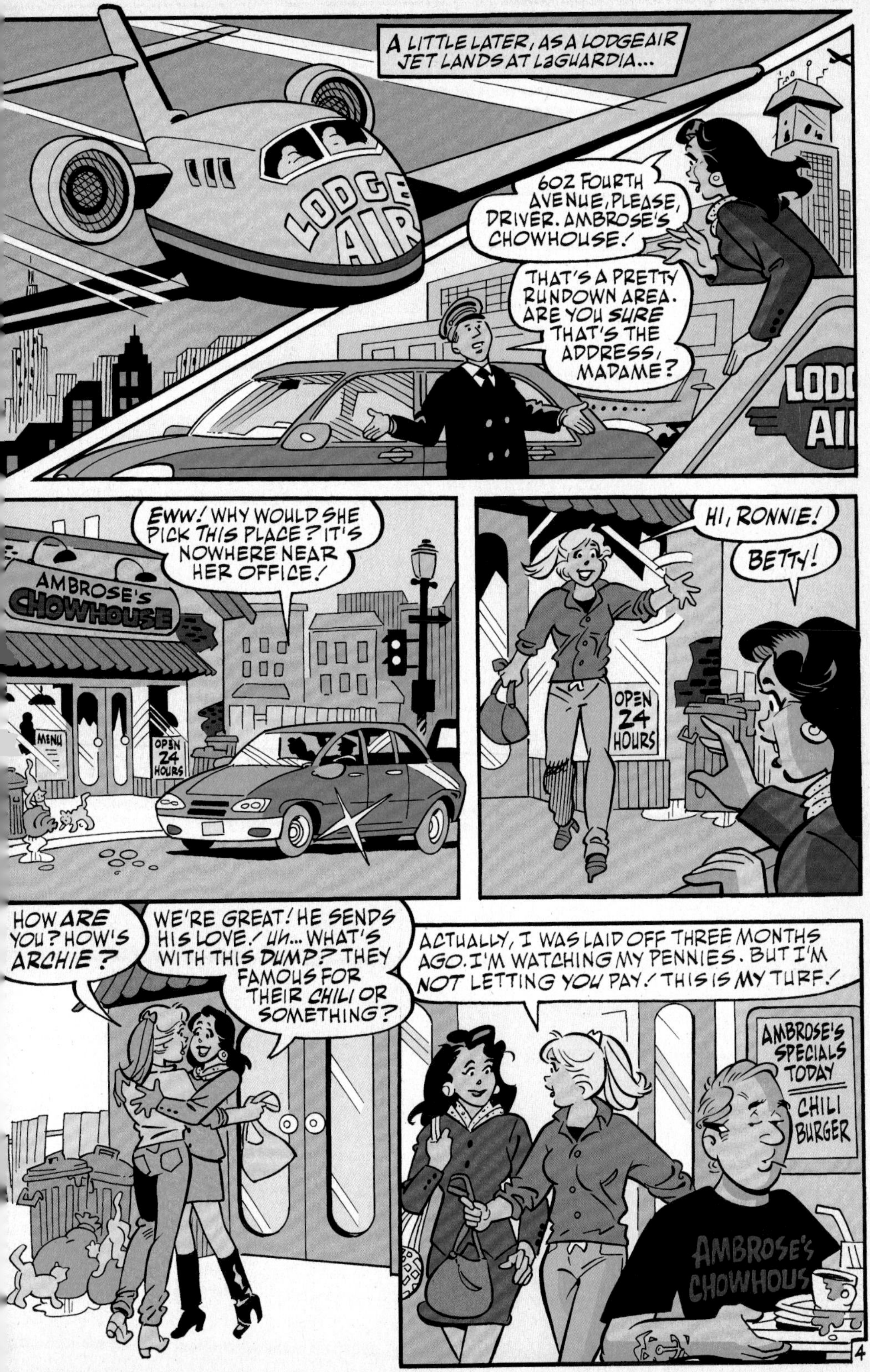
A LITTLE LATER, AS A LODGEAIR JET LANDS AT LaGUARDIA...
LODGE AIR
602 FOURTH AVENUE, PLEASE, DRIVER. AMBROSE'S CHOWHOUSE!
THAT'S A PRETTY RUNDOWN AREA. ARE YOU SURE THAT'S THE ADDRESS, MADAME?
EWW! WHY WOULD SHE PICK THIS PLACE? IT'S NOWHERE NEAR HER OFFICE!
AMBROSE'S CHOWHOUSE
MENU
OPEN 24 HOURS
HI, RONNIE!
BETTY!
OPEN 24 HOURS
HOW ARE YOU? HOW'S ARCHIE?
WE'RE GREAT! HE SENDS HIS LOVE! UH... WHAT'S WITH THIS DUMP? THEY FAMOUS FOR THEIR CHILI OR SOMETHING?
ACTUALLY, I WAS LAID OFF THREE MONTHS AGO. I'M WATCHING MY PENNIES. BUT I'M NOT LETTING YOU PAY! THIS IS MY TURF!
AMBROSE'S SPECIALS TODAY
CHILI BURGER
AMBROSE'S CHOWHOUS
4

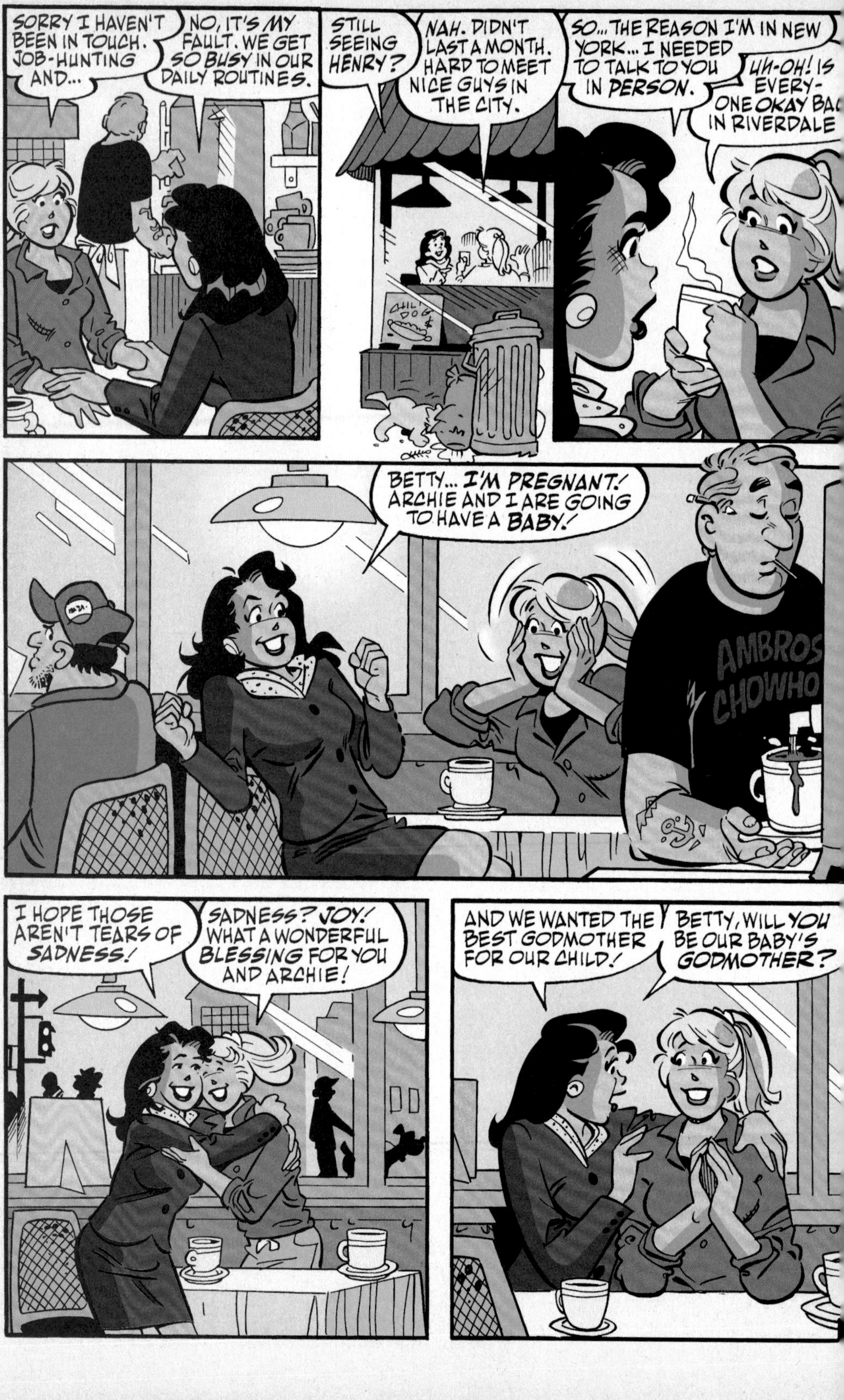
SORRY I HAVEN'T BEEN IN TOUCH. JOB-HUNTING AND...
NO, IT'S MY FAULT. WE GET SO BUSY IN OUR DAILY ROUTINES.
STILL SEEING HENRY?
NAH. DIDN'T LAST A MONTH. HARD TO MEET NICE GUYS IN THE CITY.
CHILI DOG $
SO... THE REASON I'M IN NEW YORK... I NEEDED TO TALK TO YOU IN PERSON.
UH-OH! IS EVERY-ONE OKAY BA
IN RIVERDALE
BETTY... I'M PREGNANT! ARCHIE AND I ARE GOING TO HAVE A BABY!
AMBROS CHOWHO
I HOPE THOSE AREN'T TEARS OF SADNESS!
SADNESS? JOY! WHAT A WONDERFUL BLESSING FOR YOU AND ARCHIE!
AND WE WANTED THE BEST GODMOTHER FOR OUR CHILD!
BETTY, WILL YOU BE OUR BABY'S GODMOTHER?

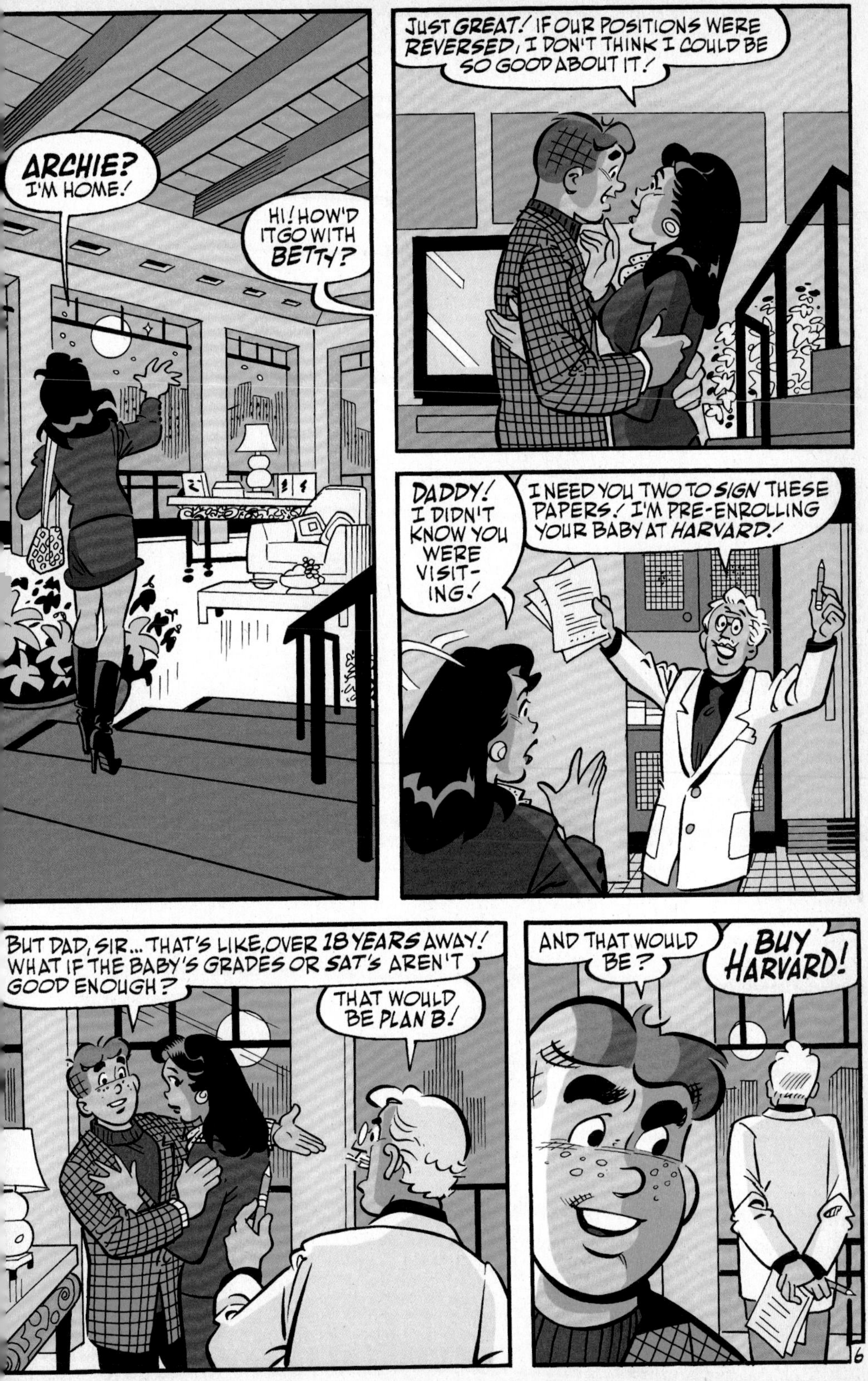
ARCHIE? I'M HOME!
HI! HOW'D IT GO WITH BETTY?
JUST GREAT! IF OUR POSITIONS WERE REVERSED, I DON'T THINK I COULD BE SO GOOD ABOUT IT!
DADDY! I DIDN'T KNOW YOU WERE VISIT-ING!
I NEED YOU TWO TO SIGN THESE PAPERS! I'M PRE-ENROLLING YOUR BABY AT HARVARD!
BUT DAD, SIR... THAT'S LIKE, OVER 18 YEARS AWAY! WHAT IF THE BABY'S GRADES OR SAT's AREN'T GOOD ENOUGH?
THAT WOULD BE PLAN B!
AND THAT WOULD BE?
BUY HARVARD!
6

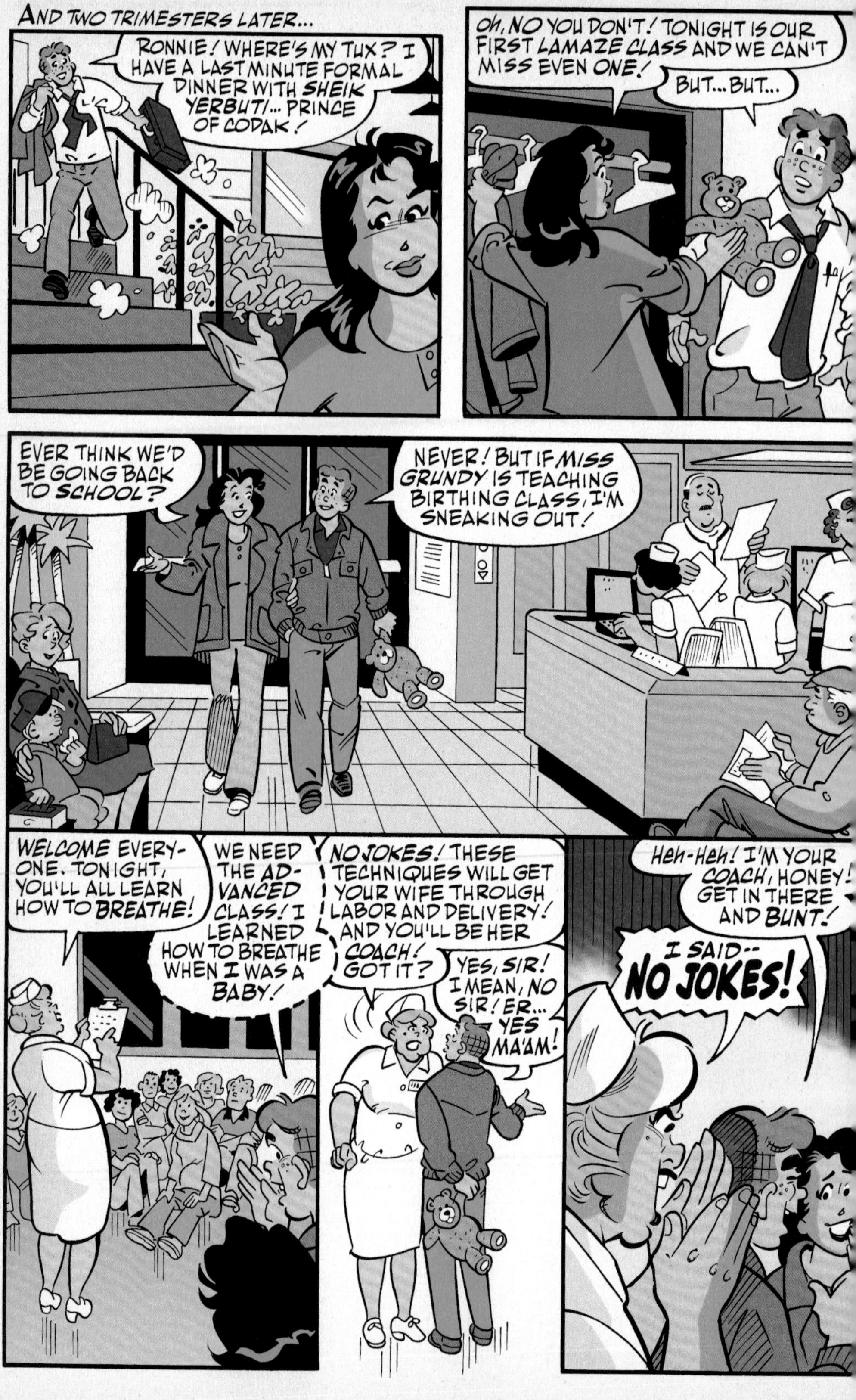
AND TWO TRIMESTERS LATER...
RONNIE! WHERE'S MY TUX? I HAVE A LAST MINUTE FORMAL DINNER WITH SHEIK YERBUTI... PRINCE OF CODAK!
OH, NO YOU DON'T! TONIGHT IS OUR FIRST LAMAZE CLASS AND WE CAN'T MISS EVEN ONE!
BUT...BUT...
EVER THINK WE'D BE GOING BACK TO SCHOOL?
NEVER! BUT IF MISS GRUNDY IS TEACHING BIRTHING CLASS, I'M SNEAKING OUT!
WELCOME EVERY-ONE. TONIGHT, YOU'LL ALL LEARN HOW TO BREATHE!
WE NEED THE AD-VANCED CLASS! I LEARNED HOW TO BREATHE WHEN I WAS A BABY!
NO JOKES! THESE TECHNIQUES WILL GET YOUR WIFE THROUGH LABOR AND DELIVERY! AND YOU'LL BE HER COACH! GOT IT?
YES, SIR! I MEAN, NO SIR! ER... YES MA'AM!
HEH-HEH! I'M YOUR COACH, HONEY! GET IN THERE AND BUNT!
I SAID-- NO JOKES!

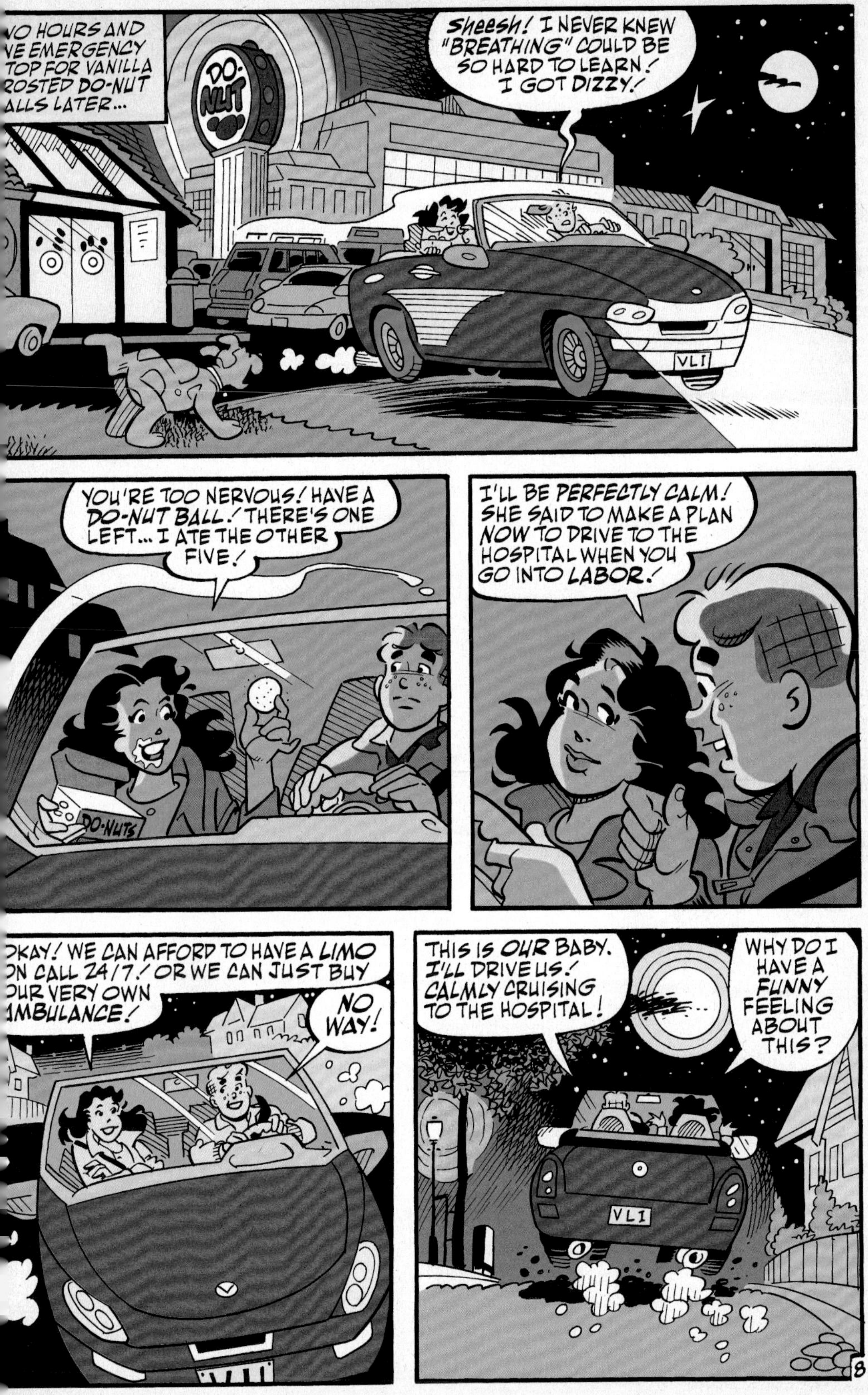
VO HOURS AND
VE EMERGENCY
TOP FOR VANILLA
ROSTED DO-NUT
ALLS LATER...
Sheesh! I NEVER KNEW "BREATHING" COULD BE SO HARD TO LEARN! I GOT DIZZY!
DO-NUT
VLI
YOU'RE TOO NERVOUS! HAVE A DO-NUT BALL! THERE'S ONE LEFT... I ATE THE OTHER FIVE!
DO-NUTS
I'LL BE PERFECTLY CALM! SHE SAID TO MAKE A PLAN NOW TO DRIVE TO THE HOSPITAL WHEN YOU GO INTO LABOR!
KAY! WE CAN AFFORD TO HAVE A LIMO
N CALL 24/7! OR WE CAN JUST BUY
UR VERY OWN
MBULANCE!
NO WAY!
THIS IS OUR BABY. I'LL DRIVE US! CALMLY CRUISING TO THE HOSPITAL!
WHY DO I HAVE A FUNNY FEELING ABOUT THIS?
VLI
8

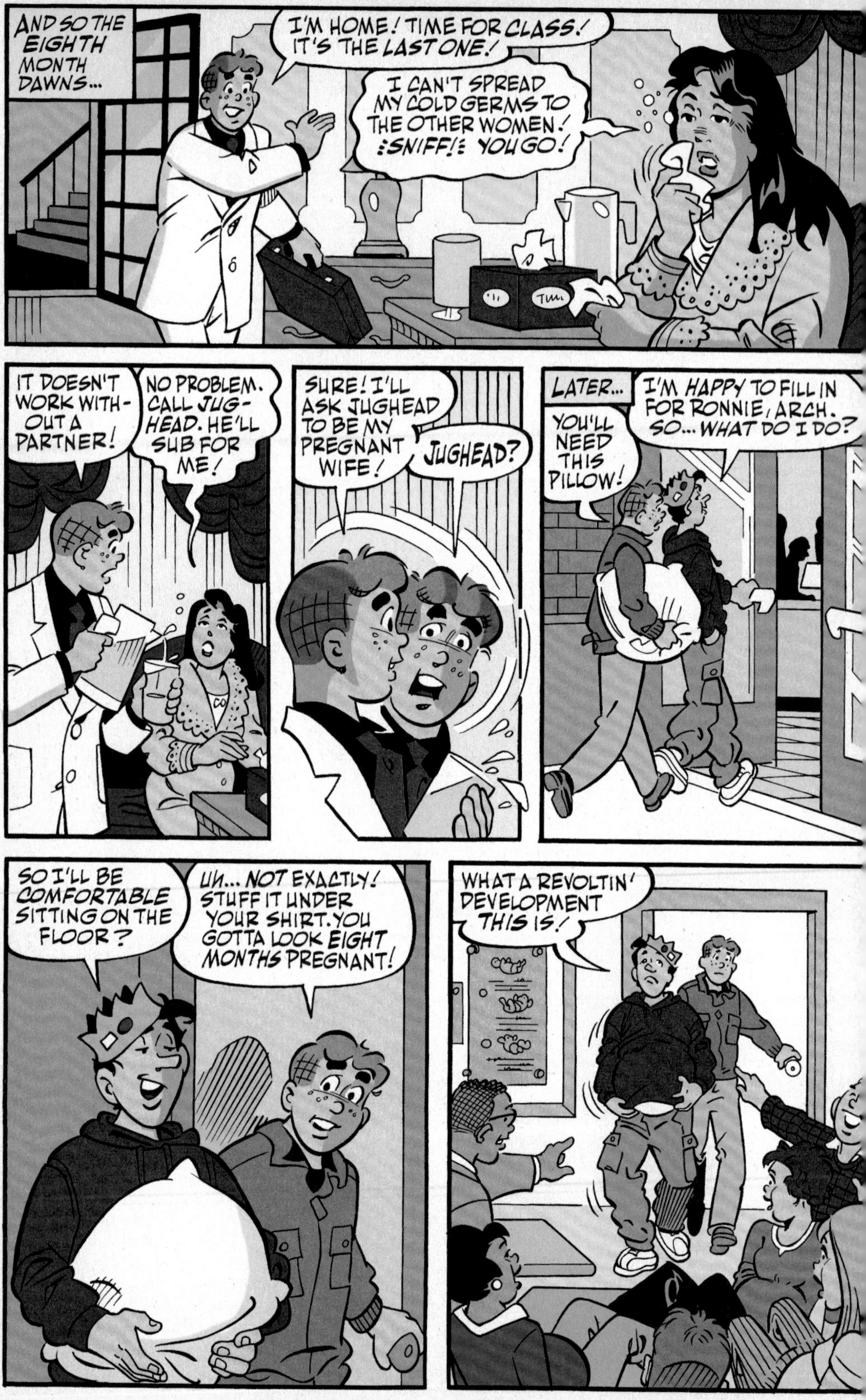
AND SO THE EIGHTH MONTH DAWNS...
I'M HOME! TIME FOR CLASS! IT'S THE LAST ONE!
I CAN'T SPREAD MY COLD GERMS TO THE OTHER WOMEN! :SNIFF!: YOU GO!
IT DOESN'T WORK WITH-OUT A PARTNER!
NO PROBLEM. CALL JUG-HEAD. HE'LL SUB FOR ME!
SURE! I'LL ASK JUGHEAD TO BE MY PREGNANT WIFE!
JUGHEAD?
LATER...
YOU'LL NEED THIS PILLOW!
I'M HAPPY TO FILL IN FOR RONNIE, ARCH. SO... WHAT DO I DO?
SO I'LL BE COMFORTABLE SITTING ON THE FLOOR?
UH... NOT EXACTLY! STUFF IT UNDER YOUR SHIRT. YOU GOTTA LOOK EIGHT MONTHS PREGNANT!
WHAT A REVOLTIN' DEVELOPMENT THIS IS!

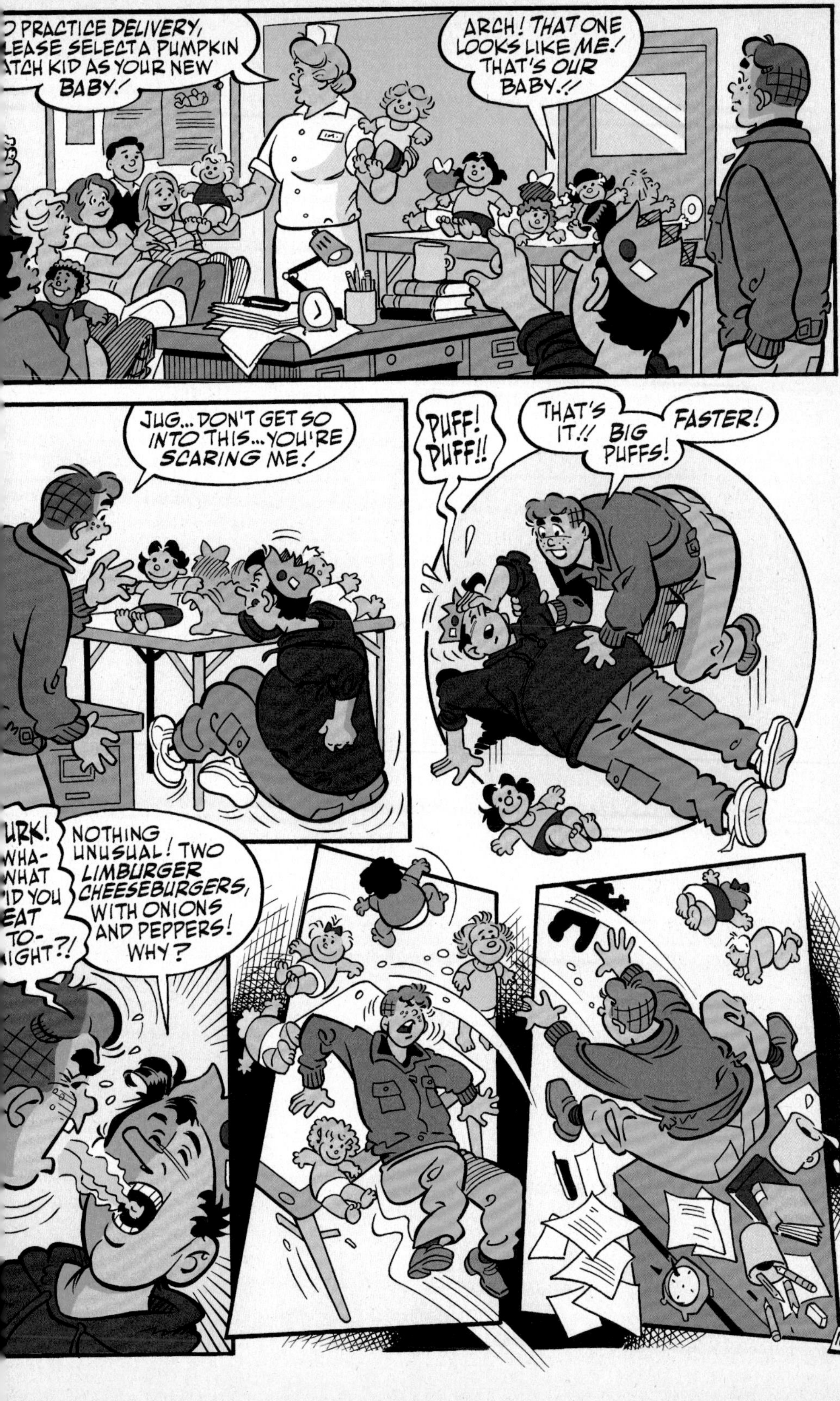
O PRACTICE DELIVERY, LEASE SELECT A PUMPKIN ATCH KID AS YOUR NEW BABY!
ARCH! THAT ONE LOOKS LIKE ME! THAT'S OUR BABY!!
JUG... DON'T GET SO INTO THIS... YOU'RE SCARING ME!
PUFF! PUFF!!
THAT'S IT!!
BIG PUFFS!
FASTER!
URK! WHA- WHAT DID YOU EAT TO- NIGHT?!
NOTHING UNUSUAL! TWO LIMBURGER CHEESEBURGERS, WITH ONIONS AND PEPPERS! WHY?
10

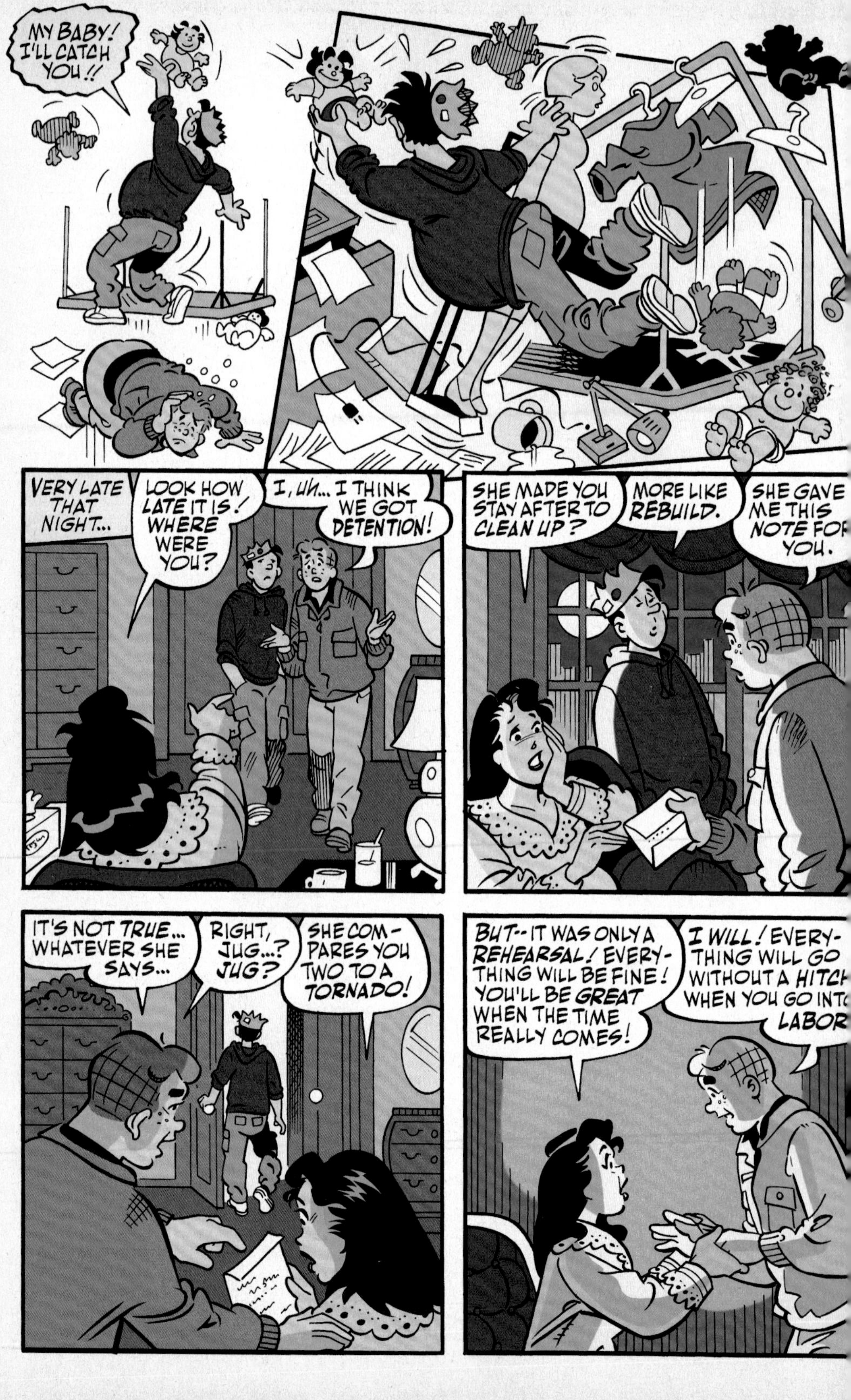
MY BABY! I'LL CATCH YOU!!
VERY LATE THAT NIGHT...
LOOK HOW LATE IT IS! WHERE WERE YOU?
I, UH... I THINK WE GOT DETENTION!
SHE MADE YOU STAY AFTER TO CLEAN UP?
MORE LIKE REBUILD.
SHE GAVE ME THIS NOTE FOR YOU.
IT'S NOT TRUE... WHATEVER SHE SAYS...
RIGHT, JUG...? JUG?
SHE COMPARES YOU TWO TO A TORNADO!
BUT-- IT WAS ONLY A REHEARSAL! EVERYTHING WILL BE FINE! YOU'LL BE GREAT WHEN THE TIME REALLY COMES!
I WILL! EVERYTHING WILL GO WITHOUT A HITCH WHEN YOU GO INTO LABOR

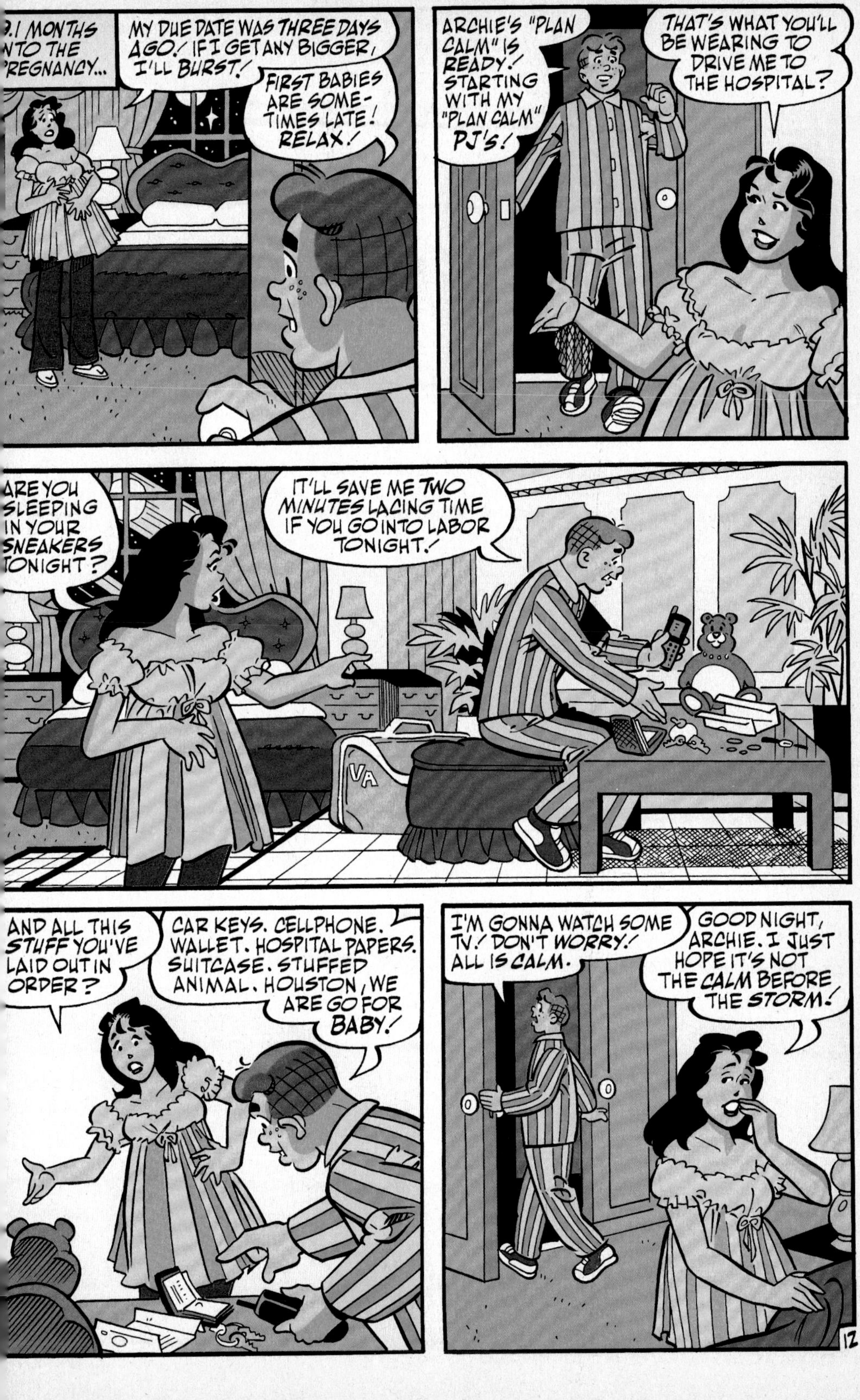
9.1 MONTHS INTO THE PREGNANCY...
MY DUE DATE WAS THREE DAYS AGO! IF I GET ANY BIGGER, I'LL BURST!
FIRST BABIES ARE SOMETIMES LATE! RELAX!
ARCHIE'S "PLAN CALM" IS READY! STARTING WITH MY "PLAN CALM" PJ's!
THAT'S WHAT YOU'LL BE WEARING TO DRIVE ME TO THE HOSPITAL?
ARE YOU SLEEPING IN YOUR SNEAKERS TONIGHT?
IT'LL SAVE ME TWO MINUTES LACING TIME IF YOU GO INTO LABOR TONIGHT!
VA
AND ALL THIS STUFF YOU'VE LAID OUT IN ORDER?
CAR KEYS. CELLPHONE. WALLET. HOSPITAL PAPERS. SUITCASE. STUFFED ANIMAL. HOUSTON, WE ARE GO FOR BABY!
I'M GONNA WATCH SOME TV! DON'T WORRY! ALL IS CALM.
GOOD NIGHT, ARCHIE. I JUST HOPE IT'S NOT THE CALM BEFORE THE STORM!
12

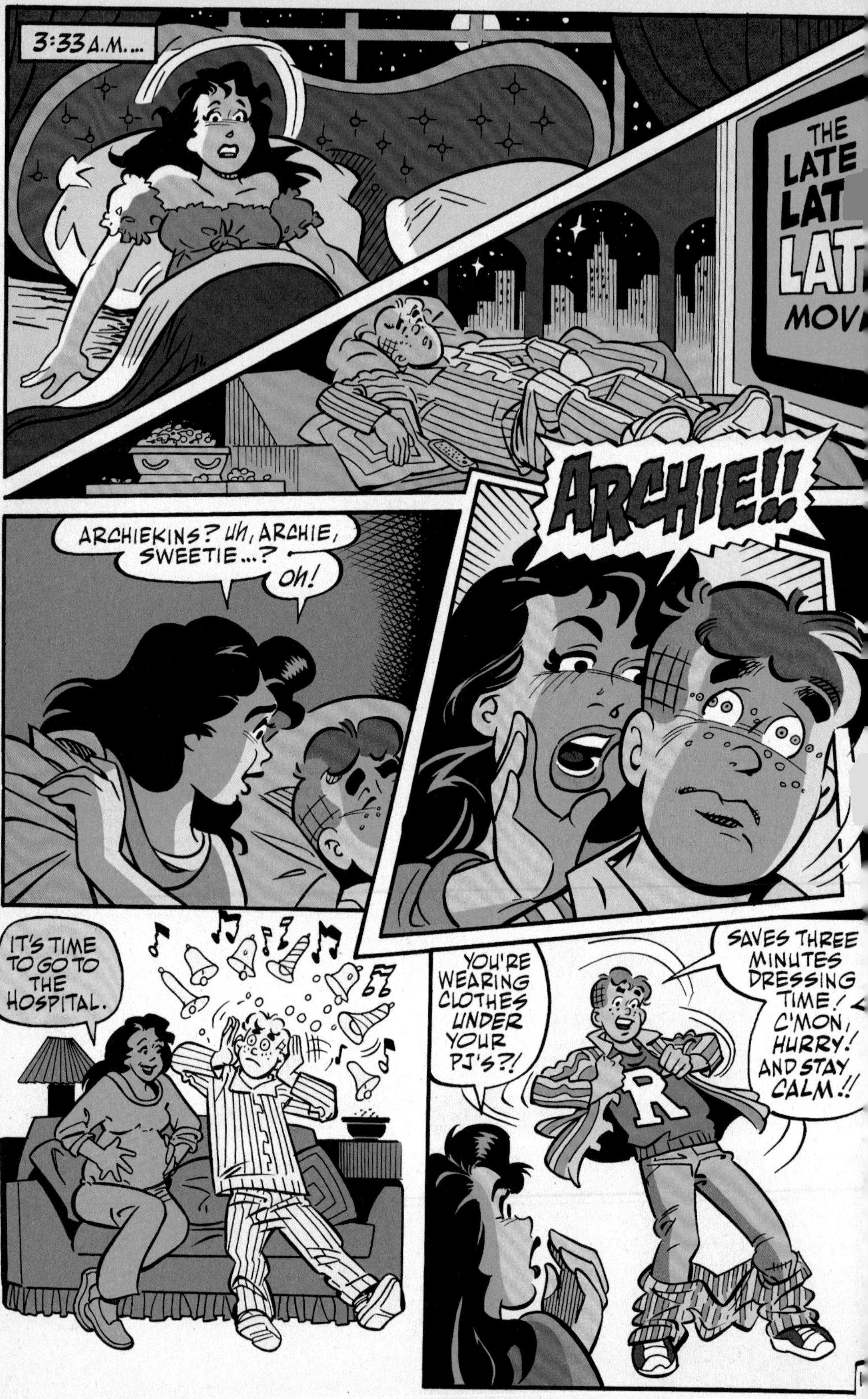
3:33 A.M. ...
THE LATE LAT LAT MOV
ARCHIE!!
ARCHIEKINS? UH, ARCHIE, SWEETIE...?
OH!
IT'S TIME TO GO TO THE HOSPITAL.
YOU'RE WEARING CLOTHES UNDER YOUR PJ'S?!
SAVES THREE MINUTES DRESSING TIME! C'MON, HURRY! AND STAY CALM!!

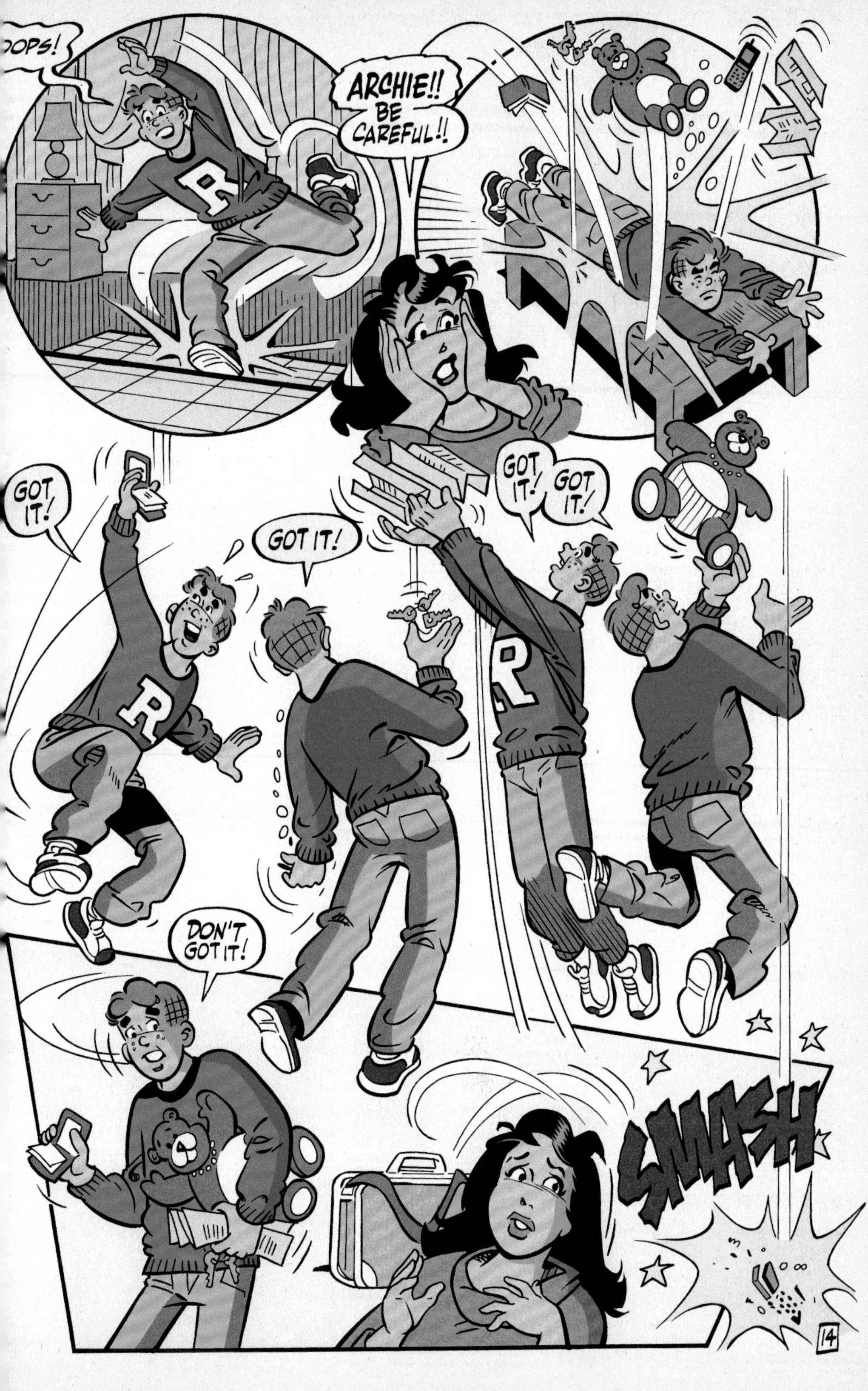
OPS!
ARCHIE!! BE CAREFUL!!
GOT IT!
GOT IT!
GOT IT!
GOT IT!
DON'T GOT IT!
SMASH
14

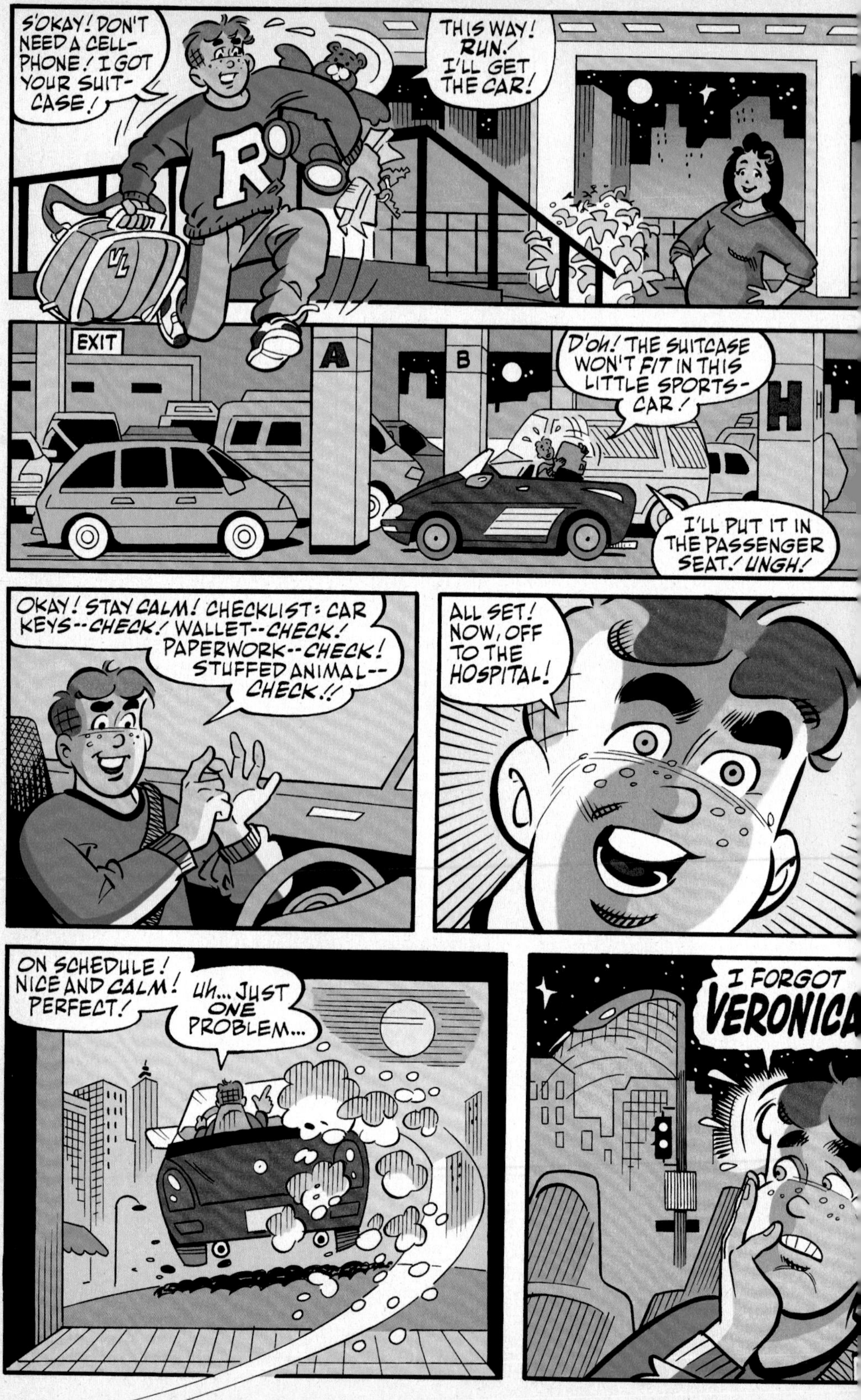
S'OKAY! DON'T NEED A CELL-PHONE! I GOT YOUR SUIT-CASE!
THIS WAY! RUN! I'LL GET THE CAR!
EXIT
A
B
H
D'OH! THE SUITCASE WON'T FIT IN THIS LITTLE SPORTS-CAR!
I'LL PUT IT IN THE PASSENGER SEAT! UNGH!
OKAY! STAY CALM! CHECKLIST: CAR KEYS--CHECK! WALLET--CHECK! PAPERWORK--CHECK! STUFFED ANIMAL--CHECK!!
ALL SET! NOW, OFF TO THE HOSPITAL!
ON SCHEDULE! NICE AND CALM! PERFECT!
UH... JUST ONE PROBLEM...
I FORGOT VERONICA

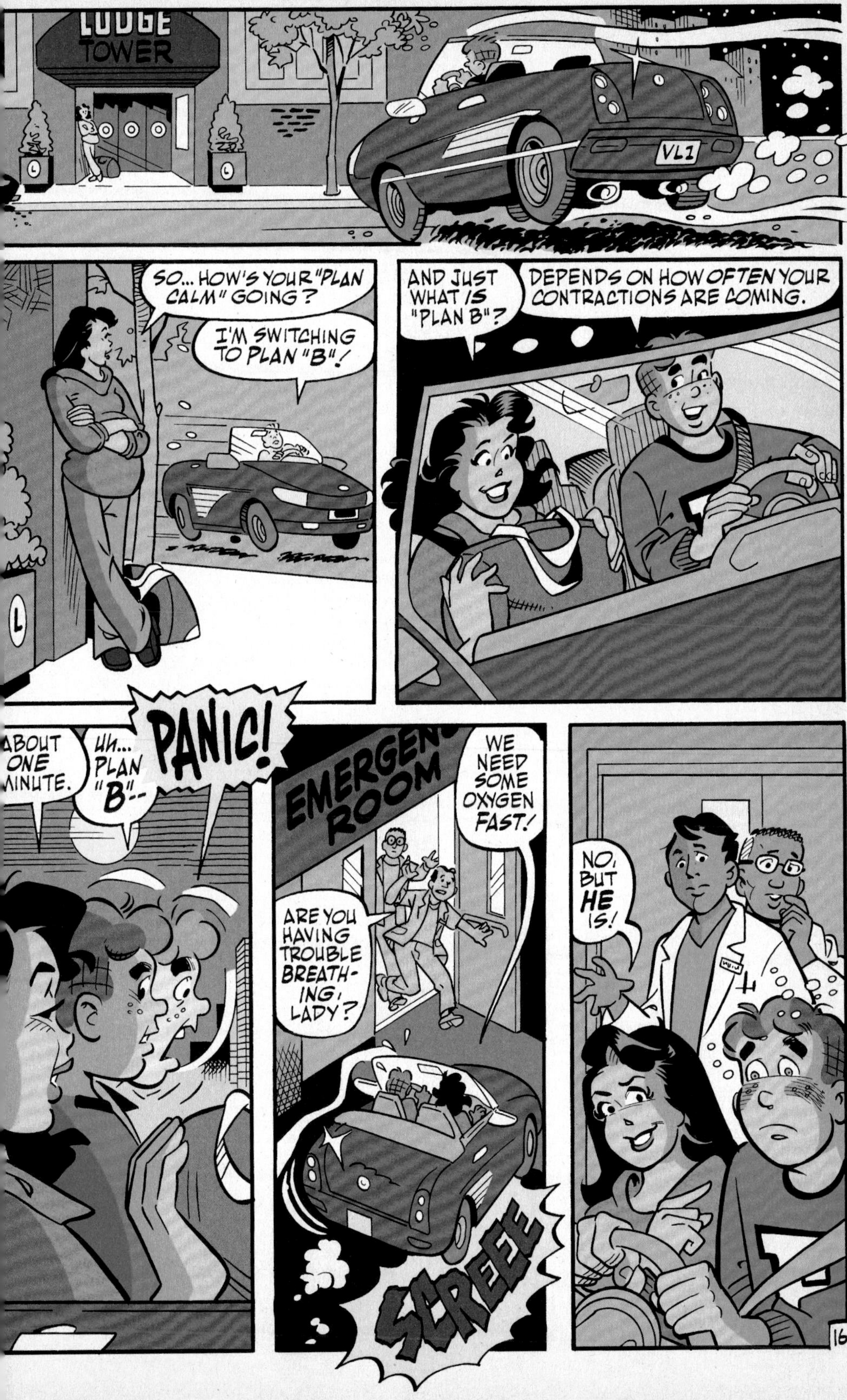
LODGE TOWER
VL1
SO... HOW'S YOUR "PLAN CALM" GOING?
I'M SWITCHING TO PLAN "B"!
AND JUST WHAT IS "PLAN B"?
DEPENDS ON HOW OFTEN YOUR CONTRACTIONS ARE COMING.
ABOUT ONE MINUTE.
UH... PLAN "B"--
PANIC!
EMERGEN ROOM
WE NEED SOME OXYGEN FAST!
ARE YOU HAVING TROUBLE BREATHING, LADY?
SCREEE
NO, BUT HE IS!

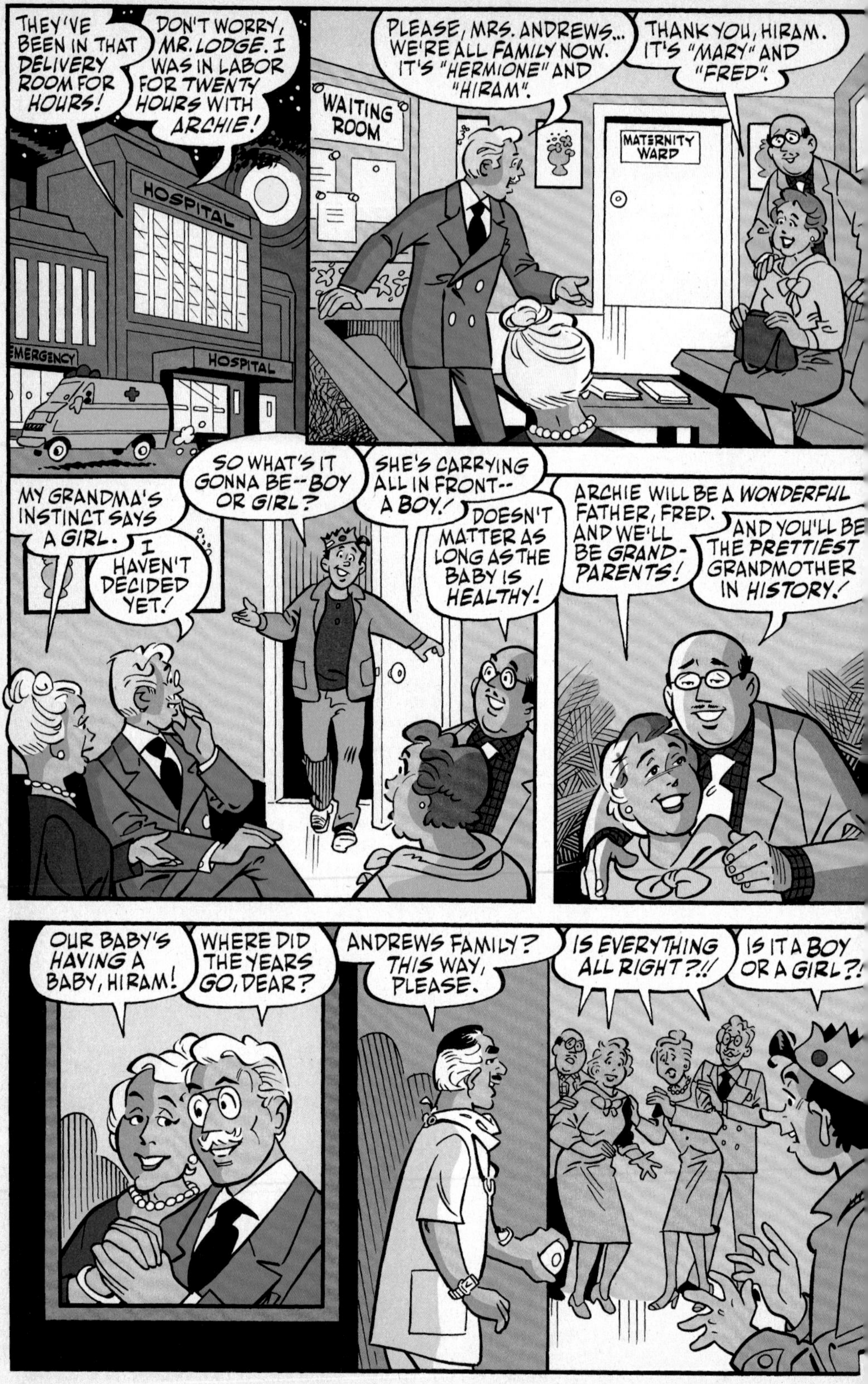
THEY'VE BEEN IN THAT DELIVERY ROOM FOR HOURS!
DON'T WORRY, MR. LODGE. I WAS IN LABOR FOR TWENTY HOURS WITH ARCHIE!
HOSPITAL
EMERGENCY
HOSPITAL
PLEASE, MRS. ANDREWS... WE'RE ALL FAMILY NOW. IT'S "HERMIONE" AND "HIRAM".
THANK YOU, HIRAM. IT'S "MARY" AND "FRED".
WAITING ROOM
MATERNITY WARD
MY GRANDMA'S INSTINCT SAYS A GIRL.
I HAVEN'T DECIDED YET!
SO WHAT'S IT GONNA BE--BOY OR GIRL?
SHE'S CARRYING ALL IN FRONT-- A BOY!
DOESN'T MATTER AS LONG AS THE BABY IS HEALTHY!
ARCHIE WILL BE A WONDERFUL FATHER, FRED. AND WE'LL BE GRAND-PARENTS!
AND YOU'LL BE THE PRETTIEST GRANDMOTHER IN HISTORY!
OUR BABY'S HAVING A BABY, HIRAM!
WHERE DID THE YEARS GO, DEAR?
ANDREWS FAMILY? THIS WAY, PLEASE.
IS EVERYTHING ALL RIGHT?!!
IS IT A BOY OR A GIRL?!

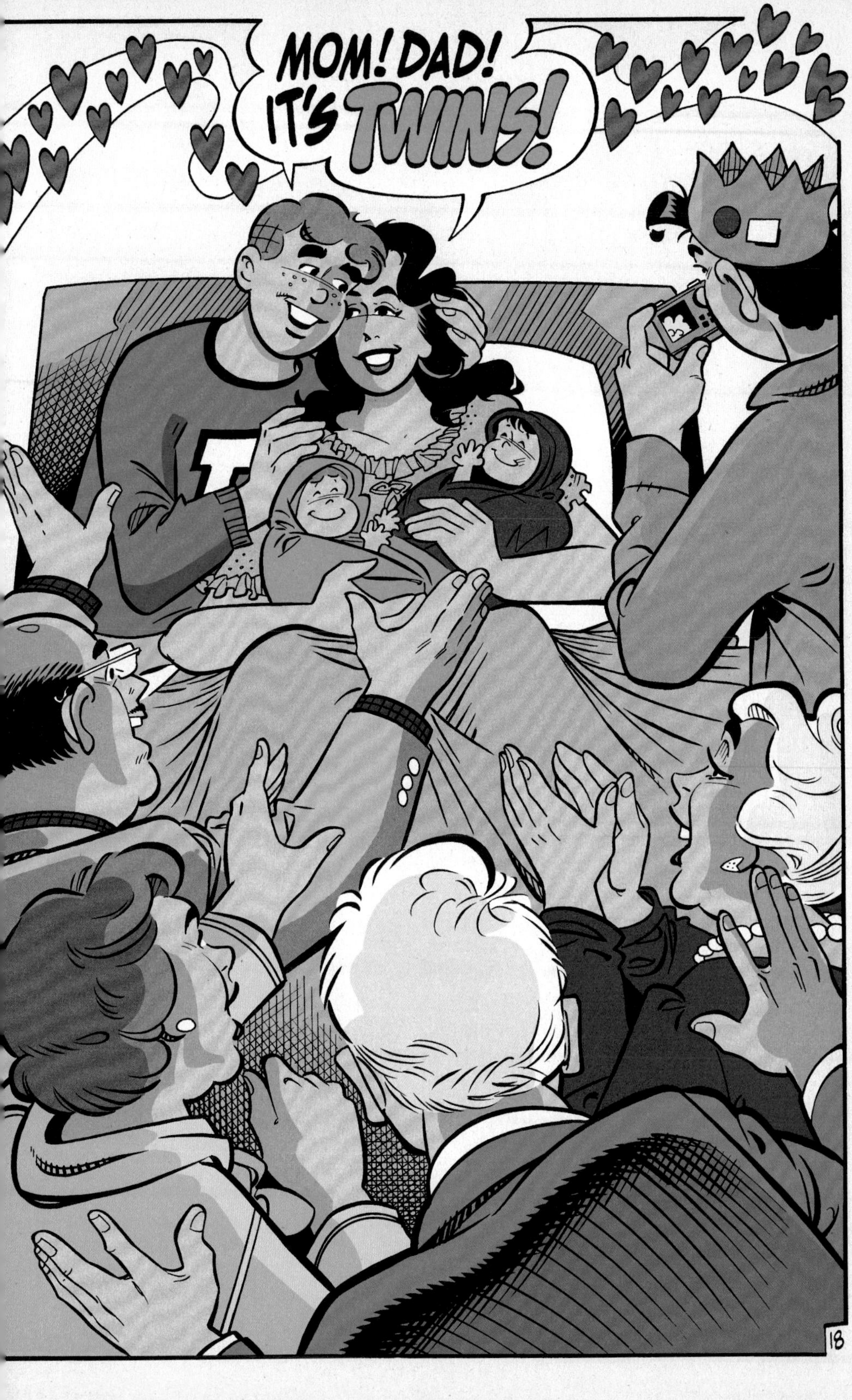
MOM! DAD! IT'S TWINS!
18

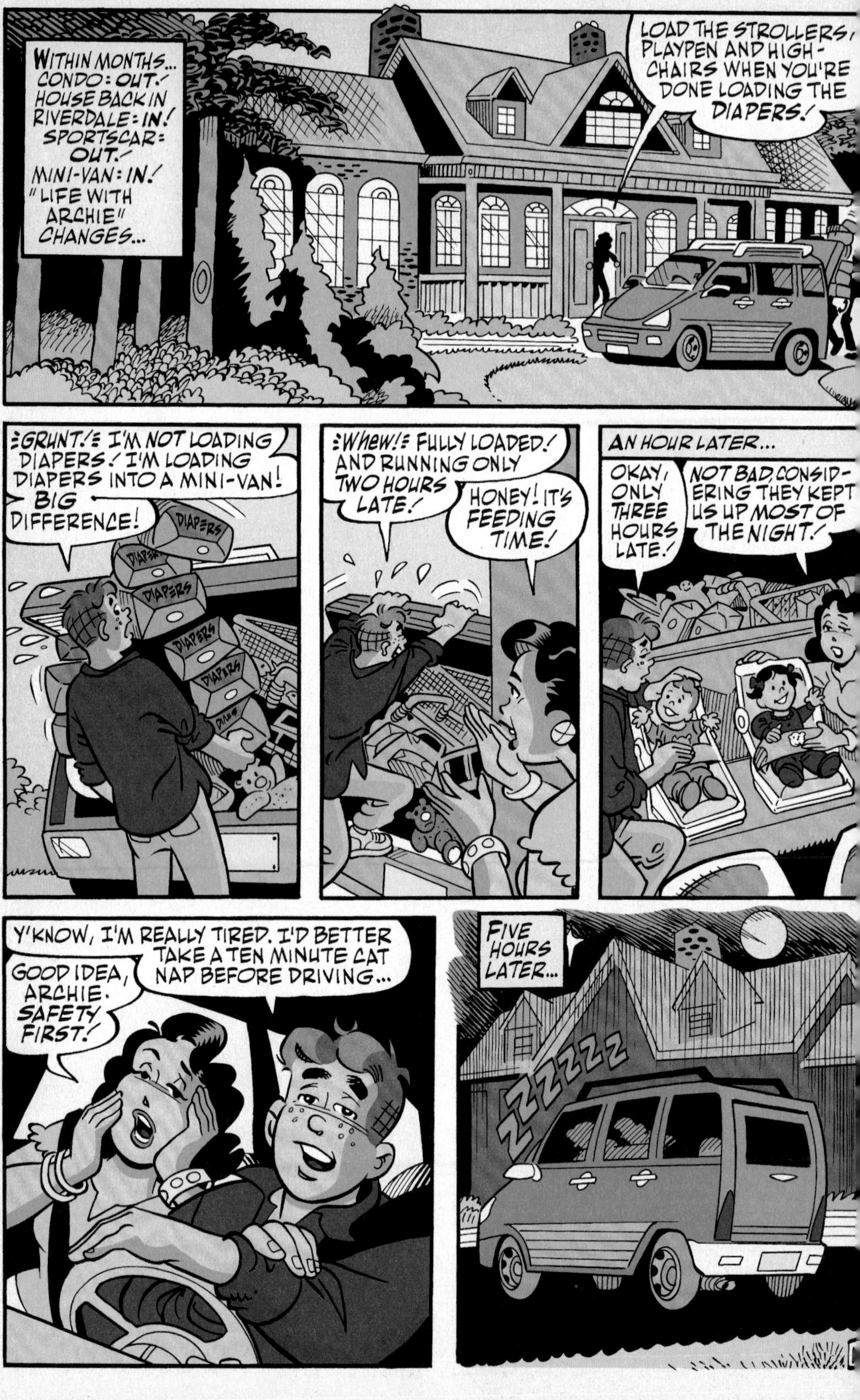
WITHIN MONTHS... CONDO: OUT! HOUSE BACK IN RIVERDALE: IN! SPORTSCAR: OUT! MINI-VAN: IN! "LIFE WITH ARCHIE" CHANGES...
LOAD THE STROLLERS, PLAYPEN AND HIGH-CHAIRS WHEN YOU'RE DONE LOADING THE DIAPERS!
:GRUNT!: I'M NOT LOADING DIAPERS! I'M LOADING DIAPERS INTO A MINI-VAN! BIG DIFFERENCE!
DIAPERS
:WHEW!: FULLY LOADED! AND RUNNING ONLY TWO HOURS LATE!
HONEY! IT'S FEEDING TIME!
AN HOUR LATER...
OKAY, ONLY THREE HOURS LATE!
NOT BAD, CONSIDERING THEY KEPT US UP MOST OF THE NIGHT!
Y'KNOW, I'M REALLY TIRED. I'D BETTER TAKE A TEN MINUTE CAT NAP BEFORE DRIVING...
GOOD IDEA, ARCHIE. SAFETY FIRST!
FIVE HOURS LATER...
ZZZZZZ

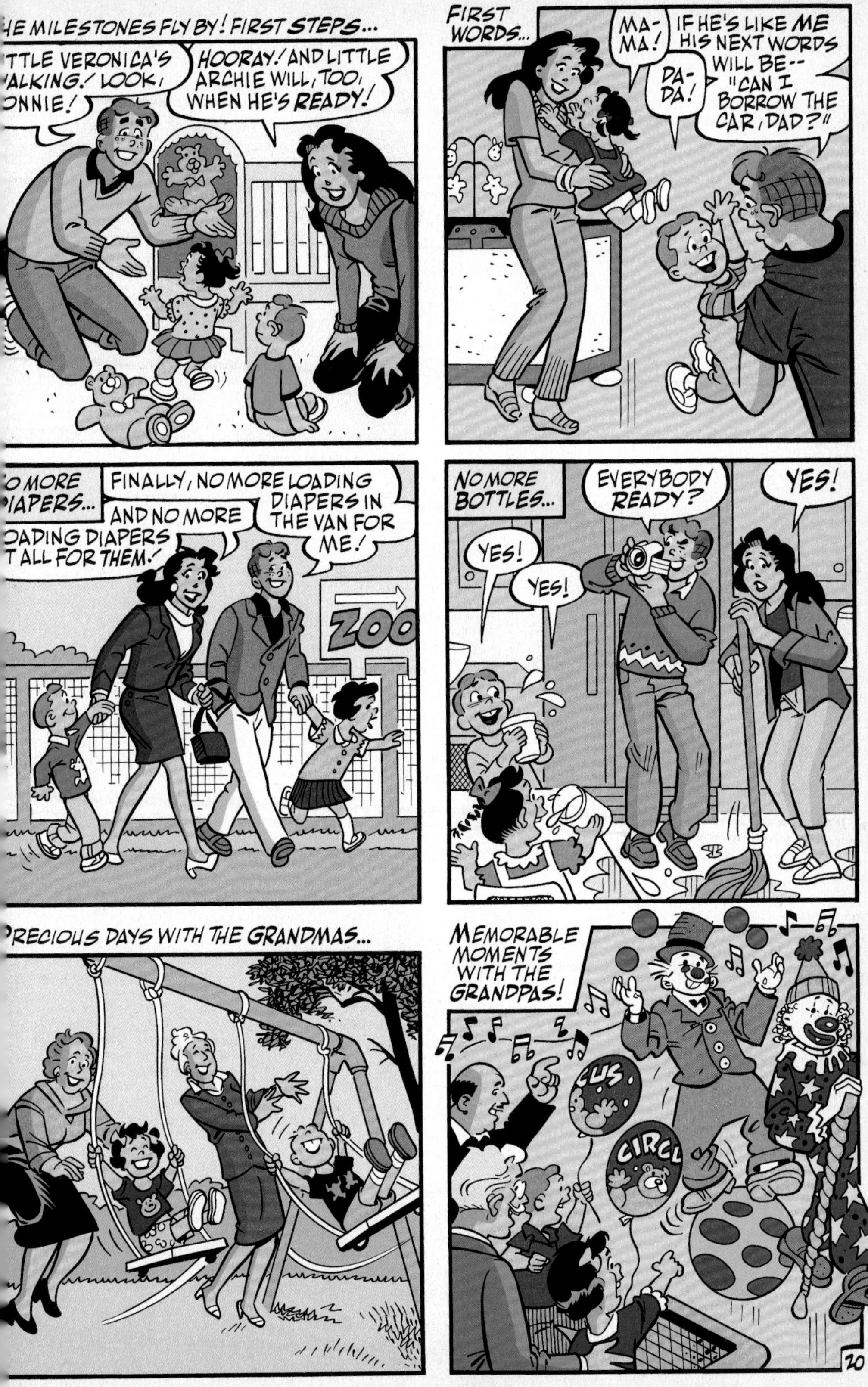
HE MILESTONES FLY BY! FIRST STEPS...
TTLE VERONICA'S ALKING! LOOK, ONNIE!
HOORAY! AND LITTLE ARCHIE WILL, TOO, WHEN HE'S READY!
FIRST WORDS...
MA-MA!
DA-DA!
IF HE'S LIKE ME HIS NEXT WORDS WILL BE-- "CAN I BORROW THE CAR, DAD?"
O MORE IAPERS...
FINALLY, NO MORE LOADING DIAPERS IN THE VAN FOR ME!
AND NO MORE OADING DIAPERS T ALL FOR THEM!
ZOO
NO MORE BOTTLES...
EVERYBODY READY?
YES!
YES!
YES!
RECIOUS DAYS WITH THE GRANDMAS...
MEMORABLE MOMENTS WITH THE GRANDPAS!
CUS
CIRCU
20

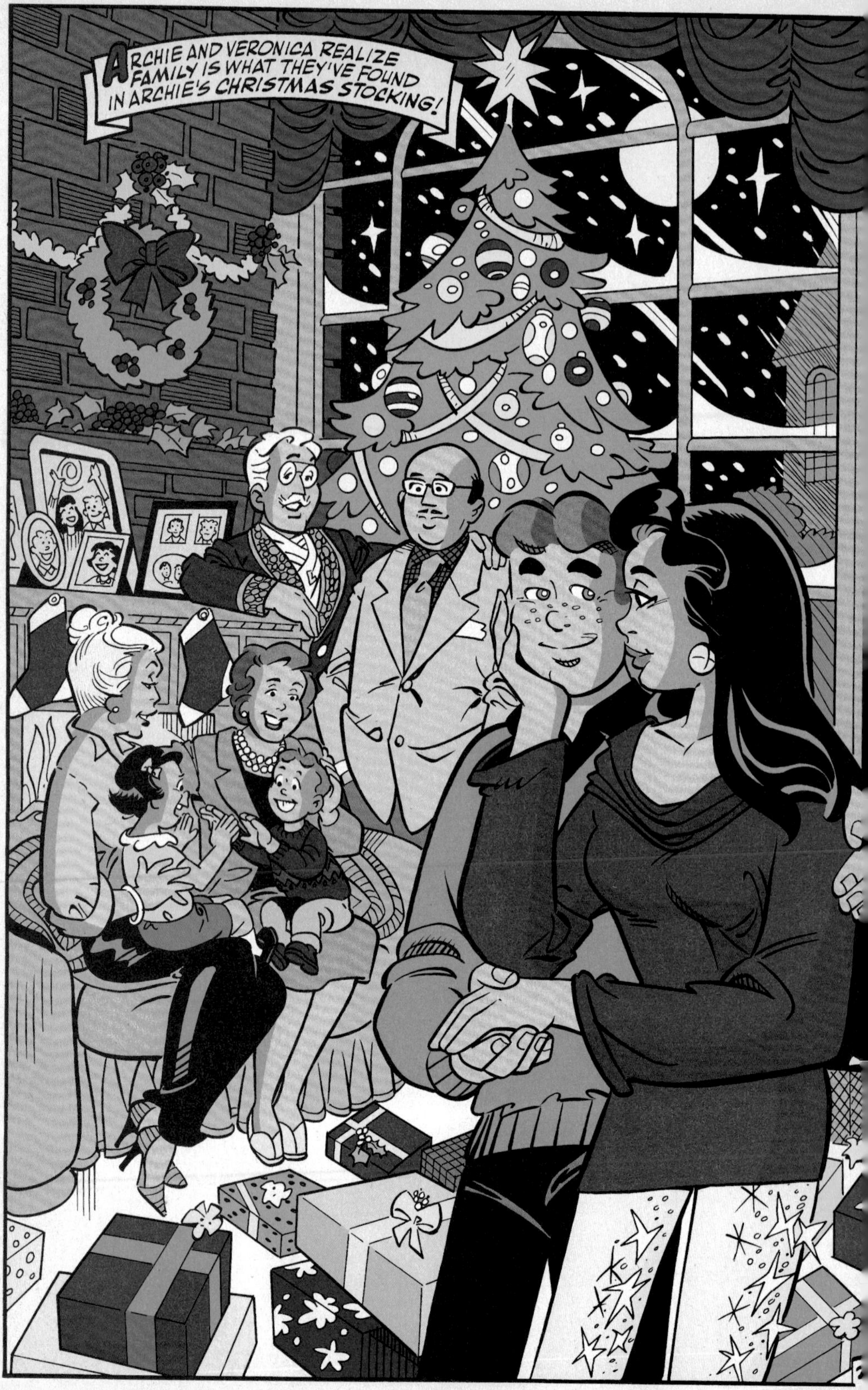
ARCHIE AND VERONICA REALIZE FAMILY IS WHAT THEY'VE FOUND IN ARCHIE'S CHRISTMAS STOCKING!

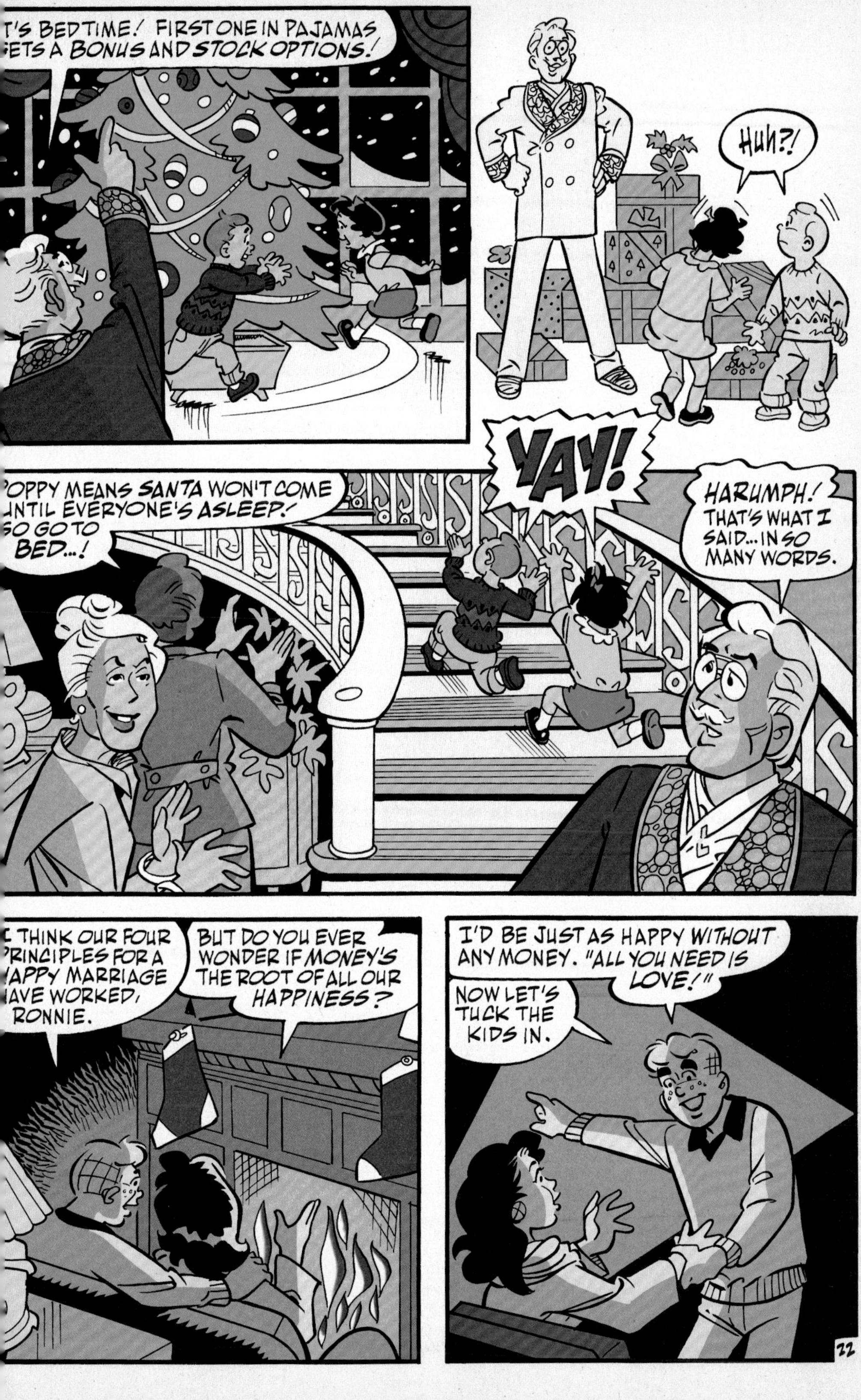
T'S BEDTIME! FIRST ONE IN PAJAMAS
ETS A BONUS AND STOCK OPTIONS!
HUH?!
YAY!
POPPY MEANS SANTA WON'T COME UNTIL EVERYONE'S ASLEEP! SO GO TO BED...!
HARUMPH! THAT'S WHAT I SAID... IN SO MANY WORDS.
I THINK OUR FOUR PRINCIPLES FOR A HAPPY MARRIAGE HAVE WORKED, RONNIE.
BUT DO YOU EVER WONDER IF MONEY'S THE ROOT OF ALL OUR HAPPINESS?
I'D BE JUST AS HAPPY WITHOUT ANY MONEY. "ALL YOU NEED IS LOVE!"
NOW LET'S TUCK THE KIDS IN.
22

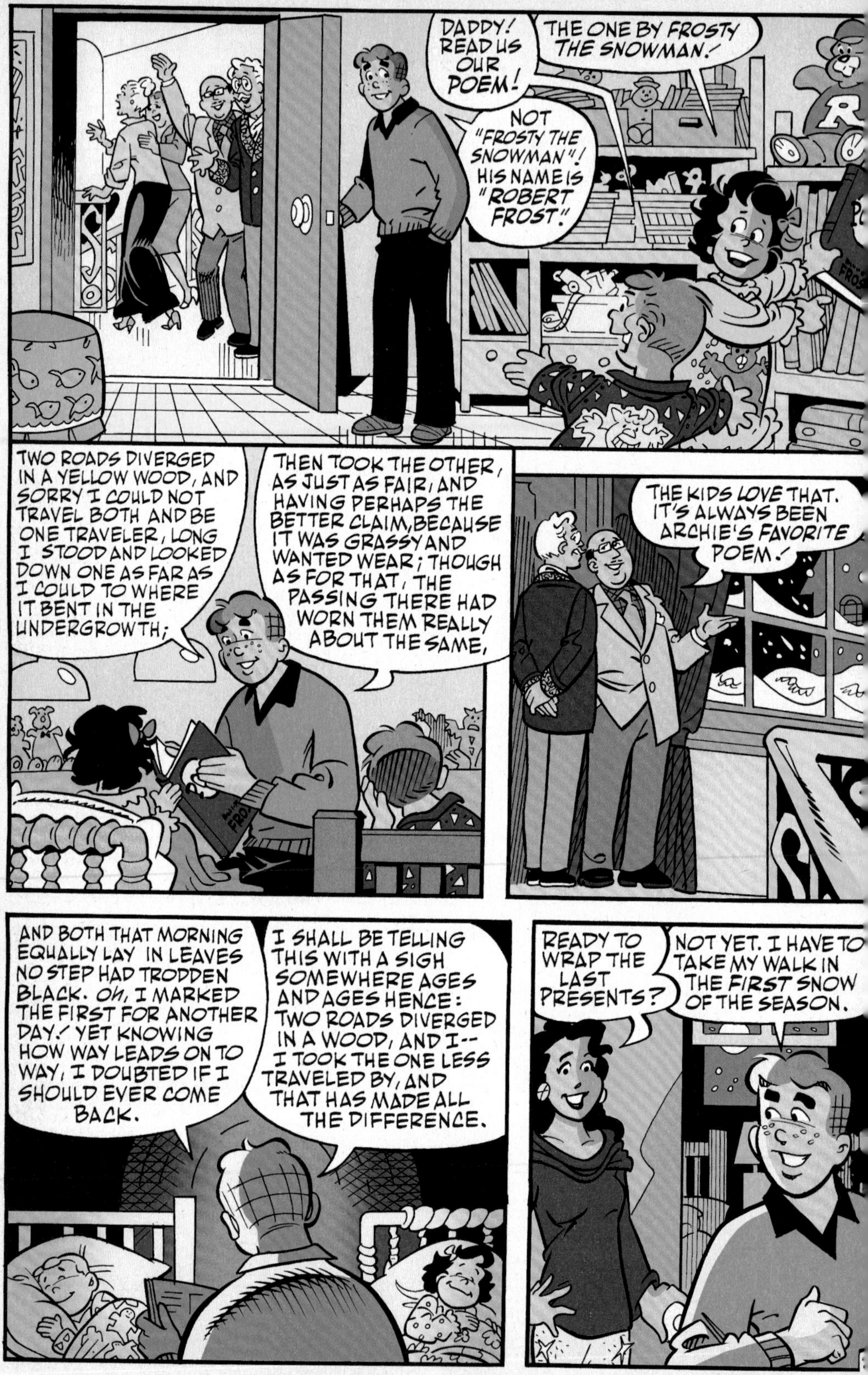
DADDY! READ US OUR POEM!
THE ONE BY FROSTY THE SNOWMAN!
NOT "FROSTY THE SNOWMAN"! HIS NAME IS "ROBERT FROST!"
TWO ROADS DIVERGED IN A YELLOW WOOD, AND SORRY I COULD NOT TRAVEL BOTH AND BE ONE TRAVELER, LONG I STOOD AND LOOKED DOWN ONE AS FAR AS I COULD TO WHERE IT BENT IN THE UNDERGROWTH;
THEN TOOK THE OTHER, AS JUST AS FAIR, AND HAVING PERHAPS THE BETTER CLAIM, BECAUSE IT WAS GRASSY AND WANTED WEAR; THOUGH AS FOR THAT, THE PASSING THERE HAD WORN THEM REALLY ABOUT THE SAME,
THE KIDS LOVE THAT. IT'S ALWAYS BEEN ARCHIE'S FAVORITE POEM!
AND BOTH THAT MORNING EQUALLY LAY IN LEAVES NO STEP HAD TRODDEN BLACK. OH, I MARKED THE FIRST FOR ANOTHER DAY! YET KNOWING HOW WAY LEADS ON TO WAY, I DOUBTED IF I SHOULD EVER COME BACK.
I SHALL BE TELLING THIS WITH A SIGH SOMEWHERE AGES AND AGES HENCE: TWO ROADS DIVERGED IN A WOOD, AND I-- I TOOK THE ONE LESS TRAVELED BY, AND THAT HAS MADE ALL THE DIFFERENCE.
READY TO WRAP THE LAST PRESENTS?
NOT YET. I HAVE TO TAKE MY WALK IN THE FIRST SNOW OF THE SEASON.

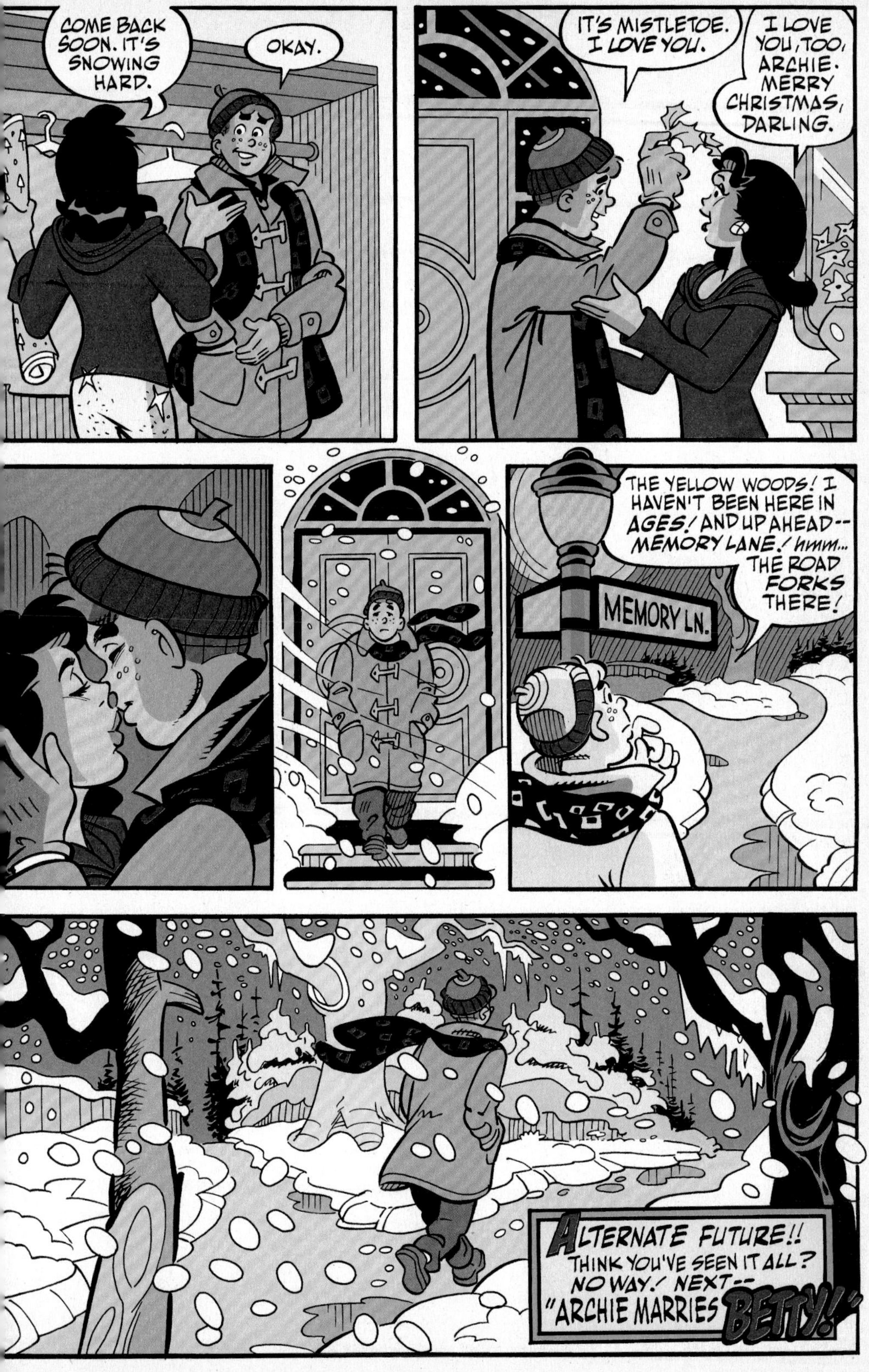
COME BACK SOON. IT'S SNOWING HARD.
OKAY.
IT'S MISTLETOE. I LOVE YOU.
I LOVE YOU, TOO, ARCHIE. MERRY CHRISTMAS, DARLING.
THE YELLOW WOODS! I HAVEN'T BEEN HERE IN AGES! AND UP AHEAD-- MEMORY LANE! hmm... THE ROAD FORKS THERE!
MEMORY LN.
ALTERNATE FUTURE!! THINK YOU'VE SEEN IT ALL? NO WAY! NEXT-- "ARCHIE MARRIES BETTY!"

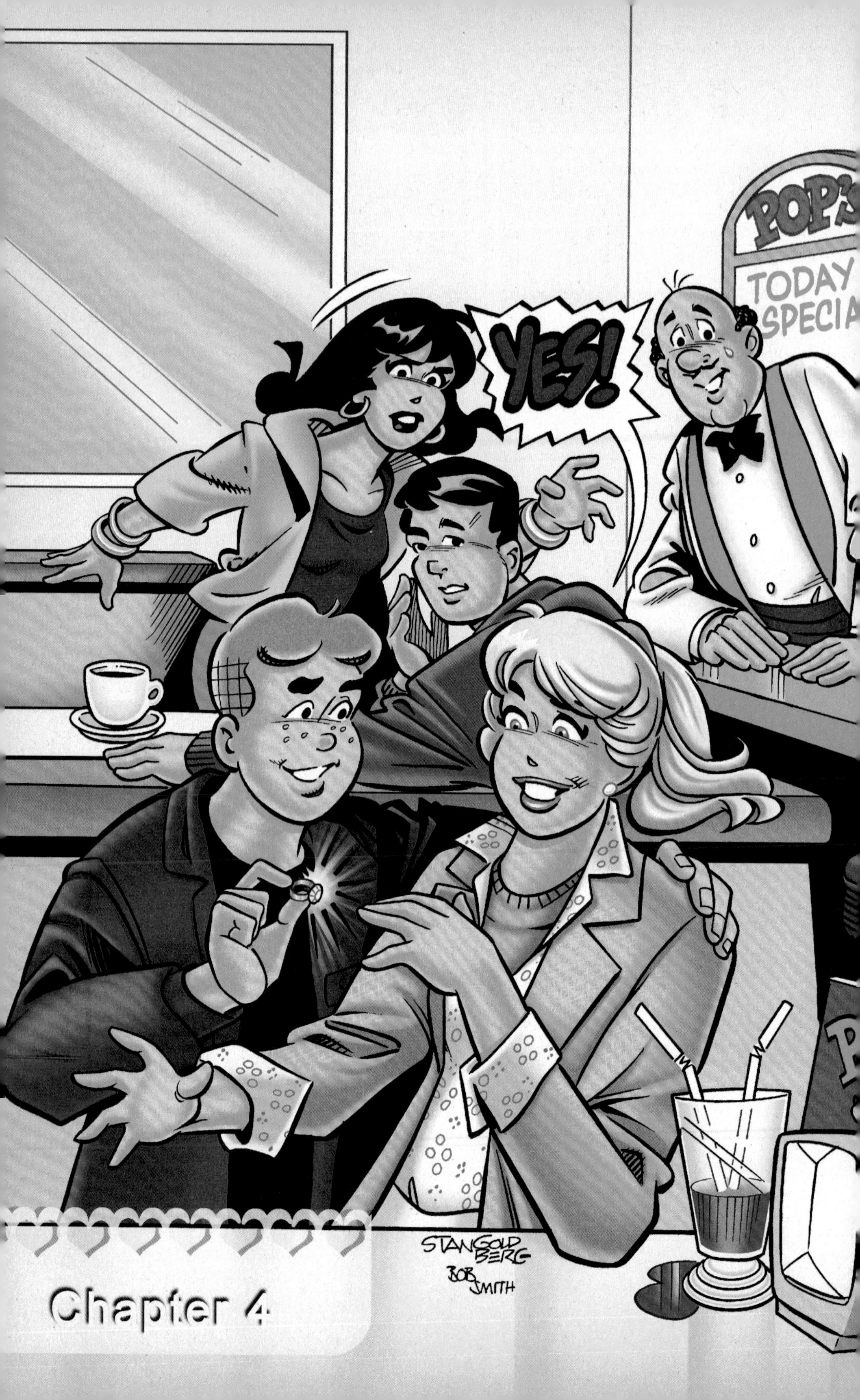
YES!
POP'S
TODAY SPECIA
STAN GOLDBERG
BOB SMITH

Chapter 4

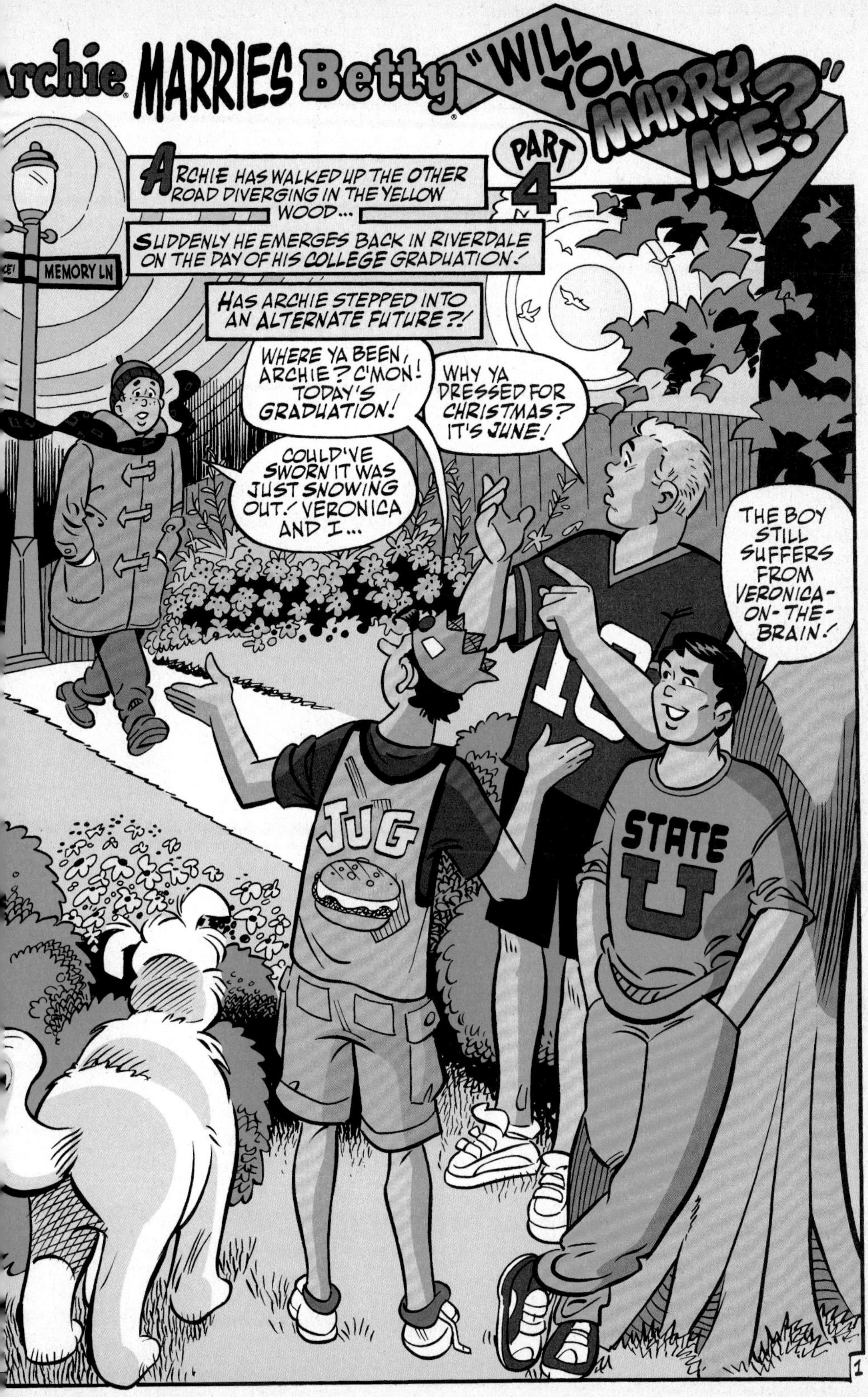
Archie MARRIES Betty
"WILL YOU MARRY ME?"
PART 4
ARCHIE HAS WALKED UP THE OTHER ROAD DIVERGING IN THE YELLOW WOOD...
SUDDENLY HE EMERGES BACK IN RIVERDALE ON THE DAY OF HIS COLLEGE GRADUATION!
HAS ARCHIE STEPPED INTO AN ALTERNATE FUTURE?!
MEMORY LN
WHERE YA BEEN, ARCHIE? C'MON! TODAY'S GRADUATION!
WHY YA DRESSED FOR CHRISTMAS? IT'S JUNE!
COULD'VE SWORN IT WAS JUST SNOWING OUT! VERONICA AND I...
THE BOY STILL SUFFERS FROM VERONICA-ON-THE-BRAIN!
JUG
STATE U
1

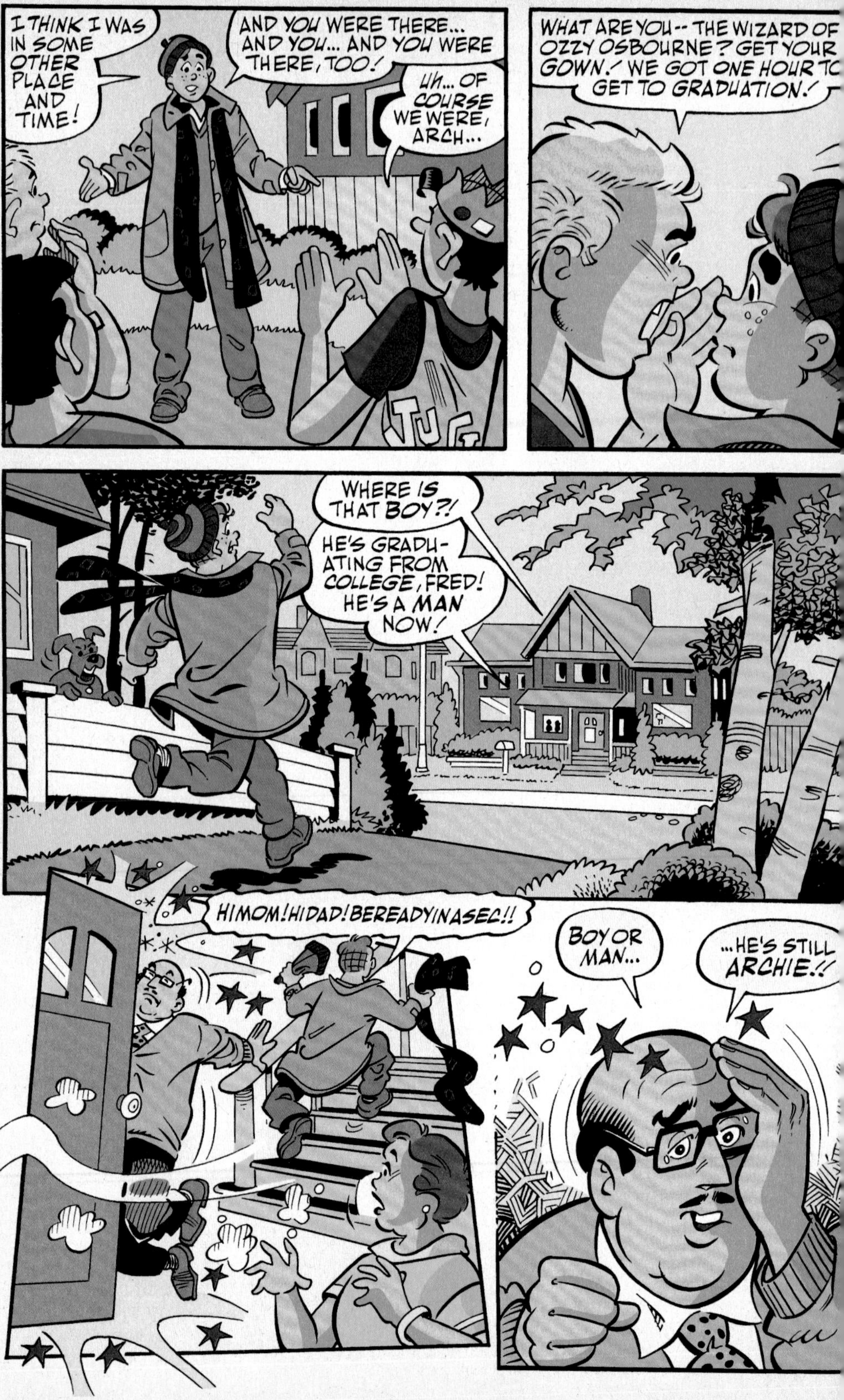
I THINK I WAS IN SOME OTHER PLACE AND TIME!
AND YOU WERE THERE... AND YOU... AND YOU WERE THERE, TOO!
UH... OF COURSE WE WERE, ARCH...
WHAT ARE YOU-- THE WIZARD OF OZZY OSBOURNE? GET YOUR GOWN! WE GOT ONE HOUR TO GET TO GRADUATION!
WHERE IS THAT BOY?!
HE'S GRADUATING FROM COLLEGE, FRED! HE'S A MAN NOW!
HI MOM! HI DAD! BE READY IN A SEC!!
BOY OR MAN...
...HE'S STILL ARCHIE!!

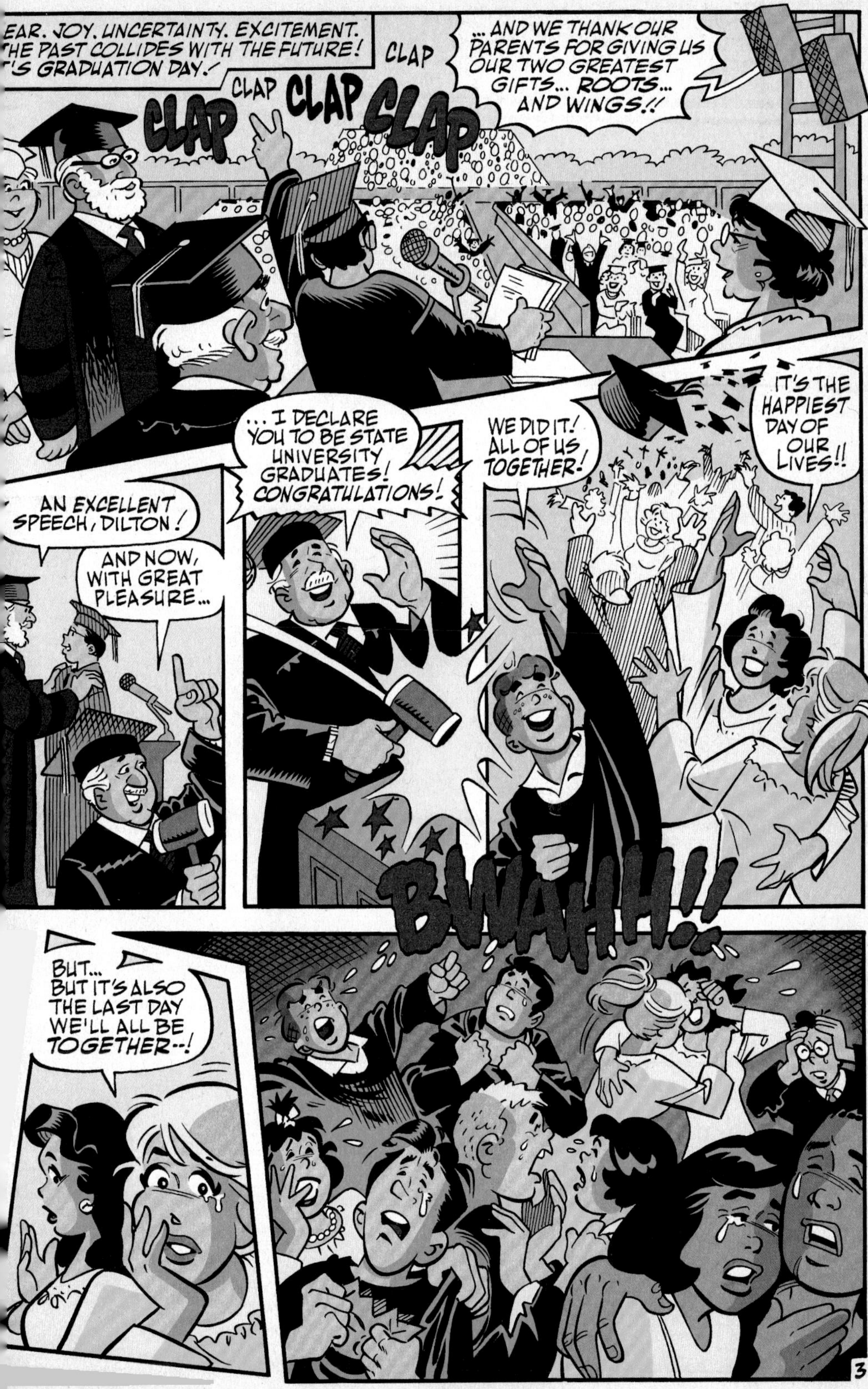
EAR. JOY. UNCERTAINTY. EXCITEMENT. THE PAST COLLIDES WITH THE FUTURE! 'T'S GRADUATION DAY!
CLAP
CLAP
CLAP
CLAP
CLAP
...AND WE THANK OUR PARENTS FOR GIVING US OUR TWO GREATEST GIFTS... ROOTS... AND WINGS!!
AN EXCELLENT SPEECH, DILTON!
AND NOW, WITH GREAT PLEASURE...
...I DECLARE YOU TO BE STATE UNIVERSITY GRADUATES! CONGRATULATIONS!
WE DID IT! ALL OF US TOGETHER!
IT'S THE HAPPIEST DAY OF OUR LIVES!!
BWAHH!!
BUT... BUT IT'S ALSO THE LAST DAY WE'LL ALL BE TOGETHER--!
3

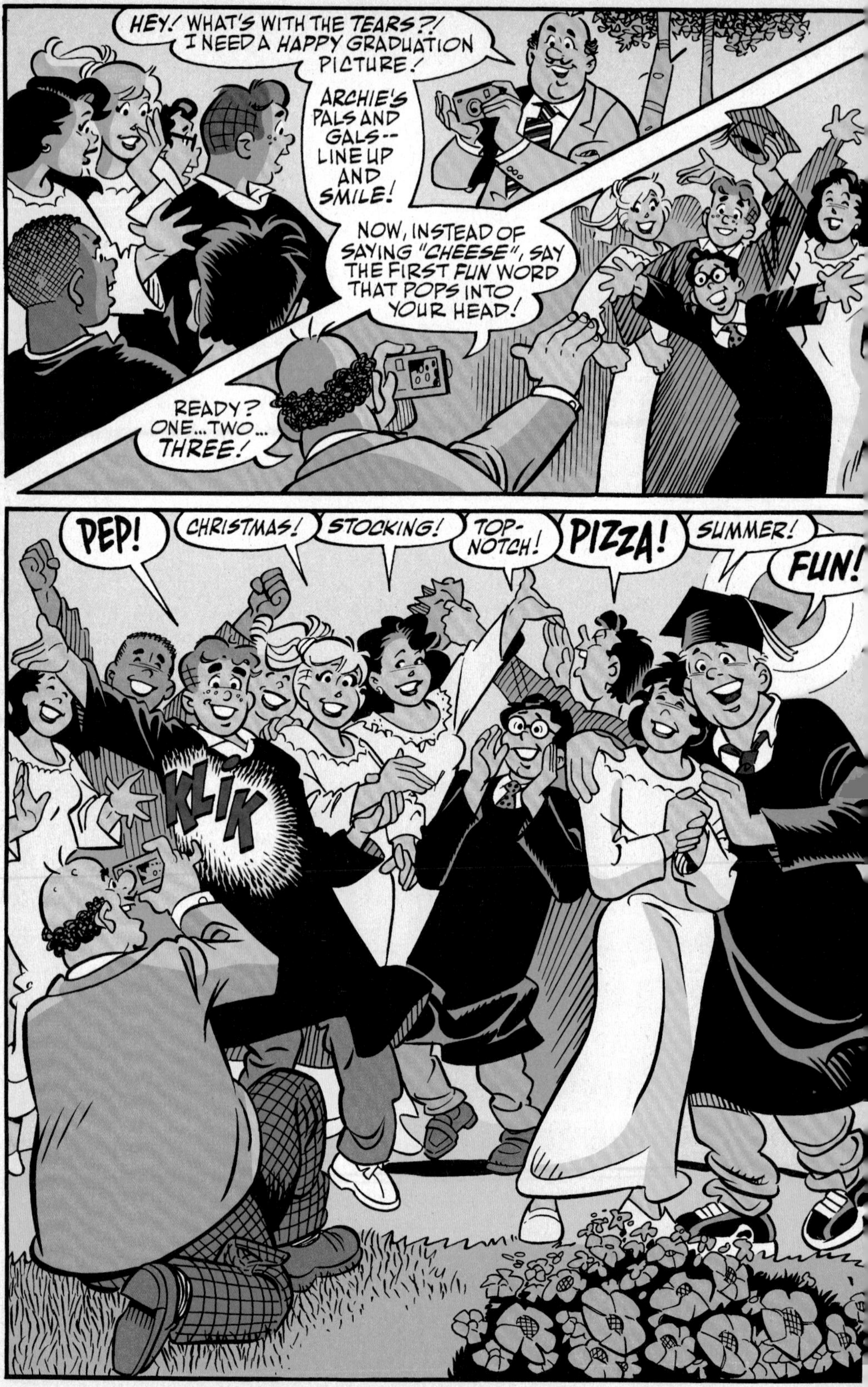
HEY! WHAT'S WITH THE TEARS?! I NEED A HAPPY GRADUATION PICTURE!
ARCHIE'S PALS AND GALS-- LINE UP AND SMILE!
NOW, INSTEAD OF SAYING "CHEESE", SAY THE FIRST FUN WORD THAT POPS INTO YOUR HEAD!
READY? ONE...TWO... THREE!
PEP!
CHRISTMAS!
STOCKING!
TOP-NOTCH!
PIZZA!
SUMMER!
FUN!
KLIK

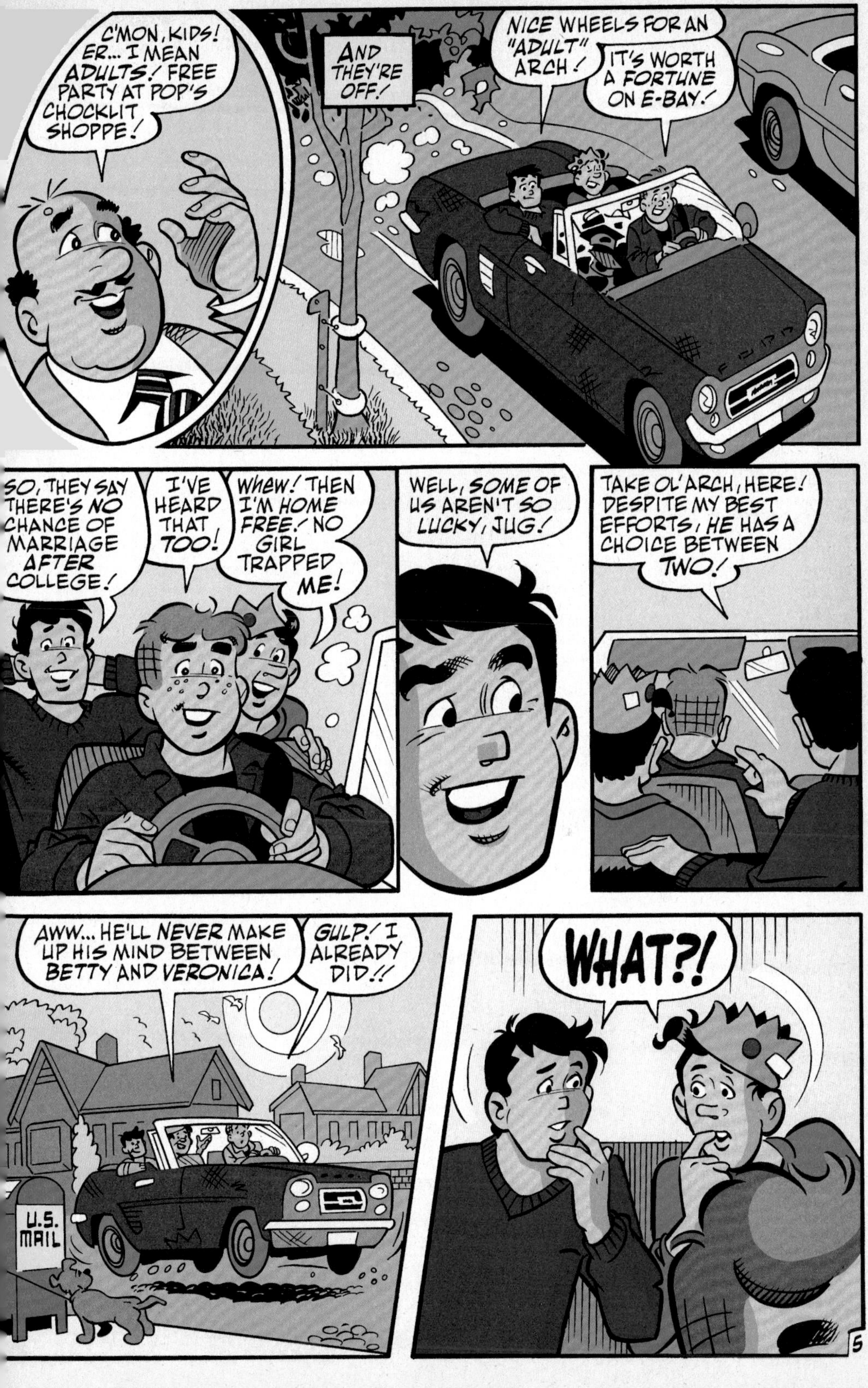
C'MON, KIDS! ER... I MEAN ADULTS! FREE PARTY AT POP'S CHOCKLIT SHOPPE!
AND THEY'RE OFF!
NICE WHEELS FOR AN "ADULT" ARCH!
IT'S WORTH A FORTUNE ON E-BAY!
SO, THEY SAY THERE'S NO CHANCE OF MARRIAGE AFTER COLLEGE!
I'VE HEARD THAT TOO!
WHEW! THEN I'M HOME FREE! NO GIRL TRAPPED ME!
WELL, SOME OF US AREN'T SO LUCKY, JUG!
TAKE OL' ARCH, HERE! DESPITE MY BEST EFFORTS, HE HAS A CHOICE BETWEEN TWO!
AWW... HE'LL NEVER MAKE UP HIS MIND BETWEEN BETTY AND VERONICA!
GULP! I ALREADY DID!!
U.S. MAIL
WHAT?!
5

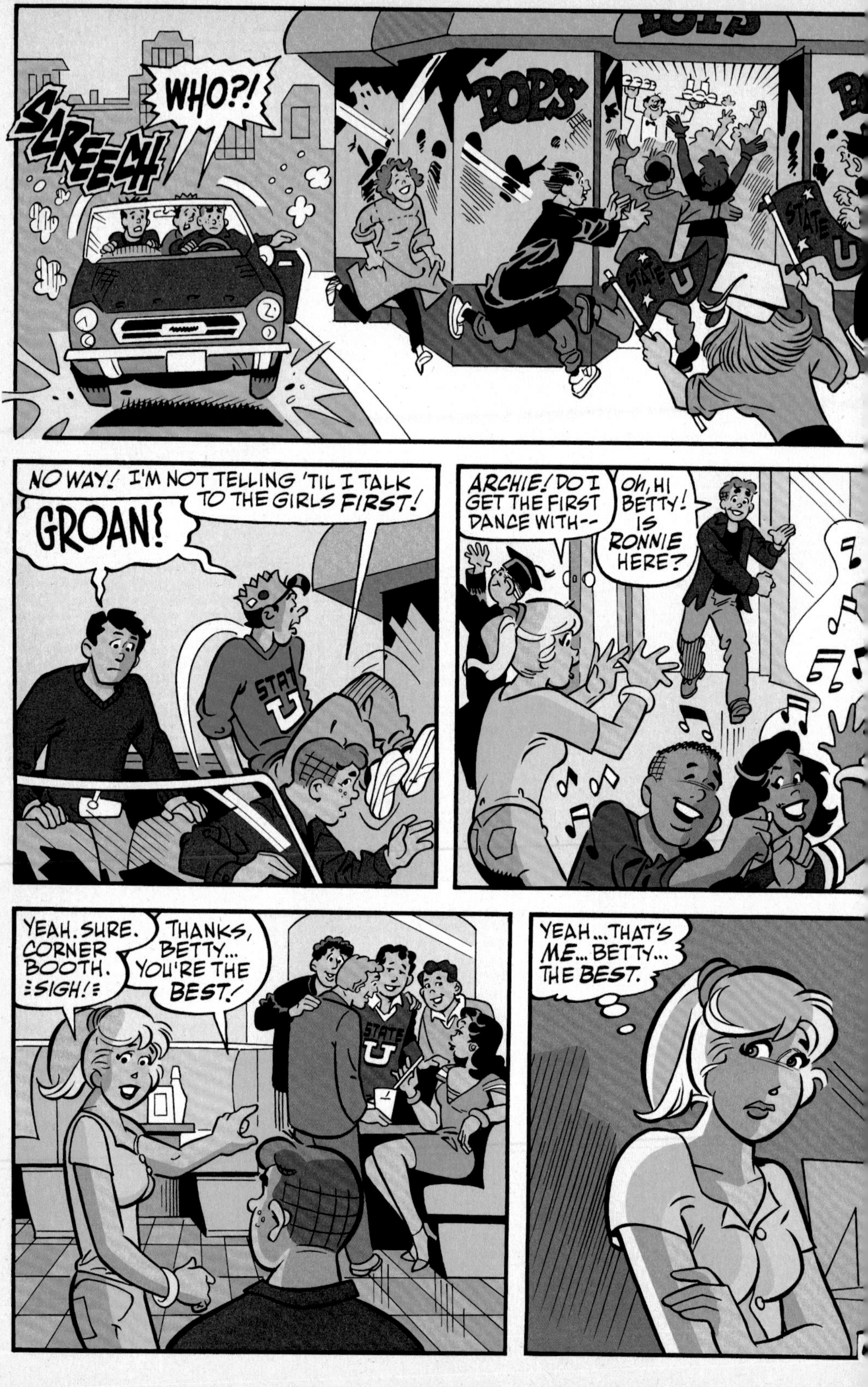
SCREECH
WHO?!
POP'S
STATE U
NO WAY! I'M NOT TELLING 'TIL I TALK TO THE GIRLS FIRST!
GROAN!
ARCHIE! DO I GET THE FIRST DANCE WITH--
OH, HI BETTY! IS RONNIE HERE?
YEAH. SURE. CORNER BOOTH. :SIGH!:
THANKS, BETTY... YOU'RE THE BEST!
YEAH... THAT'S ME... BETTY... THE BEST.

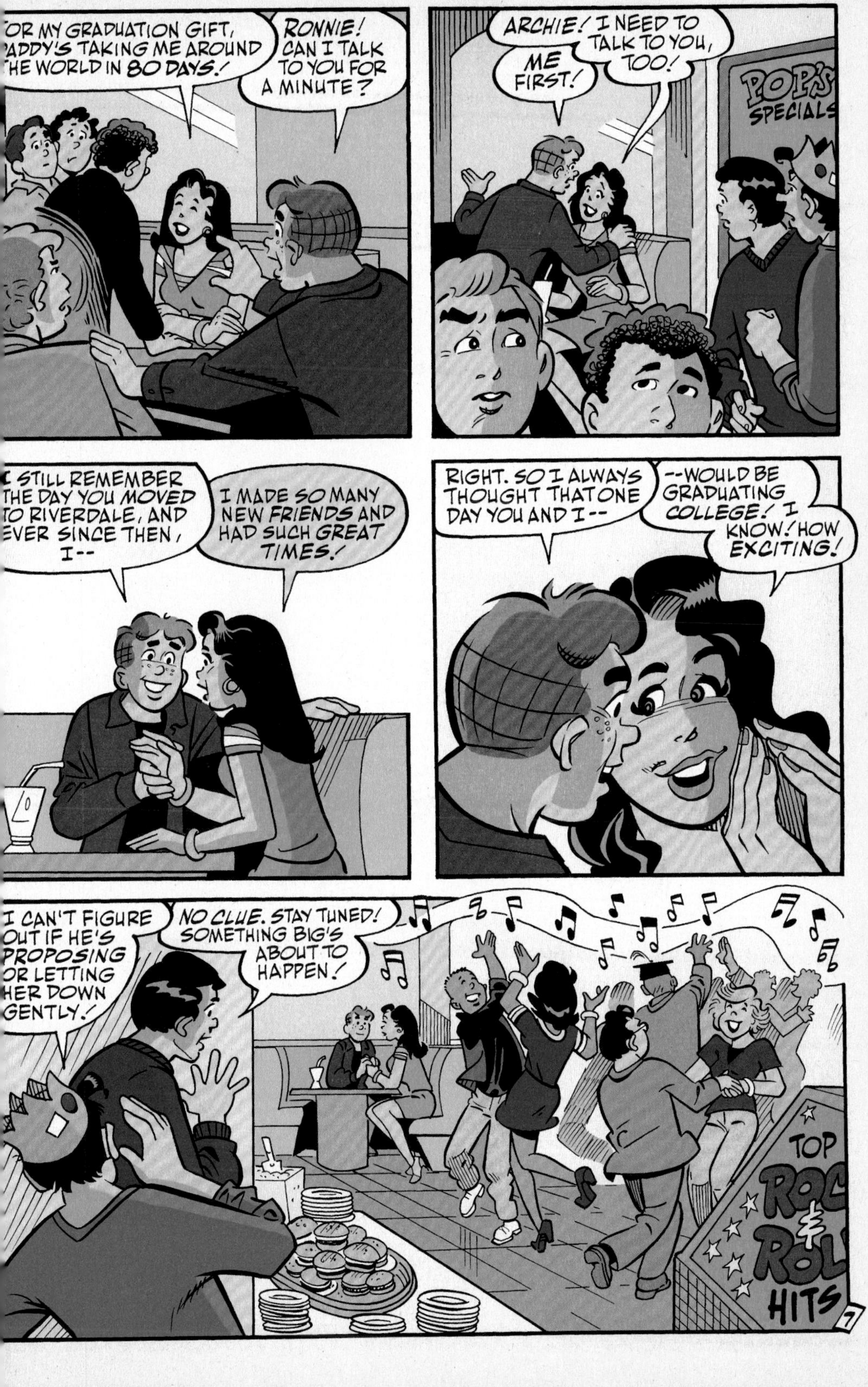
OR MY GRADUATION GIFT, ADDY'S TAKING ME AROUND HE WORLD IN 80 DAYS!
RONNIE! CAN I TALK TO YOU FOR A MINUTE?
ARCHIE! I NEED TO TALK TO YOU, TOO!
ME FIRST!
POP'S SPECIALS
STILL REMEMBER THE DAY YOU MOVED TO RIVERDALE, AND EVER SINCE THEN, I--
I MADE SO MANY NEW FRIENDS AND HAD SUCH GREAT TIMES!
RIGHT. SO I ALWAYS THOUGHT THAT ONE DAY YOU AND I--
--WOULD BE GRADUATING COLLEGE! I KNOW! HOW EXCITING!
I CAN'T FIGURE OUT IF HE'S PROPOSING OR LETTING HER DOWN GENTLY!
NO CLUE. STAY TUNED! SOMETHING BIG'S ABOUT TO HAPPEN!
TOP
HITS
7

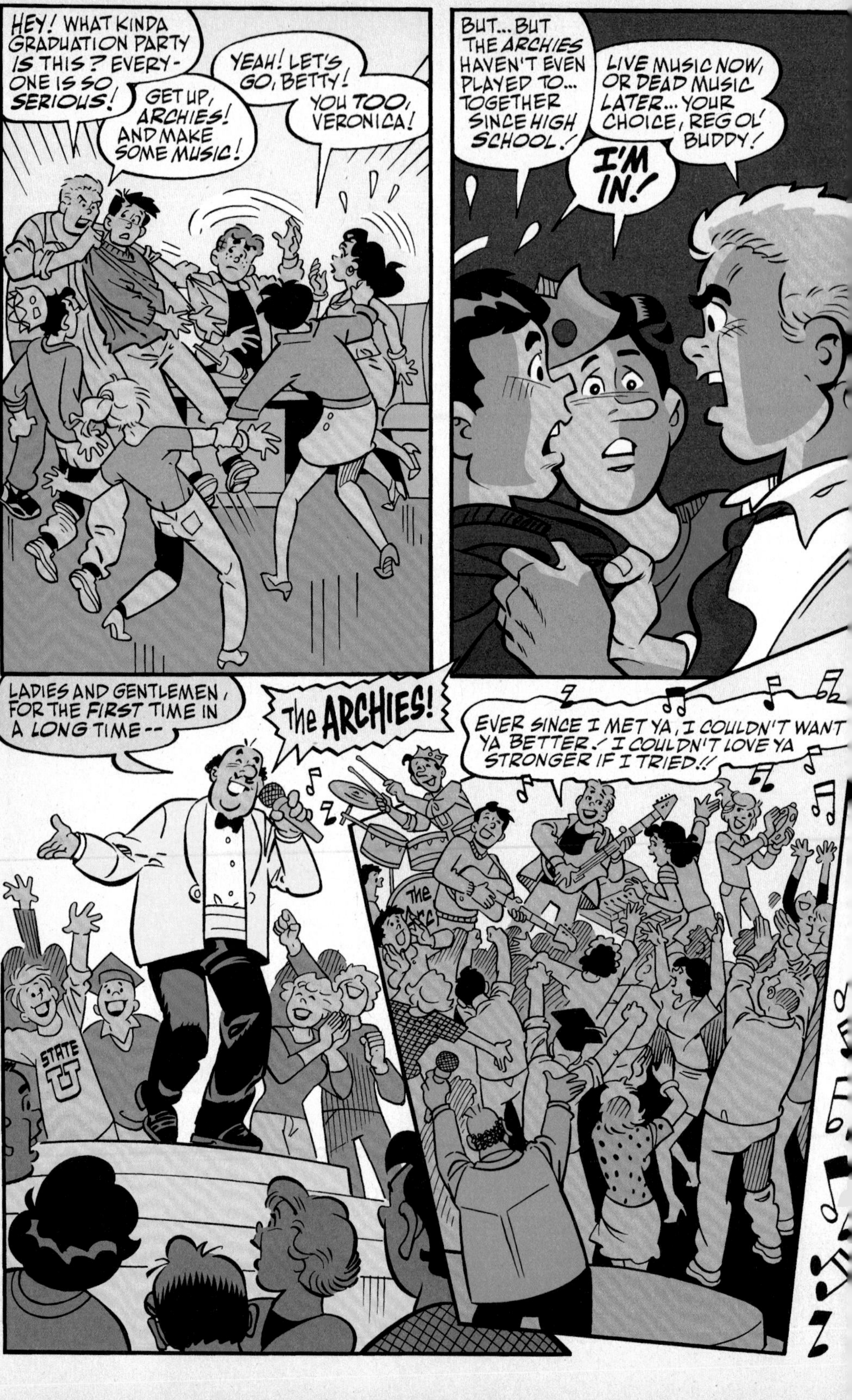
HEY! WHAT KINDA GRADUATION PARTY IS THIS? EVERY-ONE IS SO SERIOUS!
GET UP, ARCHIES! AND MAKE SOME MUSIC!
YEAH! LET'S GO, BETTY!
YOU TOO, VERONICA!
BUT... BUT THE ARCHIES HAVEN'T EVEN PLAYED TO... TOGETHER SINCE HIGH SCHOOL!
LIVE MUSIC NOW, OR DEAD MUSIC LATER... YOUR CHOICE, REG OL' BUDDY!
I'M IN!
LADIES AND GENTLEMEN, FOR THE FIRST TIME IN A LONG TIME--
The ARCHIES!
EVER SINCE I MET YA, I COULDN'T WANT YA BETTER! I COULDN'T LOVE YA STRONGER IF I TRIED!!
STATE U

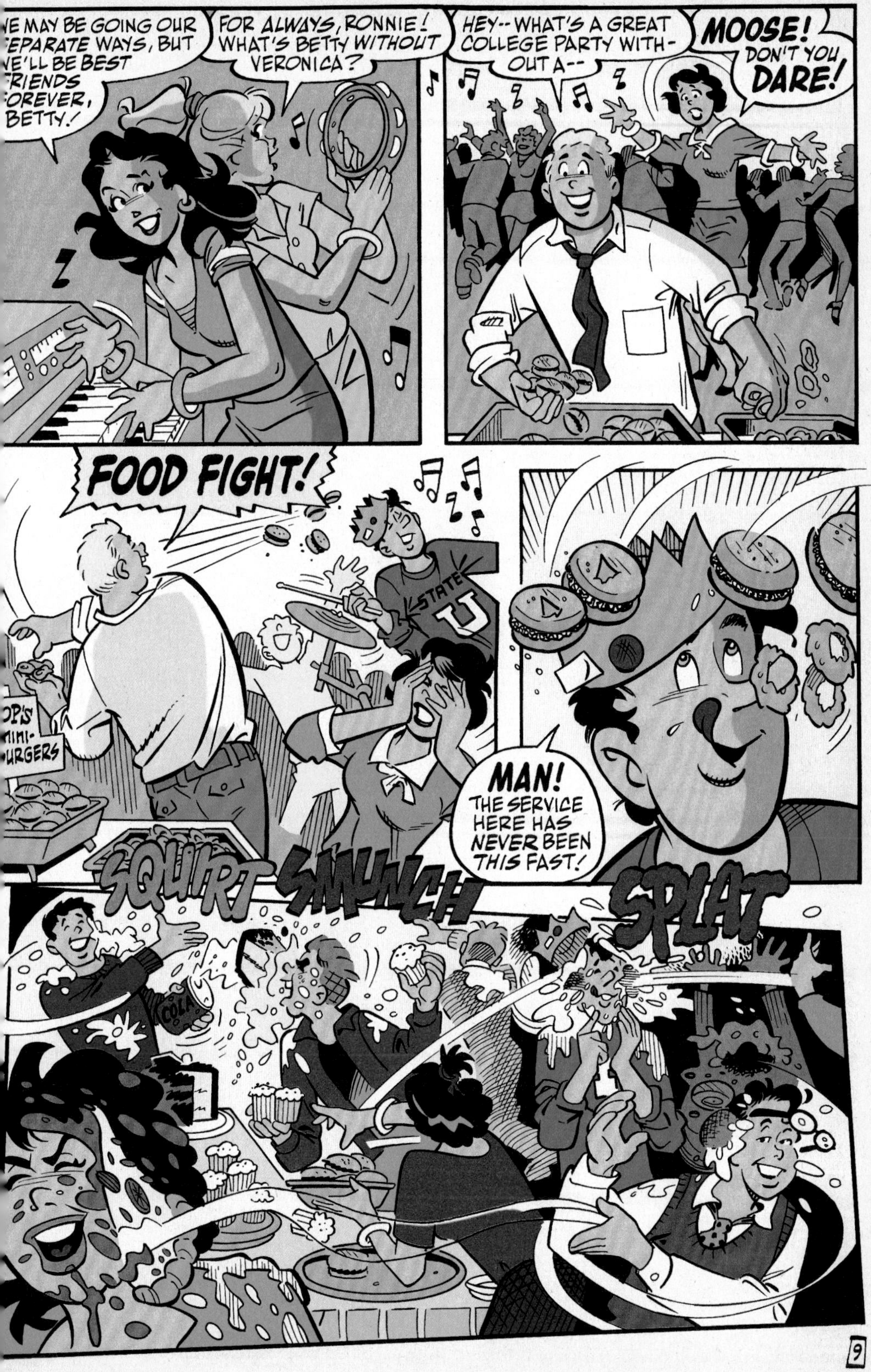

WE MAY BE GOING OUR SEPARATE WAYS, BUT WE'LL BE BEST FRIENDS FOREVER, BETTY!
FOR ALWAYS, RONNIE! WHAT'S BETTY WITHOUT VERONICA?
HEY-- WHAT'S A GREAT COLLEGE PARTY WITH-OUT A--
MOOSE! DON'T YOU DARE!
FOOD FIGHT!
STATE U
POP'S MINI-BURGERS
MAN! THE SERVICE HERE HAS NEVER BEEN THIS FAST!
SQUIRT
SMUNCH
SPLAT
COLA

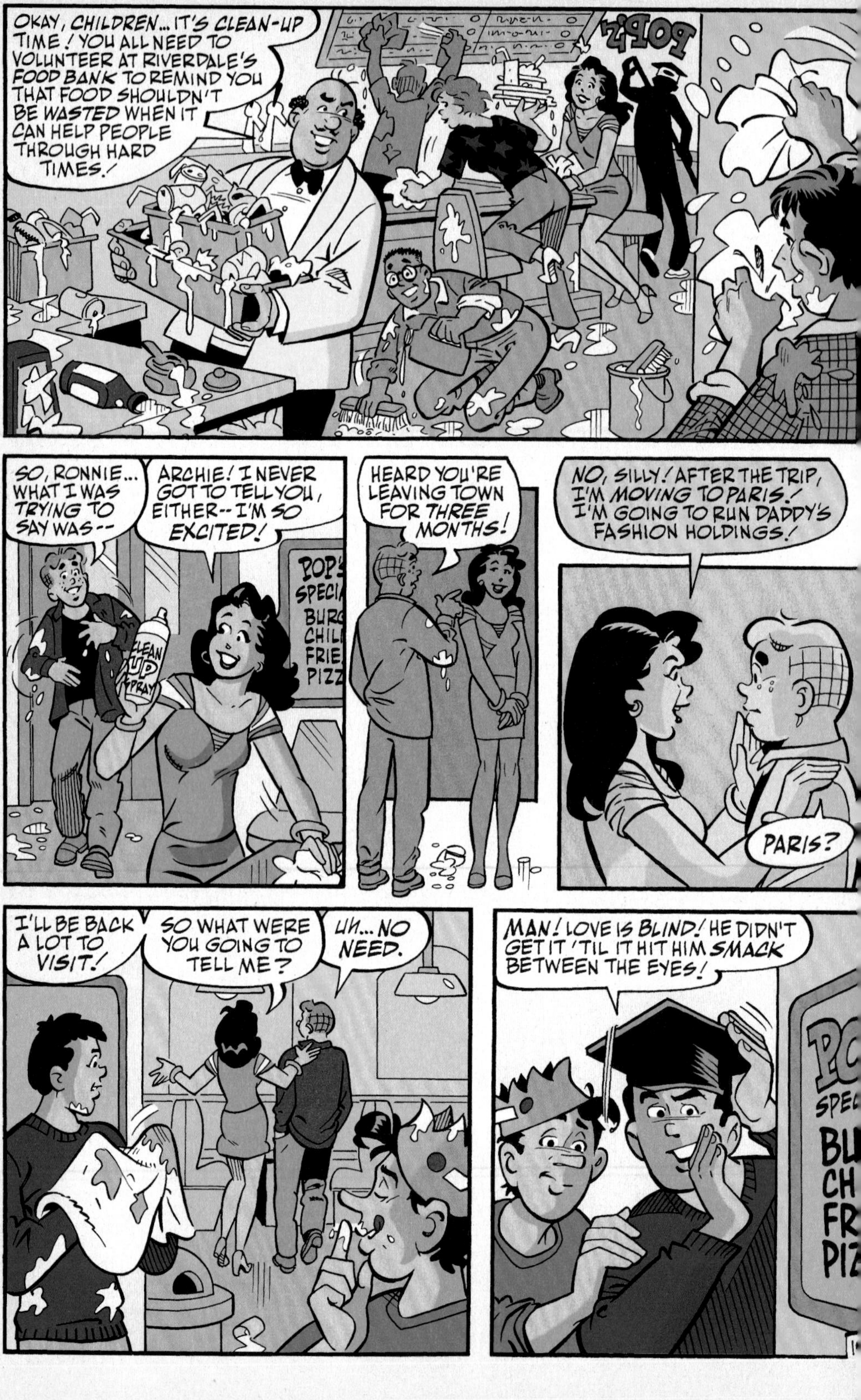
OKAY, CHILDREN... IT'S CLEAN-UP TIME! YOU ALL NEED TO VOLUNTEER AT RIVERDALE'S FOOD BANK TO REMIND YOU THAT FOOD SHOULDN'T BE WASTED WHEN IT CAN HELP PEOPLE THROUGH HARD TIMES!
POP'S
SO, RONNIE... WHAT I WAS TRYING TO SAY WAS--
ARCHIE! I NEVER GOT TO TELL YOU, EITHER-- I'M SO EXCITED!
CLEAN UP SPRAY
HEARD YOU'RE LEAVING TOWN FOR THREE MONTHS!
NO, SILLY! AFTER THE TRIP, I'M MOVING TO PARIS! I'M GOING TO RUN DADDY'S FASHION HOLDINGS!
PARIS?
I'LL BE BACK A LOT TO VISIT!
SO WHAT WERE YOU GOING TO TELL ME?
UH... NO NEED.
MAN! LOVE IS BLIND! HE DIDN'T GET IT 'TIL IT HIT HIM SMACK BETWEEN THE EYES!

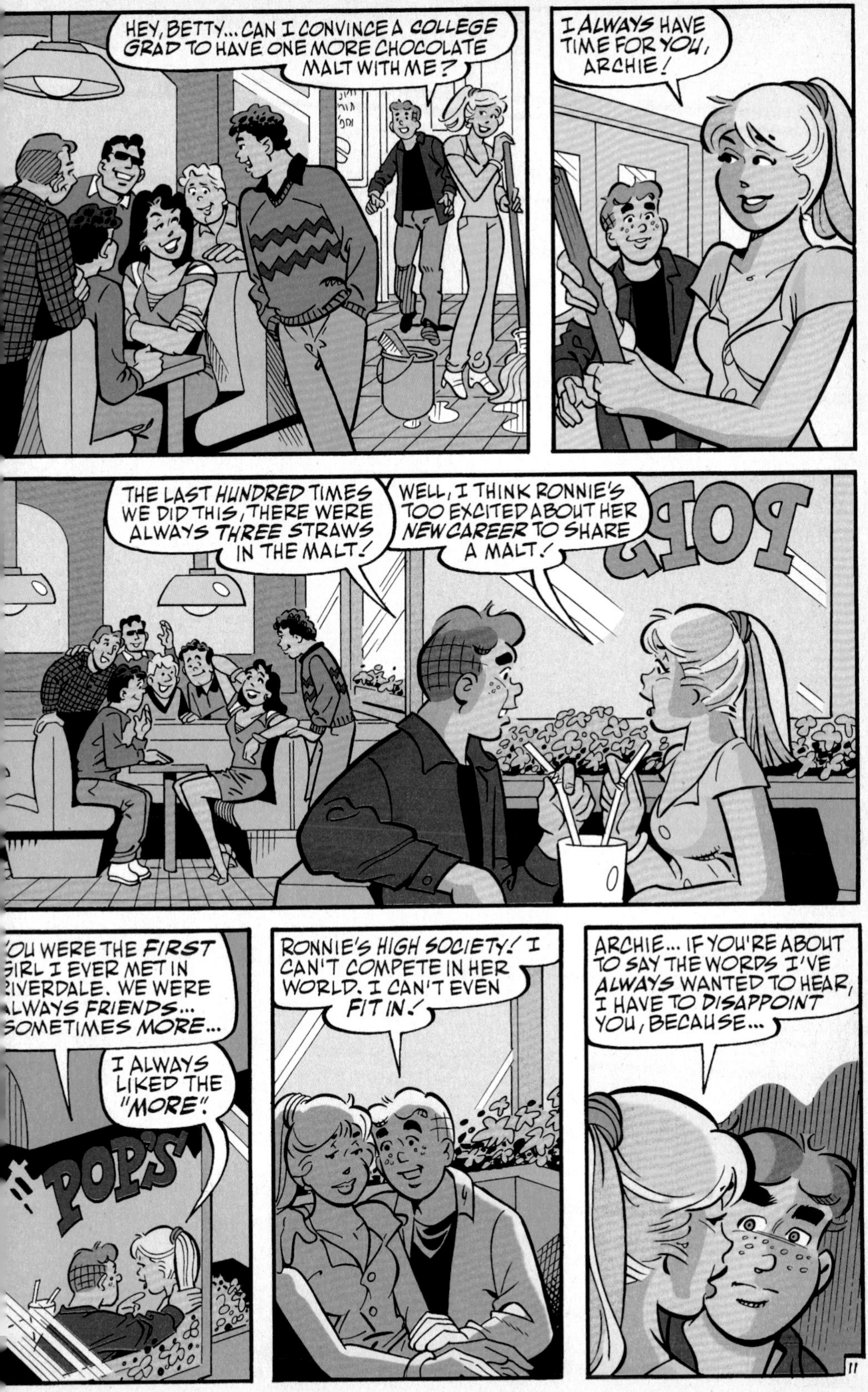
HEY, BETTY... CAN I CONVINCE A COLLEGE GRAD TO HAVE ONE MORE CHOCOLATE MALT WITH ME?
I ALWAYS HAVE TIME FOR YOU, ARCHIE!
THE LAST HUNDRED TIMES WE DID THIS, THERE WERE ALWAYS THREE STRAWS IN THE MALT!
WELL, I THINK RONNIE'S TOO EXCITED ABOUT HER NEW CAREER TO SHARE A MALT!
OU WERE THE FIRST GIRL I EVER MET IN RIVERDALE. WE WERE ALWAYS FRIENDS... SOMETIMES MORE...
I ALWAYS LIKED THE "MORE"!
POP'S
RONNIE'S HIGH SOCIETY! I CAN'T COMPETE IN HER WORLD. I CAN'T EVEN FIT IN!
ARCHIE... IF YOU'RE ABOUT TO SAY THE WORDS I'VE ALWAYS WANTED TO HEAR, I HAVE TO DISAPPOINT YOU, BECAUSE...
11

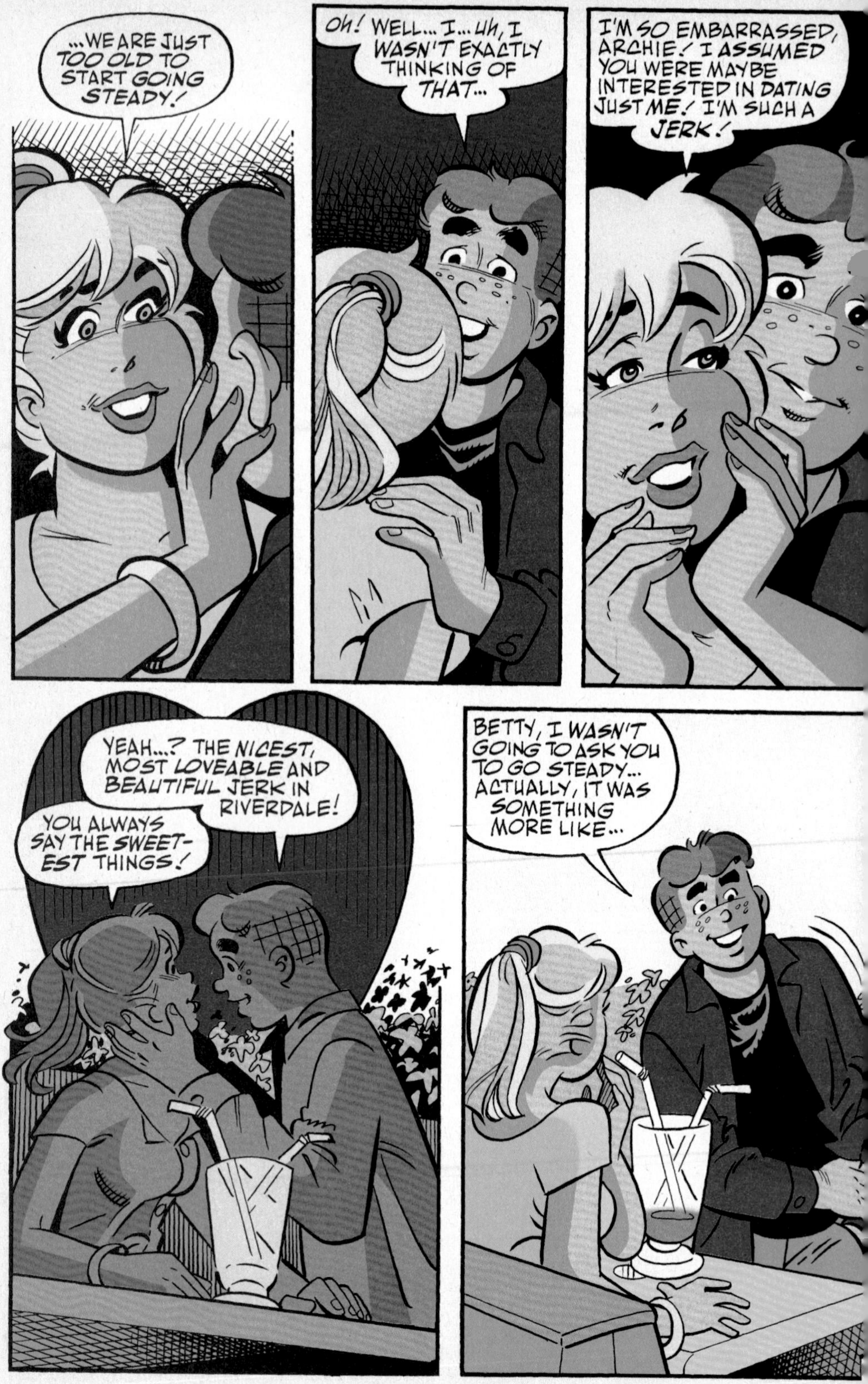
...WE ARE JUST TOO OLD TO START GOING STEADY!
OH! WELL... I... UH, I WASN'T EXACTLY THINKING OF THAT...
I'M SO EMBARRASSED, ARCHIE! I ASSUMED YOU WERE MAYBE INTERESTED IN DATING JUST ME! I'M SUCH A JERK!
YEAH...? THE NICEST, MOST LOVEABLE AND BEAUTIFUL JERK IN RIVERDALE!
YOU ALWAYS SAY THE SWEET-EST THINGS!
BETTY, I WASN'T GOING TO ASK YOU TO GO STEADY... ACTUALLY, IT WAS SOMETHING MORE LIKE...

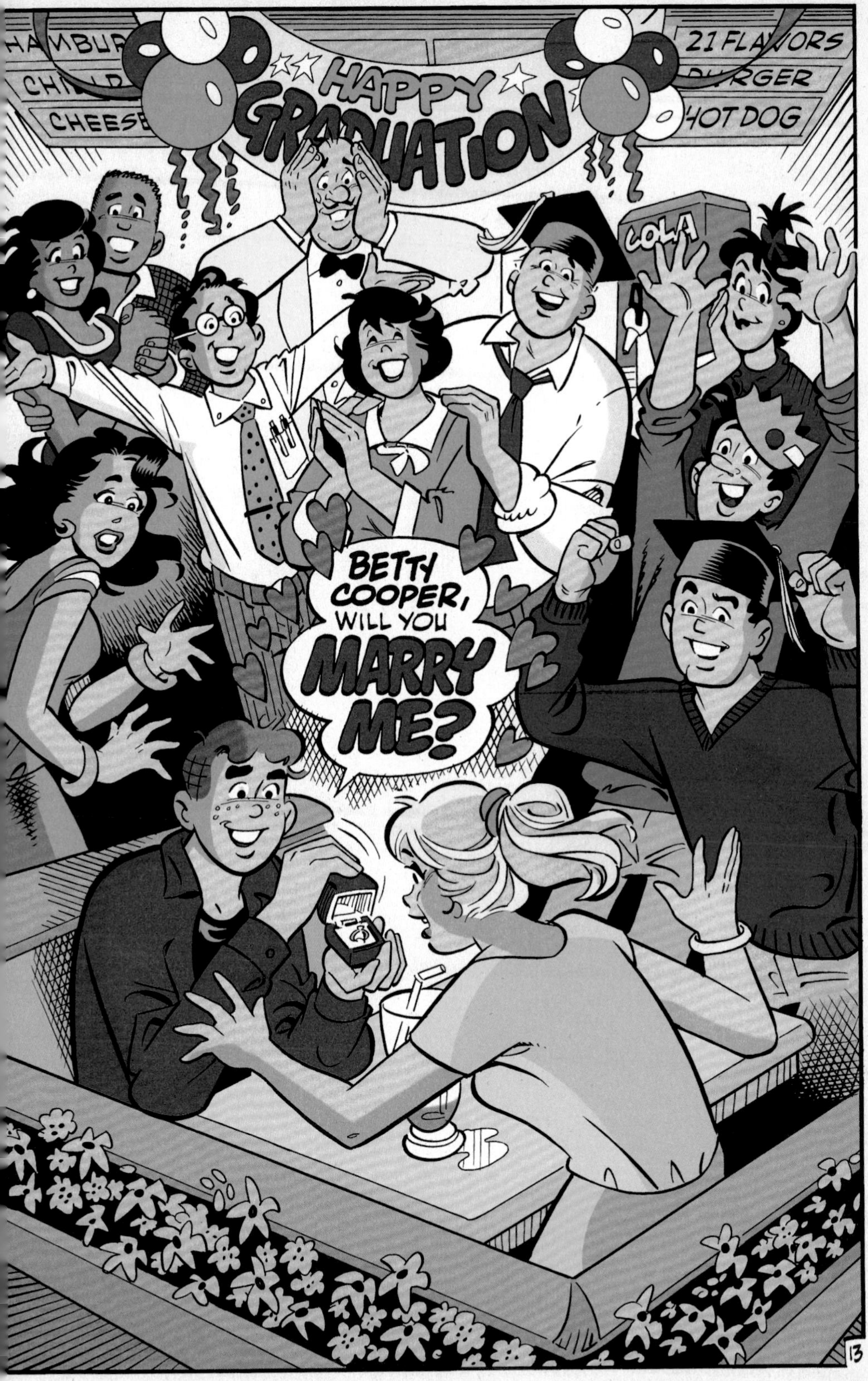
HAPPY GRADUATION
21 FLAVORS
HOT DOG
COLA
BETTY COOPER, WILL YOU MARRY ME?
13

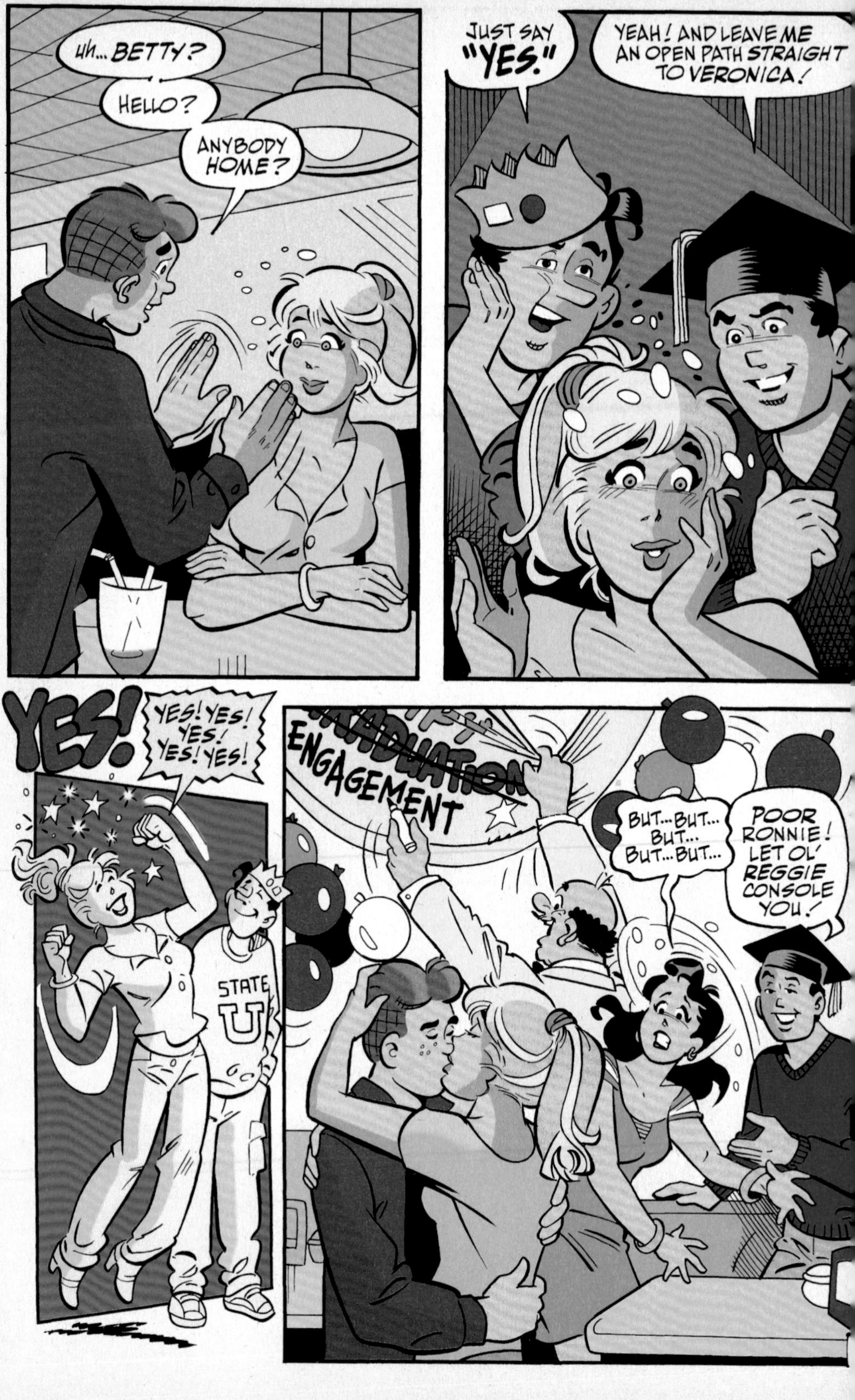
UH... BETTY?
HELLO?
ANYBODY HOME?
JUST SAY "YES."
YEAH! AND LEAVE ME AN OPEN PATH STRAIGHT TO VERONICA!
YES!
YES! YES! YES! YES! YES!
STATE U
ENGAGEMENT
BUT...BUT... BUT... BUT...BUT...
POOR RONNIE! LET OL' REGGIE CONSOLE YOU!

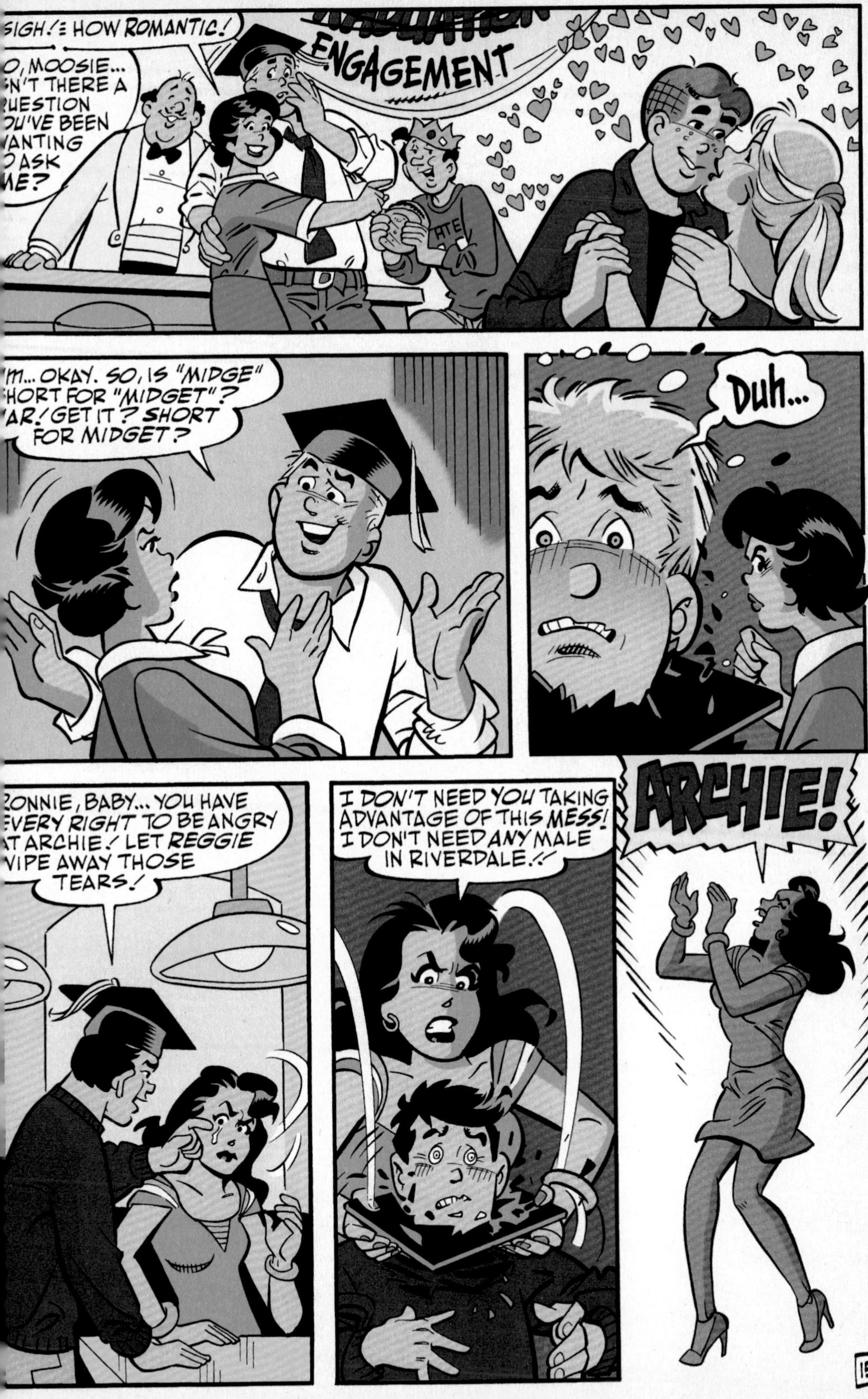
SIGH! HOW ROMANTIC!
ENGAGEMENT
O, MOOSIE... N'T THERE A UESTION OU'VE BEEN ANTING O ASK ME?
M... OKAY. SO, IS "MIDGE" HORT FOR "MIDGET"? AR! GET IT? SHORT FOR MIDGET?
Duh...
RONNIE, BABY... YOU HAVE VERY RIGHT TO BE ANGRY AT ARCHIE! LET REGGIE IPE AWAY THOSE TEARS!
I DON'T NEED YOU TAKING ADVANTAGE OF THIS MESS! I DON'T NEED ANY MALE IN RIVERDALE!!
ARCHIE!
15

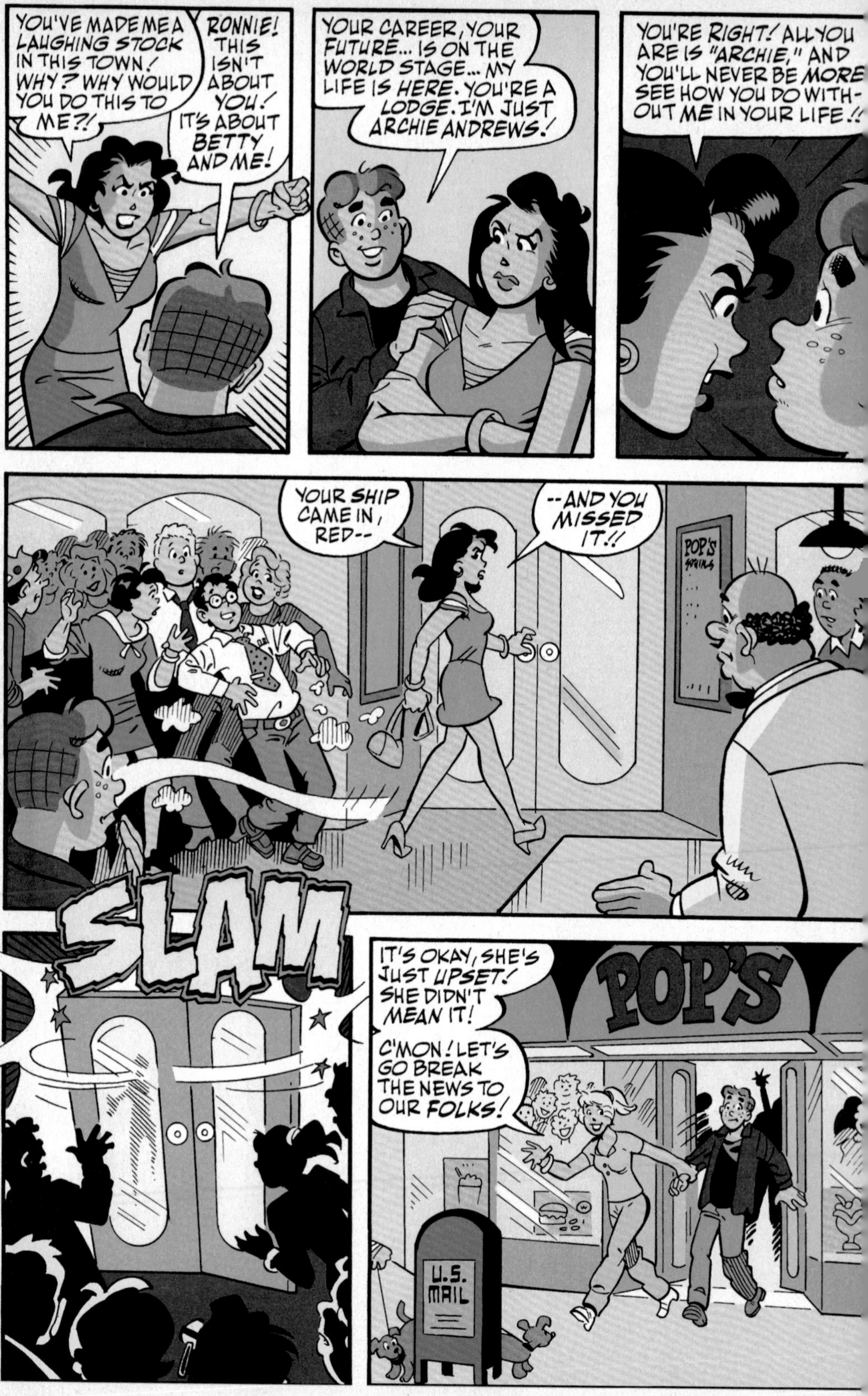
YOU'VE MADE ME A LAUGHING STOCK IN THIS TOWN! WHY? WHY WOULD YOU DO THIS TO ME?!
RONNIE! THIS ISN'T ABOUT YOU! IT'S ABOUT BETTY AND ME!
YOUR CAREER, YOUR FUTURE... IS ON THE WORLD STAGE... MY LIFE IS HERE. YOU'RE A LODGE. I'M JUST ARCHIE ANDREWS!
YOU'RE RIGHT! ALL YOU ARE IS "ARCHIE," AND YOU'LL NEVER BE MORE! SEE HOW YOU DO WITHOUT ME IN YOUR LIFE!!
YOUR SHIP CAME IN, RED--
--AND YOU MISSED IT!!
POP'S
SLAM
IT'S OKAY, SHE'S JUST UPSET! SHE DIDN'T MEAN IT!
C'MON! LET'S GO BREAK THE NEWS TO OUR FOLKS!
POP'S
U.S. MAIL

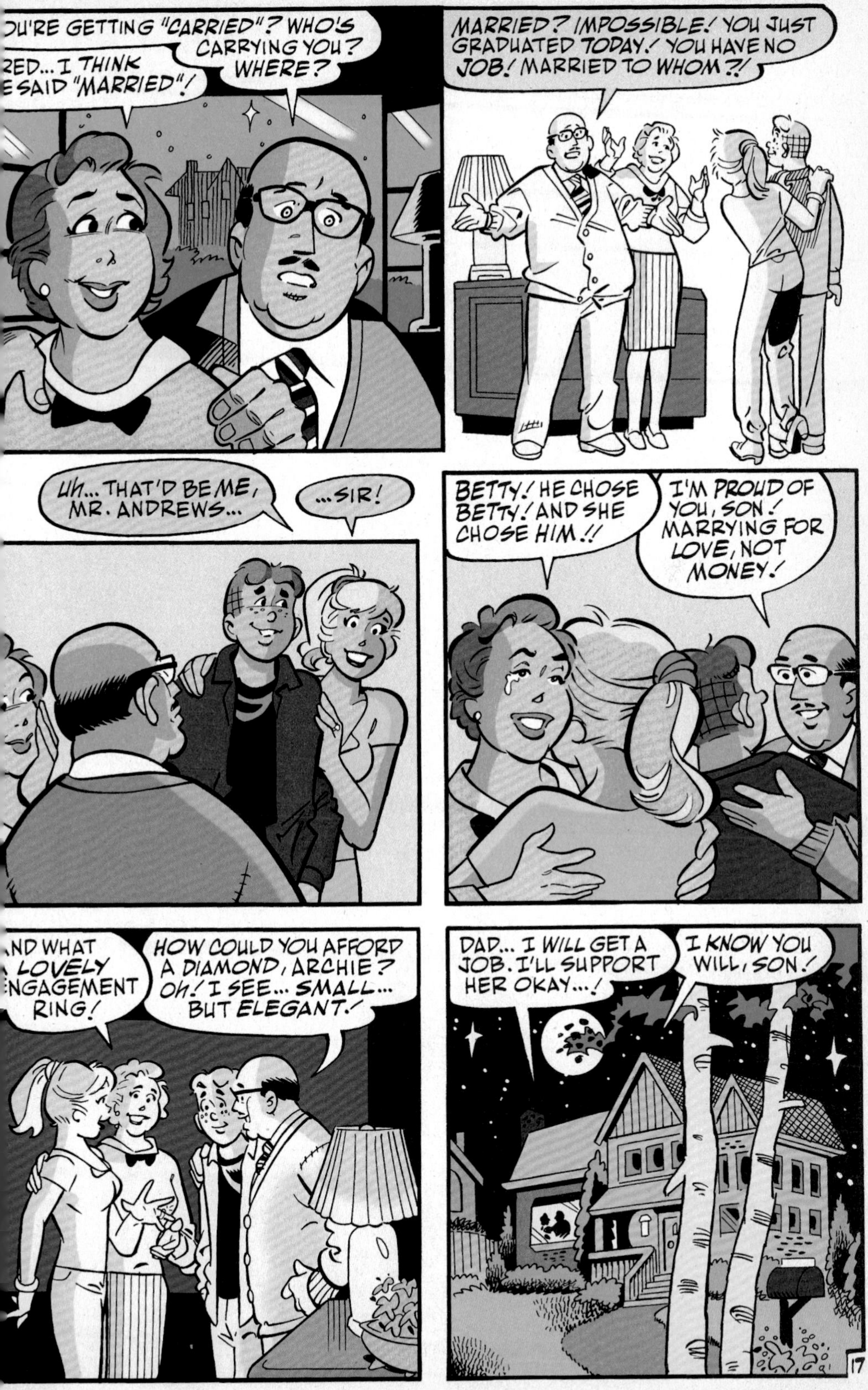
OU'RE GETTING "CARRIED"? WHO'S CARRYING YOU? WHERE?
RED... I THINK E SAID "MARRIED"!
MARRIED? IMPOSSIBLE! YOU JUST GRADUATED TODAY! YOU HAVE NO JOB! MARRIED TO WHOM?!
UH... THAT'D BE ME, MR. ANDREWS...
...SIR!
BETTY! HE CHOSE BETTY! AND SHE CHOSE HIM!!
I'M PROUD OF YOU, SON! MARRYING FOR LOVE, NOT MONEY!
ND WHAT LOVELY NGAGEMENT RING!
HOW COULD YOU AFFORD A DIAMOND, ARCHIE? OH! I SEE... SMALL... BUT ELEGANT!
DAD... I WILL GET A JOB. I'LL SUPPORT HER OKAY...!
I KNOW YOU WILL, SON!
17

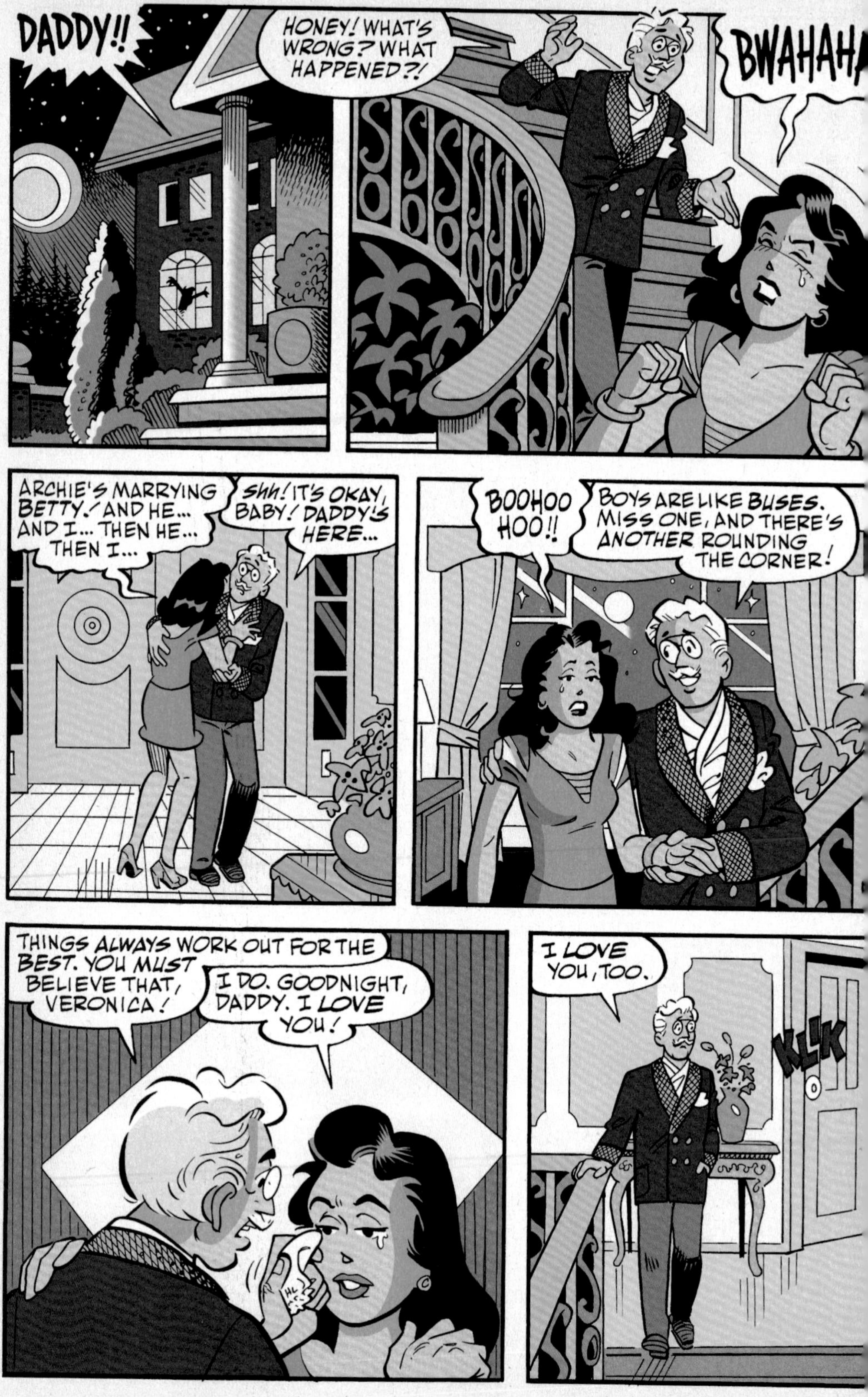
DADDY!!
HONEY! WHAT'S WRONG? WHAT HAPPENED?!
BWAHAHA
ARCHIE'S MARRYING BETTY! AND HE... AND I... THEN HE... THEN I...
SHH! IT'S OKAY, BABY! DADDY'S HERE...
BOOHOO HOO!!
BOYS ARE LIKE BUSES. MISS ONE, AND THERE'S ANOTHER ROUNDING THE CORNER!
THINGS ALWAYS WORK OUT FOR THE BEST. YOU MUST BELIEVE THAT, VERONICA!
I DO. GOODNIGHT, DADDY. I LOVE YOU!
I LOVE YOU, TOO.
KLIK

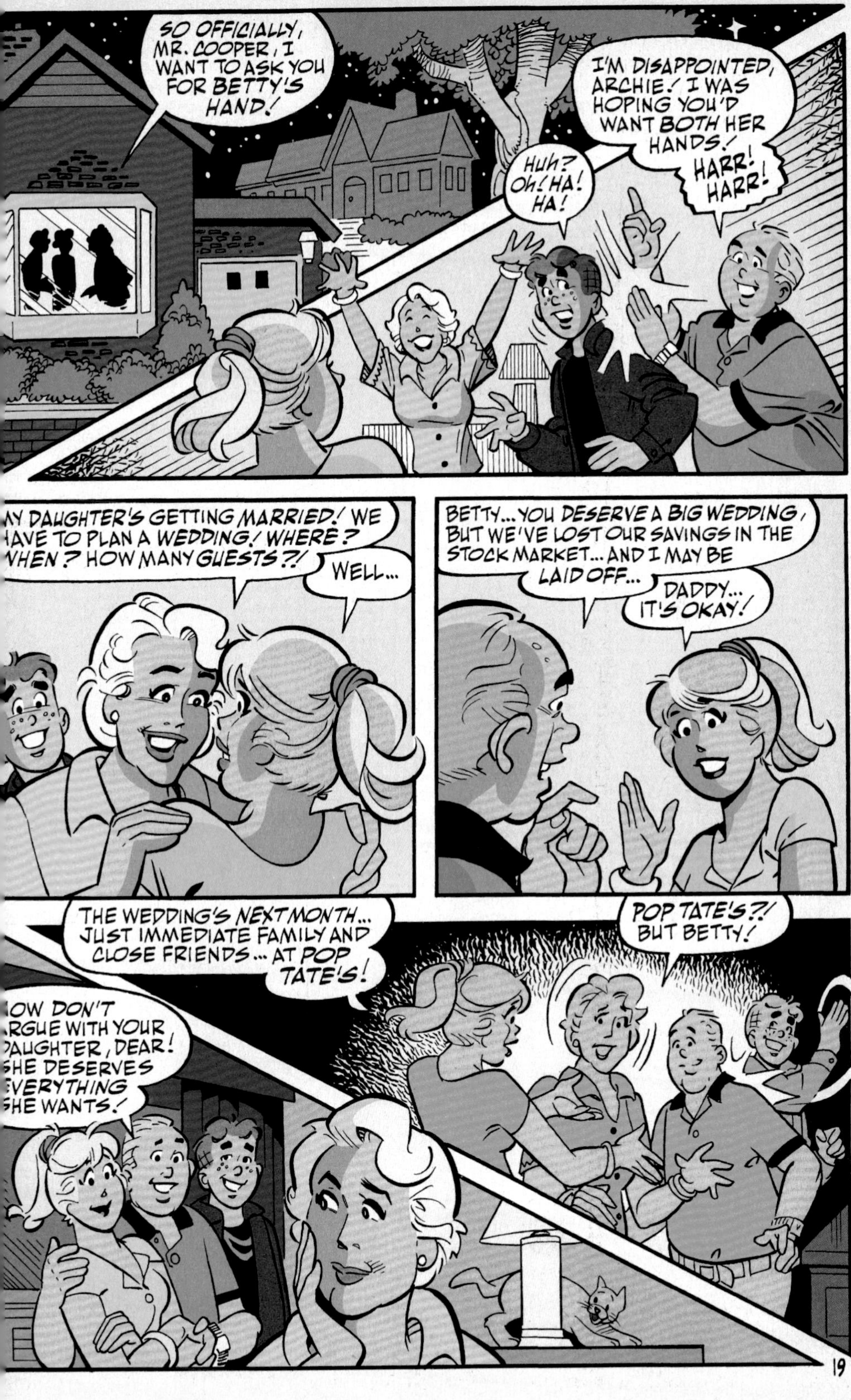
SO OFFICIALLY, MR. COOPER, I WANT TO ASK YOU FOR BETTY'S HAND!
I'M DISAPPOINTED, ARCHIE! I WAS HOPING YOU'D WANT BOTH HER HANDS!
HARR! HARR!
HUH? OH! HA! HA!
MY DAUGHTER'S GETTING MARRIED! WE HAVE TO PLAN A WEDDING! WHERE? WHEN? HOW MANY GUESTS?!
WELL...
BETTY... YOU DESERVE A BIG WEDDING, BUT WE'VE LOST OUR SAVINGS IN THE STOCK MARKET... AND I MAY BE LAID OFF...
DADDY... IT'S OKAY!
THE WEDDING'S NEXT MONTH... JUST IMMEDIATE FAMILY AND CLOSE FRIENDS... AT POP TATE'S!
POP TATE'S?! BUT BETTY!
NOW DON'T ARGUE WITH YOUR DAUGHTER, DEAR! SHE DESERVES EVERYTHING SHE WANTS!

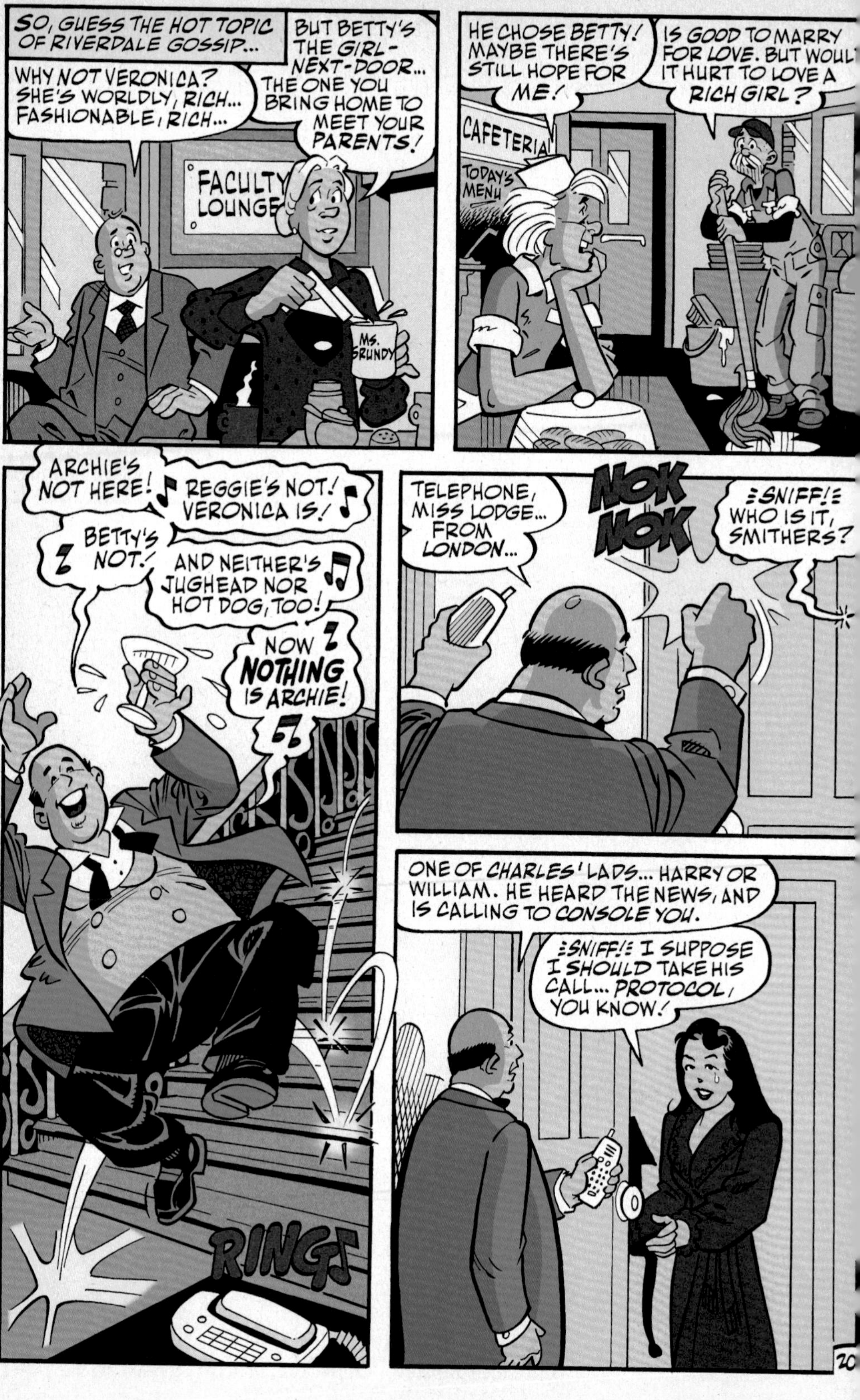
SO, GUESS THE HOT TOPIC OF RIVERDALE GOSSIP...
WHY NOT VERONICA? SHE'S WORLDLY, RICH... FASHIONABLE, RICH...
BUT BETTY'S THE GIRL-NEXT-DOOR... THE ONE YOU BRING HOME TO MEET YOUR PARENTS!
FACULTY LOUNGE
MS. GRUNDY
HE CHOSE BETTY! MAYBE THERE'S STILL HOPE FOR ME!
IS GOOD TO MARRY FOR LOVE. BUT WOUL IT HURT TO LOVE A RICH GIRL?
CAFETERIA
TODAY'S MENU
ARCHIE'S NOT HERE!
REGGIE'S NOT! VERONICA IS!
BETTY'S NOT!
AND NEITHER'S JUGHEAD NOR HOT DOG, TOO!
NOW NOTHING IS ARCHIE!
RING
TELEPHONE, MISS LODGE... FROM LONDON...
NOK NOK
SNIFF! WHO IS IT, SMITHERS?
ONE OF CHARLES' LADS... HARRY OR WILLIAM. HE HEARD THE NEWS, AND IS CALLING TO CONSOLE YOU.
SNIFF! I SUPPOSE I SHOULD TAKE HIS CALL... PROTOCOL, YOU KNOW!
20

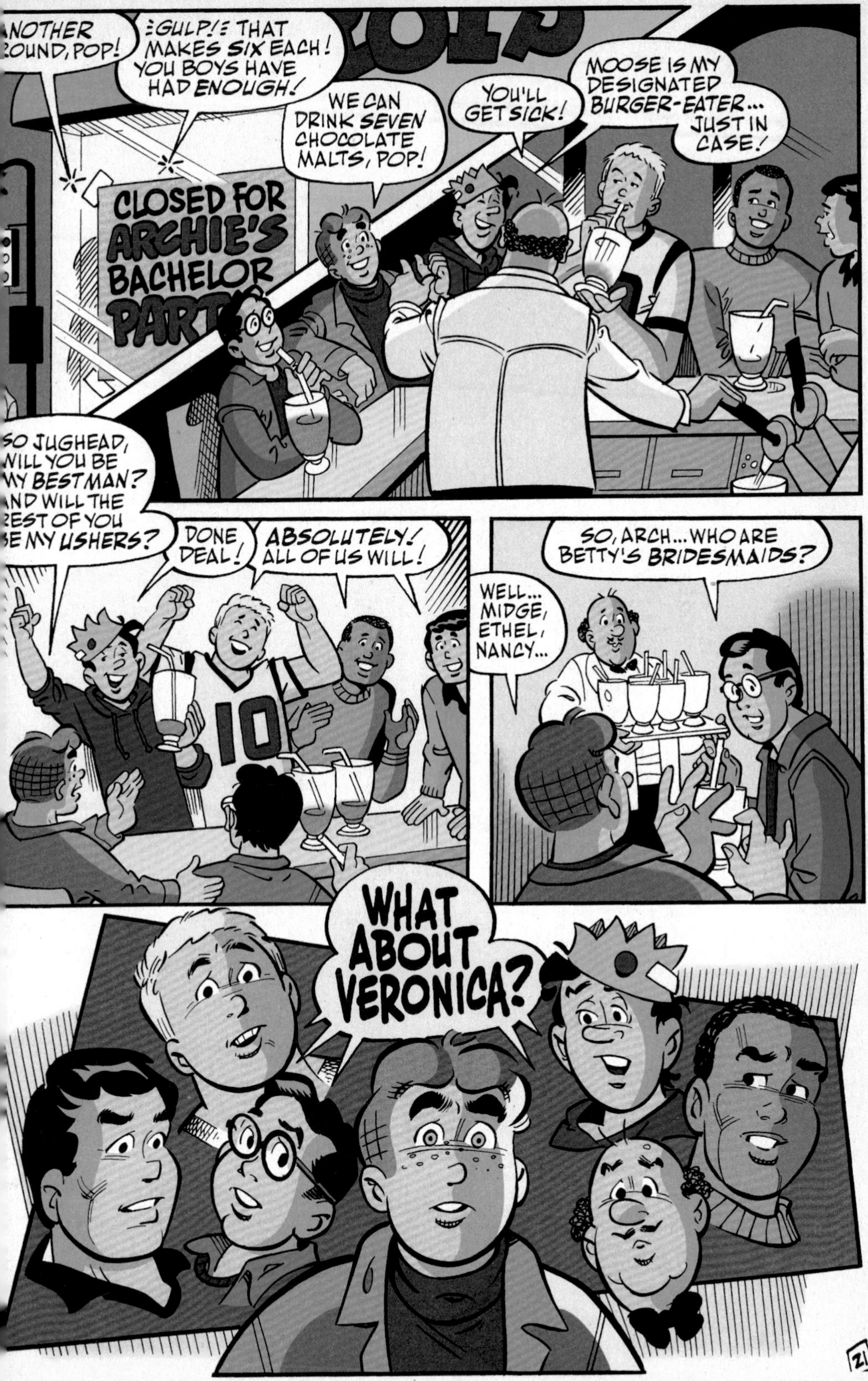

ANOTHER ROUND, POP!
GULP! THAT MAKES SIX EACH! YOU BOYS HAVE HAD ENOUGH!
WE CAN DRINK SEVEN CHOCOLATE MALTS, POP!
YOU'LL GET SICK!
MOOSE IS MY DESIGNATED BURGER-EATER... JUST IN CASE!
CLOSED FOR ARCHIE'S BACHELOR PARTY
SO JUGHEAD, WILL YOU BE MY BEST MAN? AND WILL THE REST OF YOU BE MY USHERS?
DONE DEAL!
ABSOLUTELY! ALL OF US WILL!
SO, ARCH... WHO ARE BETTY'S BRIDESMAIDS?
WELL... MIDGE, ETHEL, NANCY...
WHAT ABOUT VERONICA?

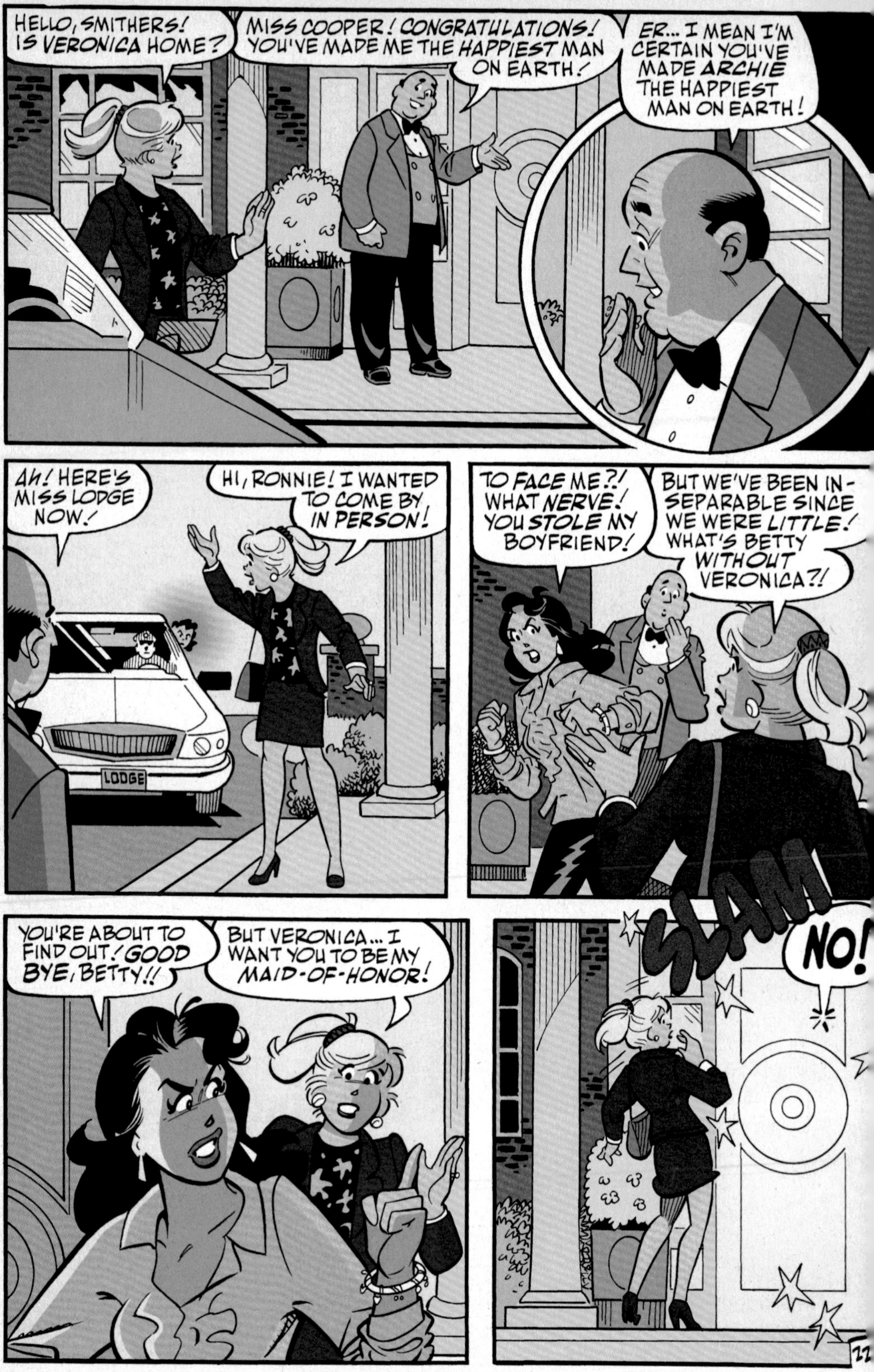
HELLO, SMITHERS! IS VERONICA HOME?
MISS COOPER! CONGRATULATIONS! YOU'VE MADE ME THE HAPPIEST MAN ON EARTH!
ER... I MEAN I'M CERTAIN YOU'VE MADE ARCHIE THE HAPPIEST MAN ON EARTH!
AH! HERE'S MISS LODGE NOW!
HI, RONNIE! I WANTED TO COME BY IN PERSON!
LODGE
TO FACE ME?! WHAT NERVE! YOU STOLE MY BOYFRIEND!
BUT WE'VE BEEN IN-SEPARABLE SINCE WE WERE LITTLE! WHAT'S BETTY WITHOUT VERONICA?!
YOU'RE ABOUT TO FIND OUT! GOOD BYE, BETTY!!
BUT VERONICA... I WANT YOU TO BE MY MAID-OF-HONOR!
SLAM
NO!
22

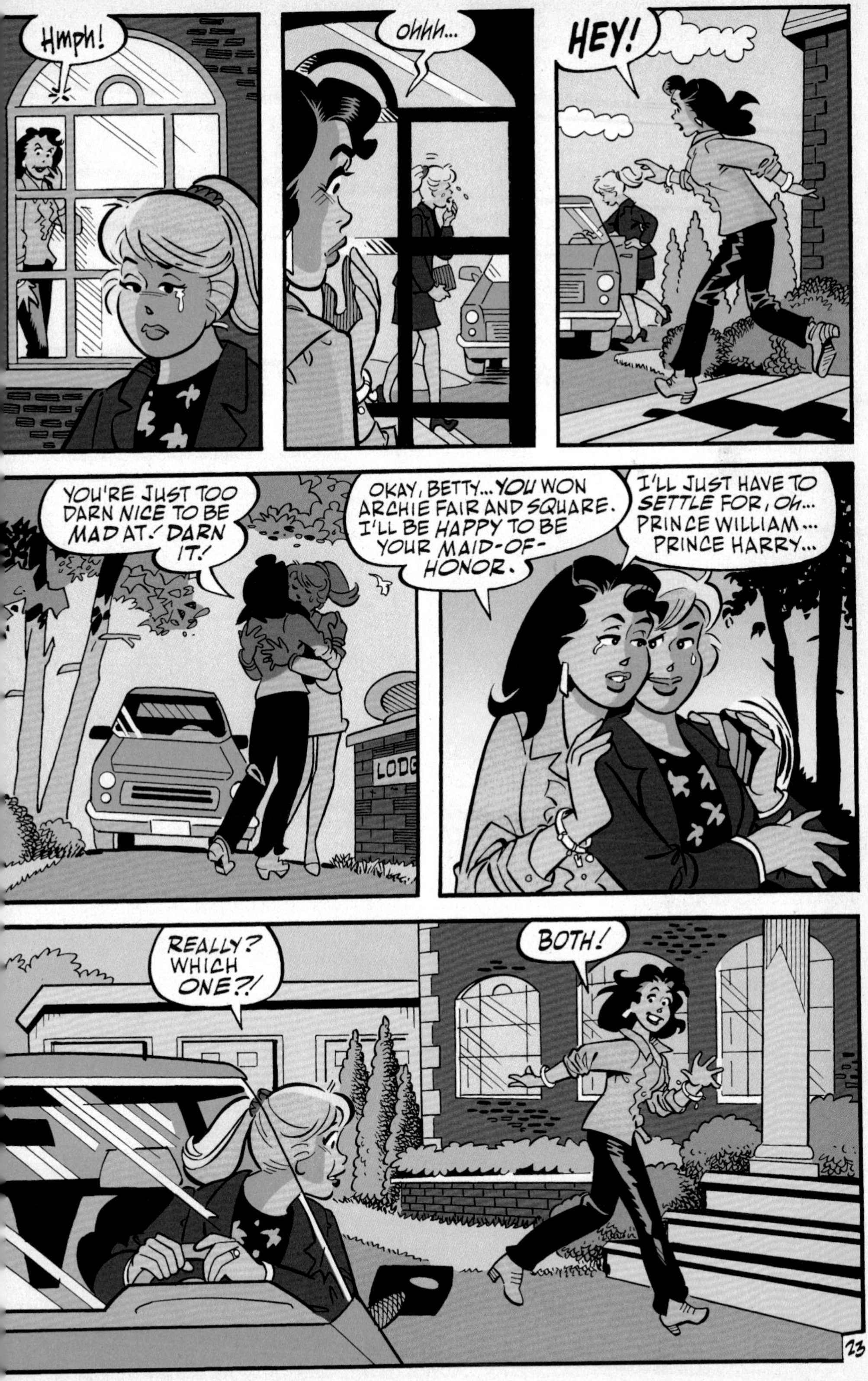
Hmph!
ohhh...
HEY!
YOU'RE JUST TOO DARN NICE TO BE MAD AT! DARN IT!
OKAY, BETTY... YOU WON ARCHIE FAIR AND SQUARE. I'LL BE HAPPY TO BE YOUR MAID-OF-HONOR.
I'LL JUST HAVE TO SETTLE FOR, OH... PRINCE WILLIAM... PRINCE HARRY...
LODG
REALLY? WHICH ONE?!
BOTH!
23

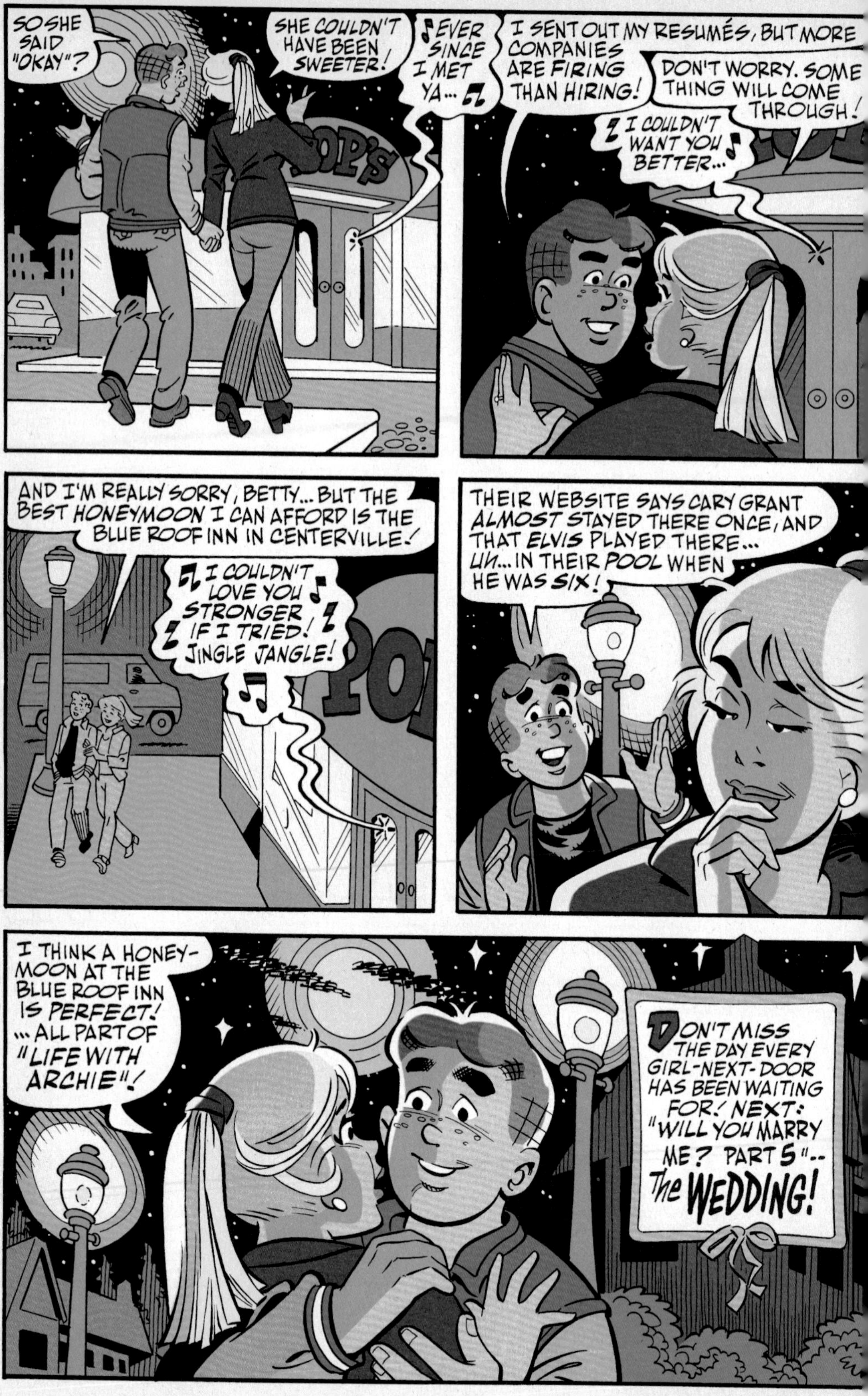
SO SHE SAID "OKAY"?
SHE COULDN'T HAVE BEEN SWEETER!
EVER SINCE I MET YA...
POP'S
I SENT OUT MY RESUMÉS, BUT MORE COMPANIES ARE FIRING THAN HIRING!
DON'T WORRY. SOME THING WILL COME THROUGH!
I COULDN'T WANT YOU BETTER...
AND I'M REALLY SORRY, BETTY... BUT THE BEST HONEYMOON I CAN AFFORD IS THE BLUE ROOF INN IN CENTERVILLE!
I COULDN'T LOVE YOU STRONGER IF I TRIED! JINGLE JANGLE!
THEIR WEBSITE SAYS CARY GRANT ALMOST STAYED THERE ONCE, AND THAT ELVIS PLAYED THERE... UH... IN THEIR POOL WHEN HE WAS SIX!
I THINK A HONEY-MOON AT THE BLUE ROOF INN IS PERFECT! ... ALL PART OF "LIFE WITH ARCHIE"!
DON'T MISS THE DAY EVERY GIRL-NEXT-DOOR HAS BEEN WAITING FOR! NEXT: "WILL YOU MARRY ME? PART 5"... The WEDDING!

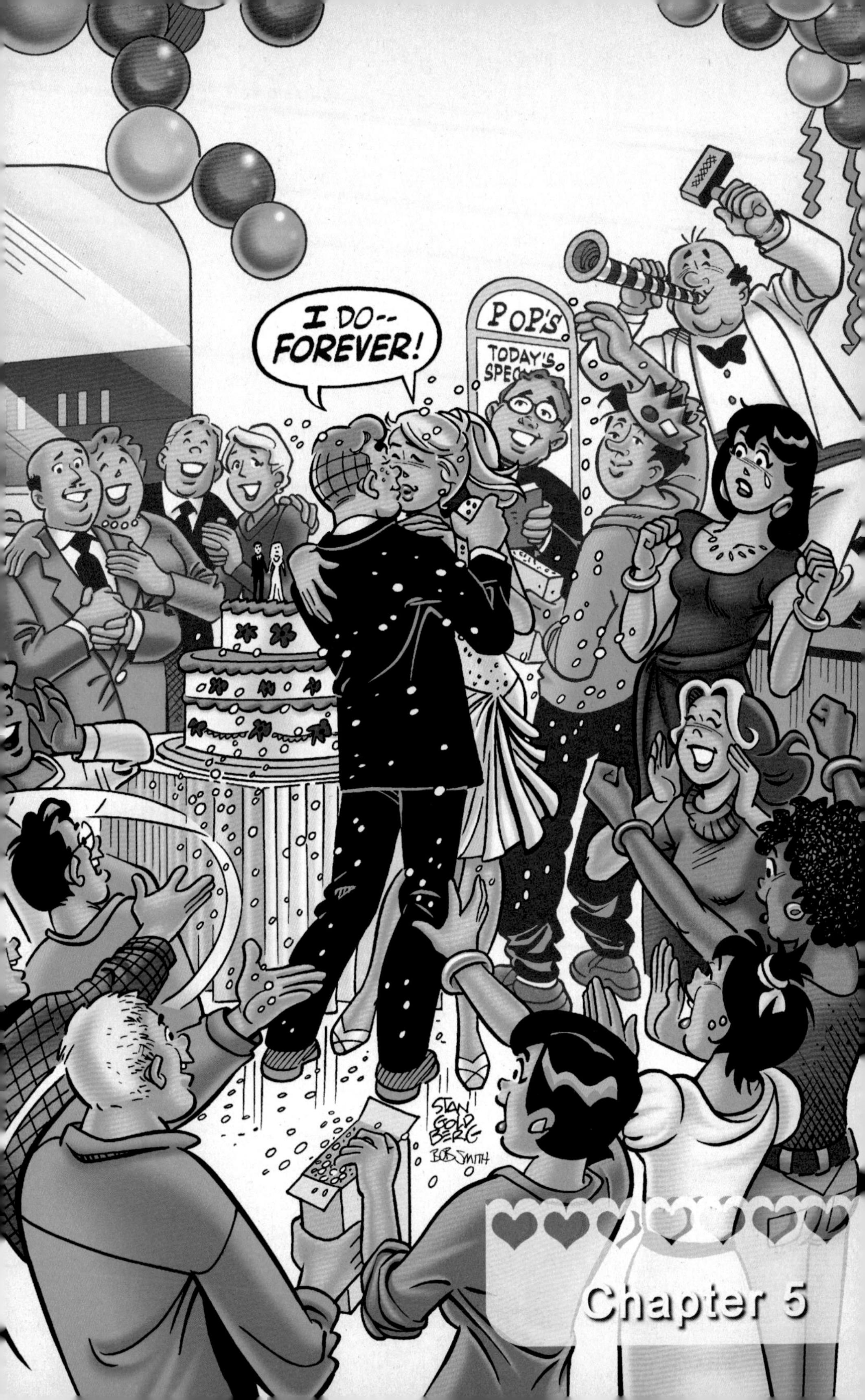
I DO--
FOREVER!
POP'S
TODAY'S
SPEC
STAN
GOLD
BERG
BOB SMITH
Chapter 5

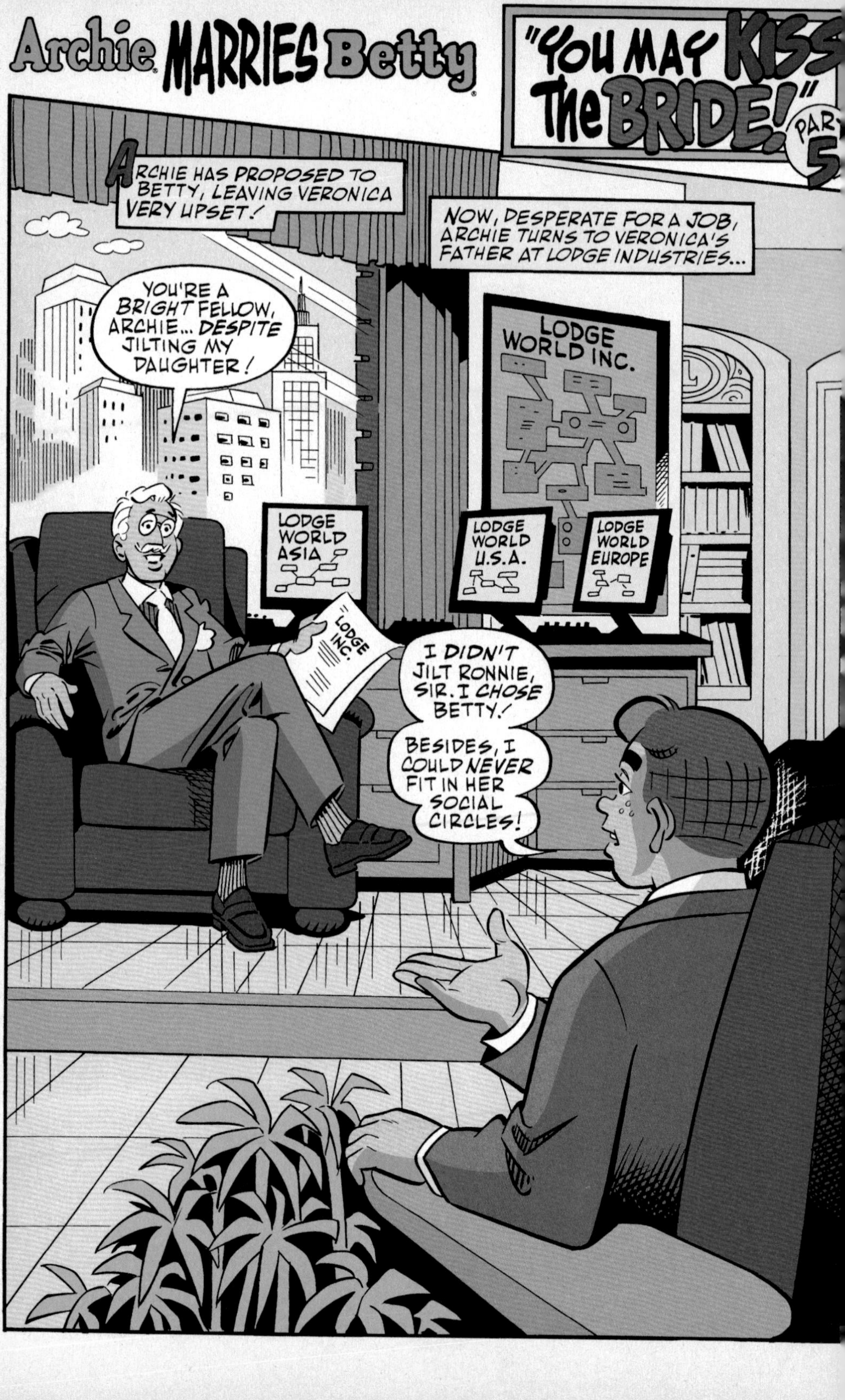
Archie MARRIES Betty
"YOU MAY KISS The BRIDE!" PART 5
ARCHIE HAS PROPOSED TO BETTY, LEAVING VERONICA VERY UPSET!
NOW, DESPERATE FOR A JOB, ARCHIE TURNS TO VERONICA'S FATHER AT LODGE INDUSTRIES...
YOU'RE A BRIGHT FELLOW, ARCHIE... DESPITE JILTING MY DAUGHTER!
LODGE WORLD INC.
LODGE WORLD ASIA
LODGE WORLD U.S.A.
LODGE WORLD EUROPE
LODGE INC.
I DIDN'T JILT RONNIE, SIR. I CHOSE BETTY!
BESIDES, I COULD NEVER FIT IN HER SOCIAL CIRCLES!

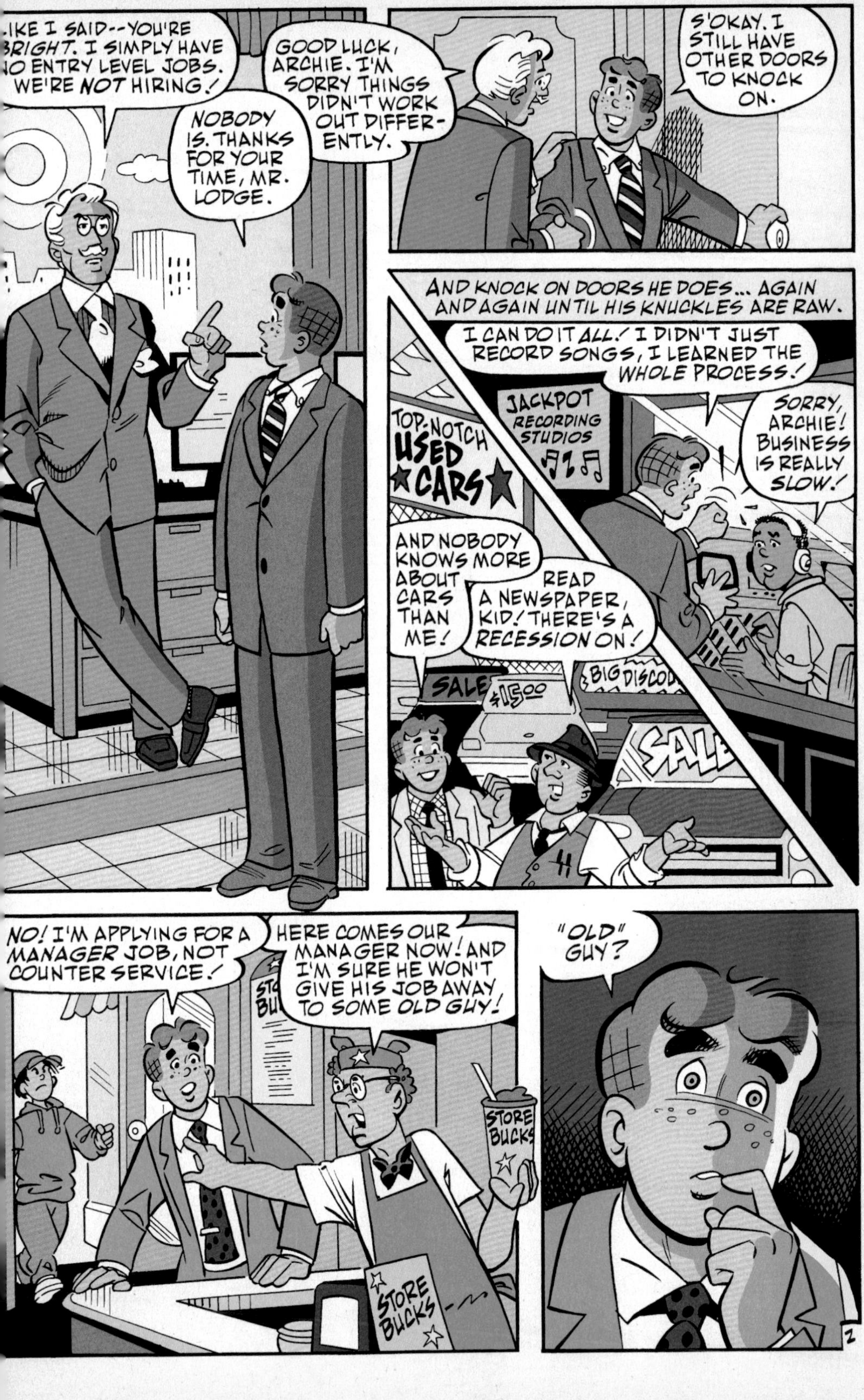
LIKE I SAID--YOU'RE BRIGHT. I SIMPLY HAVE NO ENTRY LEVEL JOBS. WE'RE NOT HIRING!
NOBODY IS. THANKS FOR YOUR TIME, MR. LODGE.
GOOD LUCK, ARCHIE. I'M SORRY THINGS DIDN'T WORK OUT DIFFERENTLY.
S'OKAY. I STILL HAVE OTHER DOORS TO KNOCK ON.
AND KNOCK ON DOORS HE DOES... AGAIN AND AGAIN UNTIL HIS KNUCKLES ARE RAW.
I CAN DO IT ALL! I DIDN'T JUST RECORD SONGS, I LEARNED THE WHOLE PROCESS!
JACKPOT RECORDING STUDIOS
SORRY, ARCHIE! BUSINESS IS REALLY SLOW!
TOP-NOTCH USED CARS
AND NOBODY KNOWS MORE ABOUT CARS THAN ME!
READ A NEWSPAPER, KID! THERE'S A RECESSION ON!
SALE
$1500
BIG DISCO
SALE
NO! I'M APPLYING FOR A MANAGER JOB, NOT COUNTER SERVICE!
HERE COMES OUR MANAGER NOW! AND I'M SURE HE WON'T GIVE HIS JOB AWAY TO SOME OLD GUY!
STORE BUCKS
STORE BUCKS
"OLD" GUY?
2

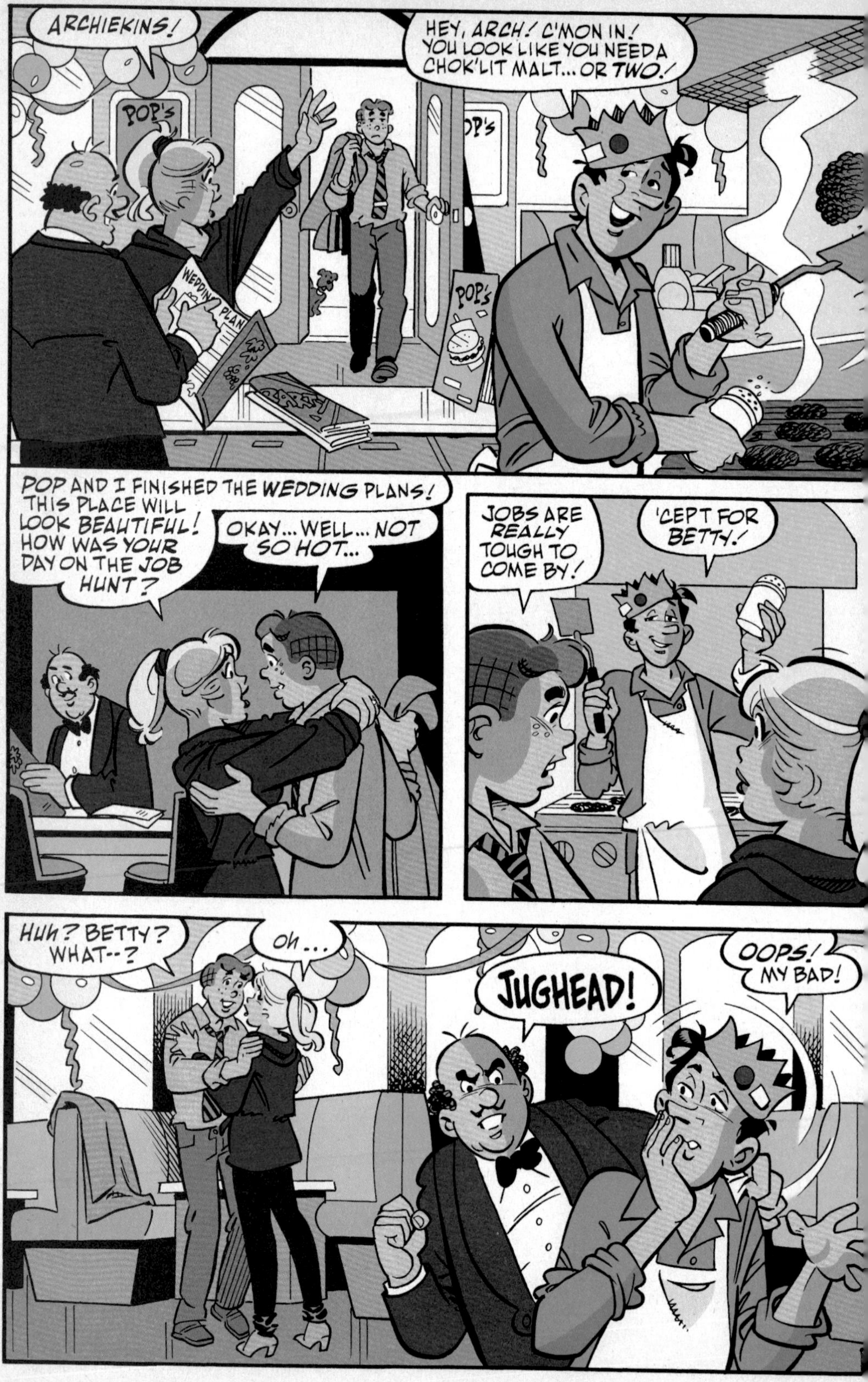
ARCHIEKINS!
HEY, ARCH! C'MON IN! YOU LOOK LIKE YOU NEED A CHOK'LIT MALT... OR TWO!
POP's
POP AND I FINISHED THE WEDDING PLANS! THIS PLACE WILL LOOK BEAUTIFUL! HOW WAS YOUR DAY ON THE JOB HUNT?
OKAY... WELL... NOT SO HOT...
JOBS ARE REALLY TOUGH TO COME BY!
'CEPT FOR BETTY!
HUH? BETTY? WHAT--?
OH...
JUGHEAD!
OOPS! MY BAD!

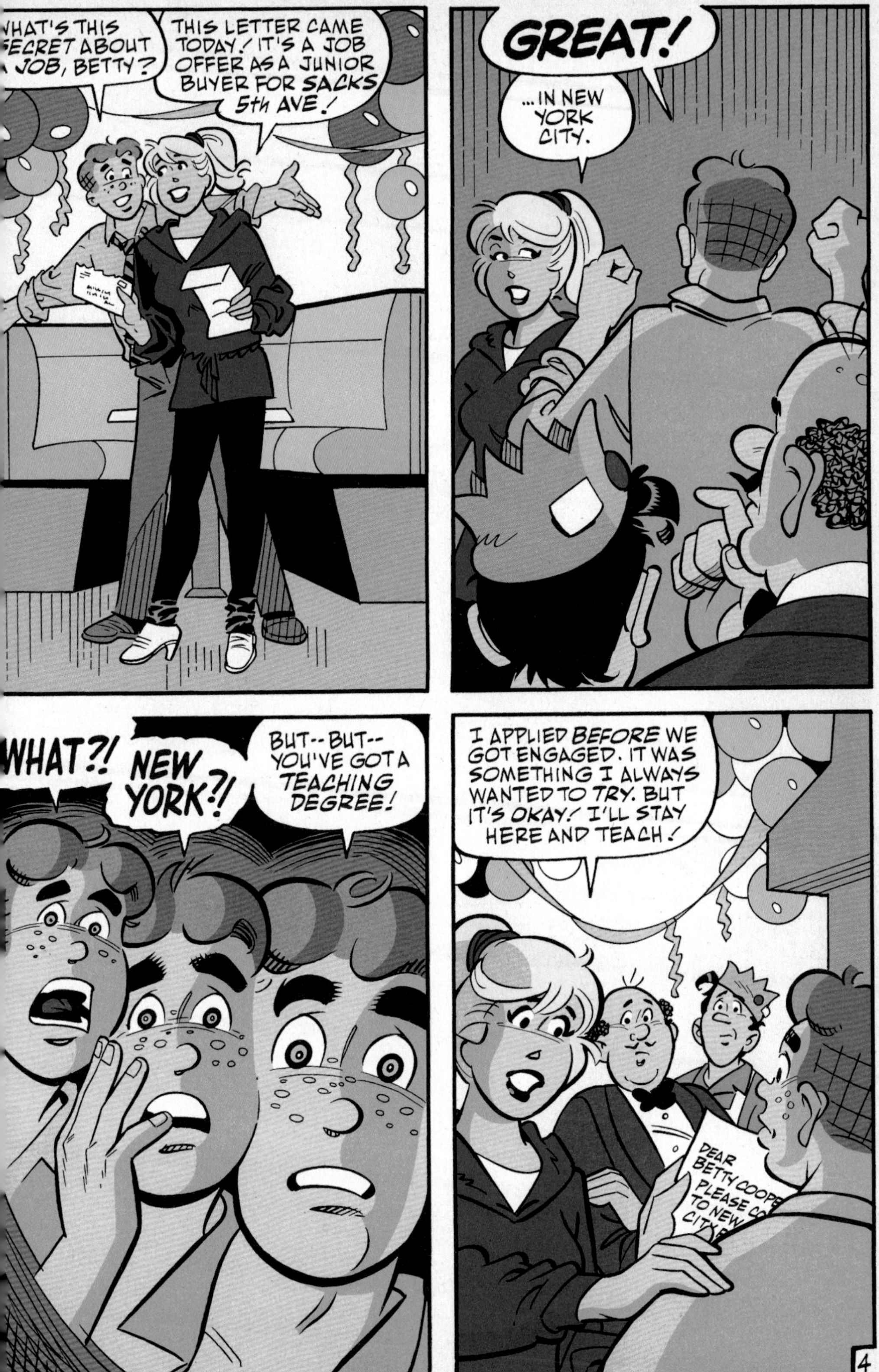
WHAT'S THIS SECRET ABOUT A JOB, BETTY?
THIS LETTER CAME TODAY! IT'S A JOB OFFER AS A JUNIOR BUYER FOR SACKS 5th AVE!
...IN NEW YORK CITY.
GREAT!
WHAT?!
NEW YORK?!
BUT--BUT-- YOU'VE GOT A TEACHING DEGREE!
I APPLIED BEFORE WE GOT ENGAGED. IT WAS SOMETHING I ALWAYS WANTED TO TRY. BUT IT'S OKAY! I'LL STAY HERE AND TEACH!
DEAR BETTY COOPE
PLEASE CO
TO NEW
CITY
4

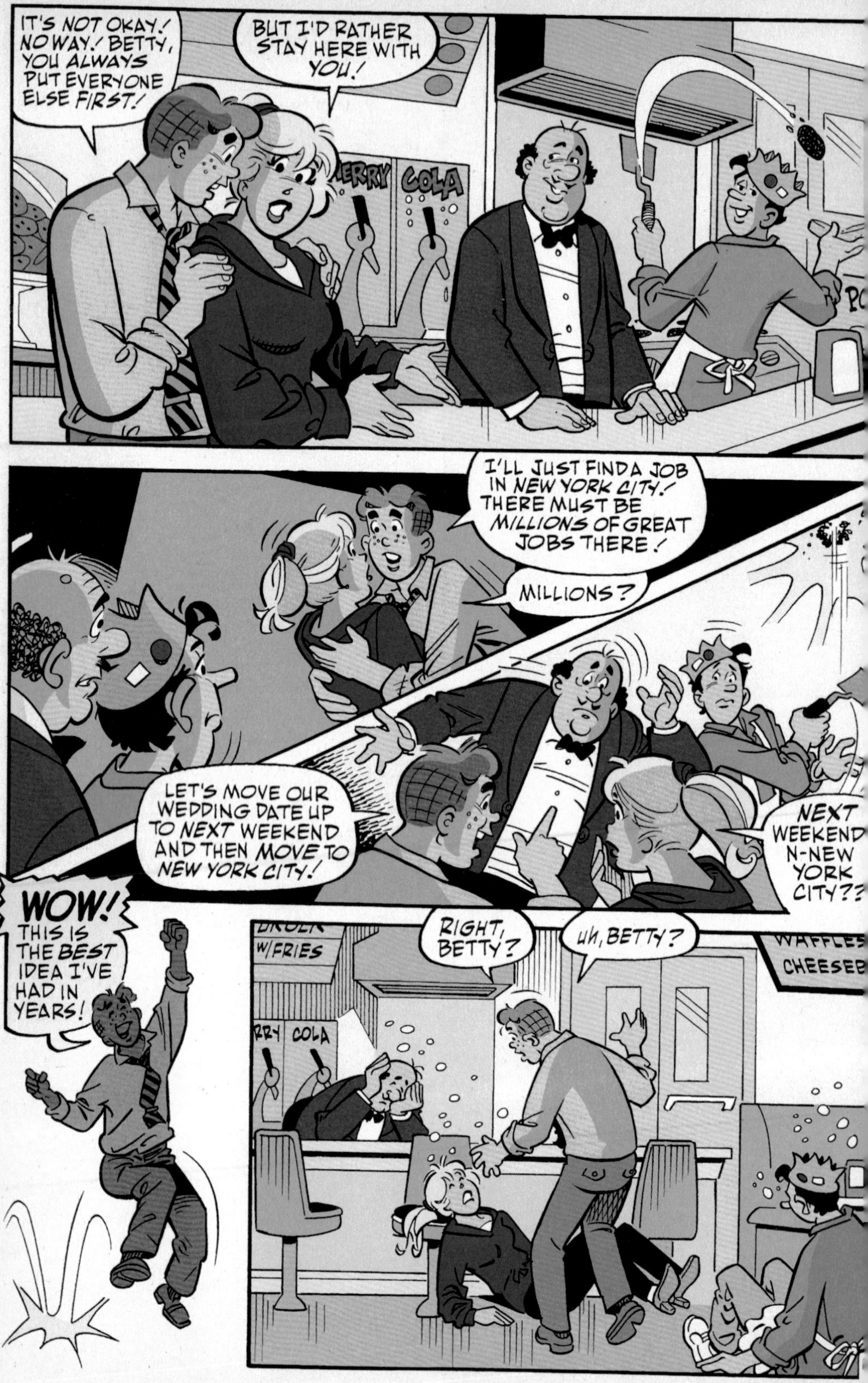
IT'S NOT OKAY! NO WAY! BETTY, YOU ALWAYS PUT EVERYONE ELSE FIRST!
BUT I'D RATHER STAY HERE WITH YOU!
COLA
I'LL JUST FIND A JOB IN NEW YORK CITY! THERE MUST BE MILLIONS OF GREAT JOBS THERE!
MILLIONS?
LET'S MOVE OUR WEDDING DATE UP TO NEXT WEEKEND AND THEN MOVE TO NEW YORK CITY!
NEXT WEEKEND N-NEW YORK CITY??
WOW! THIS IS THE BEST IDEA I'VE HAD IN YEARS!
W/FRIES
RIGHT, BETTY?
uh, BETTY?
CHEESEB
COLA

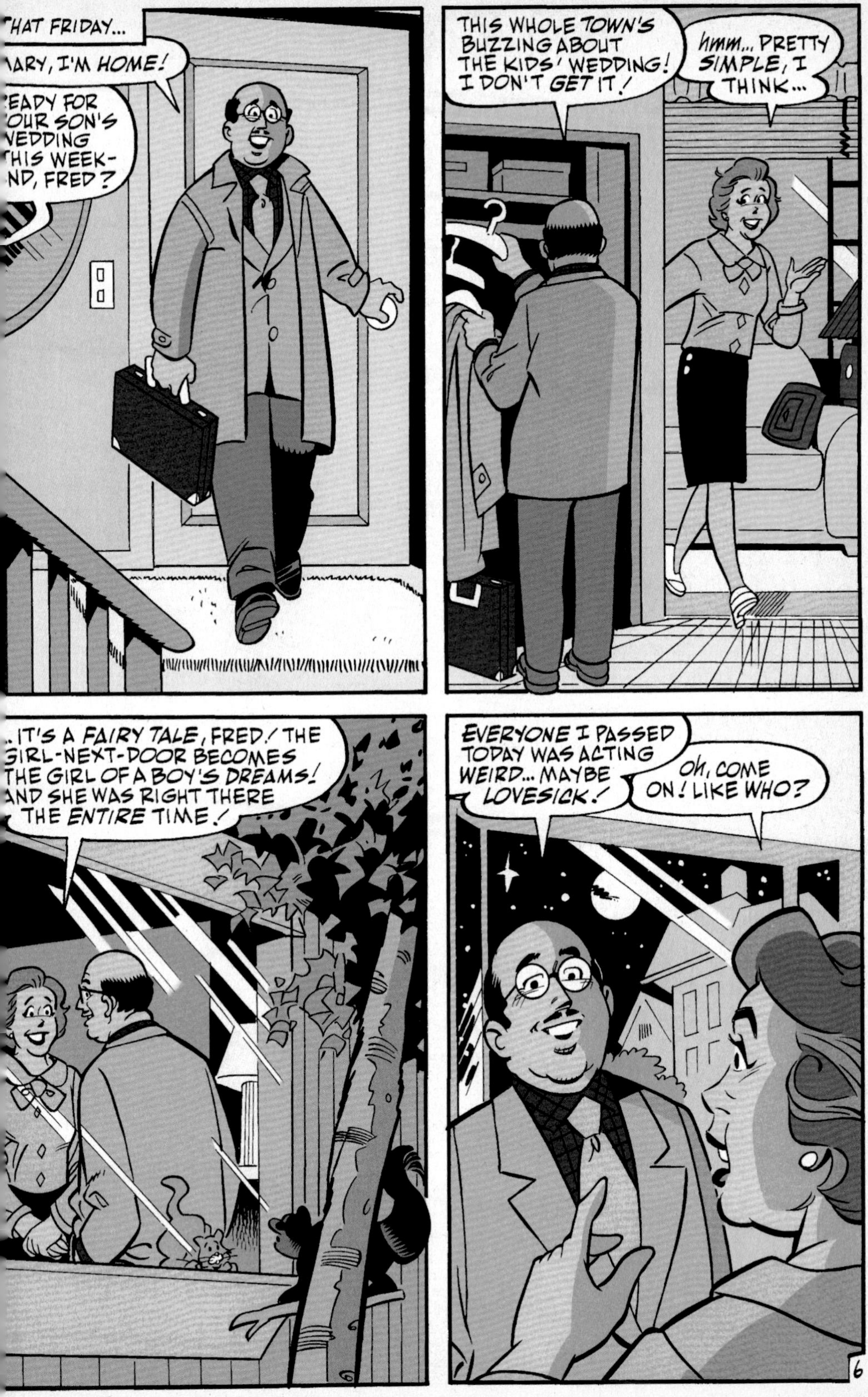
HAT FRIDAY...
ARY, I'M HOME!
EADY FOR OUR SON'S VEDDING THIS WEEK-ND, FRED?
THIS WHOLE TOWN'S BUZZING ABOUT THE KIDS' WEDDING! I DON'T GET IT!
hmm... PRETTY SIMPLE, I THINK...
..IT'S A FAIRY TALE, FRED! THE GIRL-NEXT-DOOR BECOMES THE GIRL OF A BOY'S DREAMS! AND SHE WAS RIGHT THERE THE ENTIRE TIME!
EVERYONE I PASSED TODAY WAS ACTING WEIRD... MAYBE LOVESICK!
Oh, COME ON! LIKE WHO?

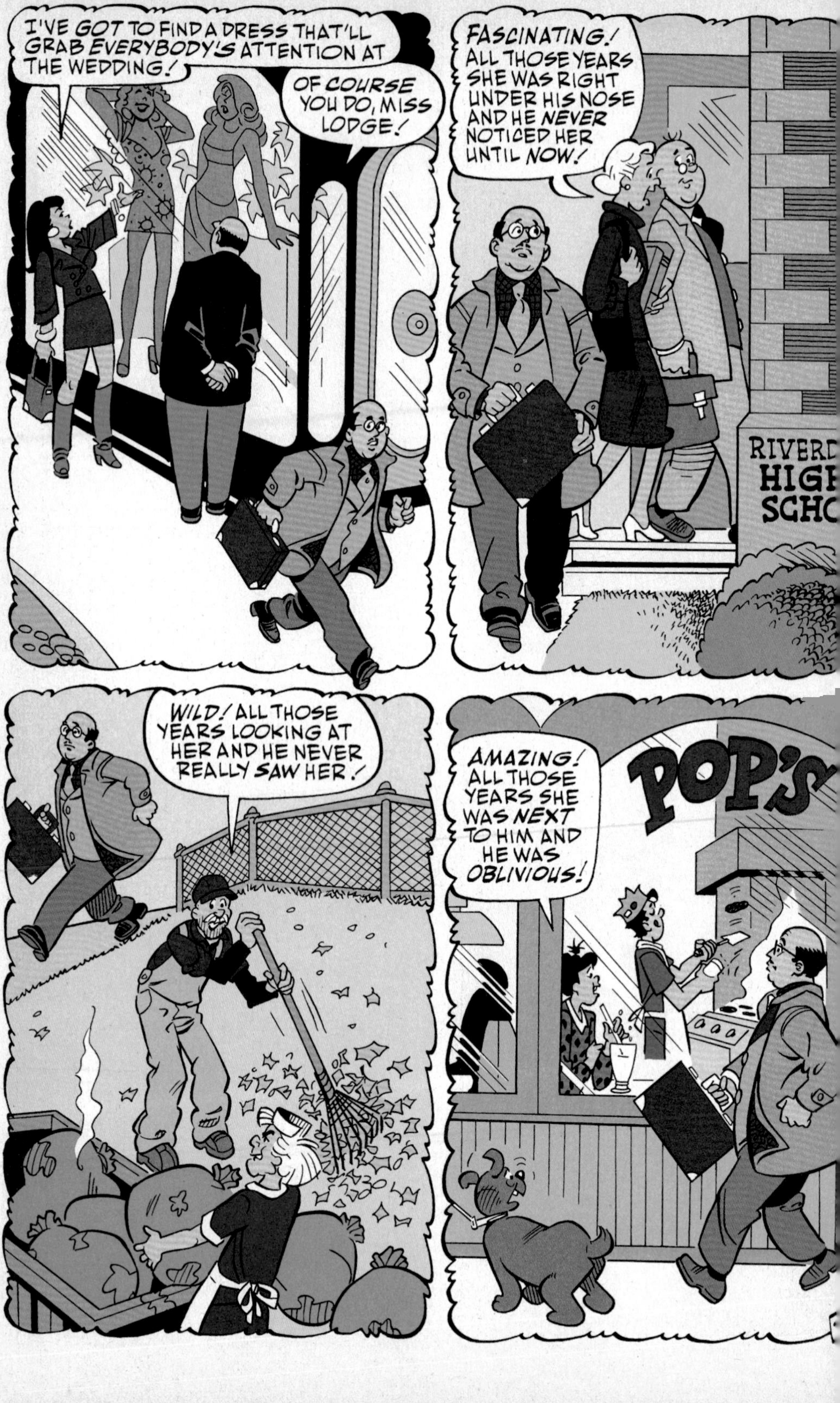
I'VE GOT TO FIND A DRESS THAT'LL GRAB EVERYBODY'S ATTENTION AT THE WEDDING!
OF COURSE YOU DO, MISS LODGE!
FASCINATING! ALL THOSE YEARS SHE WAS RIGHT UNDER HIS NOSE AND HE NEVER NOTICED HER UNTIL NOW!
RIVERD
HIGH
SCHO
WILD! ALL THOSE YEARS LOOKING AT HER AND HE NEVER REALLY SAW HER!
AMAZING! ALL THOSE YEARS SHE WAS NEXT TO HIM AND HE WAS OBLIVIOUS!
POP'S

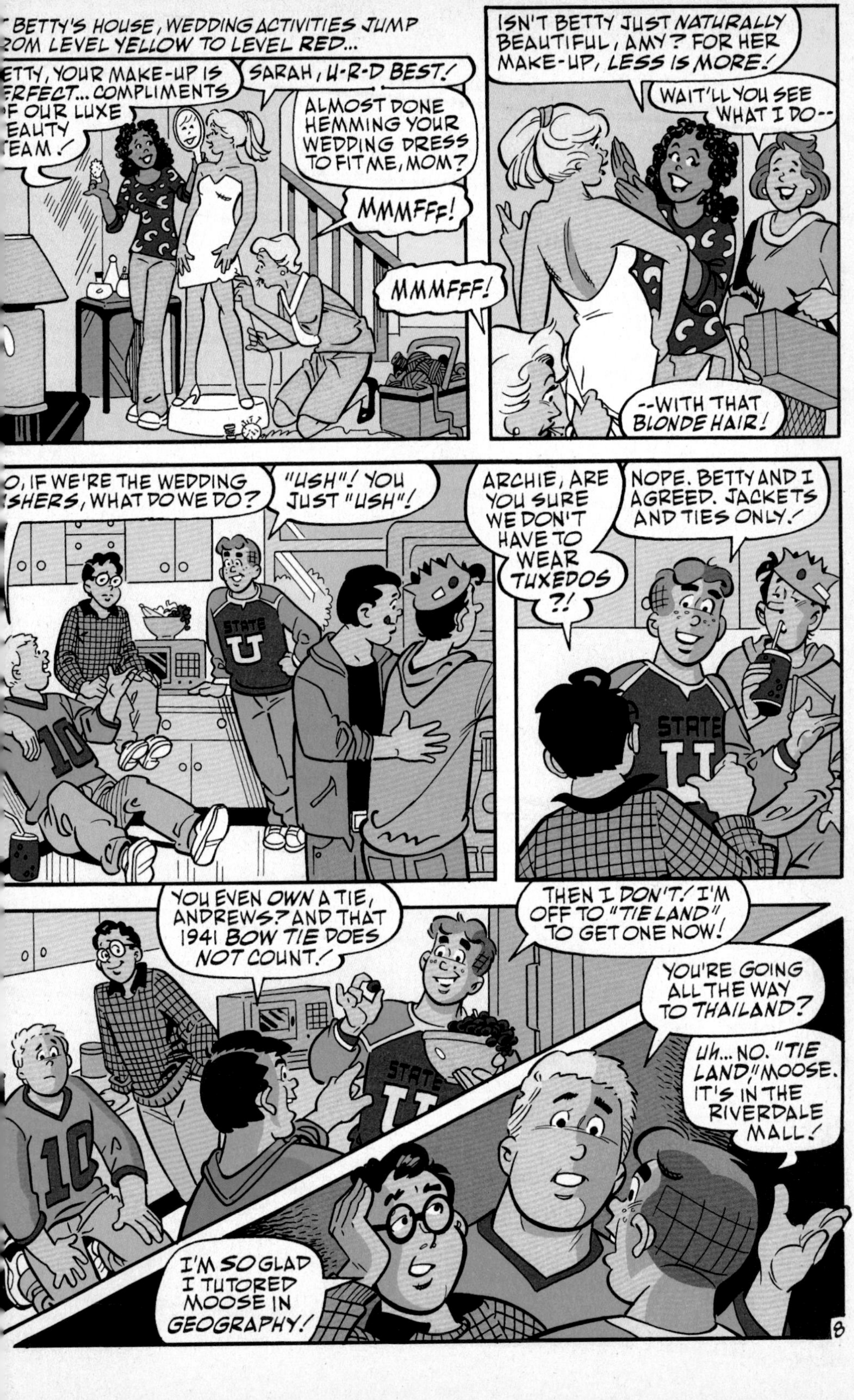
BETTY'S HOUSE, WEDDING ACTIVITIES JUMP
ROM LEVEL YELLOW TO LEVEL RED...
ETTY, YOUR MAKE-UP IS
RFECT... COMPLIMENTS
F OUR LUXE
EAUTY
TEAM!
SARAH, U-R-D BEST!
ALMOST DONE HEMMING YOUR WEDDING DRESS TO FIT ME, MOM?
MMMFFF!
MMMFFF!
ISN'T BETTY JUST NATURALLY BEAUTIFUL, AMY? FOR HER MAKE-UP, LESS IS MORE!
WAIT'LL YOU SEE WHAT I DO--
--WITH THAT BLONDE HAIR!
O, IF WE'RE THE WEDDING
SHERS, WHAT DO WE DO?
"USH"! YOU JUST "USH"!
ARCHIE, ARE YOU SURE WE DON'T HAVE TO WEAR TUXEDOS ?!
NOPE. BETTY AND I AGREED. JACKETS AND TIES ONLY!
YOU EVEN OWN A TIE, ANDREWS? AND THAT 1941 BOW TIE DOES NOT COUNT!
THEN I DON'T! I'M OFF TO "TIE LAND" TO GET ONE NOW!
YOU'RE GOING ALL THE WAY TO THAILAND?
UH... NO. "TIE LAND," MOOSE. IT'S IN THE RIVERDALE MALL!
I'M SO GLAD I TUTORED MOOSE IN GEOGRAPHY!
STATE U
10
8

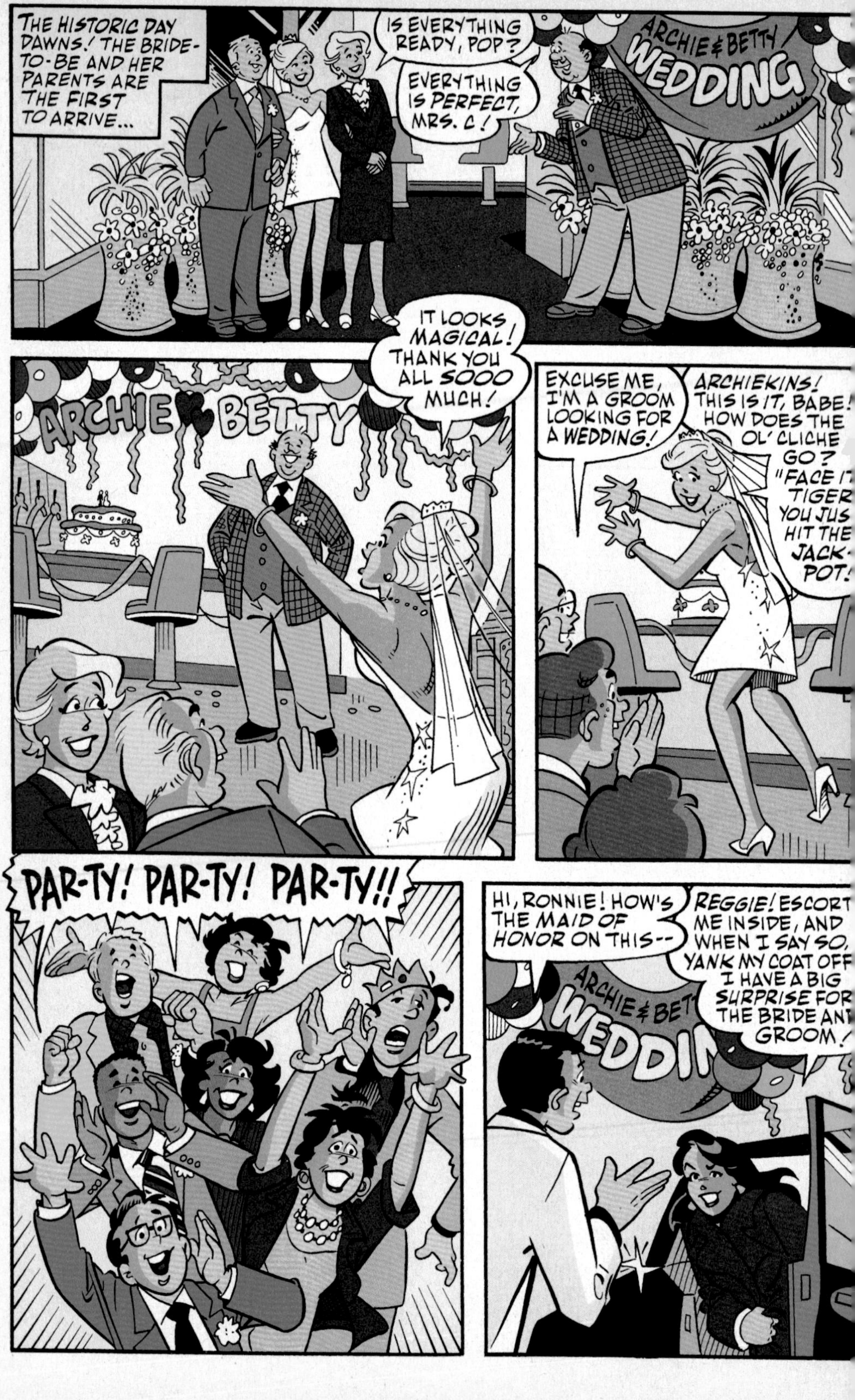
THE HISTORIC DAY DAWNS! THE BRIDE-TO-BE AND HER PARENTS ARE THE FIRST TO ARRIVE...
IS EVERYTHING READY, POP?
EVERYTHING IS PERFECT, MRS. C!
ARCHIE & BETTY WEDDING
IT LOOKS MAGICAL! THANK YOU ALL SOOO MUCH!
ARCHIE BETTY
EXCUSE ME, I'M A GROOM LOOKING FOR A WEDDING!
ARCHIEKINS! THIS IS IT, BABE! HOW DOES THE OL' CLICHE GO? "FACE IT TIGER YOU JUS HIT THE JACK-POT!
PAR-TY! PAR-TY! PAR-TY!!
HI, RONNIE! HOW'S THE MAID OF HONOR ON THIS--
REGGIE! ESCORT ME INSIDE, AND WHEN I SAY SO, YANK MY COAT OFF I HAVE A BIG SURPRISE FOR THE BRIDE AN GROOM!
ARCHIE & BET WEDDI

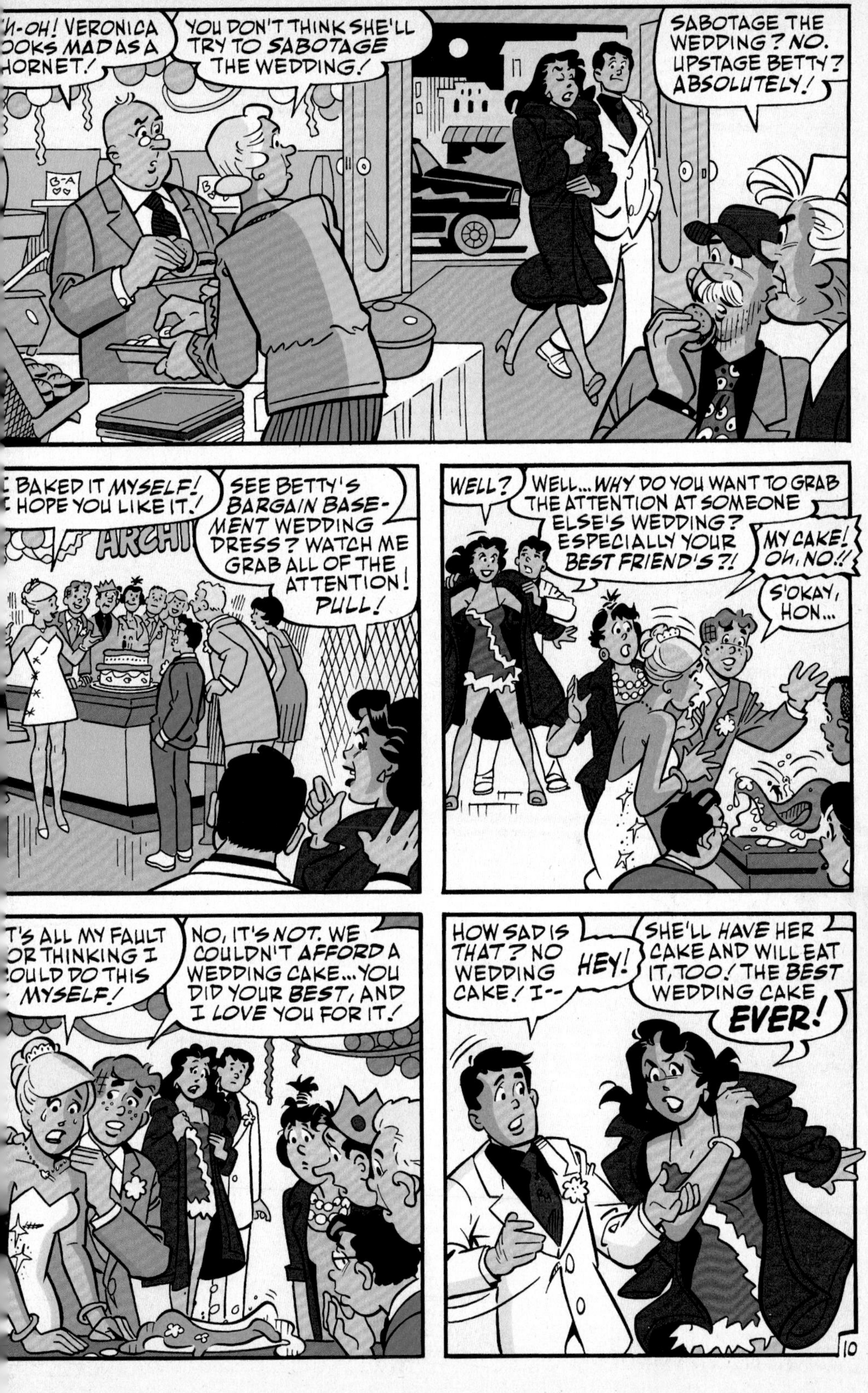

UH-OH! VERONICA LOOKS MAD AS A HORNET!
YOU DON'T THINK SHE'LL TRY TO SABOTAGE THE WEDDING!
SABOTAGE THE WEDDING? NO. UPSTAGE BETTY? ABSOLUTELY!
I BAKED IT MYSELF! I HOPE YOU LIKE IT!
ARCHI
SEE BETTY'S BARGAIN BASEMENT WEDDING DRESS? WATCH ME GRAB ALL OF THE ATTENTION! PULL!
WELL?
WELL... WHY DO YOU WANT TO GRAB THE ATTENTION AT SOMEONE ELSE'S WEDDING? ESPECIALLY YOUR BEST FRIEND'S?!
MY CAKE! OH, NO!!
S'OKAY, HON...
IT'S ALL MY FAULT FOR THINKING I COULD DO THIS MYSELF!
NO, IT'S NOT. WE COULDN'T AFFORD A WEDDING CAKE... YOU DID YOUR BEST, AND I LOVE YOU FOR IT!
HOW SAD IS THAT? NO WEDDING CAKE! I--
HEY!
SHE'LL HAVE HER CAKE AND WILL EAT IT, TOO! THE BEST WEDDING CAKE EVER!
10

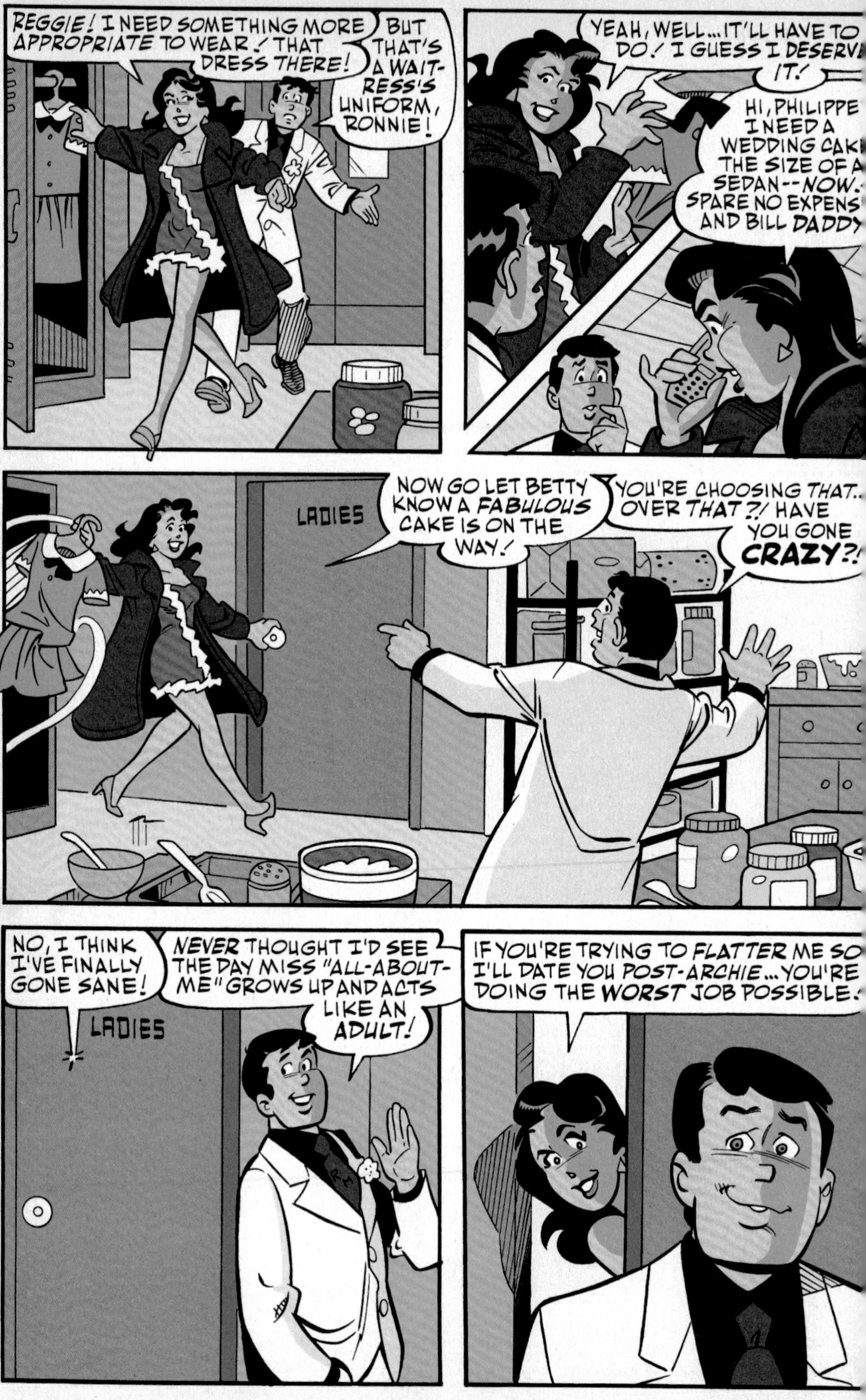
REGGIE! I NEED SOMETHING MORE APPROPRIATE TO WEAR! THAT DRESS THERE!
BUT THAT'S A WAITRESS'S UNIFORM, RONNIE!
YEAH, WELL... IT'LL HAVE TO DO! I GUESS I DESERVE IT!
HI, PHILIPPE! I NEED A WEDDING CAKE THE SIZE OF A SEDAN--NOW. SPARE NO EXPENSE AND BILL DADDY!
NOW GO LET BETTY KNOW A FABULOUS CAKE IS ON THE WAY!
YOU'RE CHOOSING THAT... OVER THAT?! HAVE YOU GONE CRAZY?!
LADIES
NO, I THINK I'VE FINALLY GONE SANE!
NEVER THOUGHT I'D SEE THE DAY MISS "ALL-ABOUT-ME" GROWS UP AND ACTS LIKE AN ADULT!
LADIES
IF YOU'RE TRYING TO FLATTER ME SO I'LL DATE YOU POST-ARCHIE... YOU'RE DOING THE WORST JOB POSSIBLE.

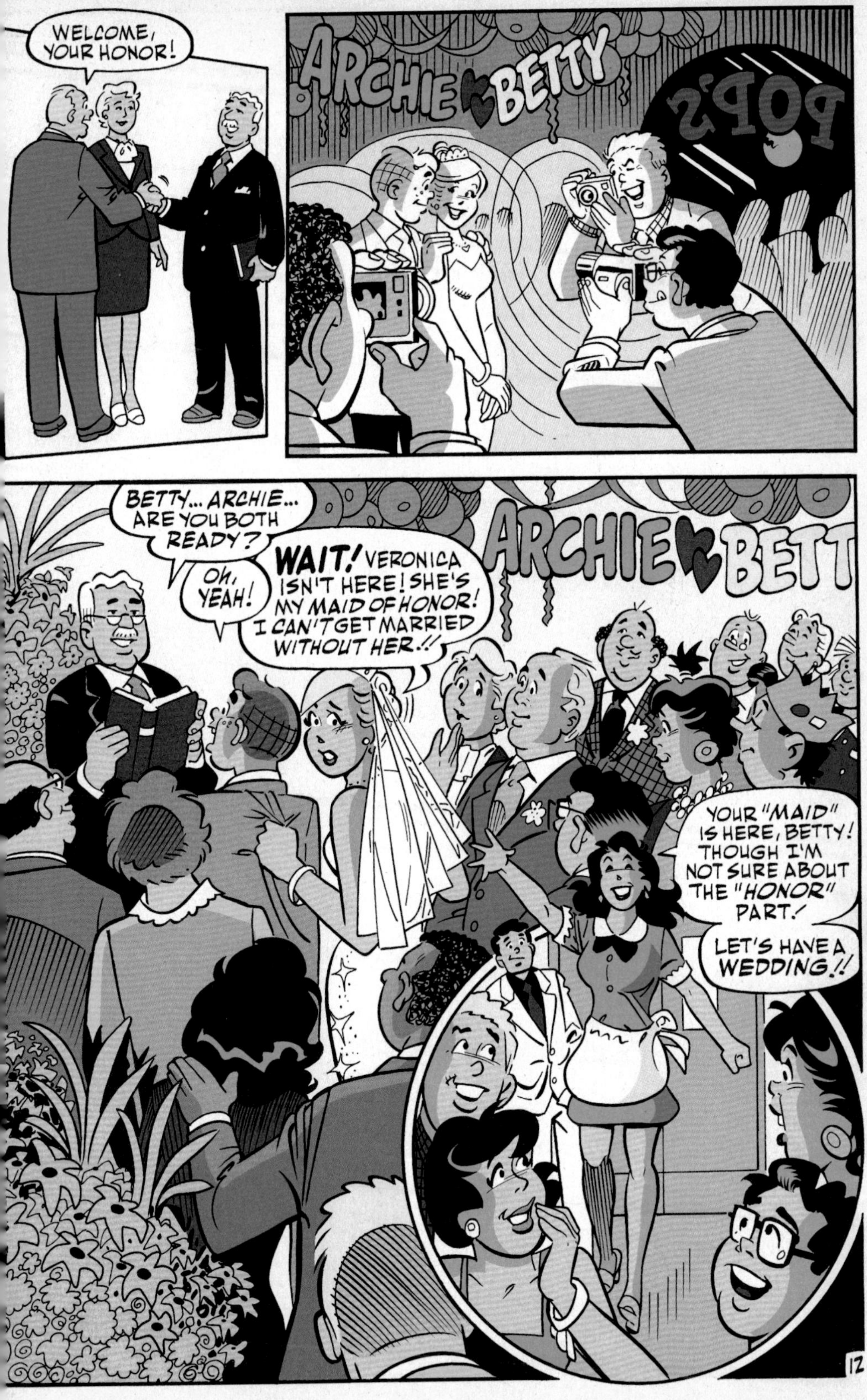

WELCOME, YOUR HONOR!
ARCHIE ♥ BETTY
POP'S
BETTY... ARCHIE... ARE YOU BOTH READY?
OH, YEAH!
WAIT! VERONICA ISN'T HERE! SHE'S MY MAID OF HONOR! I CAN'T GET MARRIED WITHOUT HER!!
ARCHIE ♥ BETT
YOUR "MAID" IS HERE, BETTY! THOUGH I'M NOT SURE ABOUT THE "HONOR" PART!
LET'S HAVE A WEDDING!!

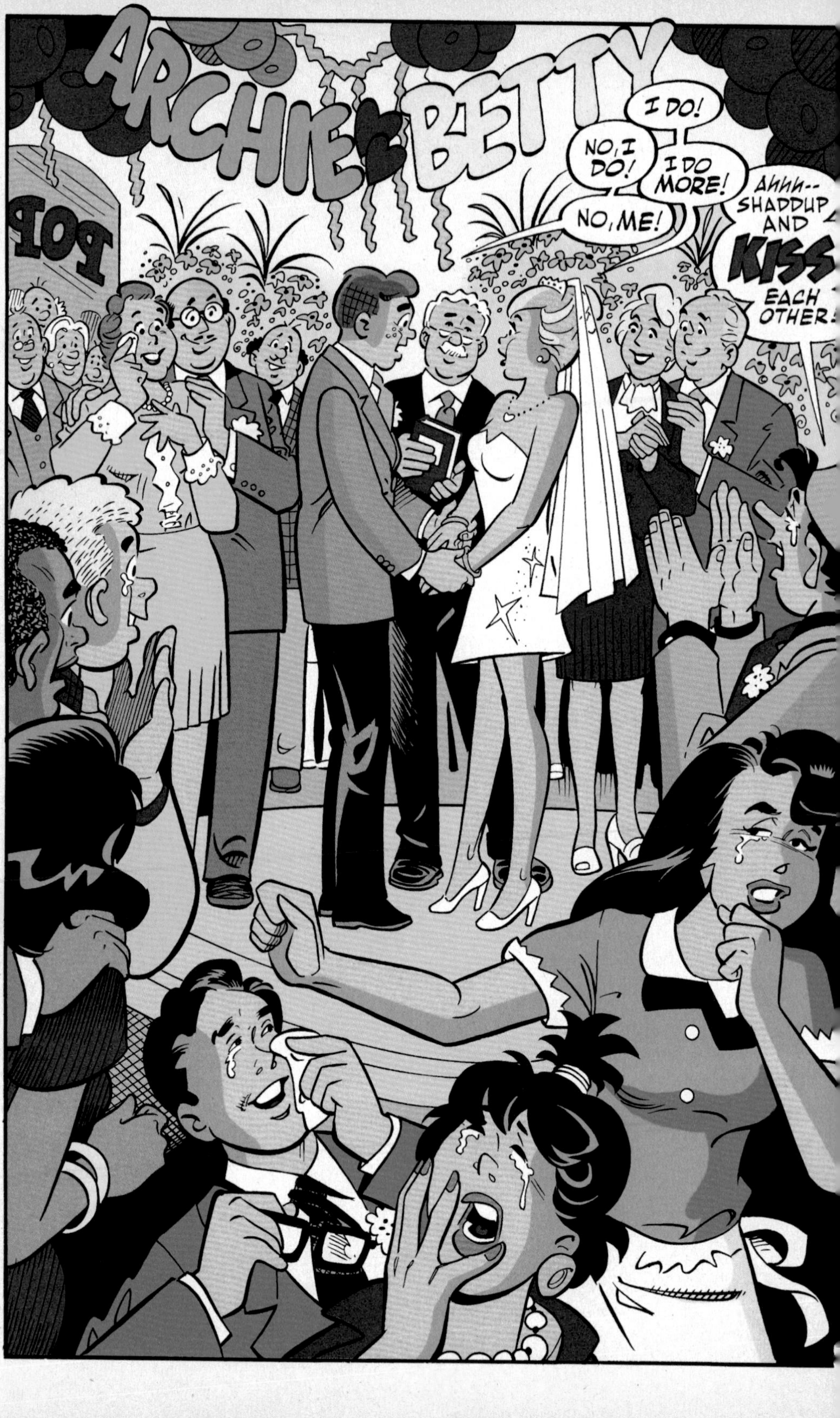
ARCHIE ♥ BETTY
POP
I DO!
NO, I DO!
I DO MORE!
NO, ME!
AHHH-- SHADDUP AND KISS EACH OTHER!

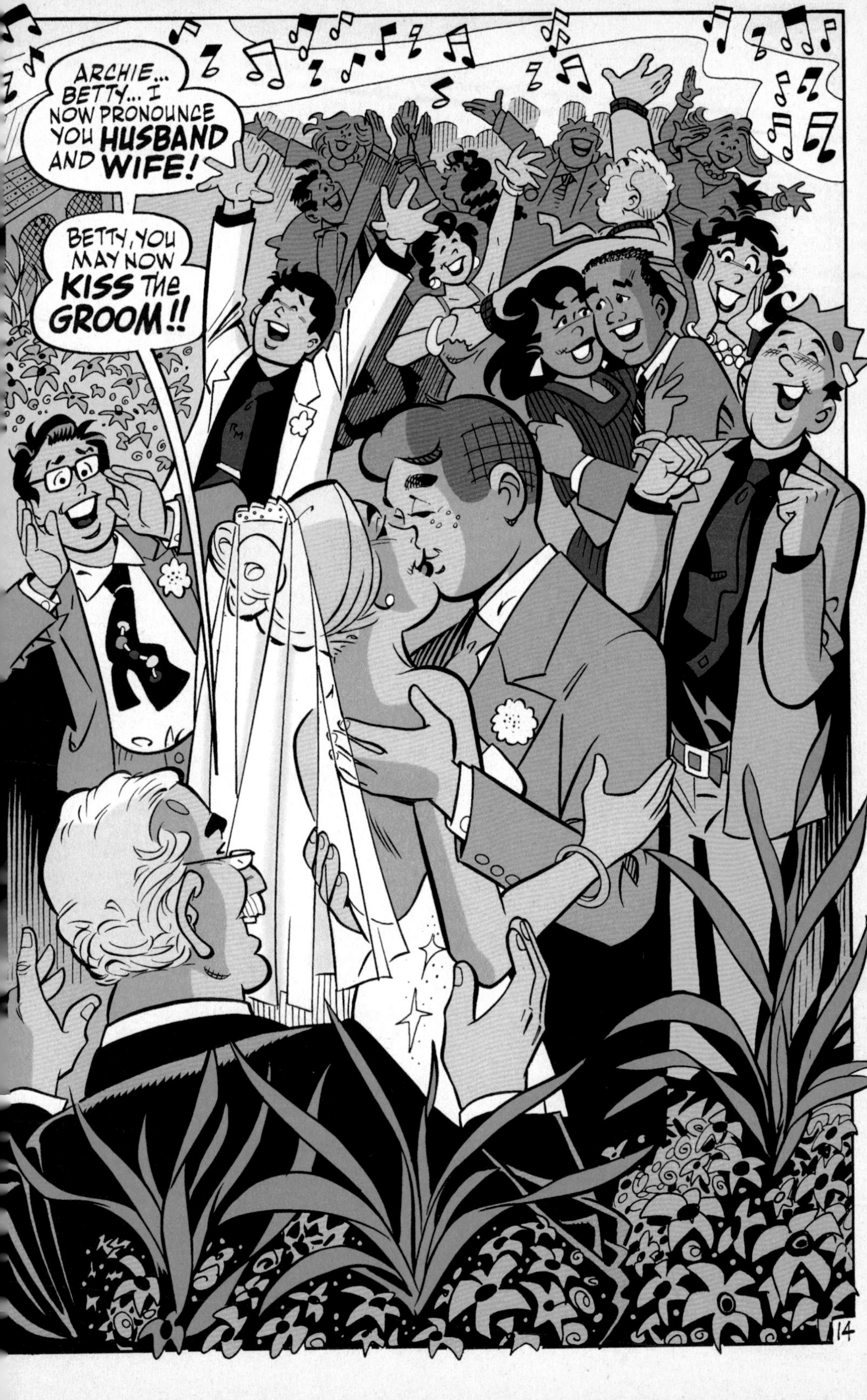
ARCHIE... BETTY... I NOW PRONOUNCE YOU HUSBAND AND WIFE!
BETTY, YOU MAY NOW KISS THE GROOM!!

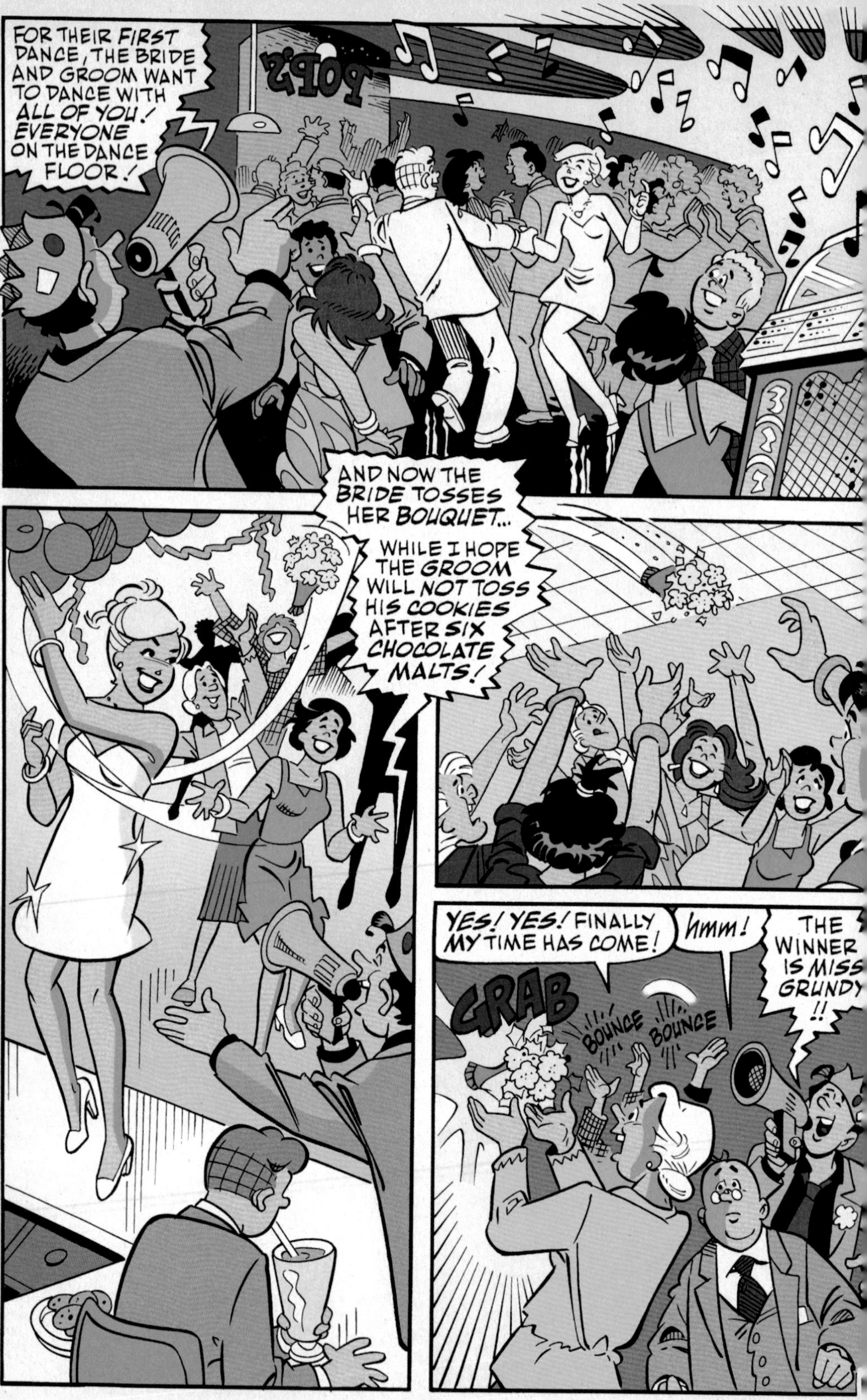
FOR THEIR FIRST DANCE, THE BRIDE AND GROOM WANT TO DANCE WITH ALL OF YOU! EVERYONE ON THE DANCE FLOOR!
POP'S
AND NOW THE BRIDE TOSSES HER BOUQUET...
WHILE I HOPE THE GROOM WILL NOT TOSS HIS COOKIES AFTER SIX CHOCOLATE MALTS!
YES! YES! FINALLY MY TIME HAS COME!
hmm!
THE WINNER IS MISS GRUNDY!!
GRAB
BOUNCE
BOUNCE

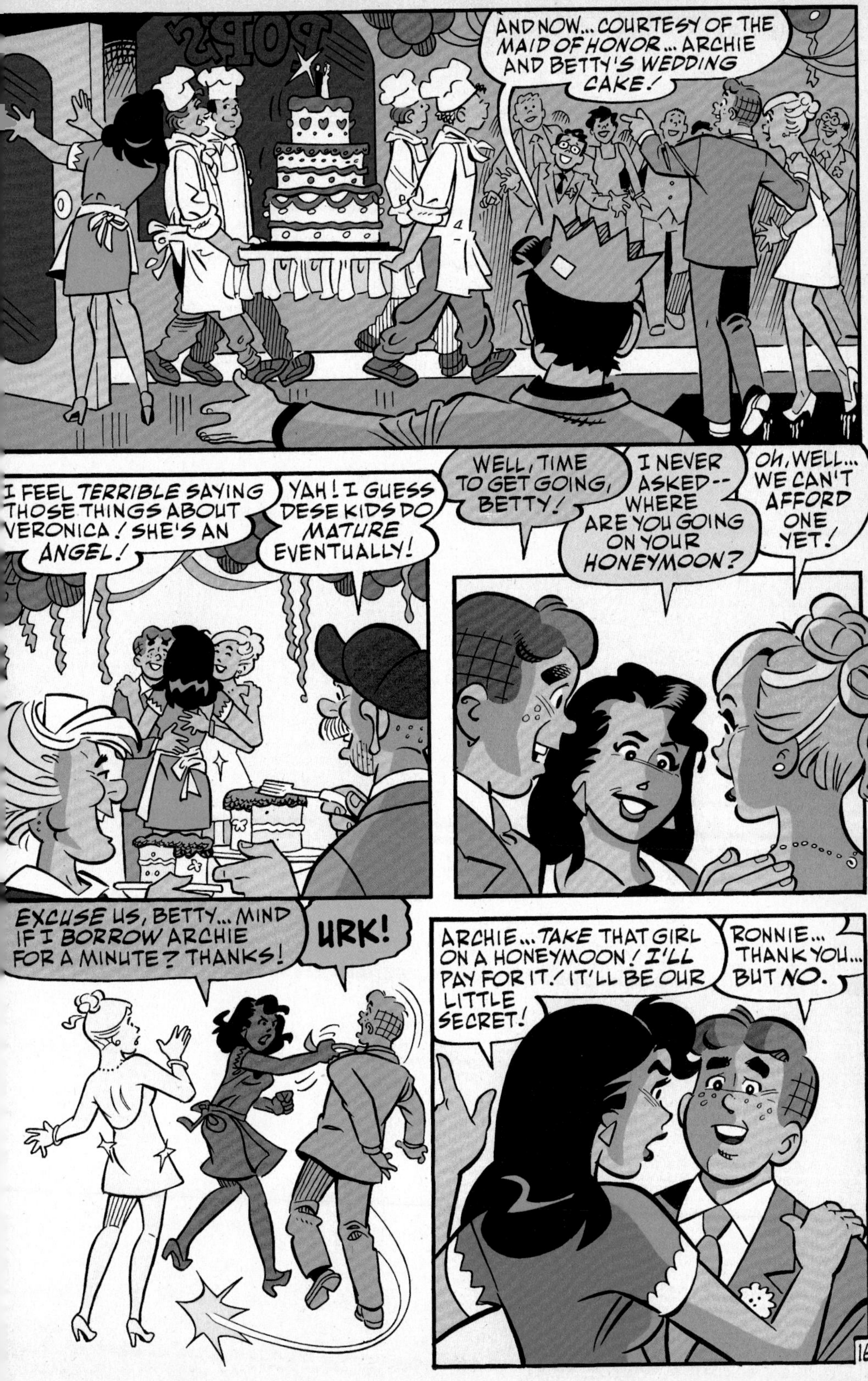
AND NOW... COURTESY OF THE MAID OF HONOR... ARCHIE AND BETTY'S WEDDING CAKE!
POP'S
I FEEL TERRIBLE SAYING THOSE THINGS ABOUT VERONICA! SHE'S AN ANGEL!
YAH! I GUESS DESE KIDS DO MATURE EVENTUALLY!
WELL, TIME TO GET GOING, BETTY!
I NEVER ASKED-- WHERE ARE YOU GOING ON YOUR HONEYMOON?
OH, WELL... WE CAN'T AFFORD ONE YET!
EXCUSE US, BETTY... MIND IF I BORROW ARCHIE FOR A MINUTE? THANKS!
URK!
ARCHIE... TAKE THAT GIRL ON A HONEYMOON! I'LL PAY FOR IT! IT'LL BE OUR LITTLE SECRET!
RONNIE... THANK YOU... BUT NO.
16

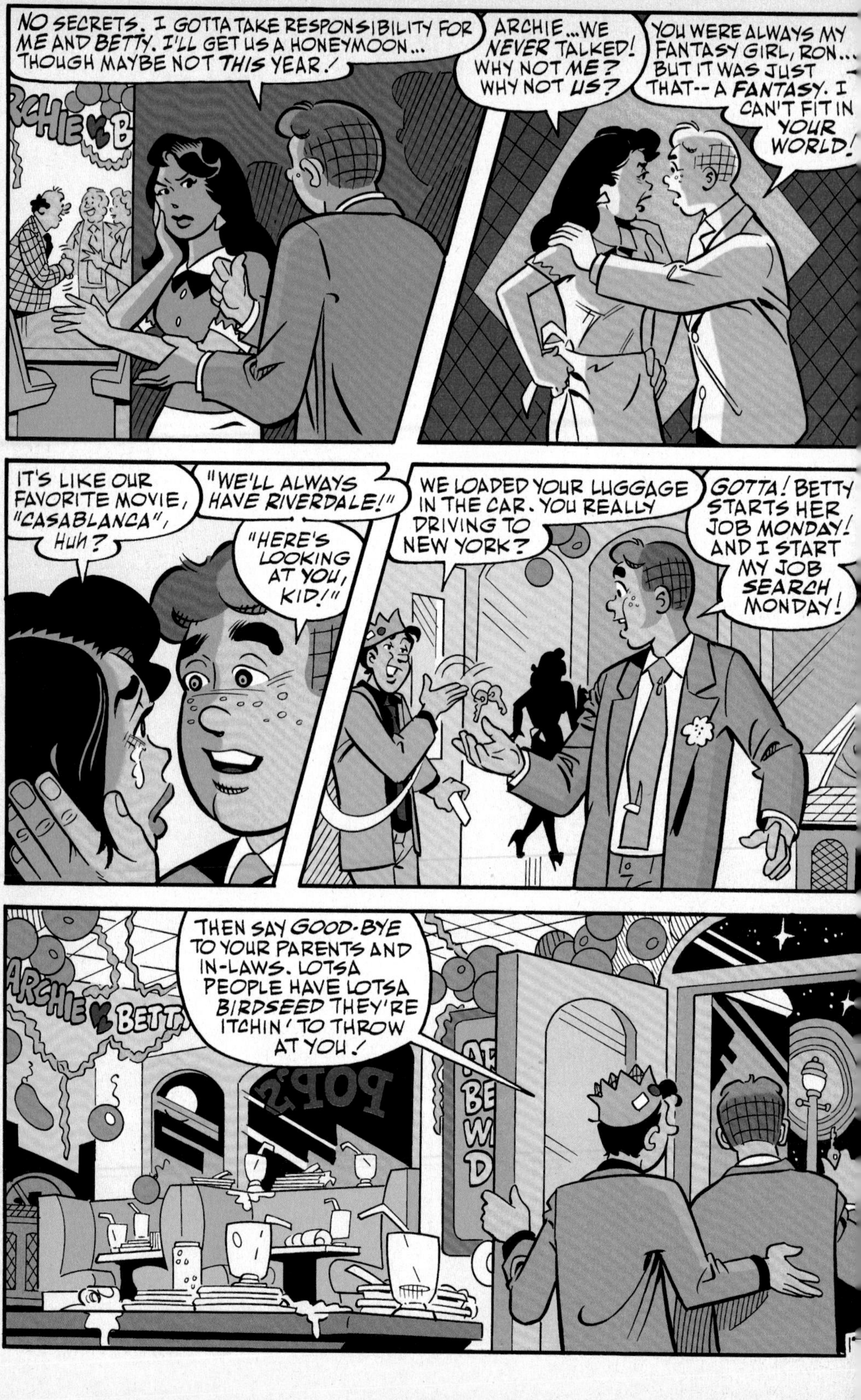
NO SECRETS. I GOTTA TAKE RESPONSIBILITY FOR ME AND BETTY. I'LL GET US A HONEYMOON... THOUGH MAYBE NOT THIS YEAR!
ARCHIE ♥ B
ARCHIE...WE NEVER TALKED! WHY NOT ME? WHY NOT US?
YOU WERE ALWAYS MY FANTASY GIRL, RON... BUT IT WAS JUST THAT-- A FANTASY. I CAN'T FIT IN YOUR WORLD!
IT'S LIKE OUR FAVORITE MOVIE, "CASABLANCA", HUH?
"WE'LL ALWAYS HAVE RIVERDALE!"
"HERE'S LOOKING AT YOU, KID!"
WE LOADED YOUR LUGGAGE IN THE CAR. YOU REALLY DRIVING TO NEW YORK?
GOTTA! BETTY STARTS HER JOB MONDAY! AND I START MY JOB SEARCH MONDAY!
ARCHIE ♥ BETTY
POP'S
THEN SAY GOOD-BYE TO YOUR PARENTS AND IN-LAWS. LOTSA PEOPLE HAVE LOTSA BIRDSEED THEY'RE ITCHIN' TO THROW AT YOU!

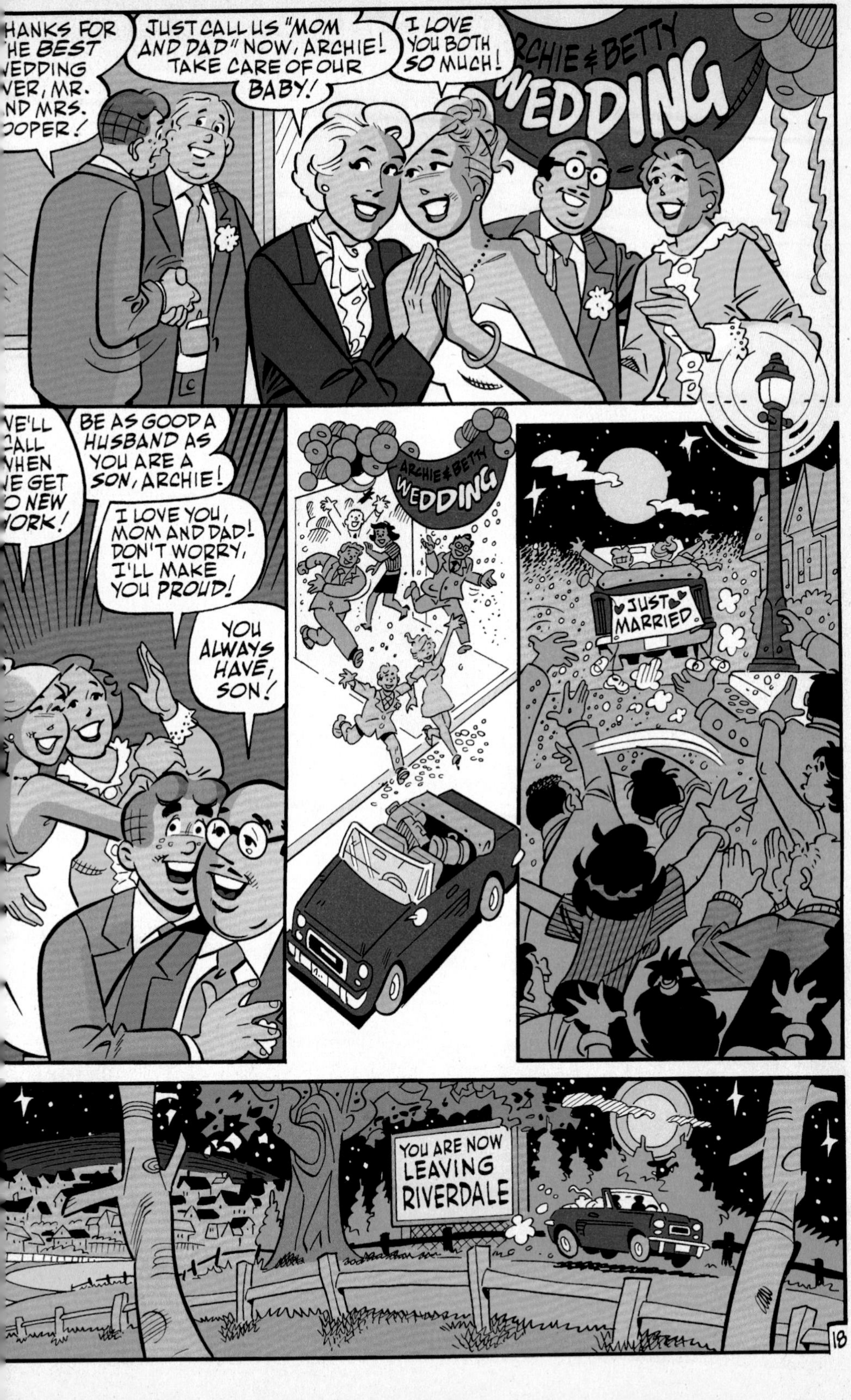
HANKS FOR
HE BEST
VEDDING
VER, MR.
ND MRS.
OOPER!
JUST CALL US "MOM AND DAD" NOW, ARCHIE! TAKE CARE OF OUR BABY!
I LOVE YOU BOTH SO MUCH!
ARCHIE & BETTY WEDDING
VE'LL
CALL
VHEN
VE GET
O NEW
YORK!
BE AS GOOD A HUSBAND AS YOU ARE A SON, ARCHIE!
I LOVE YOU, MOM AND DAD! DON'T WORRY, I'LL MAKE YOU PROUD!
YOU ALWAYS HAVE, SON!
ARCHIE & BETTY WEDDING
JUST MARRIED
YOU ARE NOW LEAVING RIVERDALE

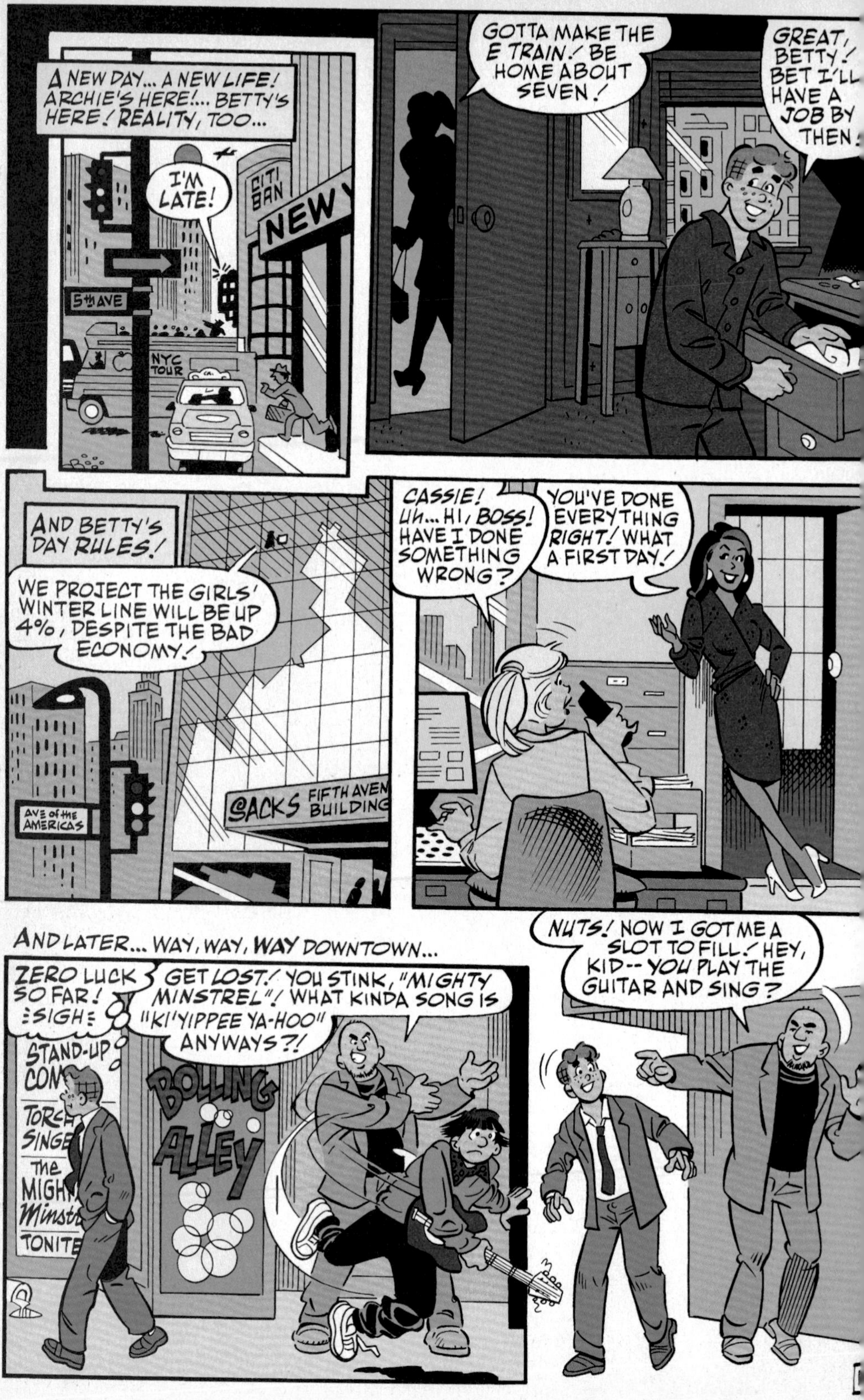
A NEW DAY... A NEW LIFE! ARCHIE'S HERE!... BETTY'S HERE! REALITY, TOO...
I'M LATE!
5th AVE
CITI BAN
NEW
NYC TOUR
GOTTA MAKE THE E TRAIN! BE HOME ABOUT SEVEN!
GREAT, BETTY! BET I'LL HAVE A JOB BY THEN!
AND BETTY'S DAY RULES!
WE PROJECT THE GIRLS' WINTER LINE WILL BE UP 4%, DESPITE THE BAD ECONOMY!
AVE of the AMERICAS
SACKS FIFTH AVEN BUILDING
CASSIE! UH... HI, BOSS! HAVE I DONE SOMETHING WRONG?
YOU'VE DONE EVERYTHING RIGHT! WHAT A FIRST DAY!
AND LATER... WAY, WAY, WAY DOWNTOWN...
ZERO LUCK SO FAR! SIGH
GET LOST! YOU STINK, "MIGHTY MINSTREL"! WHAT KINDA SONG IS "KI'YIPPEE YA-HOO" ANYWAYS?!
STAND-UP COM
TORCH SINGE
The MIGHT Minstr
TONITE
BOLLING ALLEY
NUTS! NOW I GOT ME A SLOT TO FILL! HEY, KID-- YOU PLAY THE GUITAR AND SING?

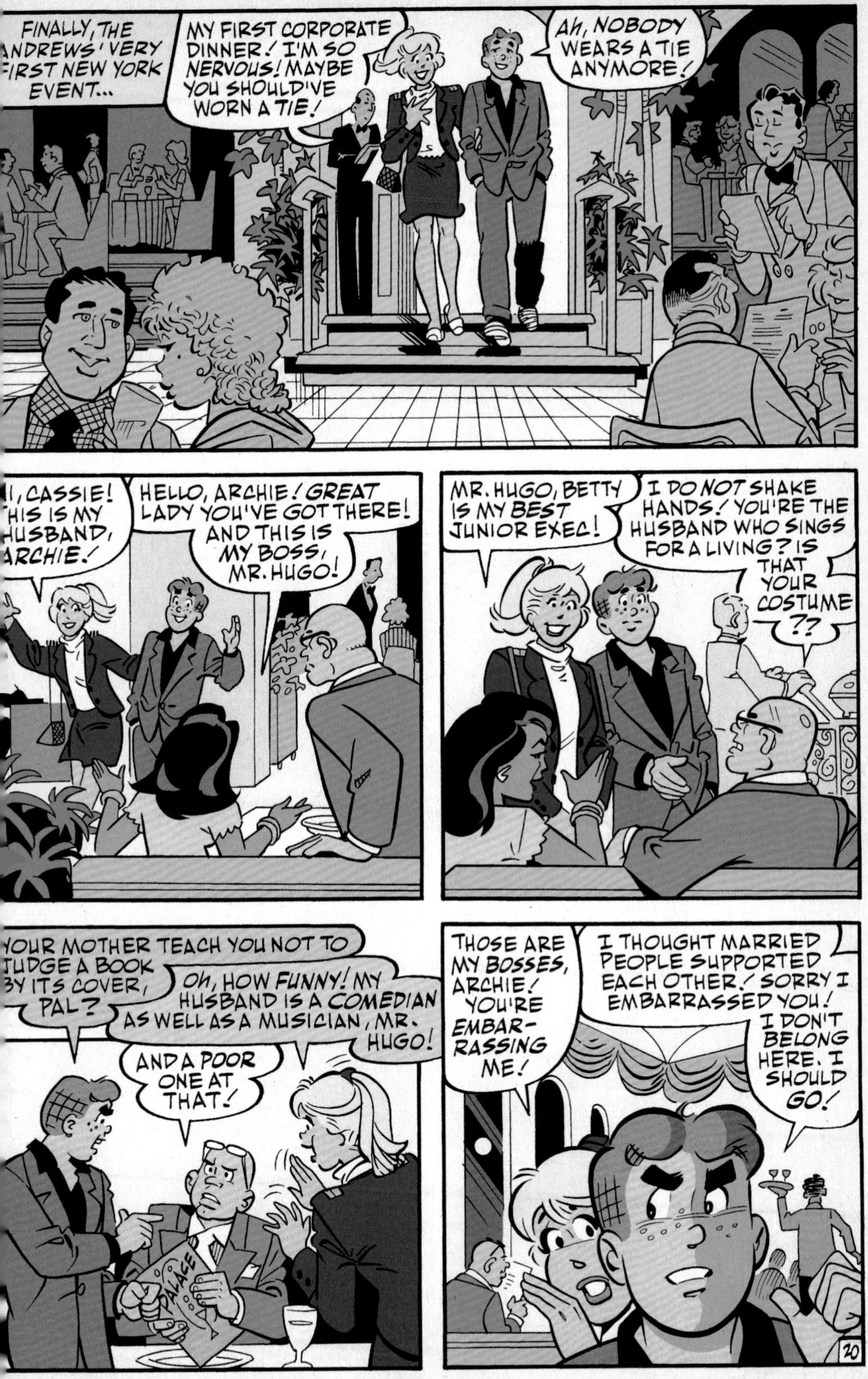

FINALLY, THE ANDREWS' VERY FIRST NEW YORK EVENT...
MY FIRST CORPORATE DINNER! I'M SO NERVOUS! MAYBE YOU SHOULD'VE WORN A TIE!
Ah, NOBODY WEARS A TIE ANYMORE!
I, CASSIE! HIS IS MY HUSBAND, RCHIE!
HELLO, ARCHIE! GREAT LADY YOU'VE GOT THERE! AND THIS IS MY BOSS, MR. HUGO!
MR. HUGO, BETTY IS MY BEST JUNIOR EXEC!
I DO NOT SHAKE HANDS! YOU'RE THE HUSBAND WHO SINGS FOR A LIVING? IS THAT YOUR COSTUME ??
YOUR MOTHER TEACH YOU NOT TO JUDGE A BOOK BY ITS COVER, PAL?
Oh, HOW FUNNY! MY HUSBAND IS A COMEDIAN AS WELL AS A MUSICIAN, MR. HUGO!
AND A POOR ONE AT THAT!
PALACE
THOSE ARE MY BOSSES, ARCHIE! YOU'RE EMBARRASSING ME!
I THOUGHT MARRIED PEOPLE SUPPORTED EACH OTHER! SORRY I EMBARRASSED YOU!
I DON'T BELONG HERE. I SHOULD GO!
20

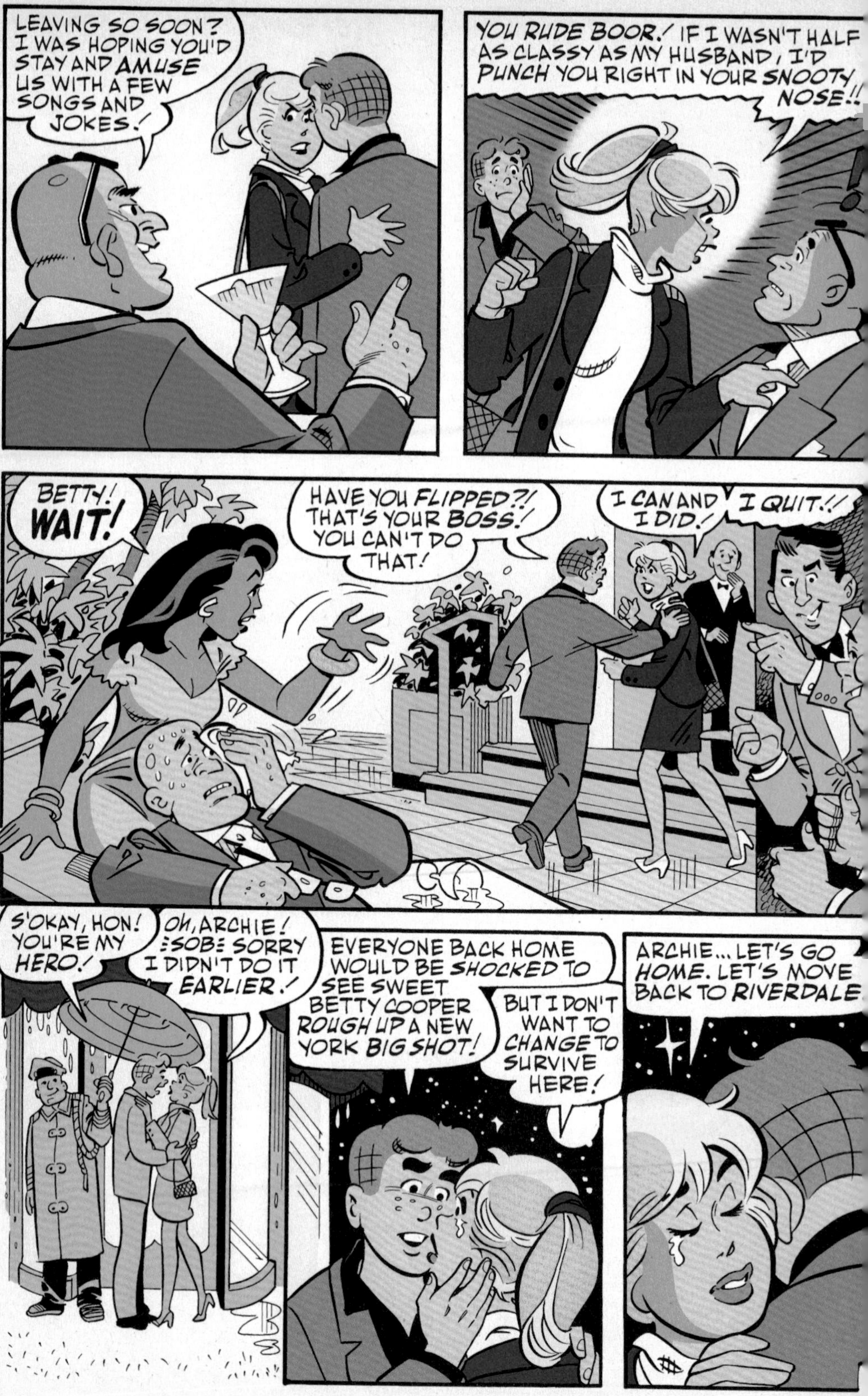
LEAVING SO SOON? I WAS HOPING YOU'D STAY AND AMUSE US WITH A FEW SONGS AND JOKES!
YOU RUDE BOOR! IF I WASN'T HALF AS CLASSY AS MY HUSBAND, I'D PUNCH YOU RIGHT IN YOUR SNOOTY NOSE!!
BETTY! WAIT!
HAVE YOU FLIPPED?! THAT'S YOUR BOSS! YOU CAN'T DO THAT!
I CAN AND I DID!
I QUIT!!
S'OKAY, HON! YOU'RE MY HERO!
OH, ARCHIE! :SOB: SORRY I DIDN'T DO IT EARLIER!
EVERYONE BACK HOME WOULD BE SHOCKED TO SEE SWEET BETTY COOPER ROUGH UP A NEW YORK BIG SHOT!
BUT I DON'T WANT TO CHANGE TO SURVIVE HERE!
ARCHIE... LET'S GO HOME. LET'S MOVE BACK TO RIVERDALE

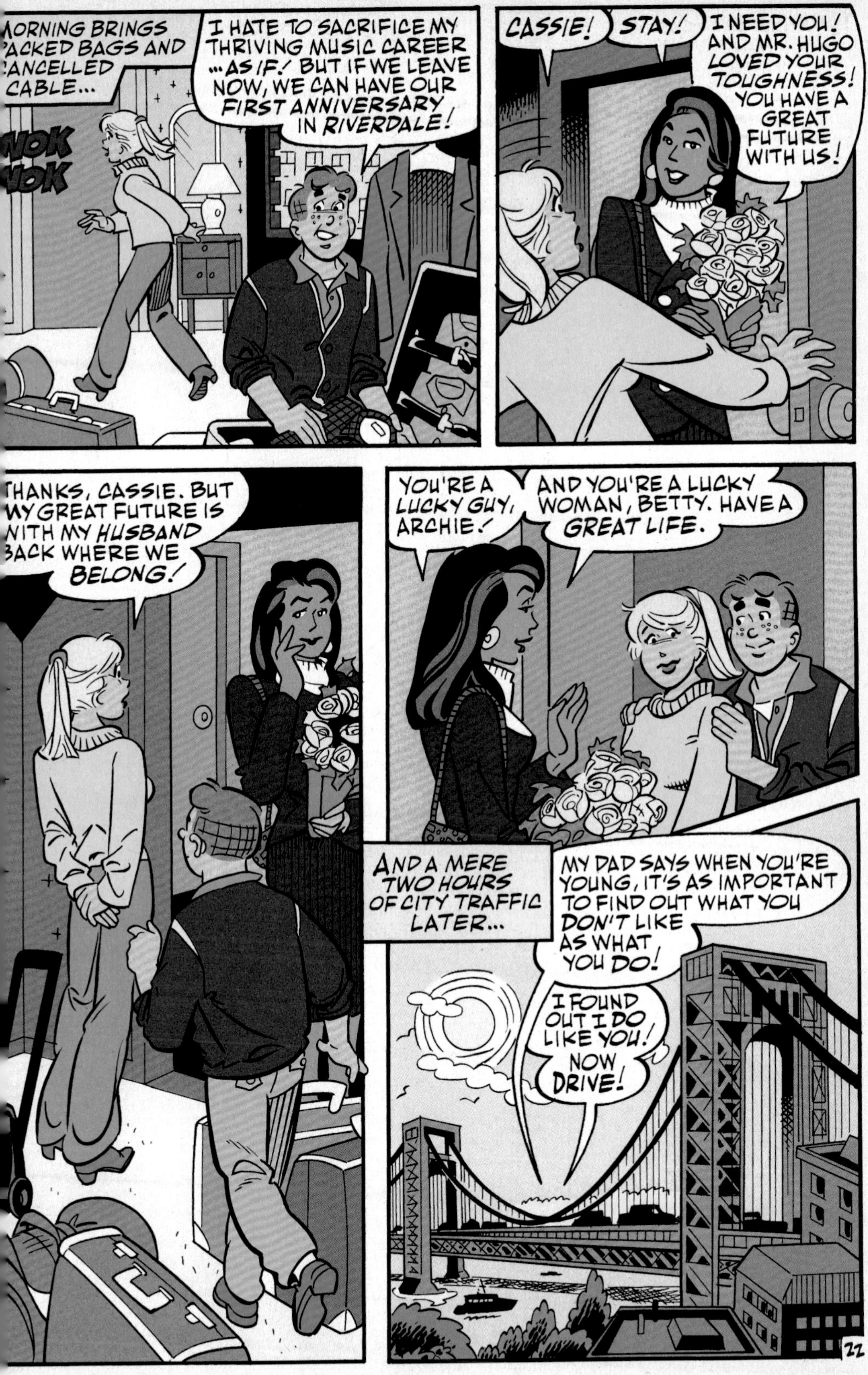
MORNING BRINGS PACKED BAGS AND CANCELLED CABLE...
NOK NOK
I HATE TO SACRIFICE MY THRIVING MUSIC CAREER ...AS IF! BUT IF WE LEAVE NOW, WE CAN HAVE OUR FIRST ANNIVERSARY IN RIVERDALE!
CASSIE!
STAY!
I NEED YOU! AND MR. HUGO LOVED YOUR TOUGHNESS! YOU HAVE A GREAT FUTURE WITH US!
THANKS, CASSIE. BUT MY GREAT FUTURE IS WITH MY HUSBAND BACK WHERE WE BELONG!
YOU'RE A LUCKY GUY, ARCHIE!
AND YOU'RE A LUCKY WOMAN, BETTY. HAVE A GREAT LIFE.
AND A MERE TWO HOURS OF CITY TRAFFIC LATER...
MY DAD SAYS WHEN YOU'RE YOUNG, IT'S AS IMPORTANT TO FIND OUT WHAT YOU DON'T LIKE AS WHAT YOU DO!
I FOUND OUT I DO LIKE YOU! NOW DRIVE!
22

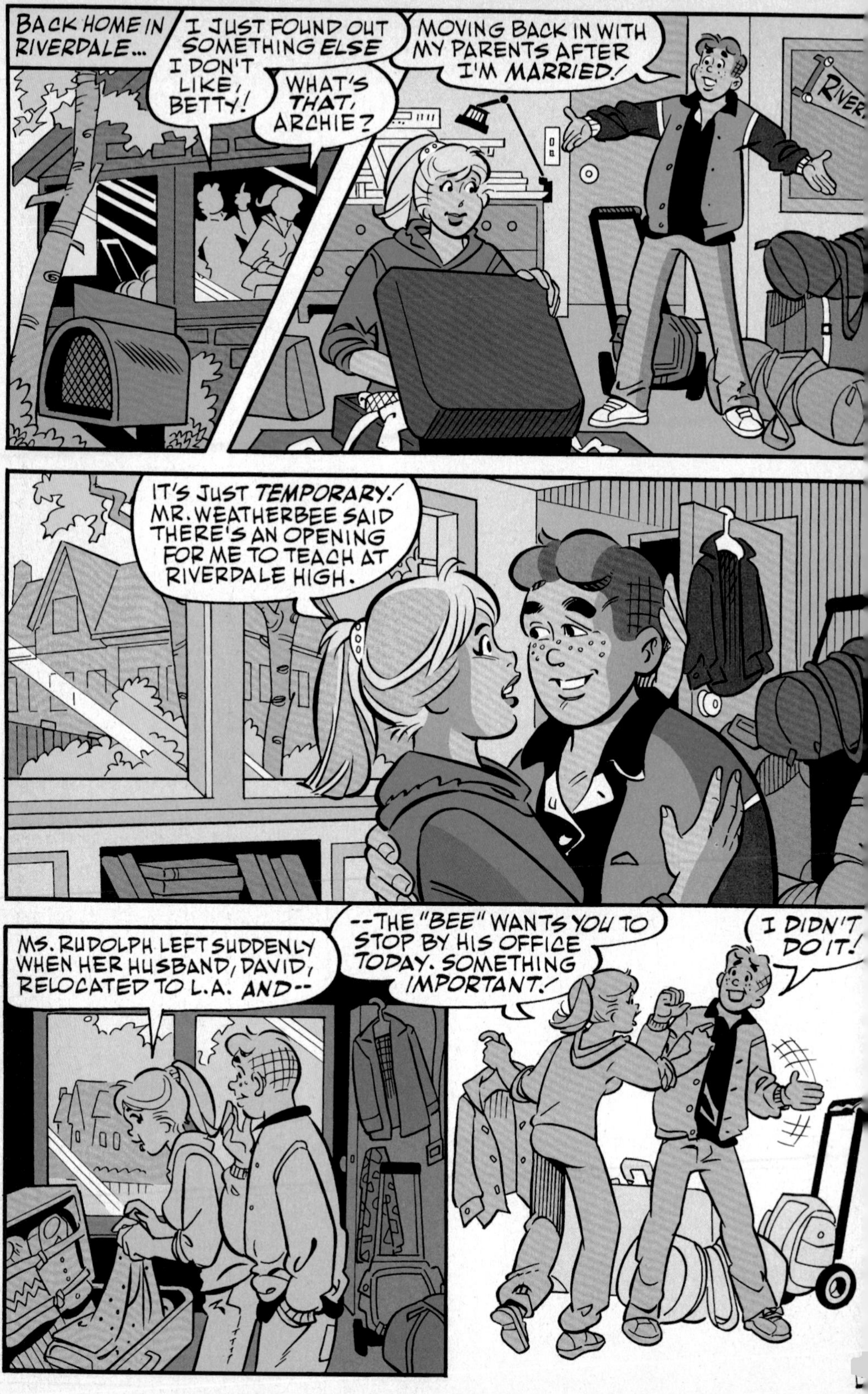
BACK HOME IN RIVERDALE...
I JUST FOUND OUT SOMETHING ELSE I DON'T LIKE, BETTY!
WHAT'S THAT, ARCHIE?
MOVING BACK IN WITH MY PARENTS AFTER I'M MARRIED!
RIVER
IT'S JUST TEMPORARY! MR. WEATHERBEE SAID THERE'S AN OPENING FOR ME TO TEACH AT RIVERDALE HIGH.
MS. RUDOLPH LEFT SUDDENLY WHEN HER HUSBAND, DAVID, RELOCATED TO L.A. AND--
--THE "BEE" WANTS YOU TO STOP BY HIS OFFICE TODAY. SOMETHING IMPORTANT!
I DIDN'T DO IT!

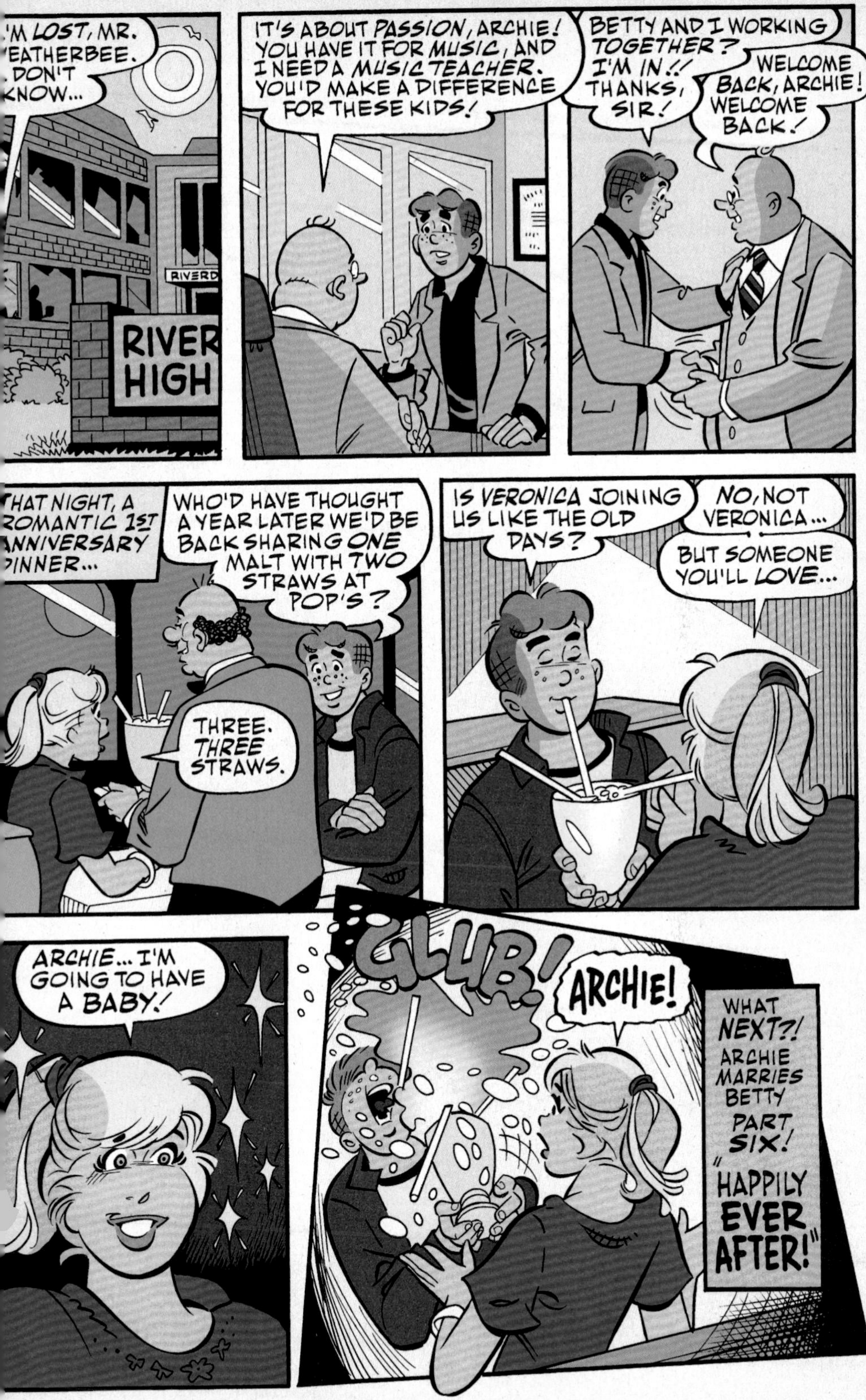
'M LOST, MR. EATHERBEE. DON'T KNOW...
RIVERD
RIVER HIGH
IT'S ABOUT PASSION, ARCHIE! YOU HAVE IT FOR MUSIC, AND I NEED A MUSIC TEACHER. YOU'D MAKE A DIFFERENCE FOR THESE KIDS!
BETTY AND I WORKING TOGETHER? I'M IN!! THANKS, SIR!
WELCOME BACK, ARCHIE! WELCOME BACK!
THAT NIGHT, A ROMANTIC 1ST ANNIVERSARY DINNER...
WHO'D HAVE THOUGHT A YEAR LATER WE'D BE BACK SHARING ONE MALT WITH TWO STRAWS AT POP'S?
THREE. THREE STRAWS.
IS VERONICA JOINING US LIKE THE OLD DAYS?
NO, NOT VERONICA...
BUT SOMEONE YOU'LL LOVE...
ARCHIE... I'M GOING TO HAVE A BABY!
GLUB!
ARCHIE!
WHAT NEXT?! ARCHIE MARRIES BETTY PART SIX! "HAPPILY EVER AFTER!"

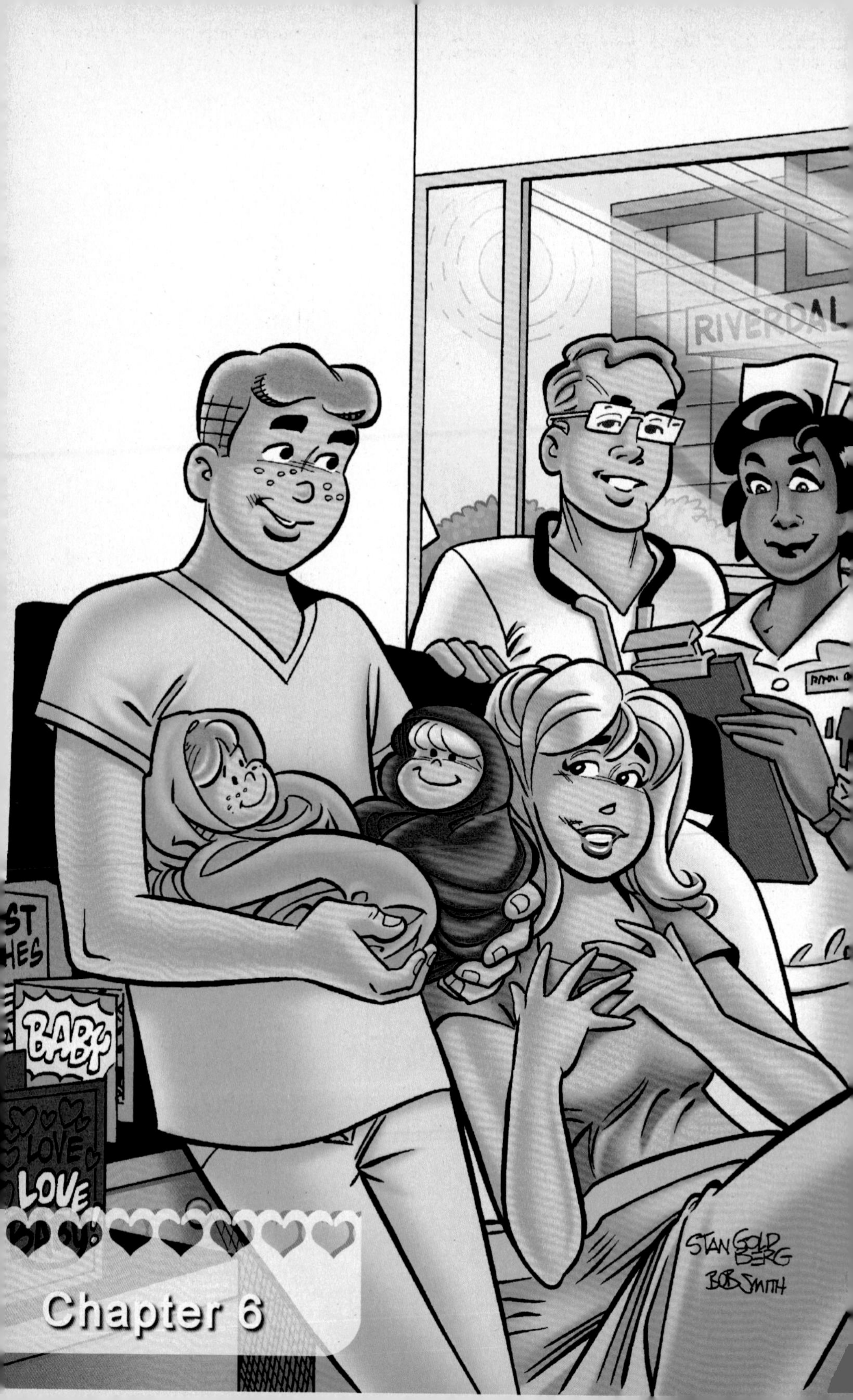

RIVERDAL
BABY
LOVE
LOVE
STAN GOLDBERG
BOB SMITH

Chapter 6

Archie MARRIES Betty

"HAPPILY EVER AFTER" PART 6

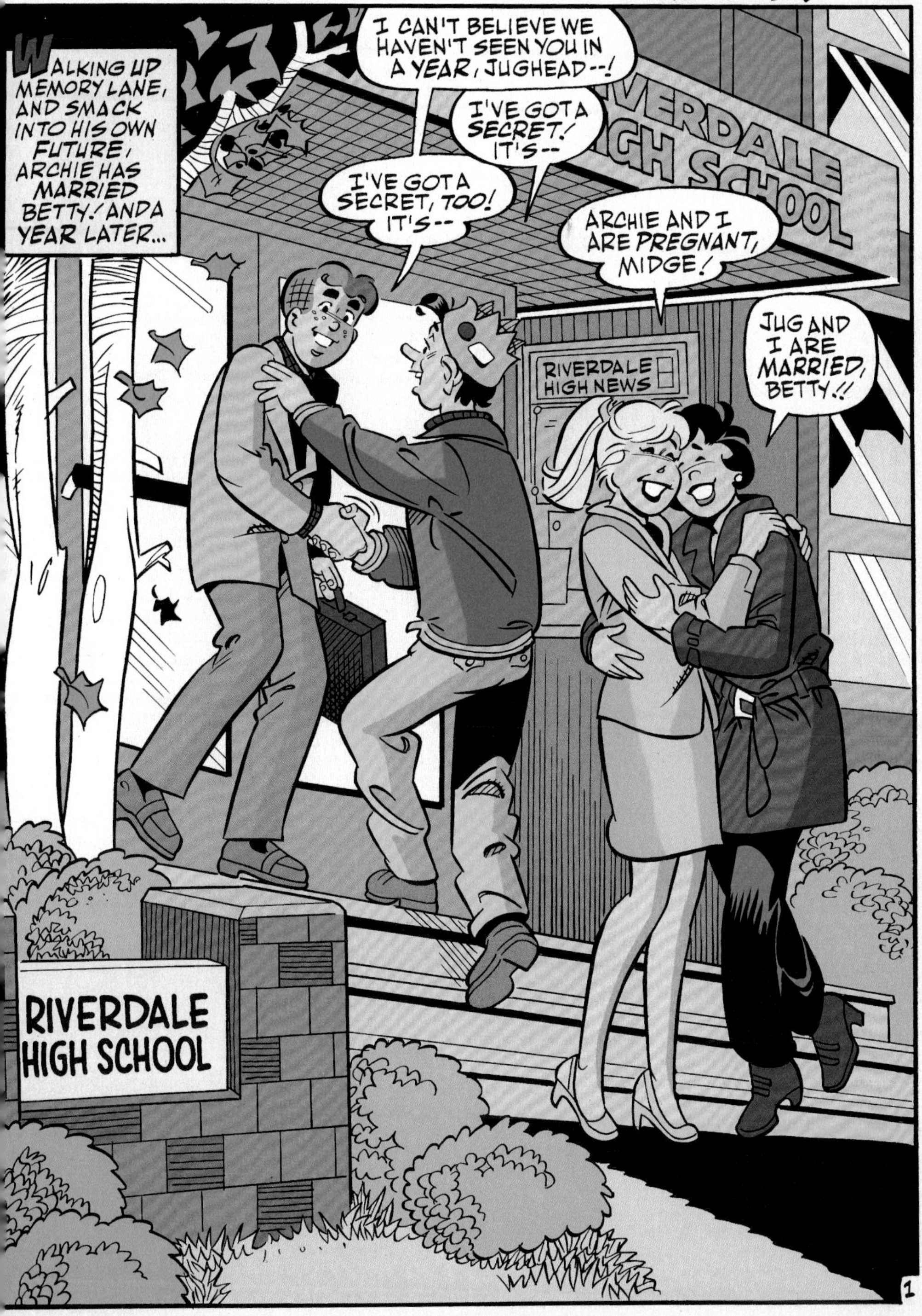
WALKING UP MEMORY LANE, AND SMACK INTO HIS OWN FUTURE, ARCHIE HAS MARRIED BETTY! AND A YEAR LATER...
I CAN'T BELIEVE WE HAVEN'T SEEN YOU IN A YEAR, JUGHEAD--!
I'VE GOT A SECRET! IT'S--
I'VE GOT A SECRET, TOO! IT'S--
RIVERDALE HIGH SCHOOL
ARCHIE AND I ARE PREGNANT, MIDGE!
JUG AND I ARE MARRIED, BETTY!!
RIVERDALE HIGH NEWS
RIVERDALE HIGH SCHOOL
1

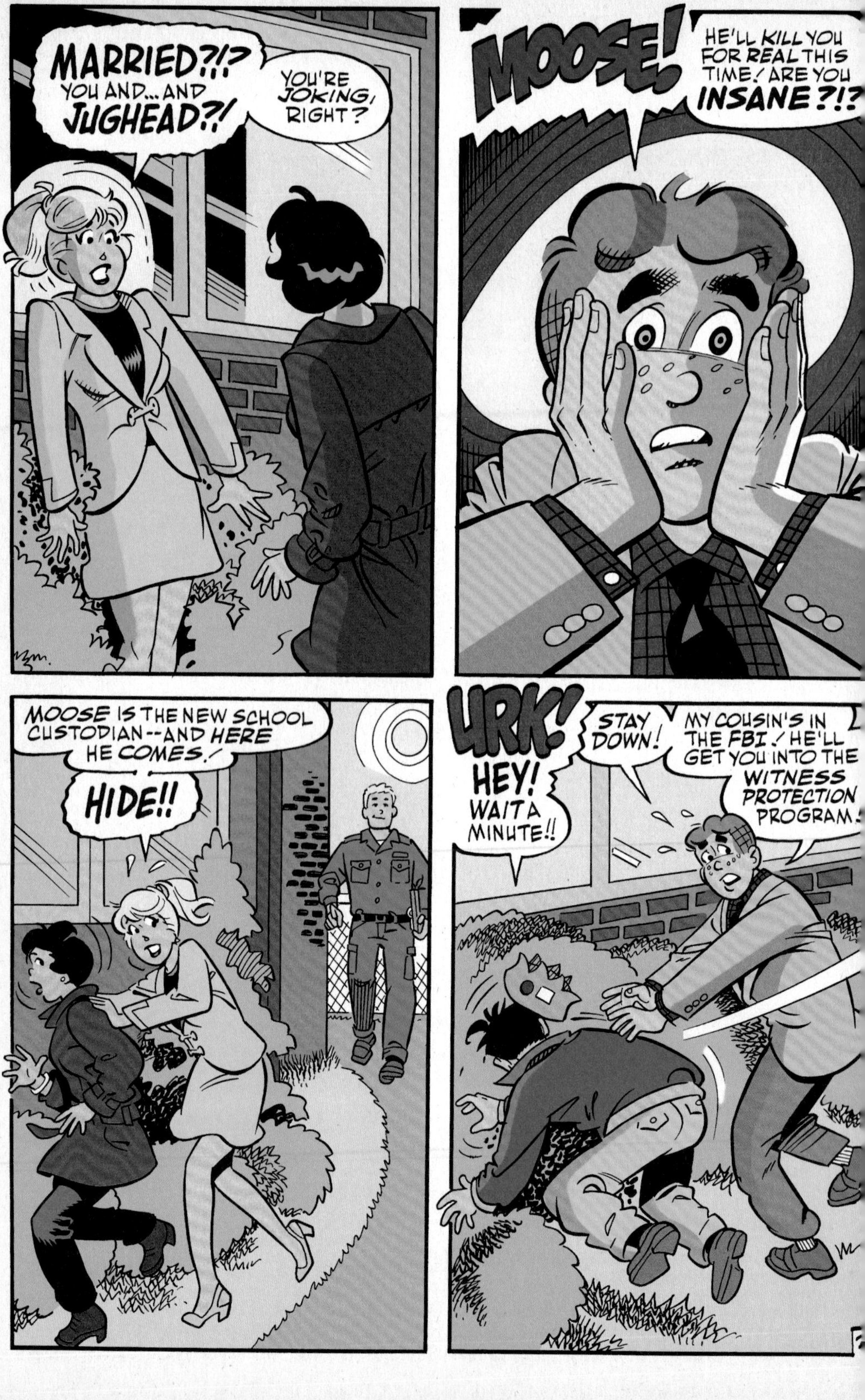
MARRIED?!? YOU AND... AND JUGHEAD?!
YOU'RE JOKING, RIGHT?
MOOSE!
HE'LL KILL YOU FOR REAL THIS TIME! ARE YOU INSANE?!?
MOOSE IS THE NEW SCHOOL CUSTODIAN--AND HERE HE COMES!
HIDE!!
URK!
HEY! WAIT A MINUTE!!
STAY DOWN!
MY COUSIN'S IN THE FBI! HE'LL GET YOU INTO THE WITNESS PROTECTION PROGRAM!

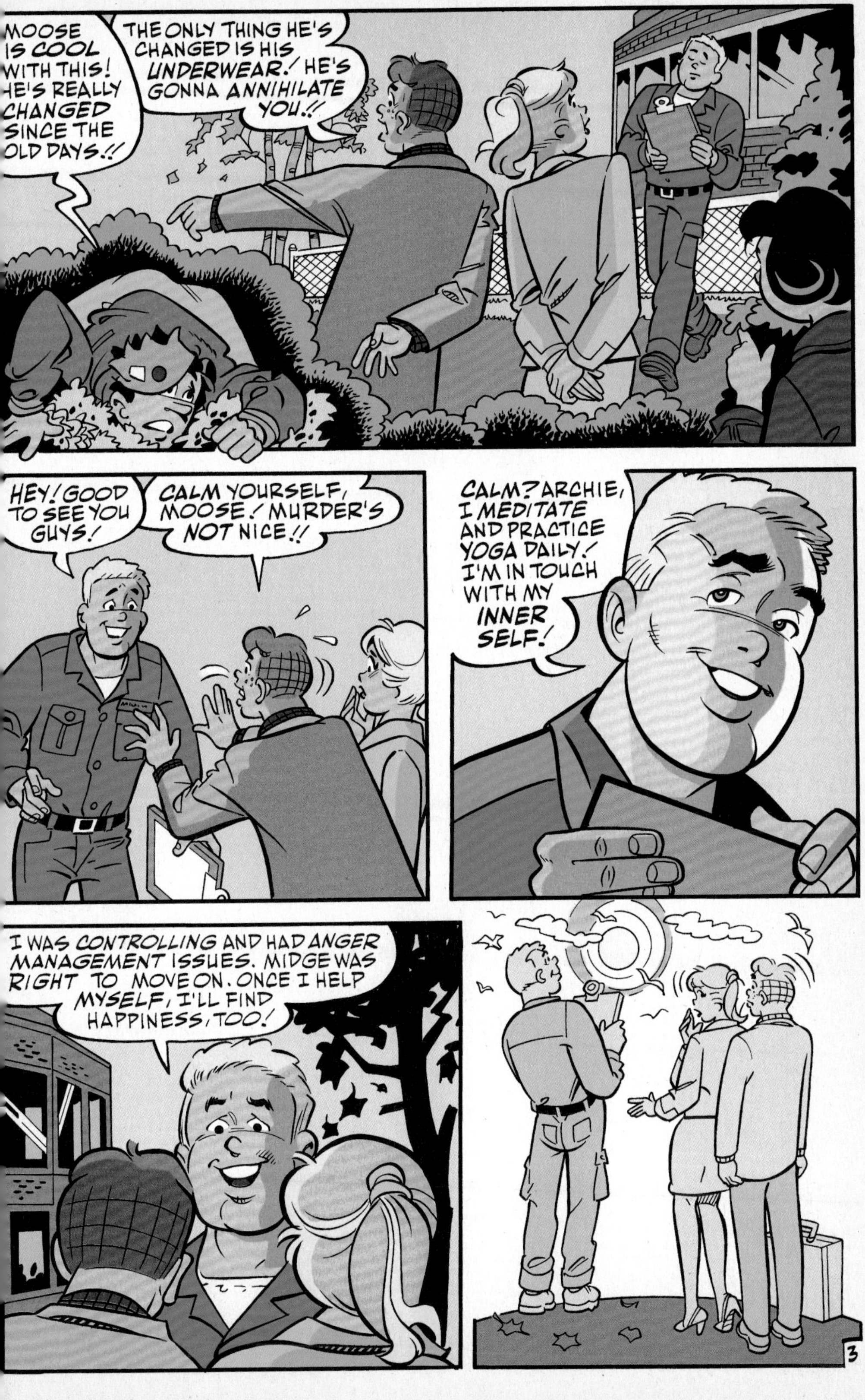
MOOSE IS COOL WITH THIS! HE'S REALLY CHANGED SINCE THE OLD DAYS.!!
THE ONLY THING HE'S CHANGED IS HIS UNDERWEAR! HE'S GONNA ANNIHILATE YOU!!
HEY! GOOD TO SEE YOU GUYS!
CALM YOURSELF, MOOSE! MURDER'S NOT NICE!!
CALM? ARCHIE, I MEDITATE AND PRACTICE YOGA DAILY! I'M IN TOUCH WITH MY INNER SELF!
I WAS CONTROLLING AND HAD ANGER MANAGEMENT ISSUES. MIDGE WAS RIGHT TO MOVE ON. ONCE I HELP MYSELF, I'LL FIND HAPPINESS, TOO!
3

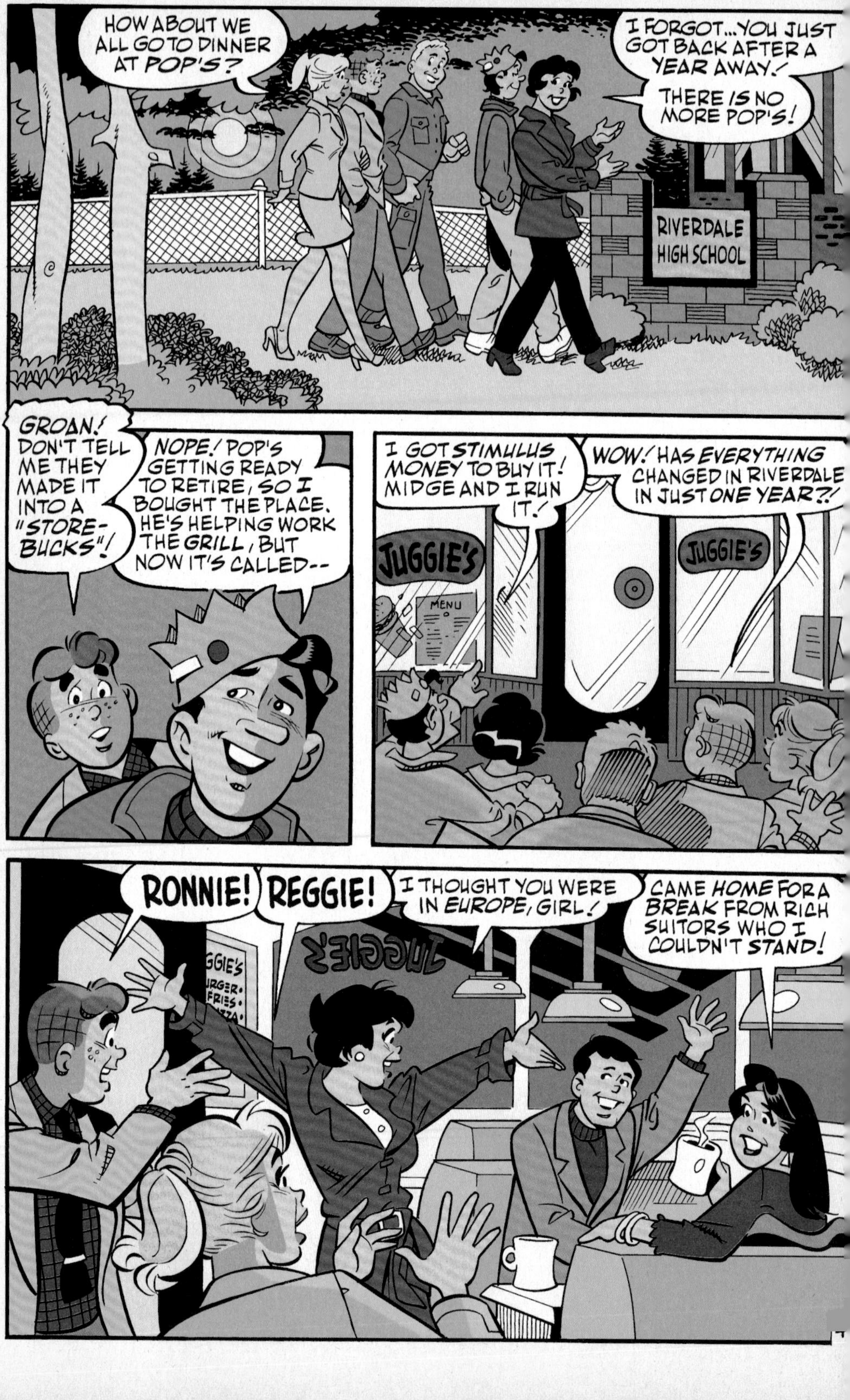
HOW ABOUT WE ALL GO TO DINNER AT POP'S?
I FORGOT...YOU JUST GOT BACK AFTER A YEAR AWAY!
THERE IS NO MORE POP'S!
RIVERDALE HIGH SCHOOL
GROAN! DON'T TELL ME THEY MADE IT INTO A "STORE-BUCKS"!
NOPE! POP'S GETTING READY TO RETIRE, SO I BOUGHT THE PLACE. HE'S HELPING WORK THE GRILL, BUT NOW IT'S CALLED--
I GOT STIMULUS MONEY TO BUY IT! MIDGE AND I RUN IT!
WOW! HAS EVERYTHING CHANGED IN RIVERDALE IN JUST ONE YEAR?!
JUGGIE'S
MENU
JUGGIE'S
RONNIE!
REGGIE!
I THOUGHT YOU WERE IN EUROPE, GIRL!
CAME HOME FOR A BREAK FROM RICH SUITORS WHO I COULDN'T STAND!

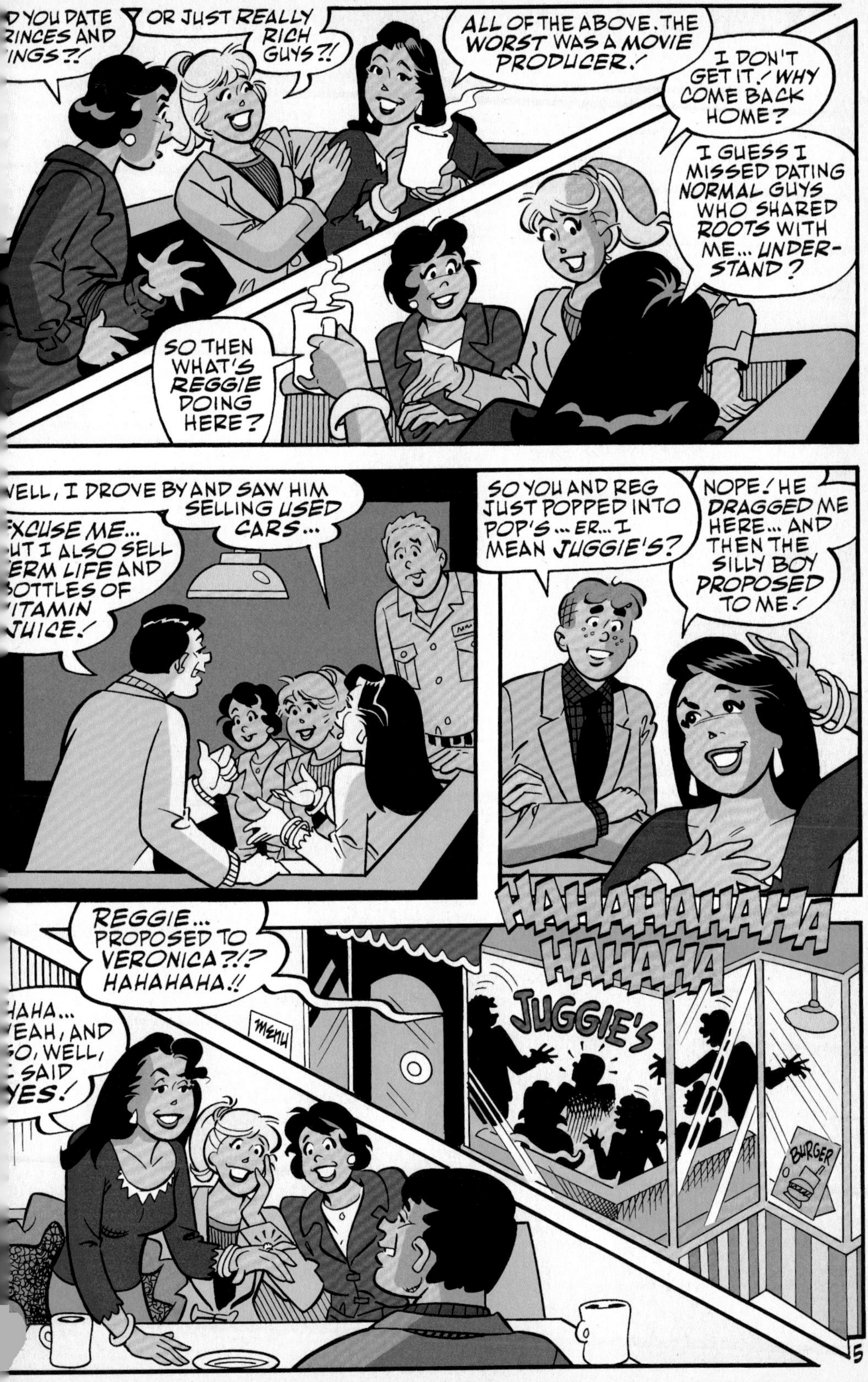
D YOU DATE RINCES AND INGS?!
OR JUST REALLY RICH GUYS?!
ALL OF THE ABOVE. THE WORST WAS A MOVIE PRODUCER!
I DON'T GET IT! WHY COME BACK HOME?
I GUESS I MISSED DATING NORMAL GUYS WHO SHARED ROOTS WITH ME... UNDER-STAND?
SO THEN WHAT'S REGGIE DOING HERE?
VELL, I DROVE BY AND SAW HIM SELLING USED CARS...
XCUSE ME... UT I ALSO SELL ERM LIFE AND OTTLES OF ITAMIN UICE!
SO YOU AND REG JUST POPPED INTO POP'S... ER... I MEAN JUGGIE'S?
NOPE! HE DRAGGED ME HERE... AND THEN THE SILLY BOY PROPOSED TO ME!
HAHAHAHAHAHA HAHAHA
REGGIE... PROPOSED TO VERONICA?!? HAHAHAHA!!
HAHA... YEAH, AND SO, WELL, SAID YES!
MENU
JUGGIE'S
BURGER
5

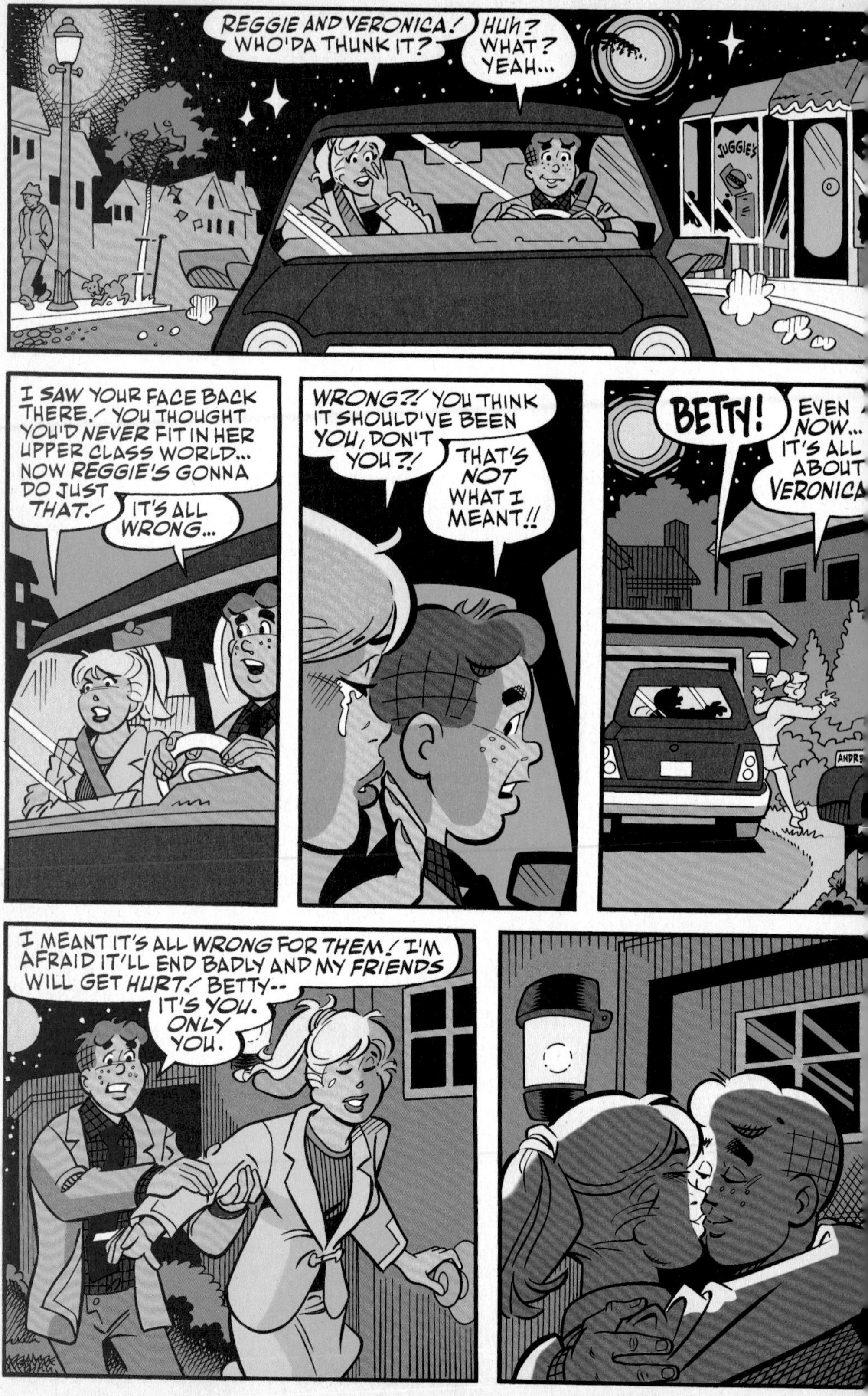
REGGIE AND VERONICA! WHO'DA THUNK IT?
HUH? WHAT? YEAH...
JUGGIE'S
I SAW YOUR FACE BACK THERE! YOU THOUGHT YOU'D NEVER FIT IN HER UPPER CLASS WORLD... NOW REGGIE'S GONNA DO JUST THAT!
IT'S ALL WRONG...
WRONG?! YOU THINK IT SHOULD'VE BEEN YOU, DON'T YOU?!
THAT'S NOT WHAT I MEANT!!
BETTY!
EVEN NOW... IT'S ALL ABOUT VERONICA
I MEANT IT'S ALL WRONG FOR THEM! I'M AFRAID IT'LL END BADLY AND MY FRIENDS WILL GET HURT! BETTY--
IT'S YOU. ONLY YOU.

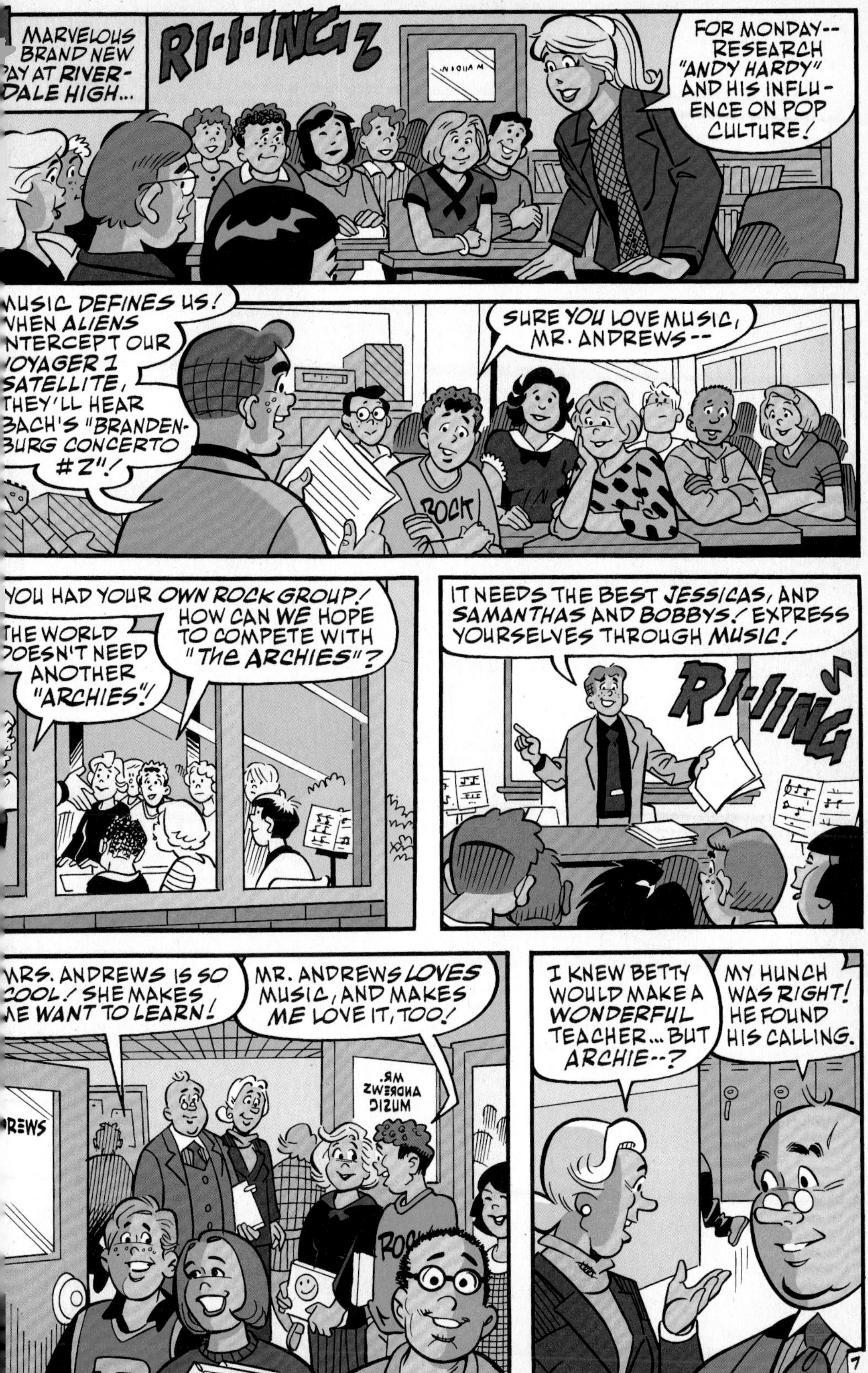
MARVELOUS BRAND NEW AY AT RIVER-DALE HIGH...
RI-I-ING
FOR MONDAY-- RESEARCH "ANDY HARDY" AND HIS INFLU-ENCE ON POP CULTURE!
USIC DEFINES US! HEN ALIENS NTERCEPT OUR OYAGER 1 SATELLITE, THEY'LL HEAR BACH'S "BRANDEN-BURG CONCERTO #2"!
SURE YOU LOVE MUSIC, MR. ANDREWS--
ROCK
YOU HAD YOUR OWN ROCK GROUP!
HOW CAN WE HOPE TO COMPETE WITH "THE ARCHIES"?
THE WORLD OESN'T NEED ANOTHER "ARCHIES"!
IT NEEDS THE BEST JESSICAS, AND SAMANTHAS AND BOBBYS! EXPRESS YOURSELVES THROUGH MUSIC!
RI-ING
RS. ANDREWS IS SO OOL! SHE MAKES E WANT TO LEARN!
MR. ANDREWS LOVES MUSIC, AND MAKES ME LOVE IT, TOO!
REWS
MR. ANDREWS MUSIC
I KNEW BETTY WOULD MAKE A WONDERFUL TEACHER... BUT ARCHIE--?
MY HUNCH WAS RIGHT! HE FOUND HIS CALLING.
7

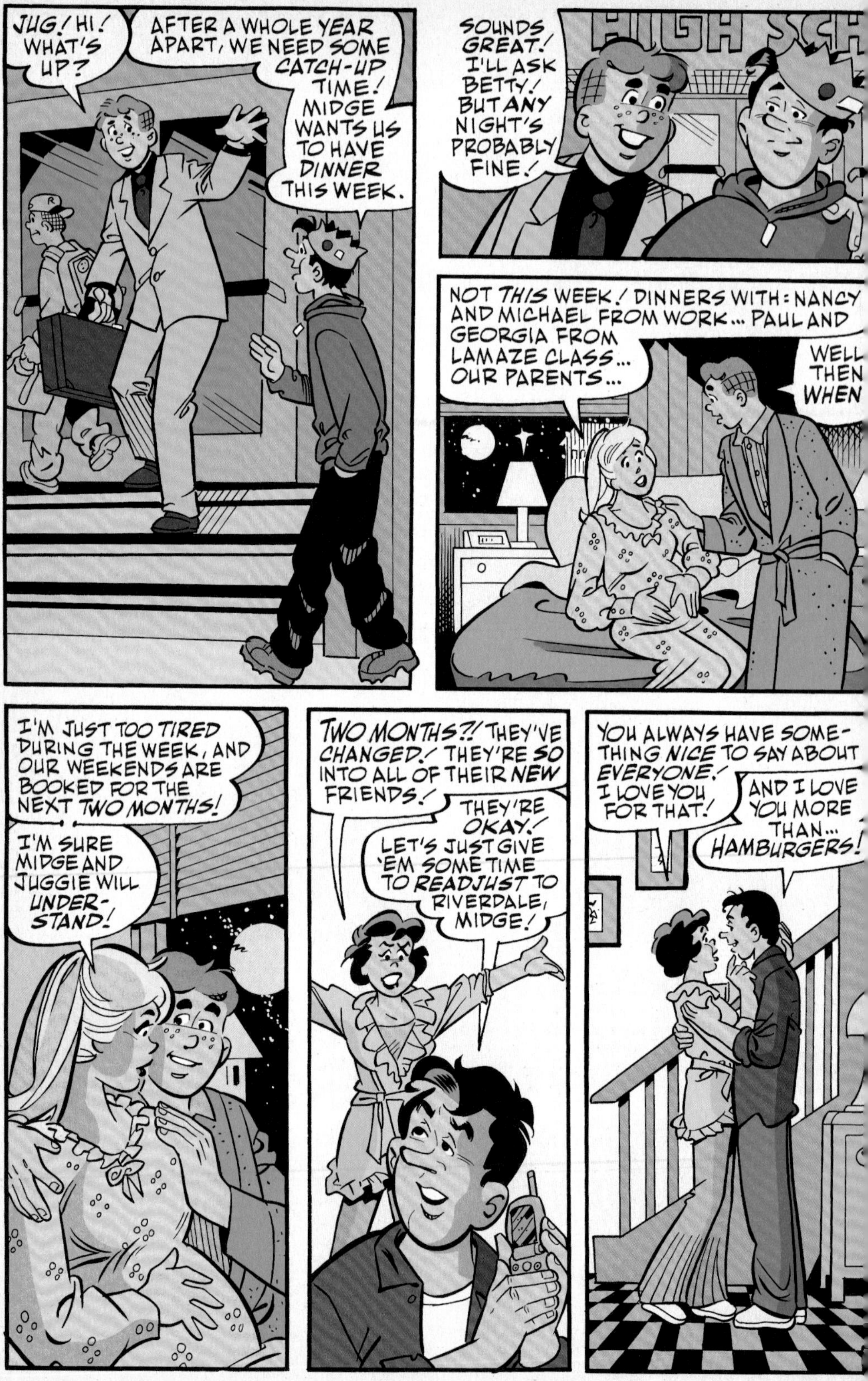
JUG! HI! WHAT'S UP?
AFTER A WHOLE YEAR APART, WE NEED SOME CATCH-UP TIME! MIDGE WANTS US TO HAVE DINNER THIS WEEK.
SOUNDS GREAT! I'LL ASK BETTY! BUT ANY NIGHT'S PROBABLY FINE!
NOT THIS WEEK! DINNERS WITH: NANCY AND MICHAEL FROM WORK... PAUL AND GEORGIA FROM LAMAZE CLASS... OUR PARENTS...
WELL THEN WHEN
I'M JUST TOO TIRED DURING THE WEEK, AND OUR WEEKENDS ARE BOOKED FOR THE NEXT TWO MONTHS!
I'M SURE MIDGE AND JUGGIE WILL UNDERSTAND!
TWO MONTHS?! THEY'VE CHANGED! THEY'RE SO INTO ALL OF THEIR NEW FRIENDS!
THEY'RE OKAY! LET'S JUST GIVE 'EM SOME TIME TO READJUST TO RIVERDALE, MIDGE!
YOU ALWAYS HAVE SOMETHING NICE TO SAY ABOUT EVERYONE! I LOVE YOU FOR THAT!
AND I LOVE YOU MORE THAN... HAMBURGERS!

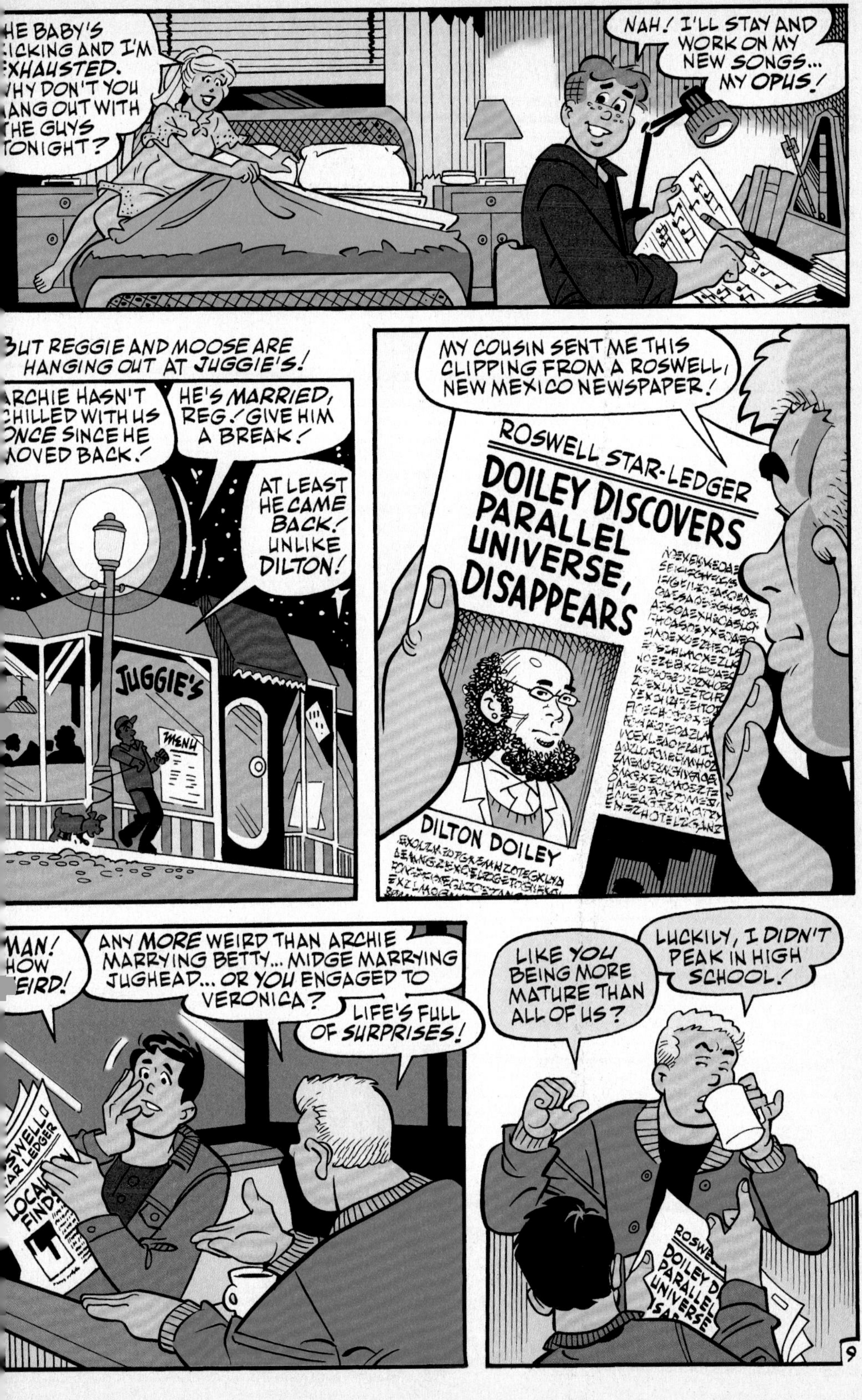
HE BABY'S ICKING AND I'M EXHAUSTED. WHY DON'T YOU HANG OUT WITH THE GUYS TONIGHT?
NAH! I'LL STAY AND WORK ON MY NEW SONGS... MY OPUS!
BUT REGGIE AND MOOSE ARE HANGING OUT AT JUGGIE'S!
ARCHIE HASN'T CHILLED WITH US ONCE SINCE HE MOVED BACK.!
HE'S MARRIED, REG.! GIVE HIM A BREAK!
AT LEAST HE CAME BACK! UNLIKE DILTON!
JUGGIE'S
MENU
MY COUSIN SENT ME THIS CLIPPING FROM A ROSWELL, NEW MEXICO NEWSPAPER!
ROSWELL STAR-LEDGER
DOILEY DISCOVERS PARALLEL UNIVERSE, DISAPPEARS
DILTON DOILEY
MAN! HOW WEIRD!
ANY MORE WEIRD THAN ARCHIE MARRYING BETTY... MIDGE MARRYING JUGHEAD... OR YOU ENGAGED TO VERONICA?
LIFE'S FULL OF SURPRISES!
LIKE YOU BEING MORE MATURE THAN ALL OF US?
LUCKILY, I DIDN'T PEAK IN HIGH SCHOOL!
9

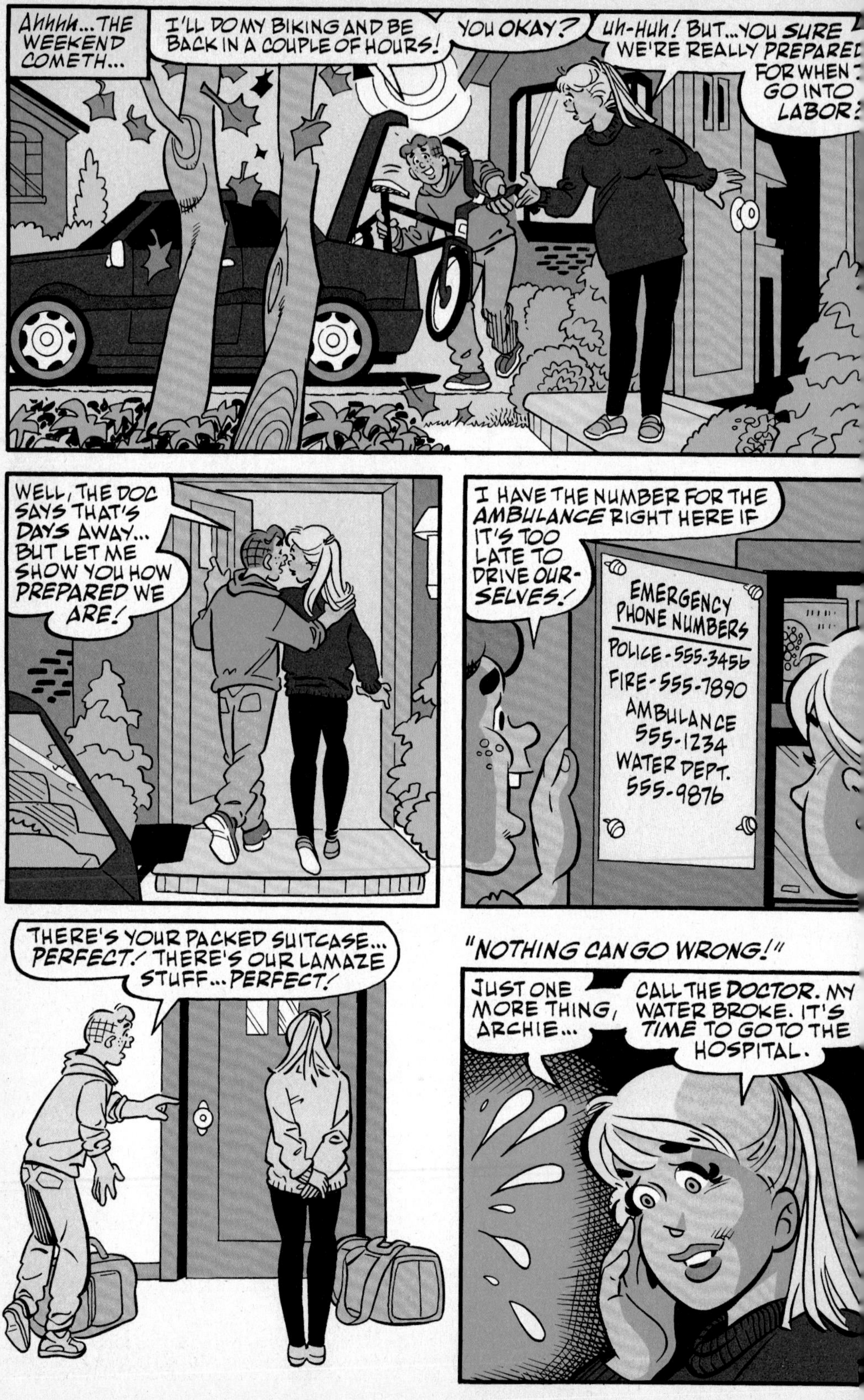
Ahhhh...THE WEEKEND COMETH...
I'LL DO MY BIKING AND BE BACK IN A COUPLE OF HOURS!
YOU OKAY?
UH-HUH! BUT...YOU SURE WE'RE REALLY PREPARED FOR WHEN I GO INTO LABOR?
WELL, THE DOC SAYS THAT'S DAYS AWAY... BUT LET ME SHOW YOU HOW PREPARED WE ARE!
I HAVE THE NUMBER FOR THE AMBULANCE RIGHT HERE IF IT'S TOO LATE TO DRIVE OURSELVES!
EMERGENCY PHONE NUMBERS
POLICE-555-3456
FIRE-555-7890
AMBULANCE 555-1234
WATER DEPT. 555-9876
THERE'S YOUR PACKED SUITCASE... PERFECT! THERE'S OUR LAMAZE STUFF...PERFECT!
"NOTHING CAN GO WRONG!"
JUST ONE MORE THING, ARCHIE...
CALL THE DOCTOR. MY WATER BROKE. IT'S TIME TO GO TO THE HOSPITAL.

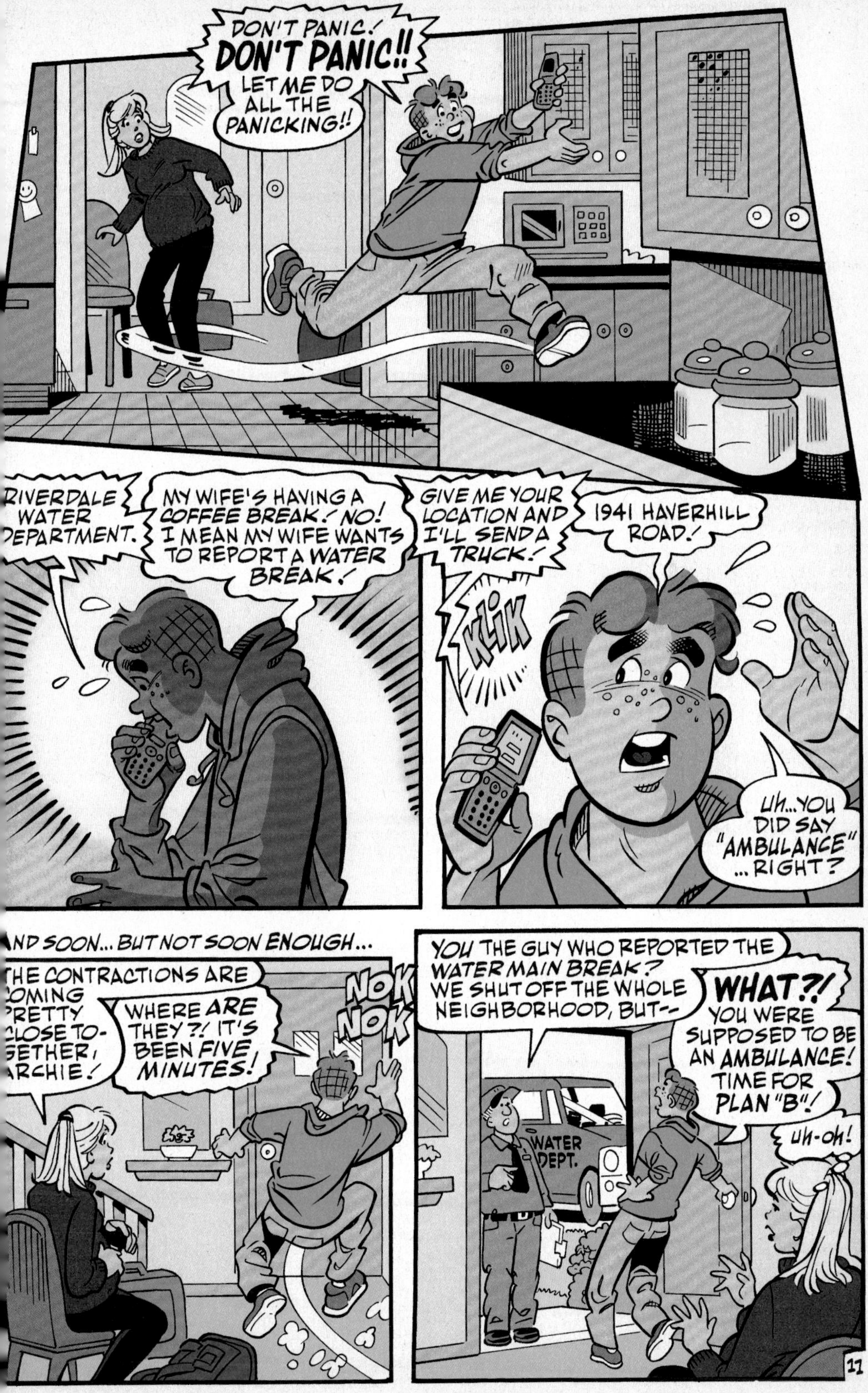
DON'T PANIC! DON'T PANIC!! LET ME DO ALL THE PANICKING!!
RIVERDALE WATER DEPARTMENT.
MY WIFE'S HAVING A COFFEE BREAK! NO! I MEAN MY WIFE WANTS TO REPORT A WATER BREAK!
GIVE ME YOUR LOCATION AND I'LL SEND A TRUCK!
1941 HAVERHILL ROAD!
KLIK
UH...YOU DID SAY "AMBULANCE" ...RIGHT?
AND SOON... BUT NOT SOON ENOUGH...
THE CONTRACTIONS ARE COMING PRETTY CLOSE TOGETHER, ARCHIE!
WHERE ARE THEY?! IT'S BEEN FIVE MINUTES!
NOK NOK
YOU THE GUY WHO REPORTED THE WATER MAIN BREAK? WE SHUT OFF THE WHOLE NEIGHBORHOOD, BUT--
WATER DEPT.
WHAT?! YOU WERE SUPPOSED TO BE AN AMBULANCE! TIME FOR PLAN "B"!
UH-OH!
11

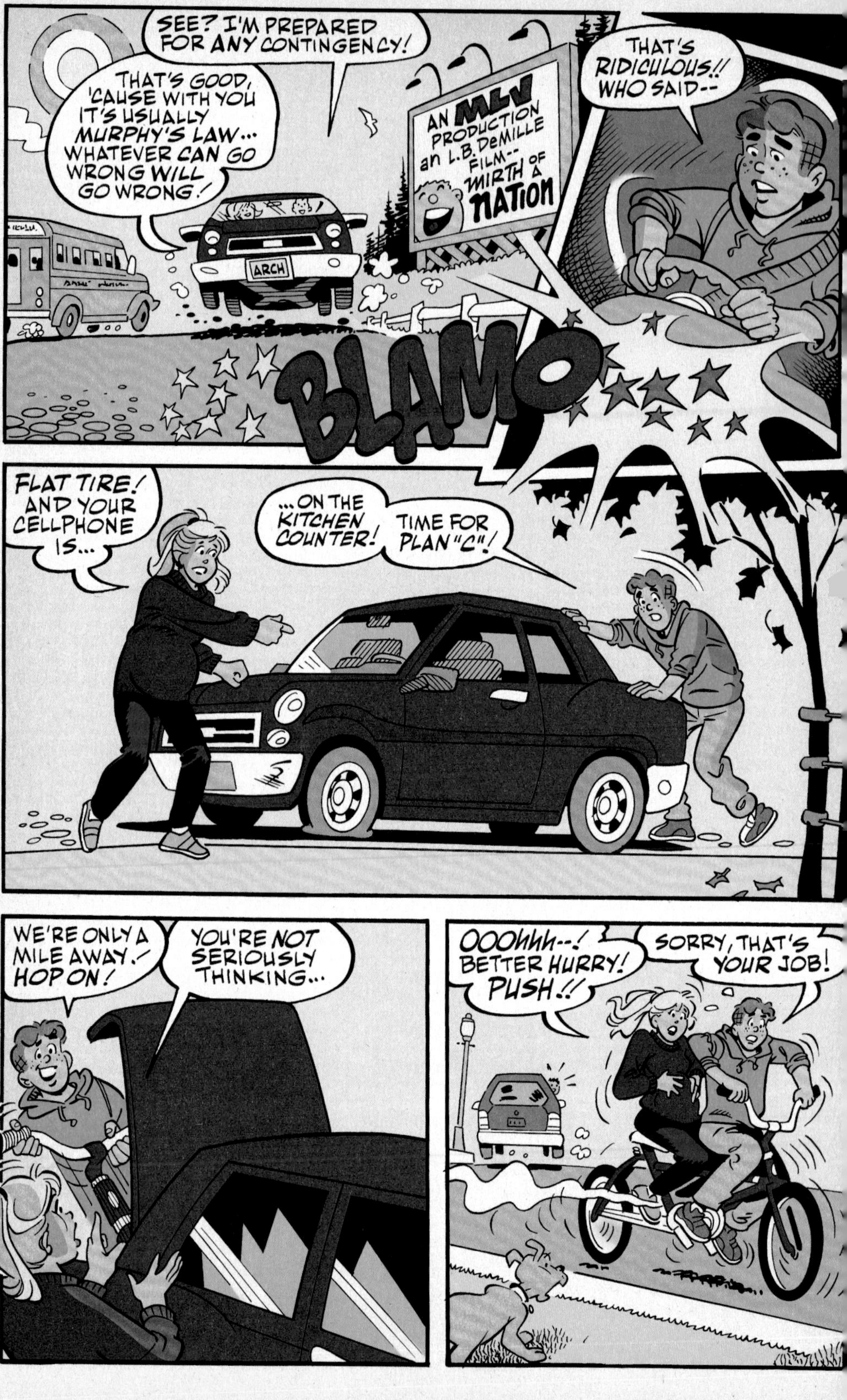
SEE? I'M PREPARED FOR ANY CONTINGENCY!
THAT'S GOOD, 'CAUSE WITH YOU IT'S USUALLY MURPHY'S LAW... WHATEVER CAN GO WRONG WILL GO WRONG!
AN MLV PRODUCTION an L.B. DeMILLE FILM-- MIRTH OF A NATION
ARCH
THAT'S RIDICULOUS!! WHO SAID--
BLAMO
FLAT TIRE! AND YOUR CELLPHONE IS...
...ON THE KITCHEN COUNTER!
TIME FOR PLAN "C"!
WE'RE ONLY A MILE AWAY. HOP ON!
YOU'RE NOT SERIOUSLY THINKING...
OOOhhh--! BETTER HURRY! PUSH!!
SORRY, THAT'S YOUR JOB!

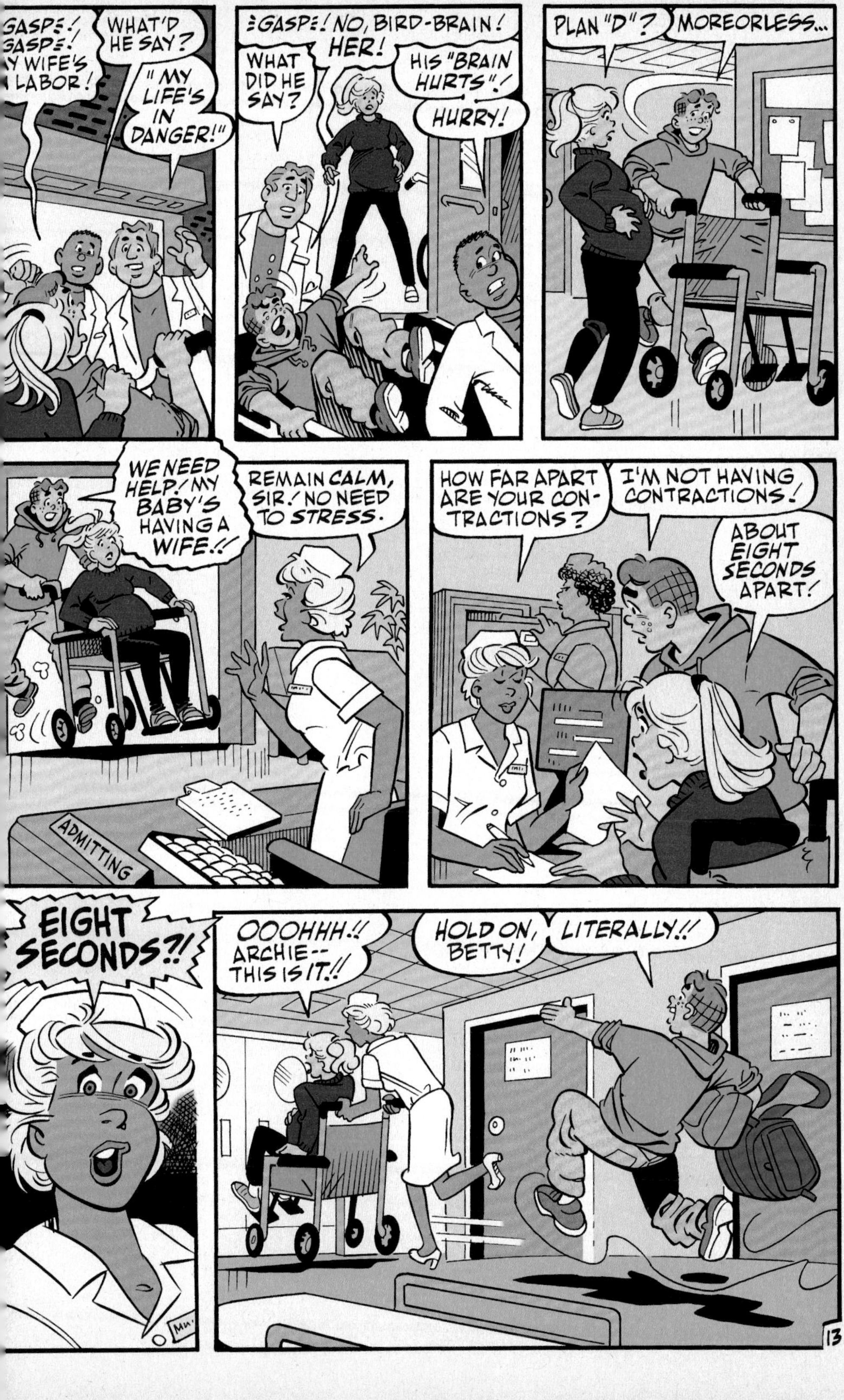
GASP! GASP! MY WIFE'S IN LABOR!
WHAT'D HE SAY?
"MY LIFE'S IN DANGER!"
GASP! NO, BIRD-BRAIN! HER!
WHAT DID HE SAY?
HIS "BRAIN HURTS"!
HURRY!
PLAN "D"?
MOREORLESS...
WE NEED HELP! MY BABY'S HAVING A WIFE!!
REMAIN CALM, SIR! NO NEED TO STRESS.
ADMITTING
HOW FAR APART ARE YOUR CONTRACTIONS?
I'M NOT HAVING CONTRACTIONS!
ABOUT EIGHT SECONDS APART!
EIGHT SECONDS?!
OOOHHH!! ARCHIE-- THIS IS IT!!
HOLD ON, BETTY!
LITERALLY!!
13

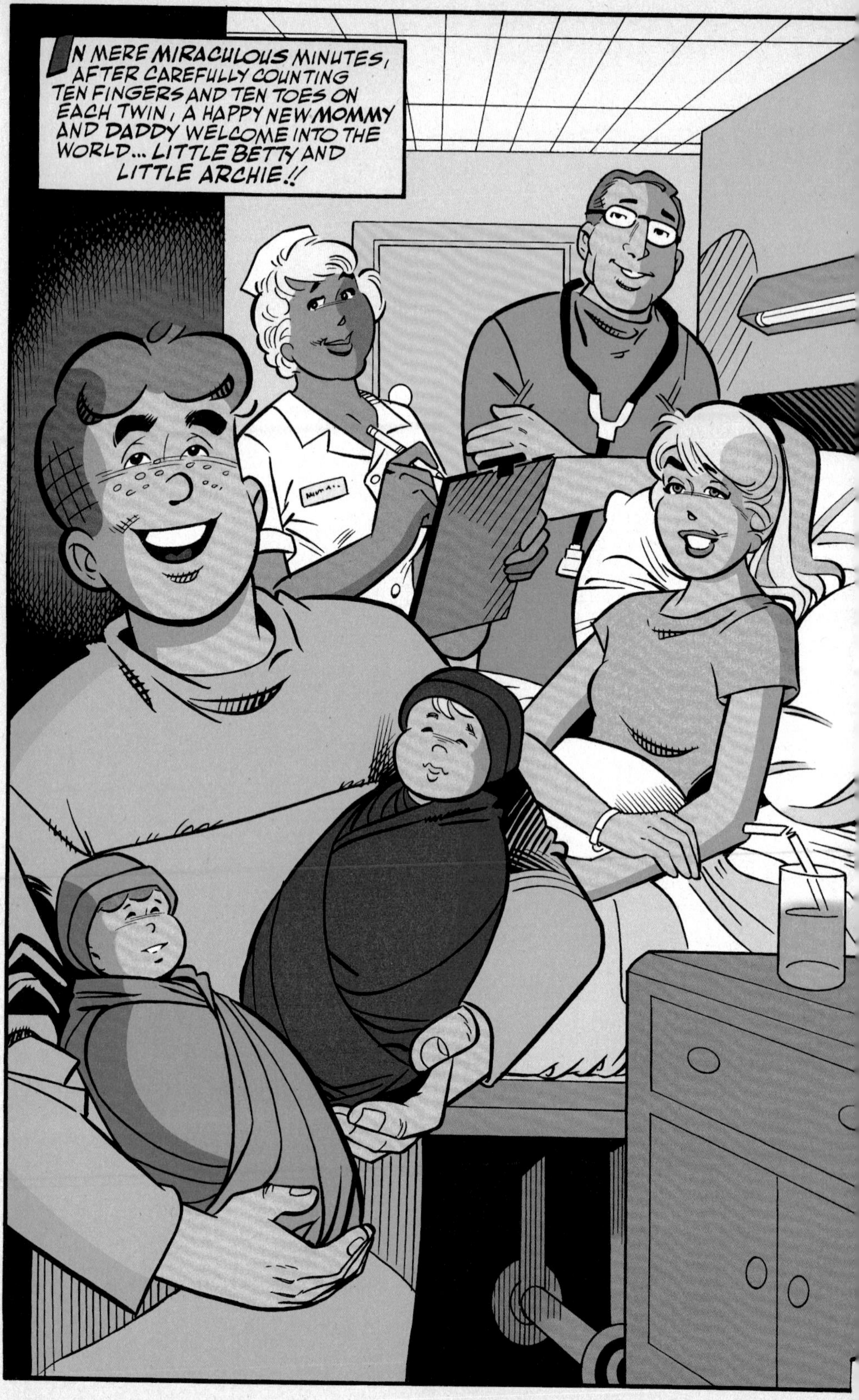
IN MERE MIRACULOUS MINUTES, AFTER CAREFULLY COUNTING TEN FINGERS AND TEN TOES ON EACH TWIN, A HAPPY NEW MOMMY AND DADDY WELCOME INTO THE WORLD... LITTLE BETTY AND LITTLE ARCHIE!!

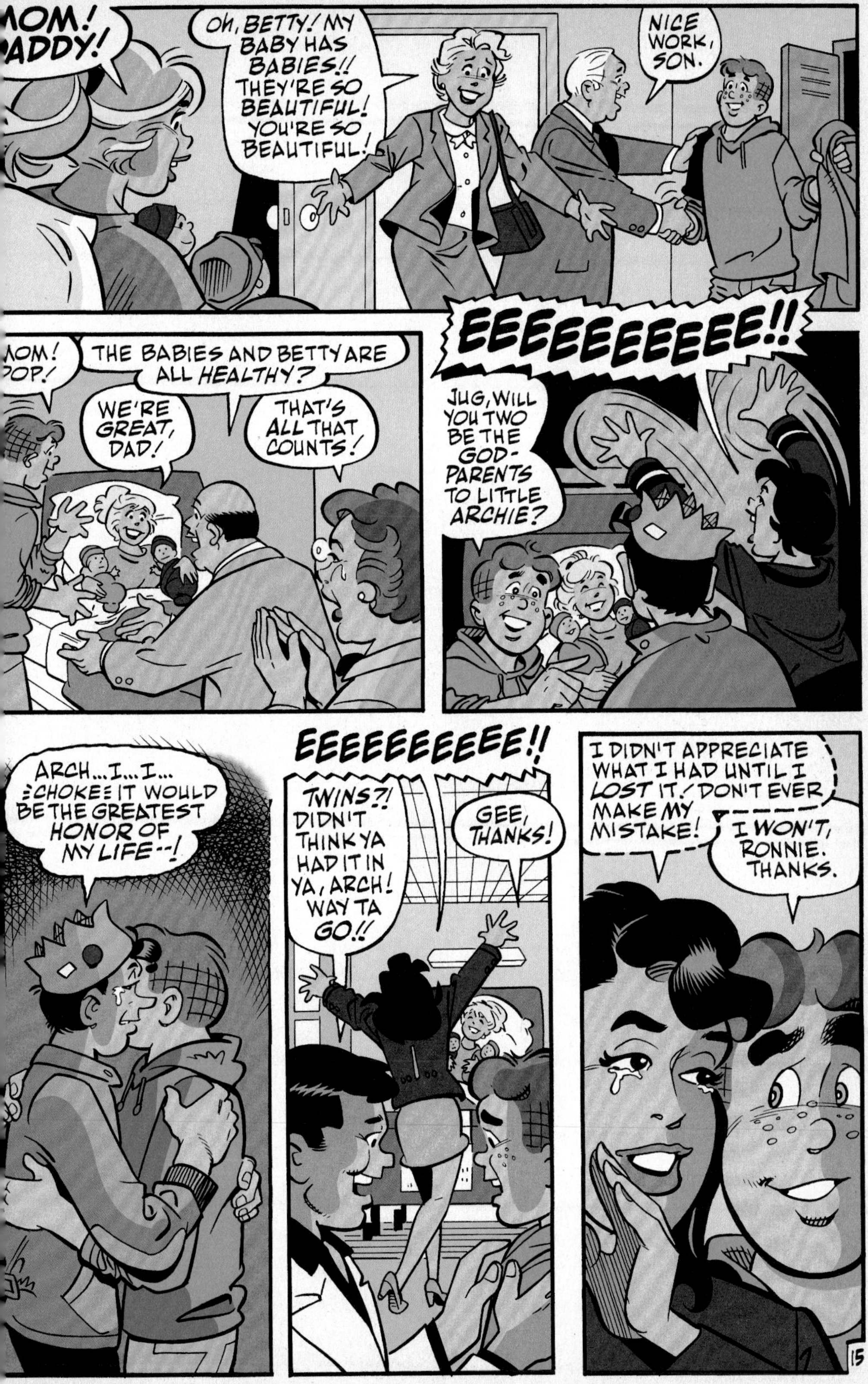
MOM! DADDY!
Oh, BETTY! MY BABY HAS BABIES!! THEY'RE SO BEAUTIFUL! YOU'RE SO BEAUTIFUL!
NICE WORK, SON.
MOM! POP!
THE BABIES AND BETTY ARE ALL HEALTHY?
WE'RE GREAT, DAD!
THAT'S ALL THAT COUNTS!
EEEEEEEEEEE!!
JUG, WILL YOU TWO BE THE GOD-PARENTS TO LITTLE ARCHIE?
ARCH... I... I... ≡CHOKE≡ IT WOULD BE THE GREATEST HONOR OF MY LIFE--!
EEEEEEEEEE!!
TWINS?! DIDN'T THINK YA HAD IT IN YA, ARCH! WAY TA GO!!
GEE, THANKS!
I DIDN'T APPRECIATE WHAT I HAD UNTIL I LOST IT. DON'T EVER MAKE MY MISTAKE!
I WON'T, RONNIE. THANKS.
15

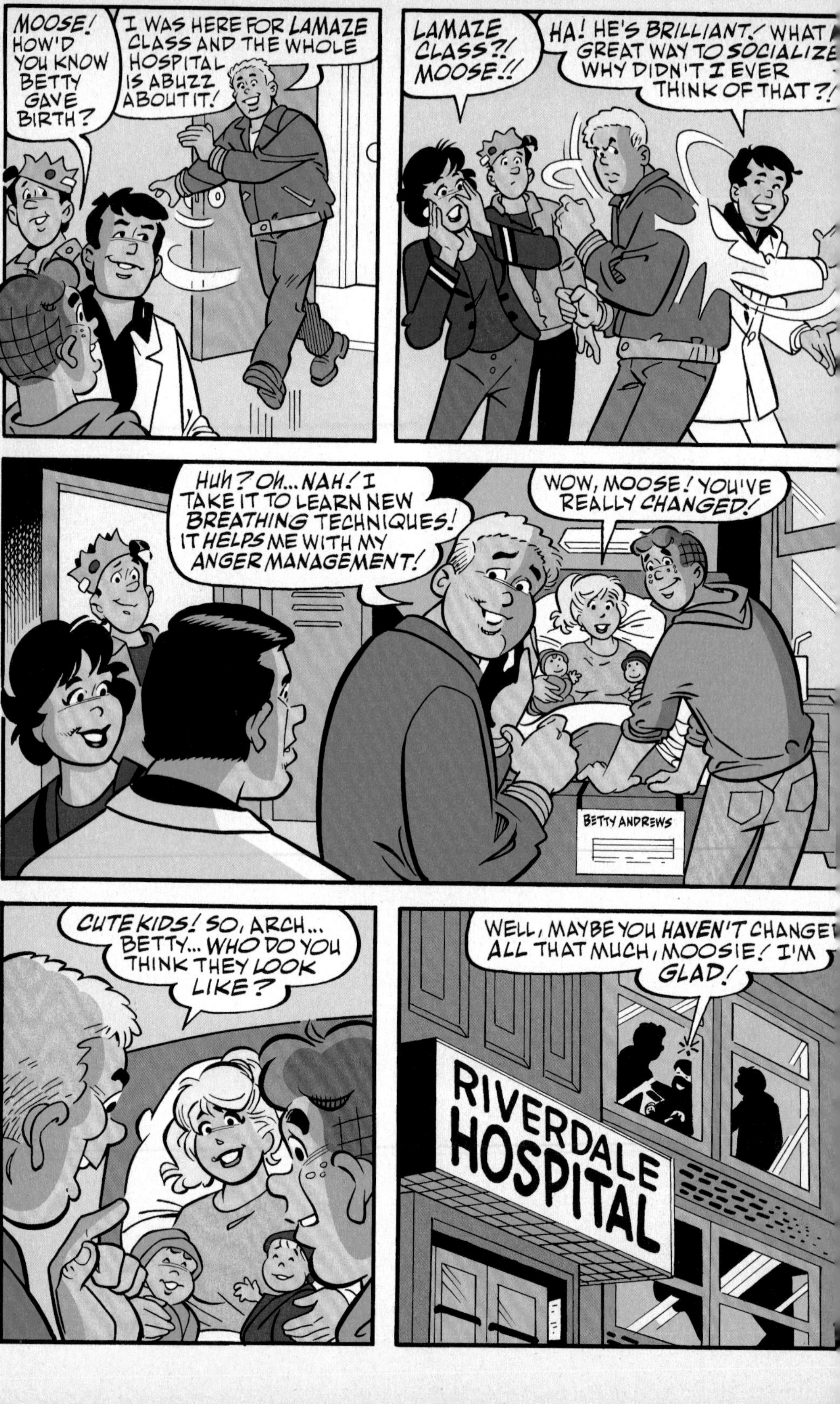
MOOSE! HOW'D YOU KNOW BETTY GAVE BIRTH?
I WAS HERE FOR LAMAZE CLASS AND THE WHOLE HOSPITAL IS ABUZZ ABOUT IT!
LAMAZE CLASS?! MOOSE!!
HA! HE'S BRILLIANT! WHAT A GREAT WAY TO SOCIALIZE! WHY DIDN'T I EVER THINK OF THAT?!
HUH? OH... NAH! I TAKE IT TO LEARN NEW BREATHING TECHNIQUES! IT HELPS ME WITH MY ANGER MANAGEMENT!
WOW, MOOSE! YOU'VE REALLY CHANGED!
BETTY ANDREWS
CUTE KIDS! SO, ARCH... BETTY... WHO DO YOU THINK THEY LOOK LIKE?
WELL, MAYBE YOU HAVEN'T CHANGED ALL THAT MUCH, MOOSIE! I'M GLAD!
RIVERDALE HOSPITAL

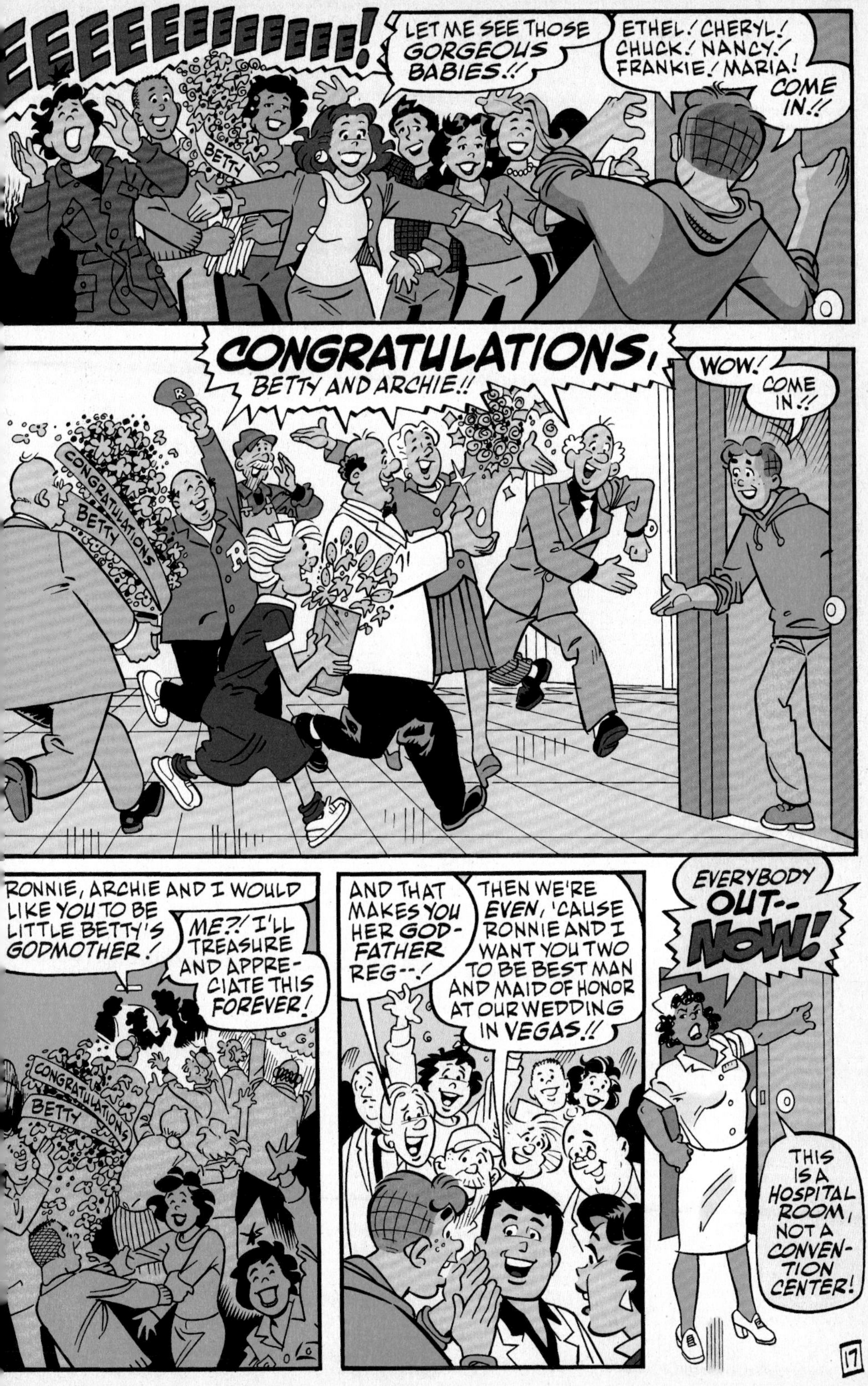
EEEEEEEEEEEEE!
LET ME SEE THOSE GORGEOUS BABIES!!
ETHEL! CHERYL! CHUCK! NANCY! FRANKIE! MARIA!
COME IN!!
BETTY
CONGRATULATIONS, BETTY AND ARCHIE!!
WOW!
COME IN!!
CONGRATULATIONS
BETTY
RONNIE, ARCHIE AND I WOULD LIKE YOU TO BE LITTLE BETTY'S GODMOTHER!
ME?! I'LL TREASURE AND APPRECIATE THIS FOREVER!
CONGRATULATIONS
BETTY
AND THAT MAKES YOU HER GOD-FATHER REG--!
THEN WE'RE EVEN, 'CAUSE RONNIE AND I WANT YOU TWO TO BE BEST MAN AND MAID OF HONOR AT OUR WEDDING IN VEGAS!!
EVERYBODY OUT-- NOW!
THIS IS A HOSPITAL ROOM, NOT A CONVENTION CENTER!
17

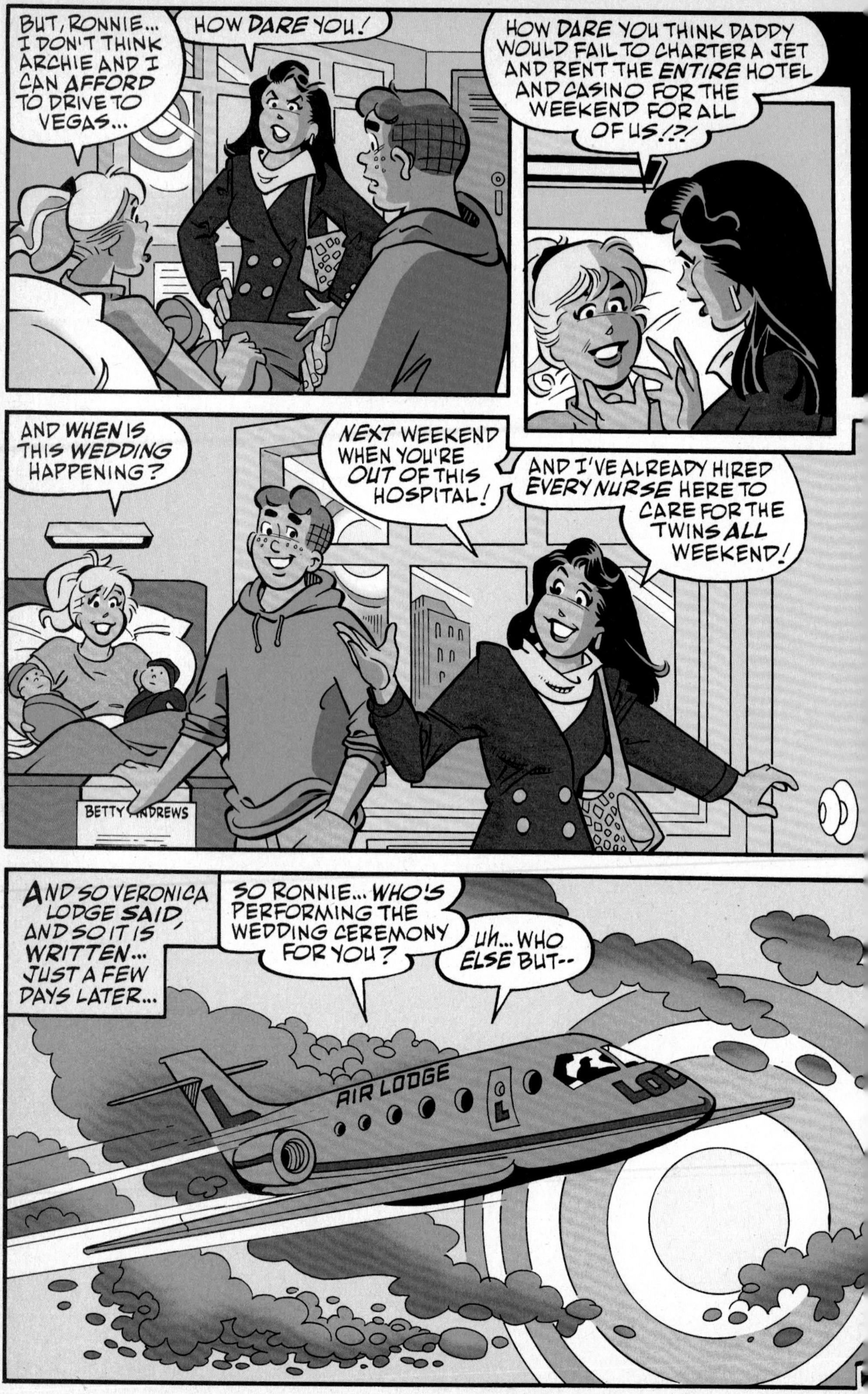
BUT, RONNIE... I DON'T THINK ARCHIE AND I CAN AFFORD TO DRIVE TO VEGAS...
HOW DARE YOU!
HOW DARE YOU THINK DADDY WOULD FAIL TO CHARTER A JET AND RENT THE ENTIRE HOTEL AND CASINO FOR THE WEEKEND FOR ALL OF US!?!
AND WHEN IS THIS WEDDING HAPPENING?
NEXT WEEKEND WHEN YOU'RE OUT OF THIS HOSPITAL!
AND I'VE ALREADY HIRED EVERY NURSE HERE TO CARE FOR THE TWINS ALL WEEKEND!
BETTY ANDREWS
AND SO VERONICA LODGE SAID, AND SO IT IS WRITTEN... JUST A FEW DAYS LATER...
SO RONNIE... WHO'S PERFORMING THE WEDDING CEREMONY FOR YOU?
UH... WHO ELSE BUT--
AIR LODGE

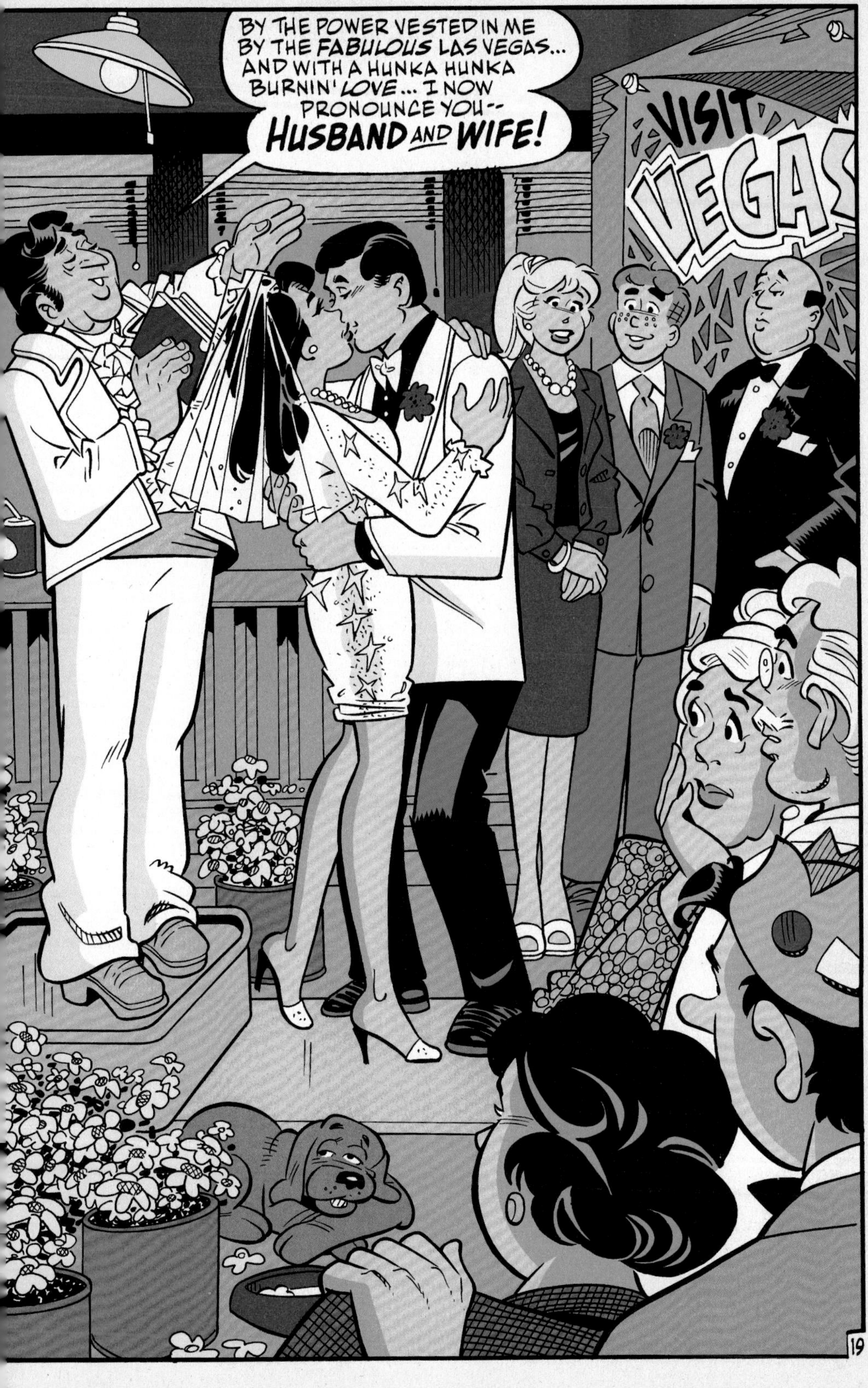
BY THE POWER VESTED IN ME BY THE FABULOUS LAS VEGAS... AND WITH A HUNKA HUNKA BURNIN' LOVE... I NOW PRONOUNCE YOU-- HUSBAND AND WIFE!
VISIT VEGAS
19

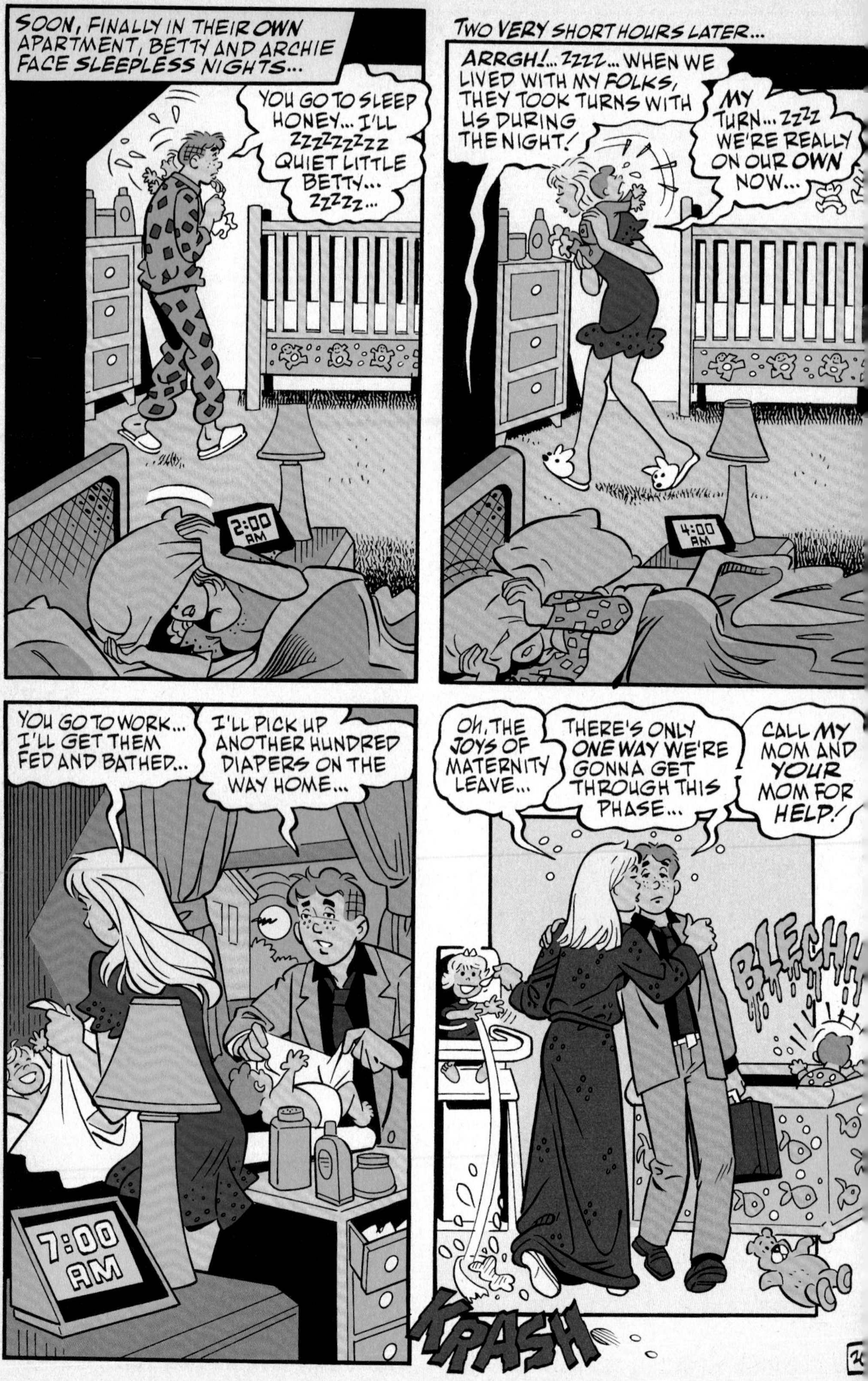
SOON, FINALLY IN THEIR OWN APARTMENT, BETTY AND ARCHIE FACE SLEEPLESS NIGHTS...
YOU GO TO SLEEP HONEY... I'LL ZZZZZZZZZ QUIET LITTLE BETTY... ZZZZZ...
2:00 AM
TWO VERY SHORT HOURS LATER...
ARRGH!... ZZZZ... WHEN WE LIVED WITH MY FOLKS, THEY TOOK TURNS WITH US DURING THE NIGHT!
MY TURN... ZZZZ WE'RE REALLY ON OUR OWN NOW...
4:00 AM
YOU GO TO WORK... I'LL GET THEM FED AND BATHED...
I'LL PICK UP ANOTHER HUNDRED DIAPERS ON THE WAY HOME...
7:00 AM
OH, THE JOYS OF MATERNITY LEAVE...
THERE'S ONLY ONE WAY WE'RE GONNA GET THROUGH THIS PHASE...
CALL MY MOM AND YOUR MOM FOR HELP!
BLECHH
KRASH

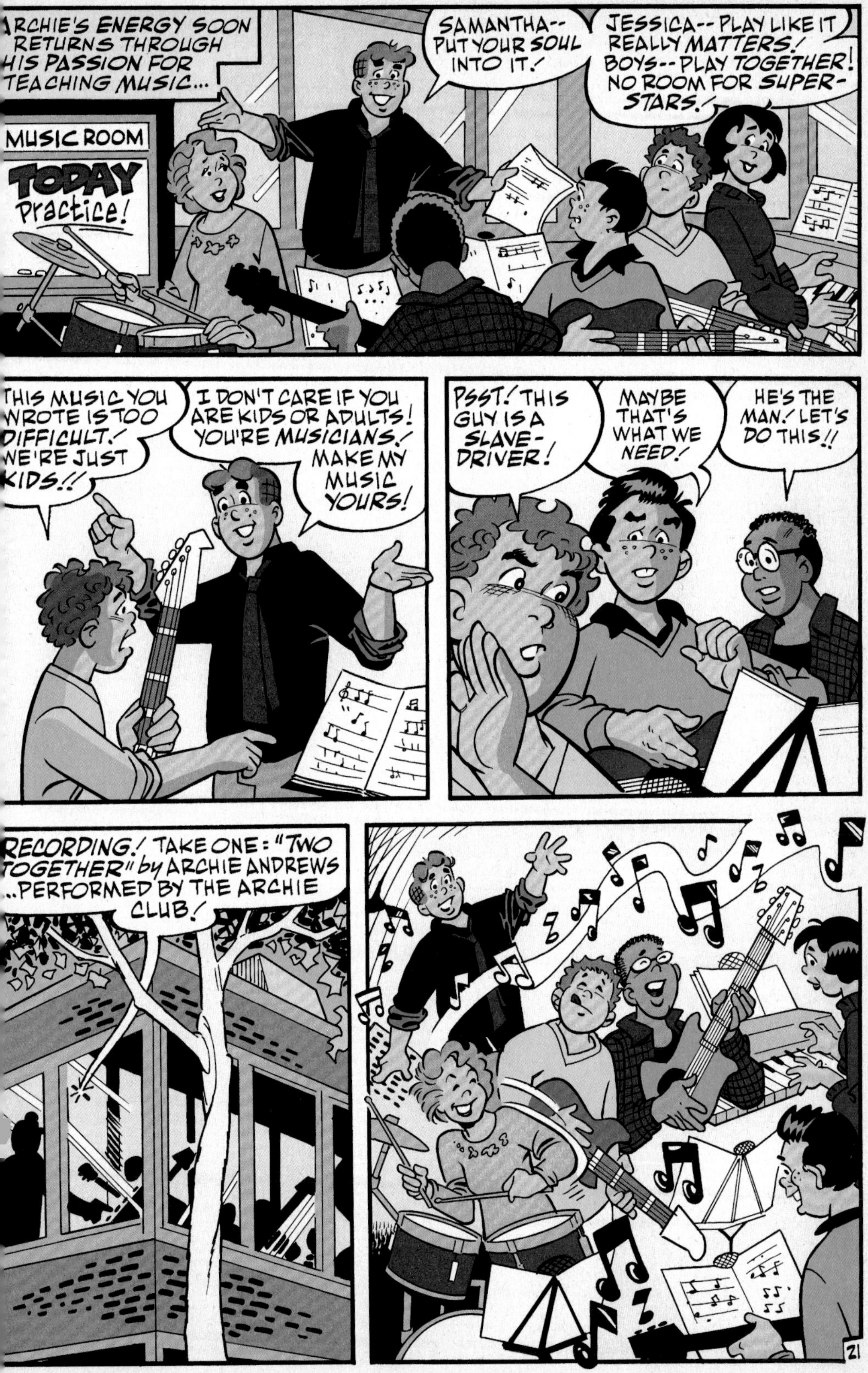

ARCHIE'S ENERGY SOON RETURNS THROUGH HIS PASSION FOR TEACHING MUSIC...
SAMANTHA-- PUT YOUR SOUL INTO IT!
JESSICA-- PLAY LIKE IT REALLY MATTERS! BOYS-- PLAY TOGETHER! NO ROOM FOR SUPER-STARS!
MUSIC ROOM
TODAY Practice!
THIS MUSIC YOU WROTE IS TOO DIFFICULT! WE'RE JUST KIDS!!
I DON'T CARE IF YOU ARE KIDS OR ADULTS! YOU'RE MUSICIANS! MAKE MY MUSIC YOURS!
PSST! THIS GUY IS A SLAVE-DRIVER!
MAYBE THAT'S WHAT WE NEED!
HE'S THE MAN! LET'S DO THIS!!
RECORDING! TAKE ONE: "TWO TOGETHER" by ARCHIE ANDREWS ...PERFORMED BY THE ARCHIE CLUB!
21

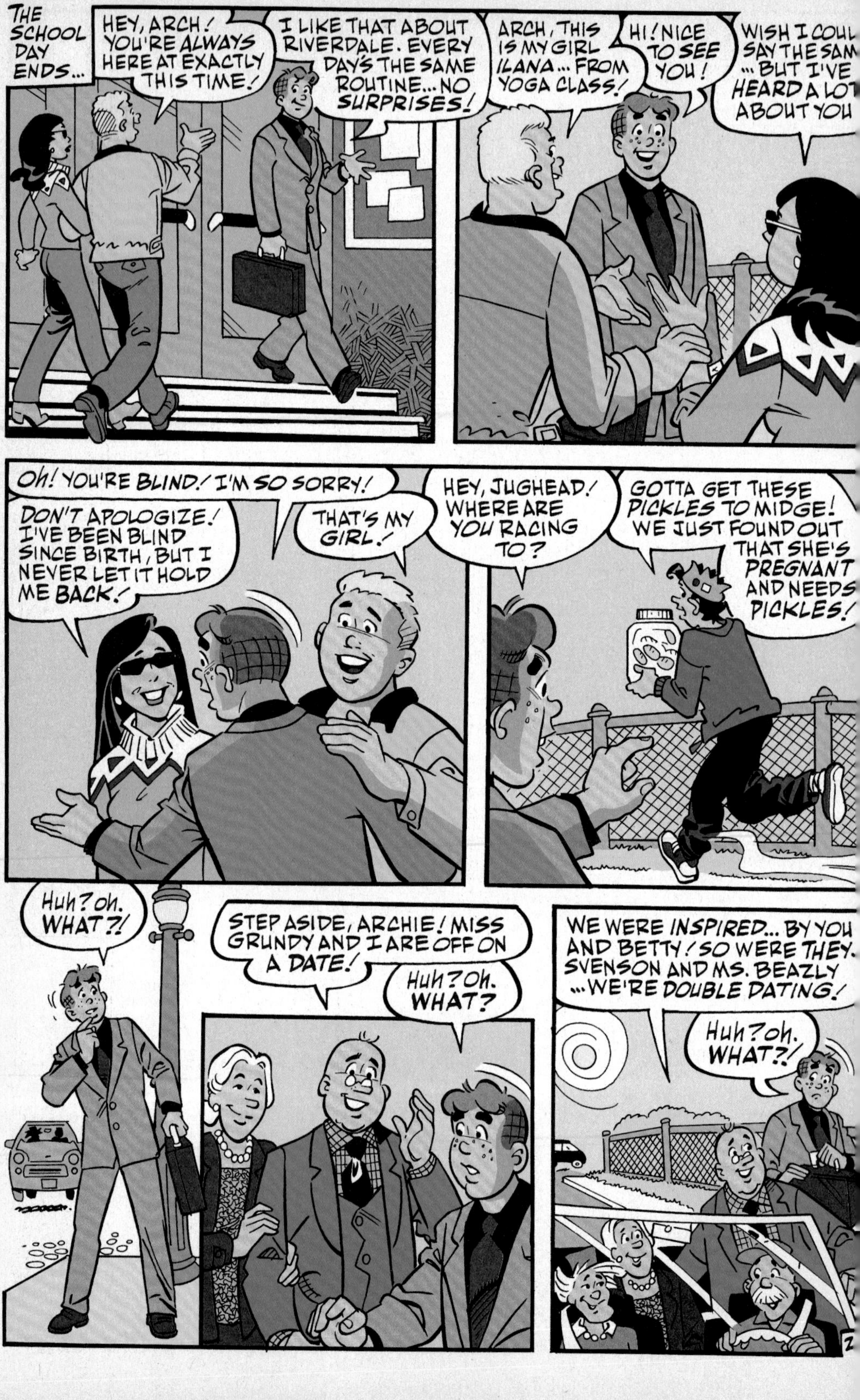
THE SCHOOL DAY ENDS...
HEY, ARCH! YOU'RE ALWAYS HERE AT EXACTLY THIS TIME!
I LIKE THAT ABOUT RIVERDALE. EVERY DAY'S THE SAME ROUTINE... NO SURPRISES!
ARCH, THIS IS MY GIRL ILANA... FROM YOGA CLASS!
HI! NICE TO SEE YOU!
WISH I COUL SAY THE SAM ... BUT I'VE HEARD A LOT ABOUT YOU
Oh! YOU'RE BLIND! I'M SO SORRY!
DON'T APOLOGIZE! I'VE BEEN BLIND SINCE BIRTH, BUT I NEVER LET IT HOLD ME BACK!
THAT'S MY GIRL!
HEY, JUGHEAD! WHERE ARE YOU RACING TO?
GOTTA GET THESE PICKLES TO MIDGE! WE JUST FOUND OUT THAT SHE'S PREGNANT AND NEEDS PICKLES!
Huh? oh. WHAT?!
STEP ASIDE, ARCHIE! MISS GRUNDY AND I ARE OFF ON A DATE!
Huh? oh. WHAT?
WE WERE INSPIRED... BY YOU AND BETTY! SO WERE THEY. SVENSON AND MS. BEAZLY ...WE'RE DOUBLE DATING!
Huh? oh. WHAT?!

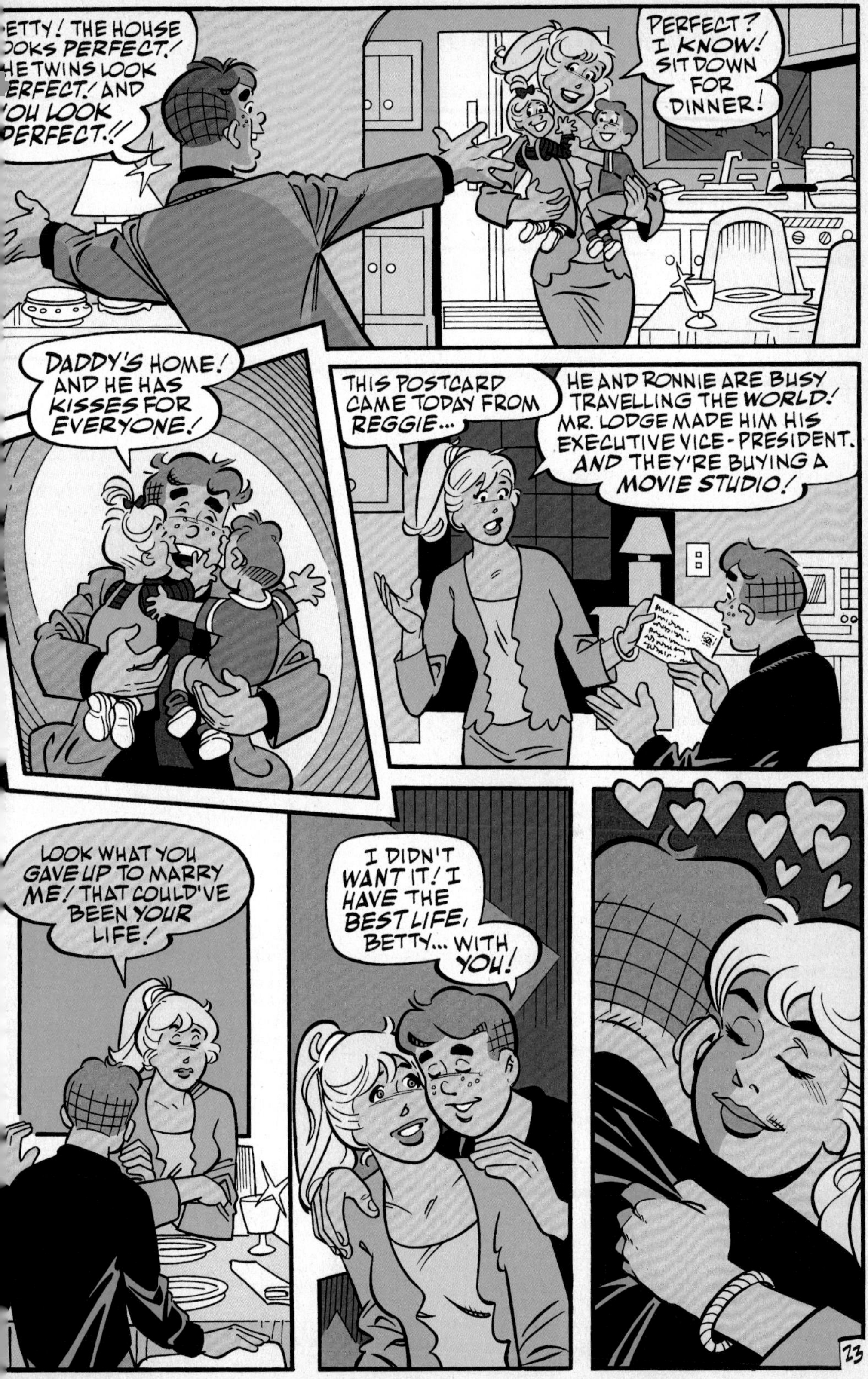
ETTY! THE HOUSE OOKS PERFECT! HE TWINS LOOK ERFECT! AND OU LOOK ERFECT!!
PERFECT? I KNOW! SIT DOWN FOR DINNER!
DADDY'S HOME! AND HE HAS KISSES FOR EVERYONE!
THIS POSTCARD CAME TODAY FROM REGGIE...
HE AND RONNIE ARE BUSY TRAVELLING THE WORLD! MR. LODGE MADE HIM HIS EXECUTIVE VICE-PRESIDENT. AND THEY'RE BUYING A MOVIE STUDIO!
LOOK WHAT YOU GAVE UP TO MARRY ME! THAT COULD'VE BEEN YOUR LIFE!
I DIDN'T WANT IT! I HAVE THE BEST LIFE, BETTY... WITH YOU!
23

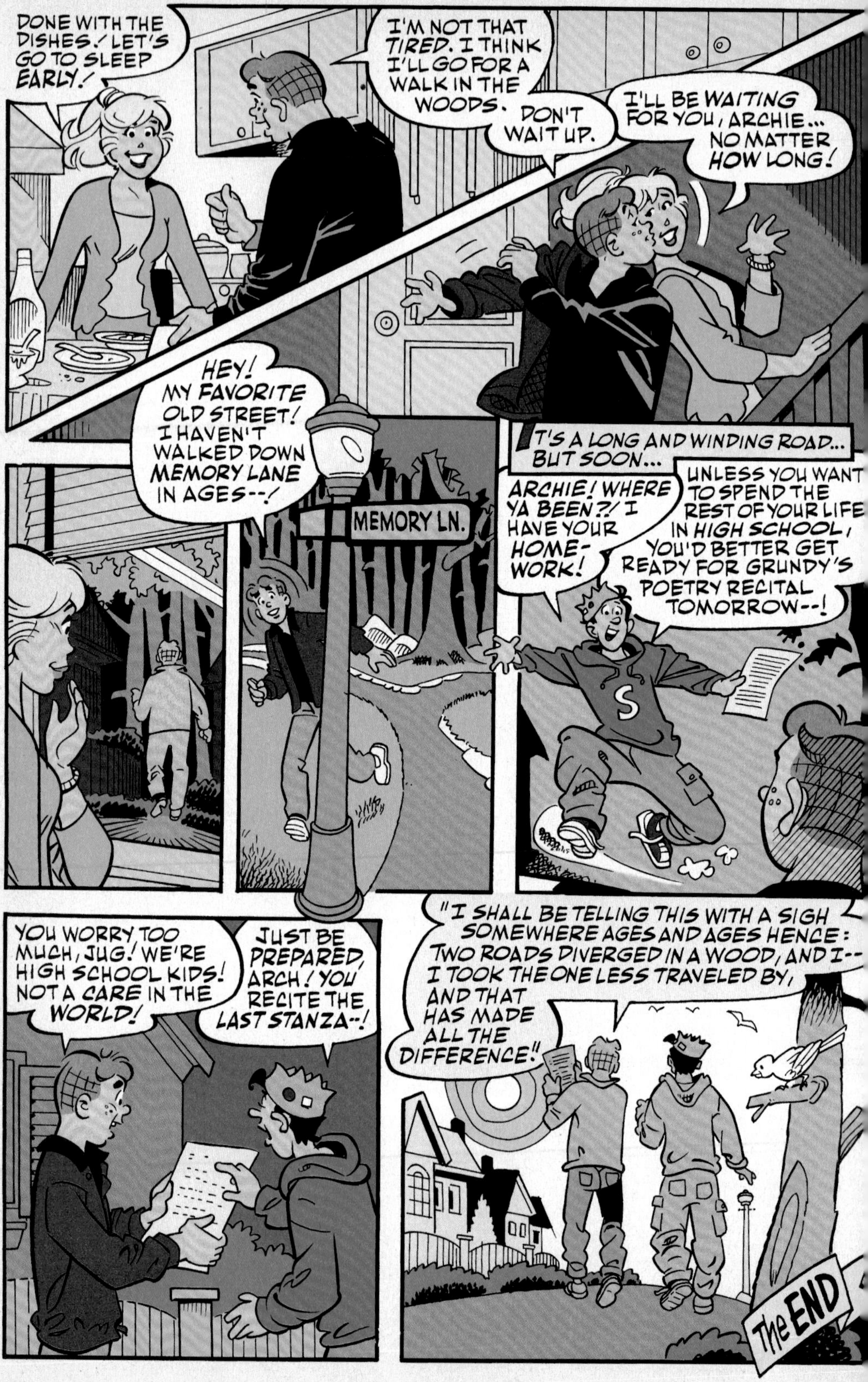
DONE WITH THE DISHES! LET'S GO TO SLEEP EARLY!
I'M NOT THAT TIRED. I THINK I'LL GO FOR A WALK IN THE WOODS.
DON'T WAIT UP.
I'LL BE WAITING FOR YOU, ARCHIE... NO MATTER HOW LONG!
HEY! MY FAVORITE OLD STREET! I HAVEN'T WALKED DOWN MEMORY LANE IN AGES--!
MEMORY LN.
IT'S A LONG AND WINDING ROAD... BUT SOON...
ARCHIE! WHERE YA BEEN?! I HAVE YOUR HOME-WORK!
UNLESS YOU WANT TO SPEND THE REST OF YOUR LIFE IN HIGH SCHOOL, YOU'D BETTER GET READY FOR GRUNDY'S POETRY RECITAL TOMORROW--!
YOU WORRY TOO MUCH, JUG! WE'RE HIGH SCHOOL KIDS! NOT A CARE IN THE WORLD!
JUST BE PREPARED, ARCH! YOU RECITE THE LAST STANZA--!
"I SHALL BE TELLING THIS WITH A SIGH SOMEWHERE AGES AND AGES HENCE: TWO ROADS DIVERGED IN A WOOD, AND I-- I TOOK THE ONE LESS TRAVELED BY, AND THAT HAS MADE ALL THE DIFFERENCE!"
The END

Epilogue

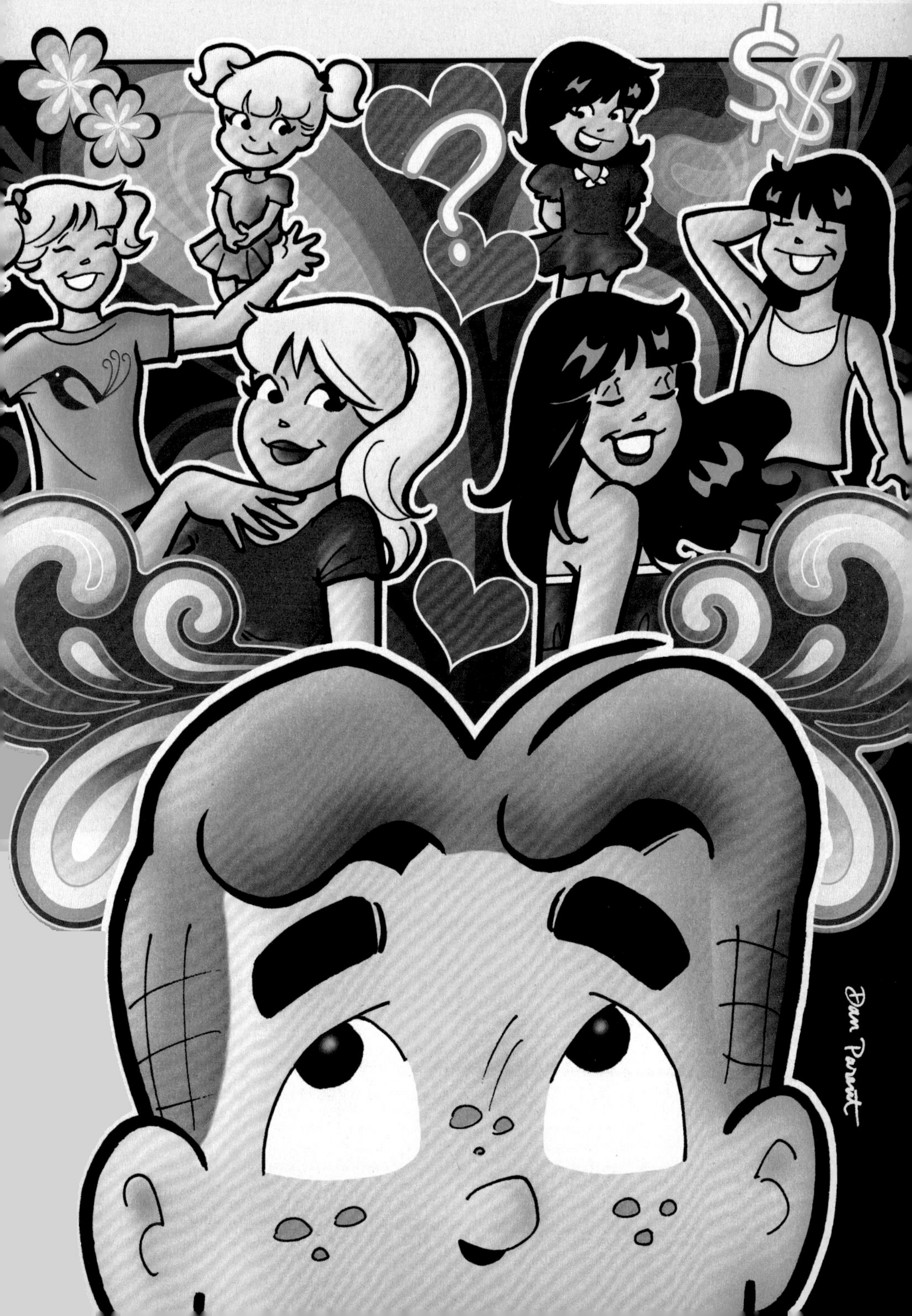
Dan Parent

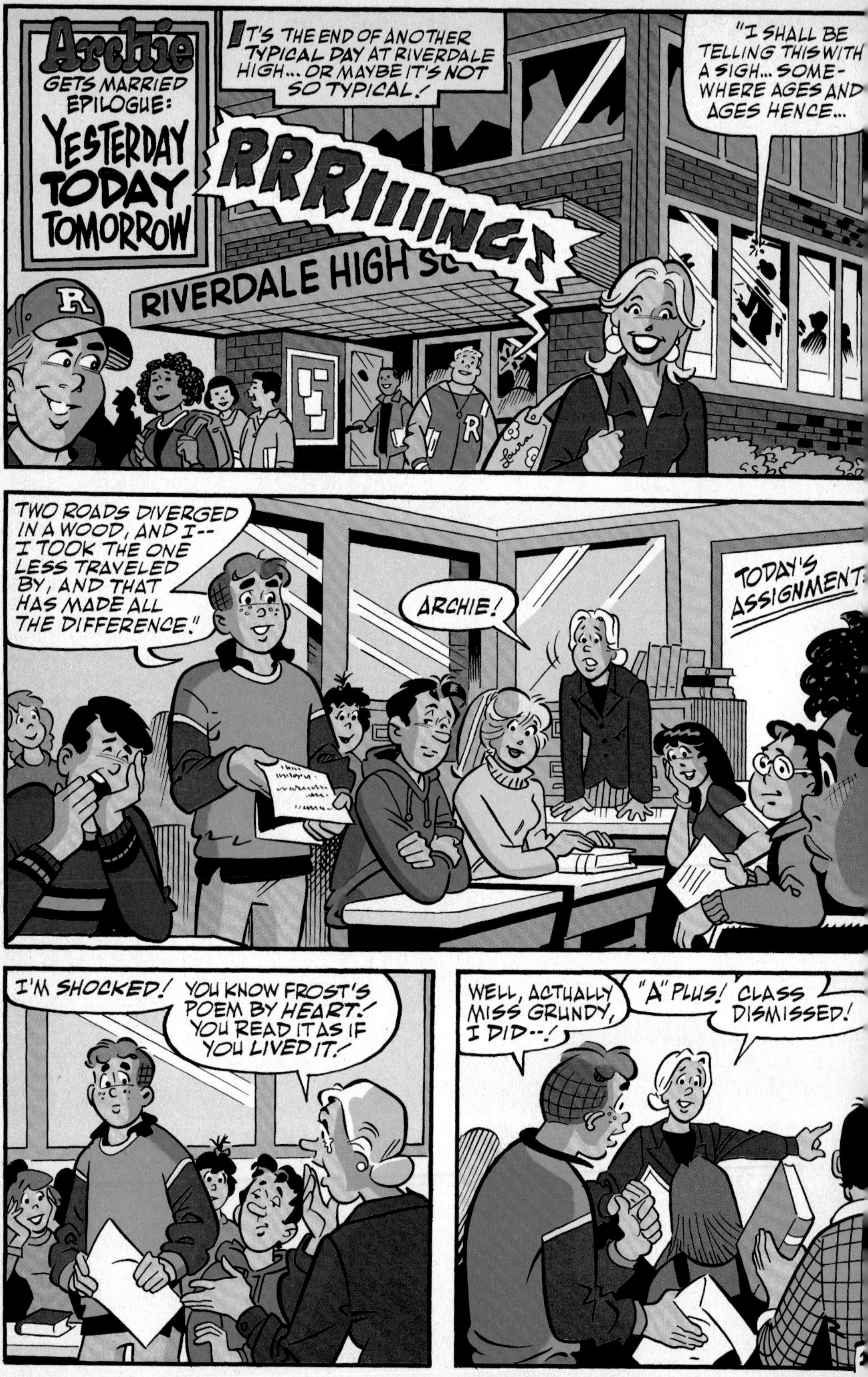
Archie
GETS MARRIED EPILOGUE:
YESTERDAY TODAY TOMORROW
IT'S THE END OF ANOTHER TYPICAL DAY AT RIVERDALE HIGH... OR MAYBE IT'S NOT SO TYPICAL!
"I SHALL BE TELLING THIS WITH A SIGH... SOMEWHERE AGES AND AGES HENCE...
RRRIIIING!
RIVERDALE HIGH SC
TWO ROADS DIVERGED IN A WOOD, AND I-- I TOOK THE ONE LESS TRAVELED BY, AND THAT HAS MADE ALL THE DIFFERENCE."
ARCHIE!
TODAY'S ASSIGNMENT
I'M SHOCKED!
YOU KNOW FROST'S POEM BY HEART! YOU READ IT AS IF YOU LIVED IT!
WELL, ACTUALLY MISS GRUNDY, I DID--!
"A" PLUS!
CLASS DISMISSED!

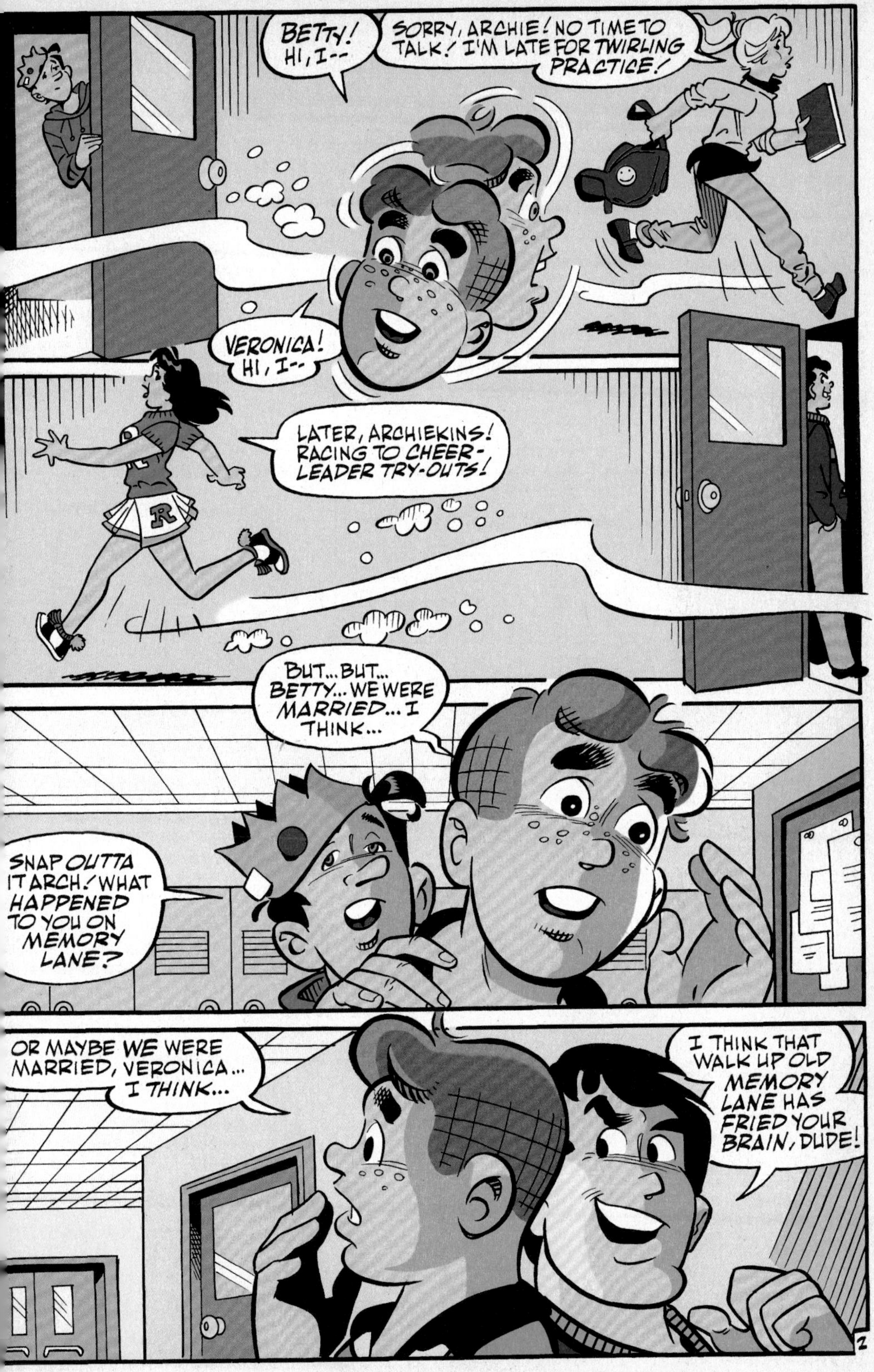
BETTY! HI, I--
SORRY, ARCHIE! NO TIME TO TALK! I'M LATE FOR TWIRLING PRACTICE!
VERONICA! HI, I--
LATER, ARCHIEKINS! RACING TO CHEER-LEADER TRY-OUTS!
BUT... BUT... BETTY... WE WERE MARRIED... I THINK...
SNAP OUTTA IT ARCH! WHAT HAPPENED TO YOU ON MEMORY LANE?
OR MAYBE WE WERE MARRIED, VERONICA... I THINK...
I THINK THAT WALK UP OLD MEMORY LANE HAS FRIED YOUR BRAIN, DUDE!
2

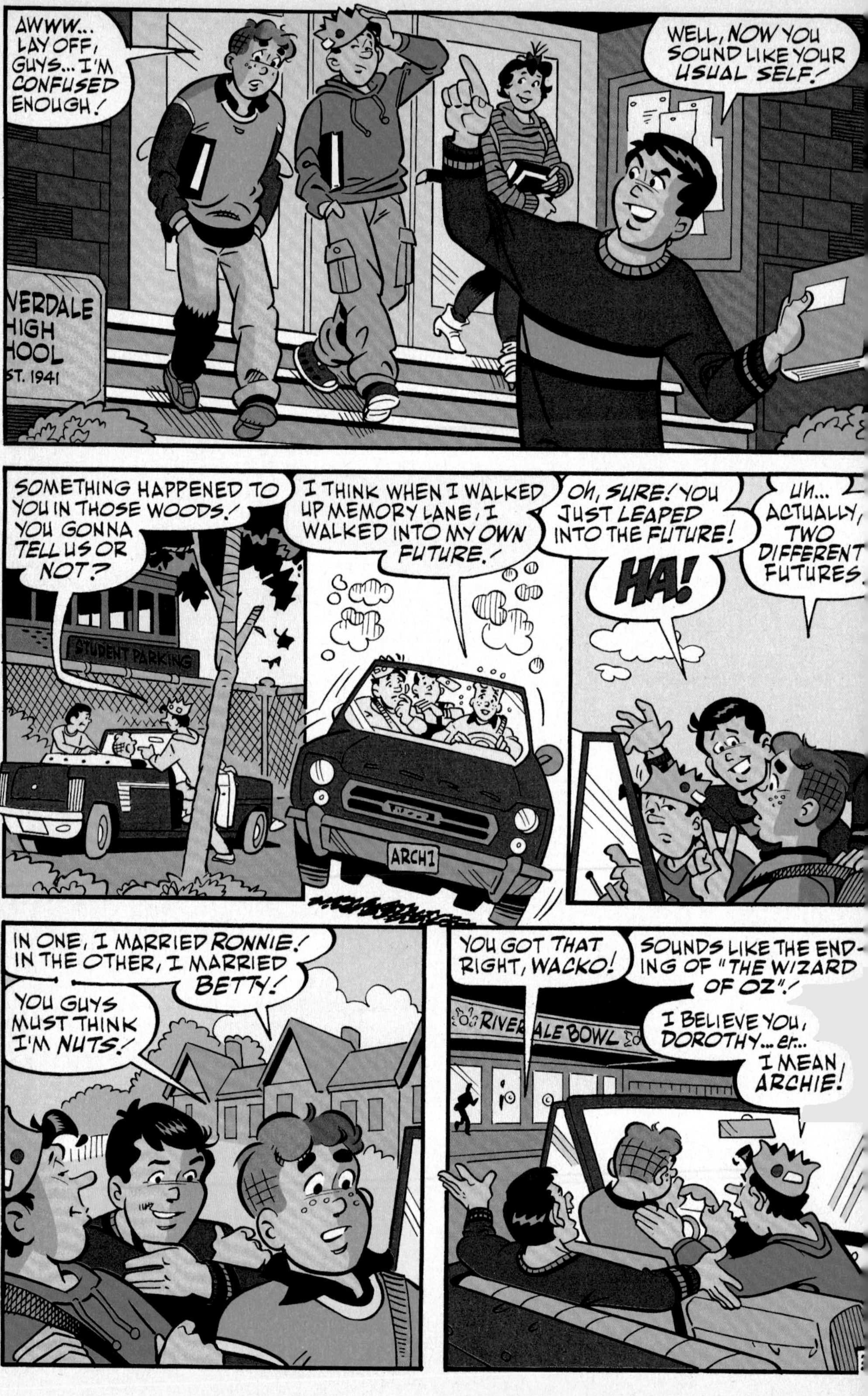
AWWW... LAY OFF, GUYS... I'M CONFUSED ENOUGH!
WELL, NOW YOU SOUND LIKE YOUR USUAL SELF!
SOMETHING HAPPENED TO YOU IN THOSE WOODS! YOU GONNA TELL US OR NOT?
STUDENT PARKING
I THINK WHEN I WALKED UP MEMORY LANE, I WALKED INTO MY OWN FUTURE.
ARCH1
OH, SURE! YOU JUST LEAPED INTO THE FUTURE!
HA!
UH... ACTUALLY, TWO DIFFERENT FUTURES.
IN ONE, I MARRIED RONNIE! IN THE OTHER, I MARRIED BETTY!
YOU GUYS MUST THINK I'M NUTS!
YOU GOT THAT RIGHT, WACKO!
SOUNDS LIKE THE ENDING OF "THE WIZARD OF OZ"!
I BELIEVE YOU, DOROTHY... er... I MEAN ARCHIE!

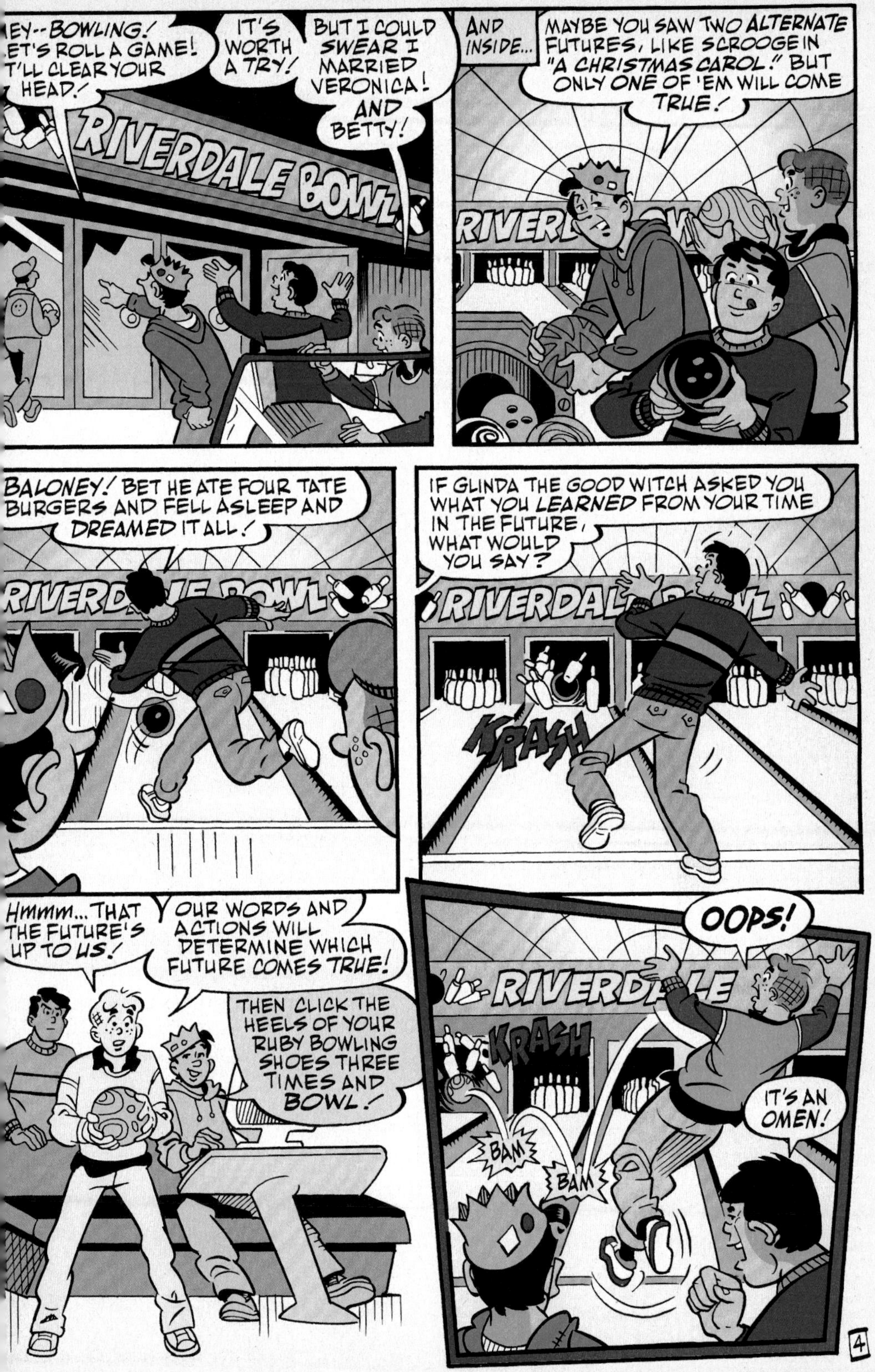

EY--BOWLING! ET'S ROLL A GAME! T'LL CLEAR YOUR HEAD!
IT'S WORTH A TRY!
BUT I COULD SWEAR I MARRIED VERONICA! AND BETTY!
RIVERDALE BOWL
AND INSIDE...
MAYBE YOU SAW TWO ALTERNATE FUTURES, LIKE SCROOGE IN "A CHRISTMAS CAROL!" BUT ONLY ONE OF 'EM WILL COME TRUE!
BALONEY! BET HE ATE FOUR TATE BURGERS AND FELL ASLEEP AND DREAMED IT ALL!
IF GLINDA THE GOOD WITCH ASKED YOU WHAT YOU LEARNED FROM YOUR TIME IN THE FUTURE, WHAT WOULD YOU SAY?
KRASH
HMMM... THAT THE FUTURE'S UP TO US!
OUR WORDS AND ACTIONS WILL DETERMINE WHICH FUTURE COMES TRUE!
THEN CLICK THE HEELS OF YOUR RUBY BOWLING SHOES THREE TIMES AND BOWL!
OOPS!
RIVERDALE
KRASH
IT'S AN OMEN!
BAM
BAM
4

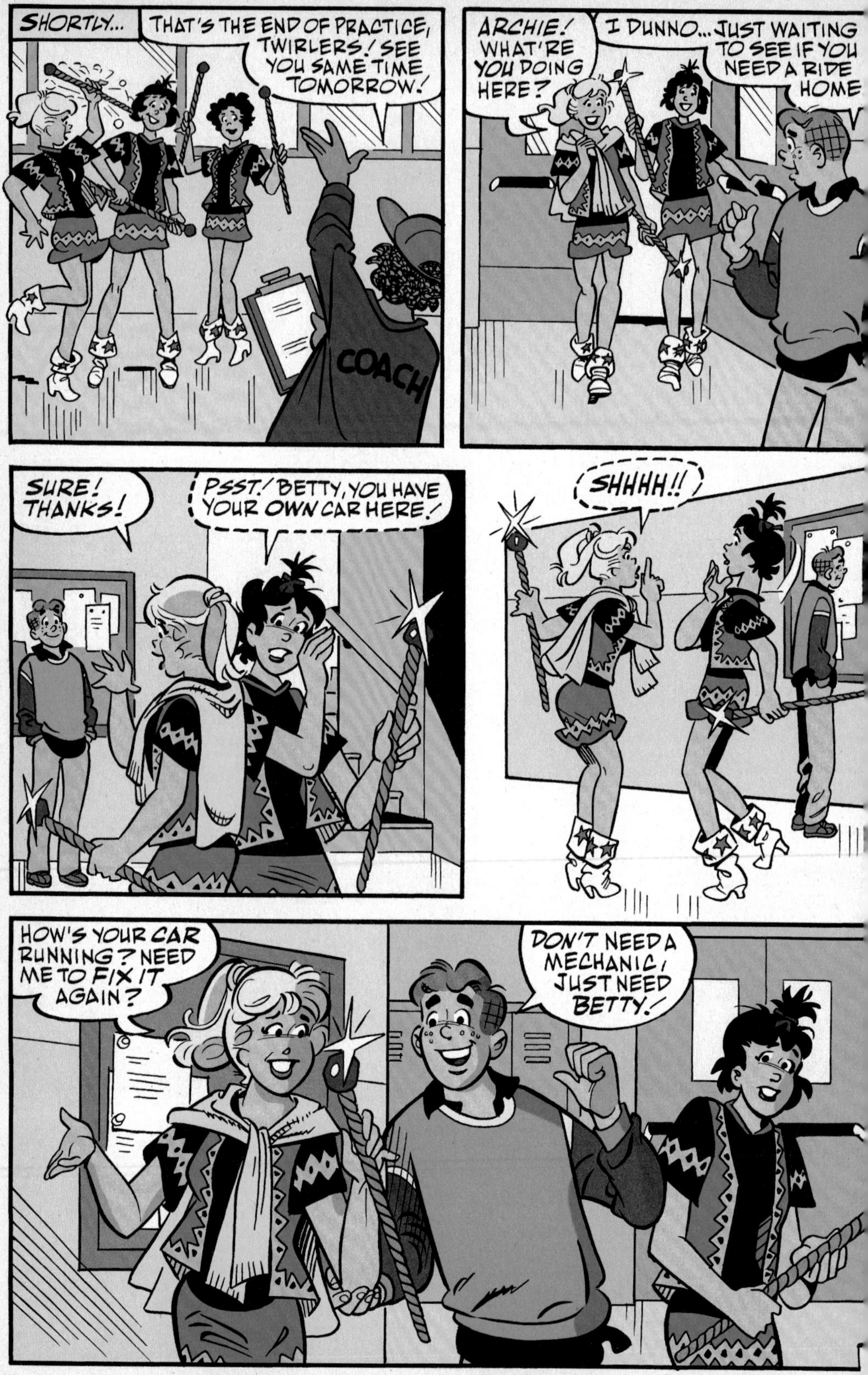
SHORTLY...
THAT'S THE END OF PRACTICE, TWIRLERS! SEE YOU SAME TIME TOMORROW!
COACH
ARCHIE! WHAT'RE YOU DOING HERE?
I DUNNO... JUST WAITING TO SEE IF YOU NEED A RIDE HOME
SURE! THANKS!
PSST! BETTY, YOU HAVE YOUR OWN CAR HERE!
SHHHH!!
HOW'S YOUR CAR RUNNING? NEED ME TO FIX IT AGAIN?
DON'T NEED A MECHANIC, JUST NEED BETTY!

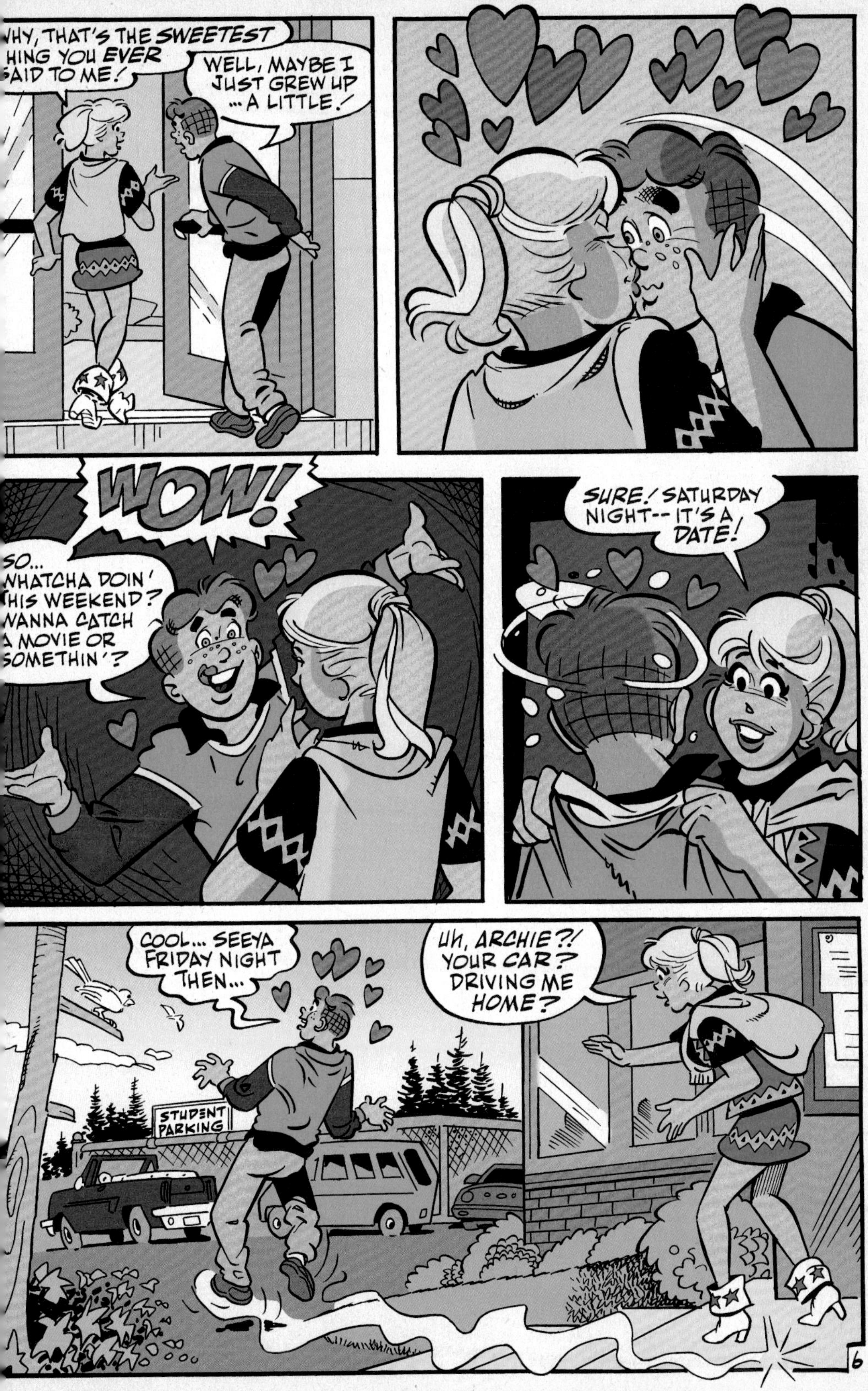
HY, THAT'S THE SWEETEST HING YOU EVER SAID TO ME!
WELL, MAYBE I JUST GREW UP ...A LITTLE!
WOW!
SO... WHATCHA DOIN' THIS WEEKEND? WANNA CATCH A MOVIE OR SOMETHIN'?
SURE! SATURDAY NIGHT-- IT'S A DATE!
COOL... SEEYA FRIDAY NIGHT THEN...
STUDENT PARKING
UH, ARCHIE?! YOUR CAR? DRIVING ME HOME?
6

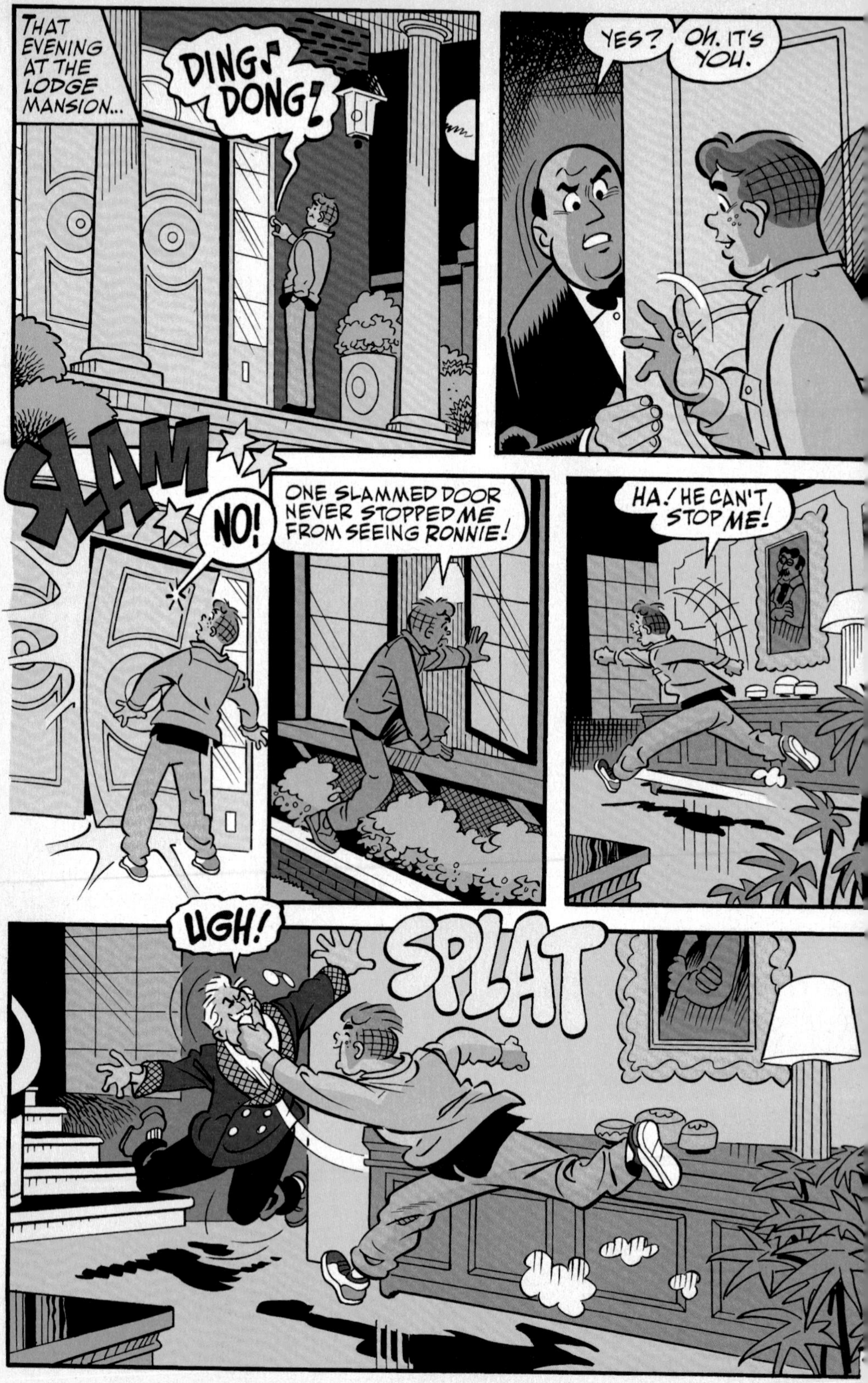
THAT EVENING AT THE LODGE MANSION...
DING DONG
YES?
OH. IT'S YOU.
SLAM
NO!
ONE SLAMMED DOOR NEVER STOPPED ME FROM SEEING RONNIE!
HA! HE CAN'T STOP ME!
UGH!
SPLAT

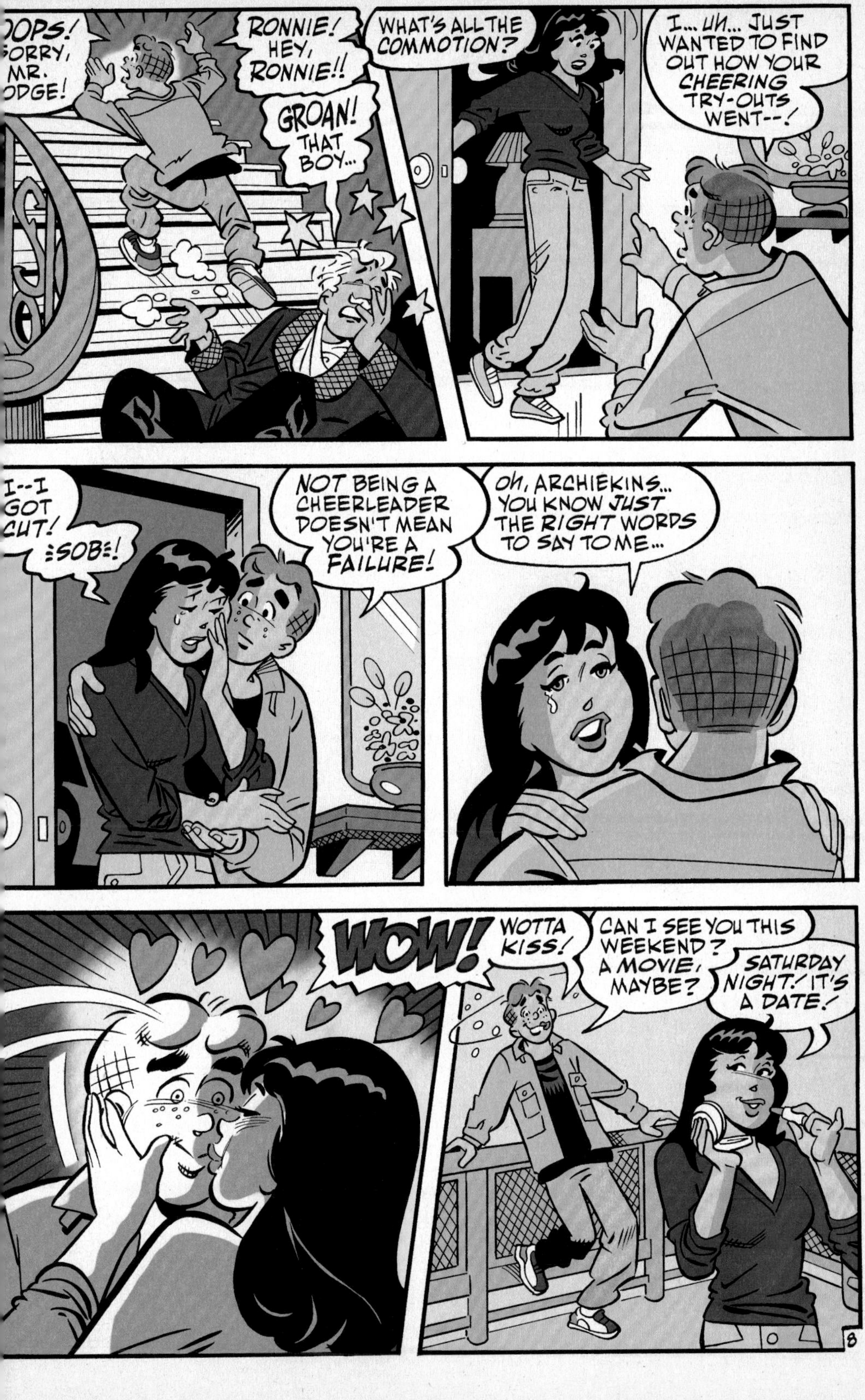
OOPS! ORRY, MR. ODGE!
RONNIE! HEY, RONNIE!!
GROAN! THAT BOY...
WHAT'S ALL THE COMMOTION?
I... UH... JUST WANTED TO FIND OUT HOW YOUR CHEERING TRY-OUTS WENT--!
I--I GOT CUT! SOB!
NOT BEING A CHEERLEADER DOESN'T MEAN YOU'RE A FAILURE!
OH, ARCHIEKINS... YOU KNOW JUST THE RIGHT WORDS TO SAY TO ME...
WOW!
WOTTA KISS!
CAN I SEE YOU THIS WEEKEND? A MOVIE, MAYBE?
SATURDAY NIGHT! IT'S A DATE!
8

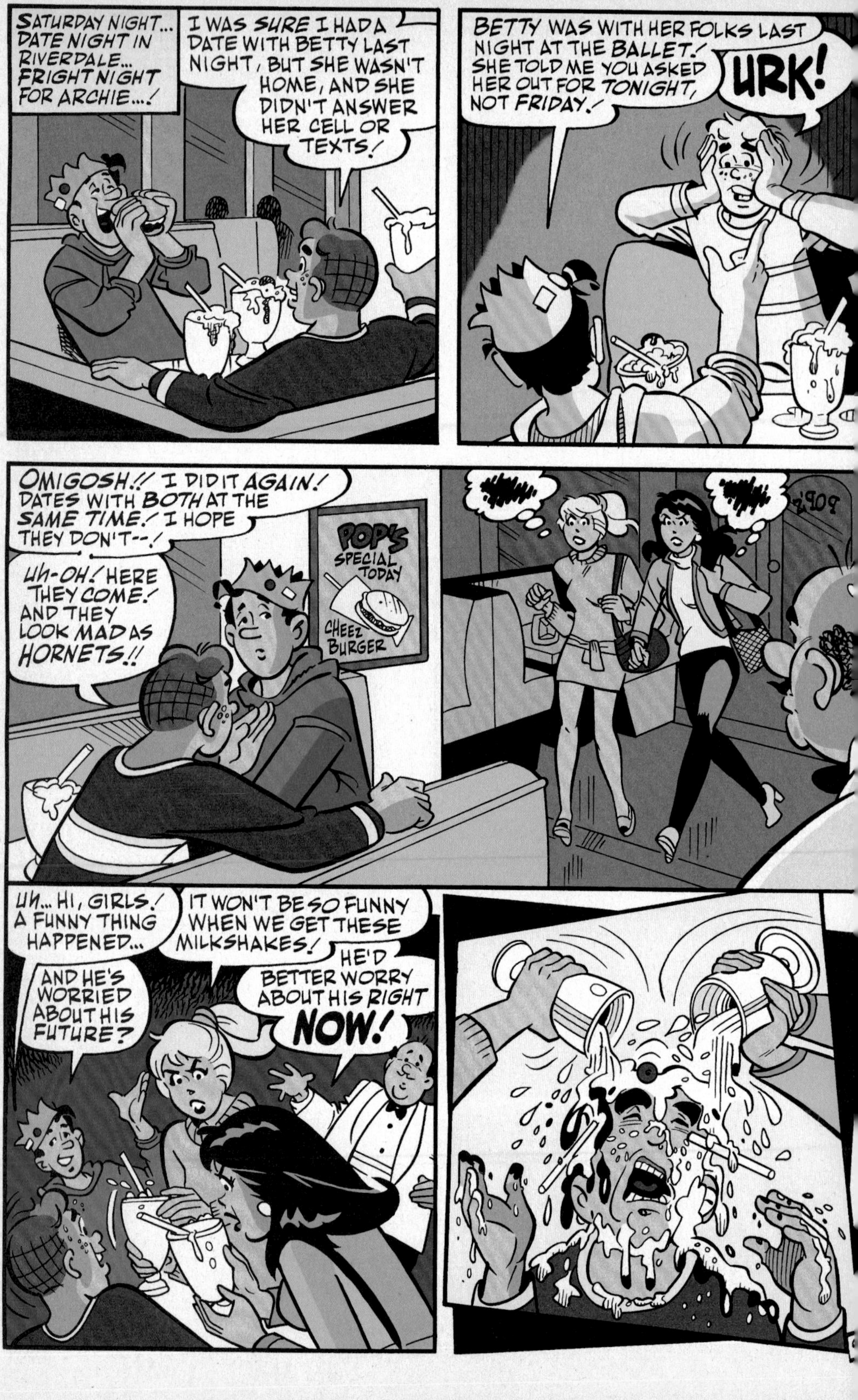
SATURDAY NIGHT... DATE NIGHT IN RIVERDALE... FRIGHT NIGHT FOR ARCHIE...!
I WAS SURE I HAD A DATE WITH BETTY LAST NIGHT, BUT SHE WASN'T HOME, AND SHE DIDN'T ANSWER HER CELL OR TEXTS!
BETTY WAS WITH HER FOLKS LAST NIGHT AT THE BALLET! SHE TOLD ME YOU ASKED HER OUT FOR TONIGHT, NOT FRIDAY!
URK!
OMIGOSH!! I DID IT AGAIN! DATES WITH BOTH AT THE SAME TIME! I HOPE THEY DON'T--!
UH-OH! HERE THEY COME! AND THEY LOOK MAD AS HORNETS!!
POP'S SPECIAL TODAY
CHEEZ BURGER
UH... HI, GIRLS! A FUNNY THING HAPPENED...
IT WON'T BE SO FUNNY WHEN WE GET THESE MILKSHAKES!
AND HE'S WORRIED ABOUT HIS FUTURE?
HE'D BETTER WORRY ABOUT HIS RIGHT NOW!

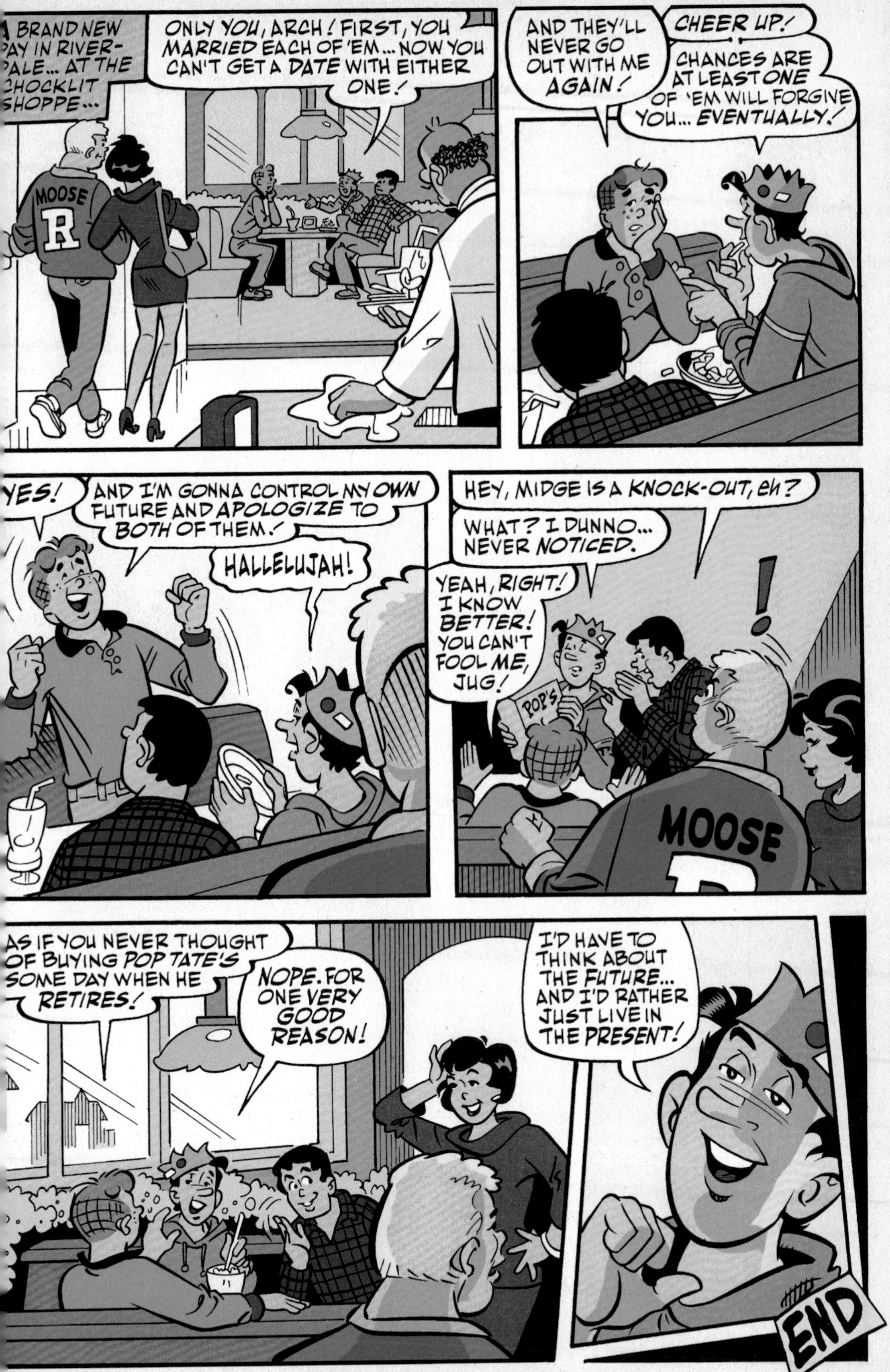
A BRAND NEW DAY IN RIVERDALE... AT THE CHOCKLIT SHOPPE...
ONLY YOU, ARCH! FIRST, YOU MARRIED EACH OF 'EM... NOW YOU CAN'T GET A DATE WITH EITHER ONE!
MOOSE
R
AND THEY'LL NEVER GO OUT WITH ME AGAIN!
CHEER UP!
CHANCES ARE AT LEAST ONE OF 'EM WILL FORGIVE YOU... EVENTUALLY!
YES!
AND I'M GONNA CONTROL MY OWN FUTURE AND APOLOGIZE TO BOTH OF THEM!
HALLELUJAH!
HEY, MIDGE IS A KNOCK-OUT, eh?
WHAT? I DUNNO... NEVER NOTICED.
YEAH, RIGHT! I KNOW BETTER! YOU CAN'T FOOL ME, JUG!
!
POP'S
MOOSE
AS IF YOU NEVER THOUGHT OF BUYING POP TATE'S SOME DAY WHEN HE RETIRES!
NOPE. FOR ONE VERY GOOD REASON!
I'D HAVE TO THINK ABOUT THE FUTURE... AND I'D RATHER JUST LIVE IN THE PRESENT!
END

THE ARCHIE WEDDING

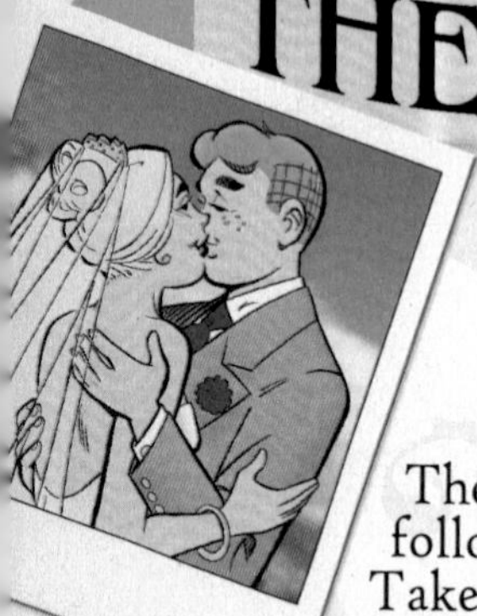

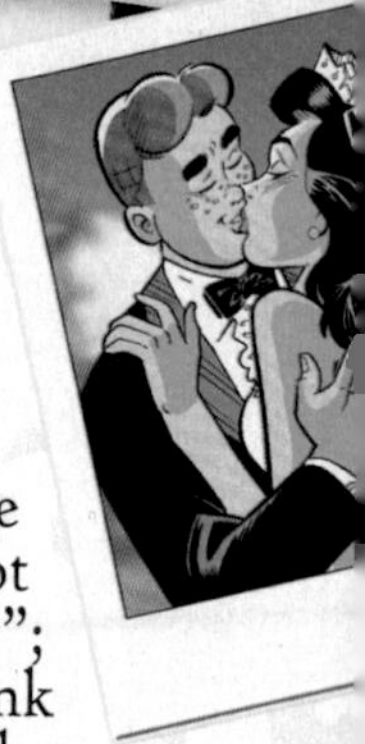

Afterword

By Michael Uslan

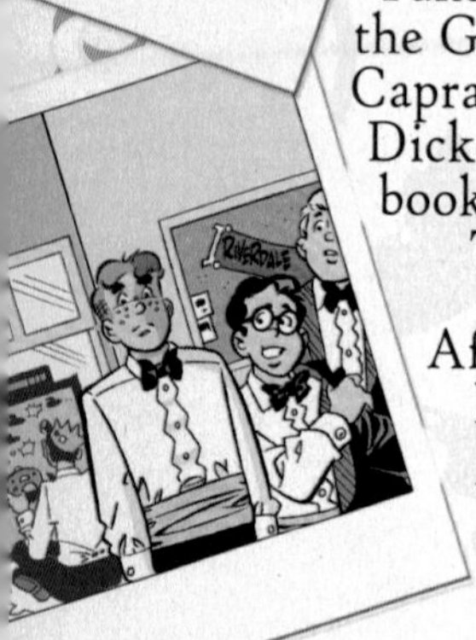
RIVERDALE

The recipe was simple—one part each of the following: Robert Frost's poem, "The Road Not Taken"; Joni Mitchell's song, "Both Sides Now"; the Gwyneth Paltrow movie, "Sliding Doors"; Frank Capra's classic, "It's a Wonderful Life"; Charles Dickens' novella, "A Christmas Carol"; L. Frank Baum's book, "The Wizard of Oz" ... and Archie, Betty & Veronica! The result was the seven chapter story you just read.

After 68 years of dating these two girls, SOMEONE had to make a decision. So, sorry, Arch, ol' pal... I did!

With all of the above as inspiration, I wanted to explore what life would be like for Archie, Betty & Veronica if he married Veronica and, in comparison, if he instead married Betty. Using the classic Archie comic book time traveling device "Memory Lane," Archie visited two different futures. We learned several important things in the process: the decision as to one's mate will cause 90% of all his or her happiness or unhappiness in life; just because Archie at age 22 made a choice, that doesn't necessarily mean it was the best choice (or even a good choice); a marriage not only changes the lives of the couple, but has a "butterfly effect" that also changes the lives of their families and friends; some people marry for love, while others marry for money or security; Betty has self-esteem and self-confidence issues she needs to explore—maybe Archie just isn't good enough for HER; a marriage may be more successful if it's based on a foundation of two people who are first and foremost best friends; some people peak in high school, while others don't evolve until later in life; money doesn't necessarily buy happiness. And who could have imagined, before the worldwide firestorm of media attention this story received, that so many people from multiple generations truly care so much about the question of IF Archie should marry at all, and if so, whether the right choice is Betty or Veronica?!

But let's be perfectly clear... ONE of these two futures for Archie, Betty and Veronica WILL indeed come to pass! As we reset Riverdale's clock to the present amid the gang's high school hi-jinx, the future depends on what these three young people do or don't do, say or fail to say to each other. That is what will determine which future will be the real one. What a great reason to closely follow every Archie story over the next five years!

The BEST thing that "The Archie Wedding" stories have done is to reawaken the interest of people of all ages and cultures to their heartfelt interest in and love for these characters. Archie and the gang truly mean something to them, and millions of people care what happens to these comic book friends. With the publication of these tales, we were inundated with letters telling us that parents and children were reading these together... often even with grandparents who also grew up reading Archie comics at camp, on the beach, or after school. Lastly, they made the worldwide general public aware that comic books are still being published and can be found in comic book stores all over. This was a good thing for the entire industry.

My personal thanks go out to Golden Agers John Goldwater, Bob Montana, Vic Bloom, Harry Shorten, Louis Silberkleit, Maurice Coyne, and all the great artists and writers from "The Greatest Generation" who bequeathed Archie to the world. And for making this historic series possible, Victor Gorelick, Jon Goldwater, Fred Mausser, Nancy Silberkleit, the legendary and great Stan Goldberg, Bob Smith, Jack Morelli, Glenn Whitmore, Mike Pellerito, Rik Offenberger, Paul Castiglia, Ellen Leonforte, Joe Pepitone, Tito Peña, Carlos Antunes, Stephen Oswald, Paul Kaminski, Joe Morciglio, Suzannah Rowntree and Duncan McLachlan. For their familial support, Nancy, David, Sarah, and Paul Uslan. To my own three real-life Jugheads (or was I THEIR Jughead?), Bobby Klein, Barry Milberg, and Marc Caplan. And to the two girls in high school who were my own Betty & Veronica (you know who you are)!

Michael Uslan
2010

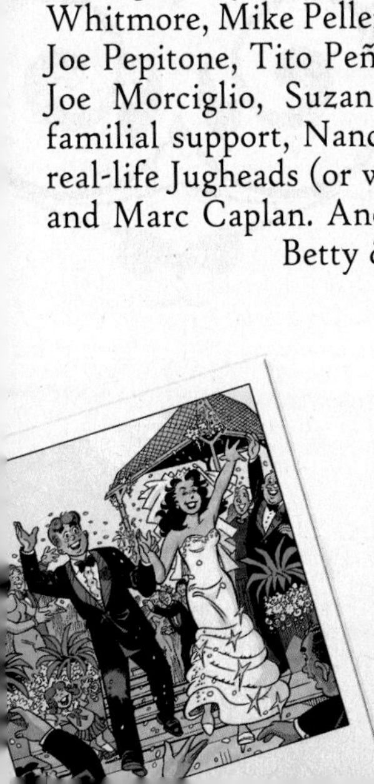

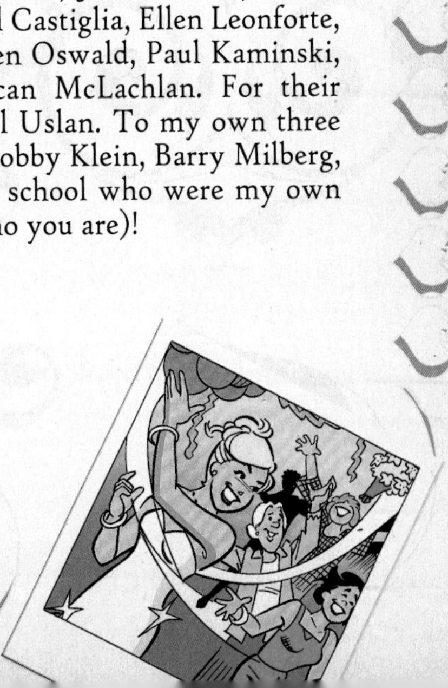

BONUS MATERIAL

From August 31 through September 5, 2009, the weekly Archie newspaper strip featured a wedding theme. It was evident at this point that Archie wedding fever had become a pandemic!

EVER THINK OF MARRIAGE, ARCH?
ARE YOU KIDDING?
© 2009 creators.com, © 2009 Archie Publ., Inc.
OF COURSE I THINK ABOUT MARRIAGE...
Visit: www.archiecomics.com
...IN THE GENERAL, ABSTRACT, THEORETICAL, NON-SPECIFIC SENSE!
8-31

BOY ARCH, WHEN YOU MENTIONED YOU THINK ABOUT MARRIAGE A LOT...
YUM!
© 2009 creators.com, © 2009 Archie Publ., Inc.
...YOU REALLY OPENED A CAN OF WORMS!
Visit: www.archiecomics.com
I DON'T THINK THEY APPRECIATED YOUR ANALOGY!
9-1

WHO DO YOU THINK YOU'D MARRY, ARCH?
HMMM... WELL... MAYBE VERONICA!
© 2009 creators.com, © 2009 Archie Publ., Inc.
EEYEEOW!
LODGE ESTATE
Visit: www.archiecomics.com
WHAT IS IT, DADDY?
I DON'T KNOW! A COLD CHILL RAN UP AND DOWN MY SPINE!
9-2

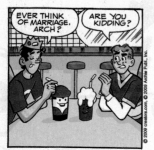

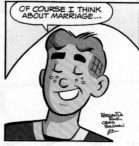

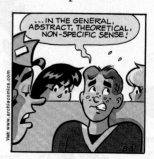

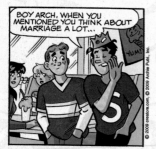

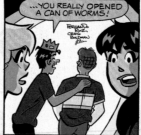

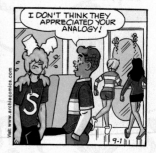

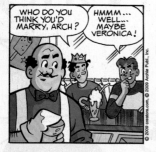

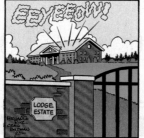

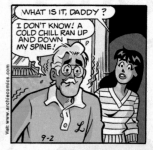

The Archie comic strip has been featured in newspapers all over the world since the mid 1940s and continues to bring joy to readers worldwide.

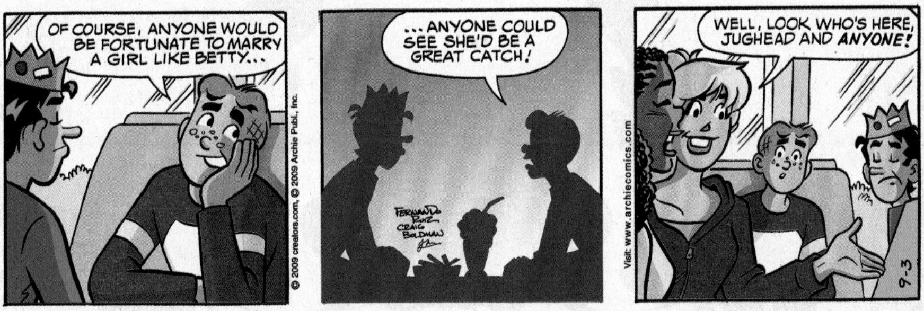
OF COURSE, ANYONE WOULD BE FORTUNATE TO MARRY A GIRL LIKE BETTY...
© 2009 creators.com, © 2009 Archie Publ., Inc.
...ANYONE COULD SEE SHE'D BE A GREAT CATCH!
WELL, LOOK WHO'S HERE, JUGHEAD AND ANYONE!
Visit: www.archiecomics.com
9-3

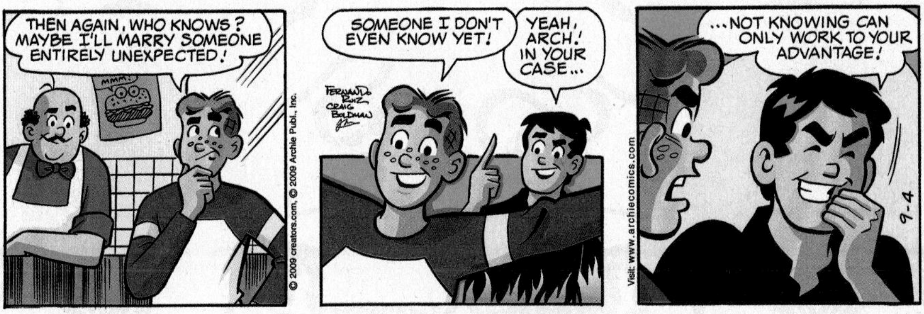
THEN AGAIN, WHO KNOWS? MAYBE I'LL MARRY SOMEONE ENTIRELY UNEXPECTED!
MMM!
© 2009 creators.com, © 2009 Archie Publ., Inc.
SOMEONE I DON'T EVEN KNOW YET!
YEAH, ARCH! IN YOUR CASE...
...NOT KNOWING CAN ONLY WORK TO YOUR ADVANTAGE!
Visit: www.archiecomics.com
9-4

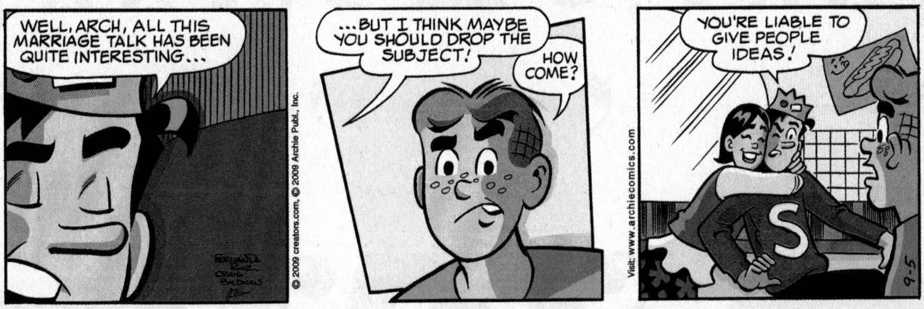
WELL, ARCH, ALL THIS MARRIAGE TALK HAS BEEN QUITE INTERESTING...
© 2009 creators.com, © 2009 Archie Publ., Inc.
...BUT I THINK MAYBE YOU SHOULD DROP THE SUBJECT!
HOW COME?
YOU'RE LIABLE TO GIVE PEOPLE IDEAS!
Visit: www.archiecomics.com
9-5

Script: Craig Boldman / Pencils: Fernando Ruiz / Inks: Bob Smith / Letters: Jon D'Agostino / Colors: Joe Morciglio

Fall in love with thes
great Archie Comics graphic novels

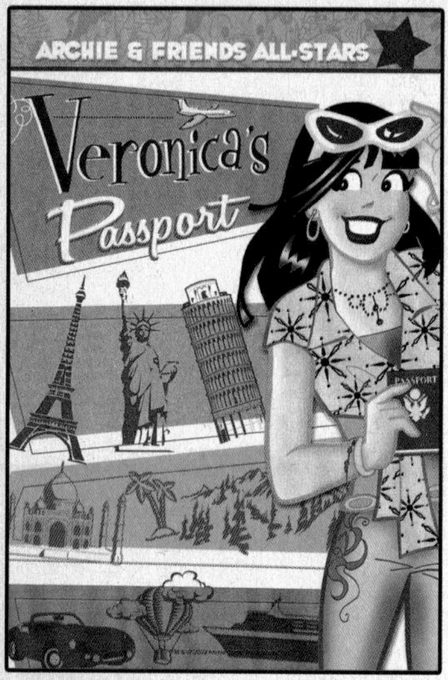
ARCHIE & FRIENDS ALL-STARS
Veronica's
Passport

Archie & Friends All-Stars Vol. 1:
Veronica's Passport
Pack your bags and take a trip across the globe with the trendiest traveller around, Veronica Lodge.
ISBN: 978-1-879794-43-6
$9.95 US / $11.95 CAN

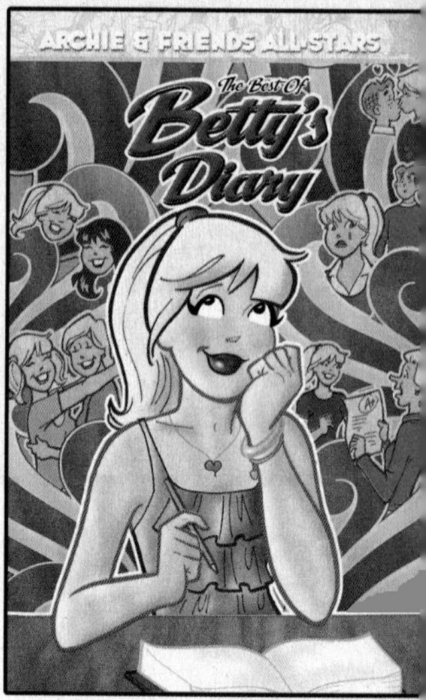
ARCHIE & FRIENDS ALL-STARS
The Best Of
Betty's
Diary

Archie & Friends All-Stars Vol. 2
The Best of Betty's Diary
Everyone thinks they know Betty Cooper, but even the girl next doc has some secrets of her own.
ISBN: 978-1-879794-46-7
$9.95 US / $11.95 CAN

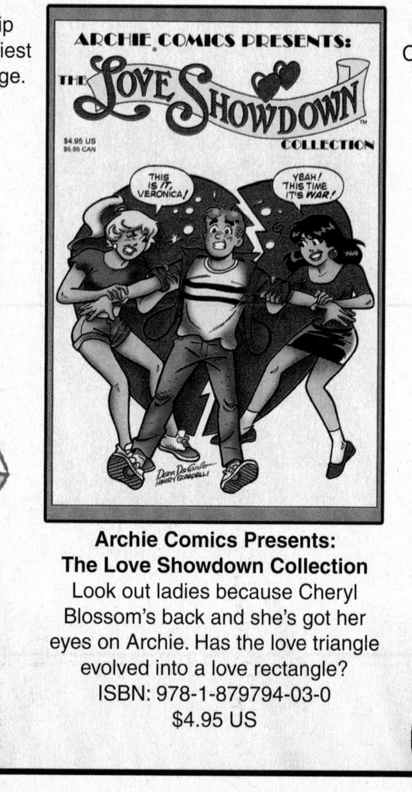
ARCHIE COMICS PRESENTS:
THE LOVE SHOWDOWN
COLLECTION
$4.95 US
$5.95 CAN
THIS IS IT, VERONICA!
YEAH! THIS TIME IT'S WAR!

Archie Comics Presents:
The Love Showdown Collection
Look out ladies because Cheryl Blossom's back and she's got her eyes on Archie. Has the love triangle evolved into a love rectangle?
ISBN: 978-1-879794-03-0
$4.95 US

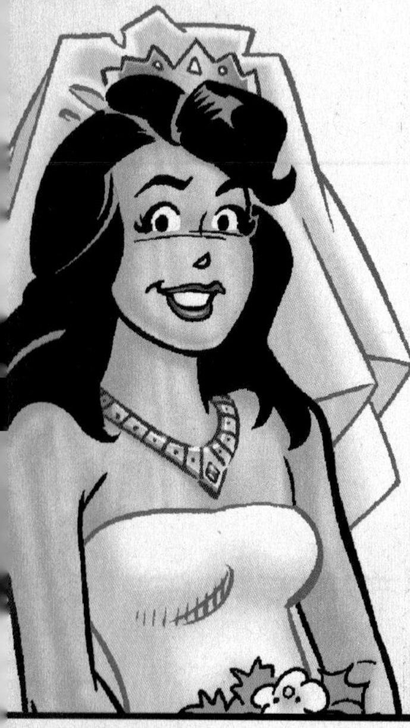

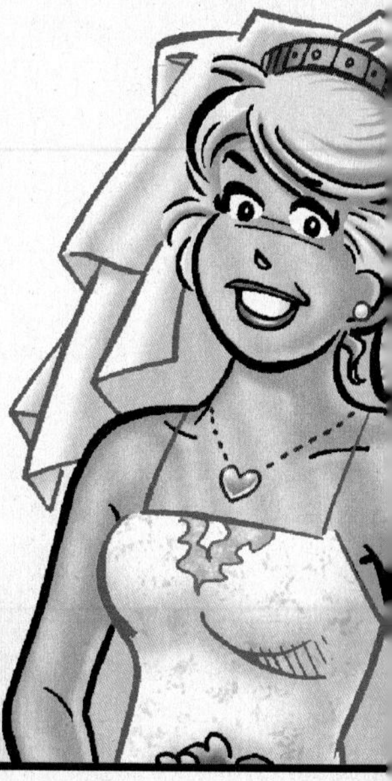

AVAILABLE AT YOUR LOCAL COMICS SHOP OR BOOKSTORE!
To find a comic shop in your area, call 1-888-266-4226.
ALSO AVAILABLE ONLINE AT ARCHIECOMICS.COM
*Price and availability subject to change without notice.